THE GREATEST WORKS
OF CHRISTIAN CIVILIZATION

DR. DAVID JOHN PAUL MARZAK EDITOR IN CHIEF

****

THOMAS AQUINAS
ETHICAL AND POLITICAL WRITINGS

Treatise on Law and Kingship
Volume 47 - III

****

Michael Stephen Mary Marzak, Associate Editor

KOLBE'S GREATEST BOOKS
OF CHRISTIAN CIVILIZATION

1 Moses

2 Joshua

3 King David

4 Homer

5 Sun Tsu

6 Confucius

7 Hippocrates

8 Aeschylus

9 Sophocles

10 Euripides

11 Herodotus

12 Thucydides

13 Aristophanes

14 Plato

15 Aristotle

16 Euclid

17 Archimedes

18 Cicero

19 Virgil

20 Flavius Josephus

21 Plutarch

22 Justin Martyr

23 Galen

24 Eusebius

25 St. Ephraem of Syria

26 St. Athanasius

27 St. Basil the Great

Politics – Philosophy – Science – Theology
Education – Literature – Math – History

KOLBE'S GREATEST BOOKS
OF CHRISTIAN CIVILIZATION

28 St. Ambrose

29 St. John Chrysostom

30 St. Augustine

31 Paulus Orosius

32 St. Patrick

33 St. Leo the Great

34 Boethius

35 Saint Benedict

36 St. Gregory the Great

37 Alfred the Great

38 Venerable Bede

39 Charlemagne

40 Song of Roland

41 St. Anselm

42 St. Bernard

43 El Cid

44 St. Francis of Assisi

45 St. Albert the Great

46 St. Bonaventure

47 St. Thomas Aquinas

48 Dante Alighieri

49 Geoffrey Chaucer

50 St. Catherine of Sienna

51 Thomas a Kempis

Politics – Philosophy – Science – Theology
Education - Literature – Math – History

Title of the English Original:

Kolbe's Greatest Books of Christian Civilization

Volume 47-III — Saint Thomas Aquinas:
Ethical and Political Writings
Treatise on Kingship

Published by The Kolbe Foundation

Cover design by Michael S. Marzak

Printed in the United States of America

Translated by
Gerald B. Phelan,
Revised by I. Th. Eschmann, O.P.
Toronto: The Pontifical Institute of Mediaeval Studies, 1949
Re-edited and chapter numbers aligned with Latin, by Joseph Kenny, O.P.

Table of Contents

Table of Contents

TREATISE ON THE KINGSHIP

De Regiminie Principium (De Regno)

BOOK ONE

Kolbe's Greatest Books
Volume Fourty Seven

By

Saint Thomas Aquinas

BOOK ONE

TO THE KING OF CYPRUS

AS I WAS TURNING over in my mind what I might present to Your Majesty as a gift at once worthy of Your Royal Highness and befitting my profession and office, it seemed to me a highly appropriate offering that, for a king, I should write a book on kingship, in which, so far as my ability permits, I should carefully expound, according to the authority of Holy Writ and the teachings of the philosophers as well as the practice of worthy princes, both the origin of kingly government and the things which pertain to the office of a king, relying for the beginning, progress and accomplishment of this work, on the help of Him, Who is King of Kings, Lord of Lords, through Whom kings rule, God the Mighty Lord, King great above all gods.

BOOK ONE

CHAPTER 1

WHAT IS MEANT BY THE WORD 'KING'

[2] The first step in our undertaking must be to set forth what is to be understood by the term king.

[3] In all things which are ordered towards an end, wherein this or that course may be adopted, some directive principle is needed through which the due end may be reached by the most direct route. A ship, for example, which moves in different directions. according to the impulse of the changing winds, would never reach its destination were it not brought to port by the skill of the pilot. Now, man has an end to which his whole life and all his actions are ordered; for man is an intelligent agent, and it is clearly the part of an intelligent agent to act in view of an end. Men also adopt different methods in proceeding towards their proposed end, as the diversity of men's pursuits and actions clearly indicates. Consequently man needs some directive principle to guide him towards his end.

[4] To be sure, the light of reason is placed by nature in every man, to guide him in his acts towards his end. Wherefore, if man were intended to live alone, as many animals do, he would require no other guide to his end. Each man would be a king unto himself, under God, the highest King, inasmuch as he would direct himself in his acts by the light of reason given him from on high. Yet it is natural for man, more than for any other animal, to be a social and political animal, to live in a group.

[5] This is clearly a necessity of man's nature. For all other animals, nature has prepared food, hair as a covering, teeth, horns, claws as means of defence or at least speed in flight, while man alone was made without any natural provisions for these things. Instead of all these, man was endowed with reason, by the use of which he could procure all these things for himself by the work of his hands. Now, one man alone is not able to procure them all for himself, for one man could not sufficiently provide for life, unassisted. It is therefore natural that man should live in the society of many.

[6] Moreover, all other animals are able to, discern, by inborn skill, what is useful and what is injurious, even as the sheep naturally regards the wolf as his enemy. Some animals also recognize by natural skill certain medicinal herbs and other things necessary for their life. Man, on the contrary, has a natural knowledge of the things which are essential for his. life only in a general fashion, inasmuch as he is able to attain knowledge of the particular things necessary for human life by reasoning from natural principles. But it is not possible for one man to arrive at a knowledge of all these things by his own individual reason. It is therefore necessary for man to live in a multitude so that each one may assist his fellows, and different men may be occupied in seeking, by their reason, to make different discoveries—one, for example, in medicine, one in this and another in that.

[7] This point is further and most plainly evidenced by the fact that the. use of speech is a prerogative proper to man. By this means, one man is able fully to express his conceptions to others. Other animals, it is true, express their feelings to one another in a general way, as a dog may express anger by barking and other animals give vent to other feelings in various fashions. But man communicates with his kind more completely than any other animal known to be gregarious, such as the crane, the ant or the bee. — With this in mind, Solomon says: "It is better that there be two than one; for they have the advantage of their company."'

[8] If, then, it is natural for man to live in the society of many, it is necessary that there exist among men some means by which the group may be governed. For where there are many men together and each one is looking after his own interest, the multitude would be broken up and scattered unless there were also an agency to take care of what appertains to the commonweal. In like manner, the body of a man or any other animal would disintegrate unless there were a general ruling force within the body which watches over the common good of all members. With this in mind, Solomon says [Eccl. 4:9]: "Where there is no governor, the people shall fall."

[9] Indeed it is reasonable that this should happen, for what is proper and what is common are not identical. Things differ by what is proper to each: they are united by what they have in common. But diversity of effects is due to diversity of causes. Consequently, there must exist something which impels towards the common good of the many, over and above that which impels towards the particular good of each individual. Wherefore also in all things that are ordained

9

towards one end, one thing is found to rule the rest. Thus in the corporeal universe, by the first body, i.e. the celestial body, the other bodies are regulated according to the order of Divine Providence; and all bodies are ruled by a rational creature. So, too in the individual man, the soul rules the body; and among the parts of the soul, the irascible and the concupiscible parts are ruled by reason. Likewise, among the members of a body, one, such as the heart or the head, is the principal and moves all the others. Therefore in every multitude there must be some governing power.

[handwritten annotations: Just / unjust — Monarchy / aristocracy / Polity / Democracy / oligarcy / tyrany]

CHAPTER 2

DIFFERENT KINDS OF RULE

[10] Now it happens in certain things which are, ordained towards an end that one may proceed in a right way and also in a wrong way. So, too, in the government of a multitude there is a distinction between right and wrong. A thing is rightly directed when it is led towards a befitting end; wrongly when it is led towards an unbefitting end. Now the end which befits a multitude of free men is different from that which befits a multitude of slaves, for the free man is one who exists for his own sake, while the slave, as such, exists for the sake of another. If, therefore, a multitude of free men is ordered by the ruler towards the common good of the multitude, that rulership will be right and just, as is suitable to free men. If, on the other hand, a rulership aims, not at the common good of the multitude, but at the private good of the ruler, it will be an unjust and perverted rulership. The Lord, therefore, threatens such rulers, saying by the mouth of Ezekiel: "Woe to the shepherds that feed themselves (seeking, that is, their own interest) : should not the flocks be fed by the shepherd?" Shepherds indeed should seek the good of their flocks, and every ruler, the good of the multitude subject to him.

[11] If an unjust government is carried on by one man alone, who seeks his own benefit from his rule and not the good of the multitude subject to him, such a ruler is called a tyrant—a word derived from *strength*—because he oppresses by might instead of ruling by justice. Thus among the ancients all powerful men were called tyrants. If an. unjust government is carried on, not by one but by several, and if they be few, it is called an oligarchy, that is, the rule of a few. This occurs when a few, who differ from the tyrant only by the fact that they are more than one, oppress the people by means of their wealth. If, finally, the bad government is carried on by the multitude, it is called a democracy, i.e. control by the populace, which comes about when the plebeian people by force of numbers oppress the rich. In this way the whole people will be as one tyrant.

[12] In like manner we must divide just governments. If the government is administered by many, it is given the name common to all forms of government, viz. polity, as for instance when a group of warriors exercise dominion over a city

or province. If it is administered by a few men of virtue, this kind of government is called an aristocracy, i.e. noble governance, or governance by noble men, who for this reason are called the Optimates. And if a just government is in the hands of one man alone, he is properly called a king. Wherefore the Lord says by the mouth of Ezekiel:" "My servant, David, shall be king over them and all of them shall have one shepherd."

[13] From this it is clearly shown that the idea of king implies that he be one man who is chief and that he be a shepherd, seeking the common good of the multitude and not his own.

[14] Now since man must live in a group, because he is not sufficient unto himself to procure the necessities of life were he to remain solitary, it follows that a society will be the more perfect the more it is sufficient unto itself to procure the necessities of life. There is, to some extent, sufficiency for life in one *family of one household*, namely, insofar as pertains to the natural acts of nourishment and the begetting of offspring and other things of this kind. Self-sufficiency exists, furthermore, in one *street* with regard to those things which belong to the trade of one guild. In a *city*, which is the perfect community, it exists with regard to all the necessities of life. Still more self-sufficiency is found in a *province* because of the need of fighting together and of mutual help against enemies. Hence the man ruling a perfect community, i.e. a city or a province, is antonomastically called the king. The ruler of a household is called father, not king, although he bears a certain resemblance to the king, for which reason kings are sometimes called the fathers of their peoples.

[15] It is plain, therefore, from what has been said, that a king is one who rules the people of one city or province, and rules them for the common good. Wherefore Solomon says [Eccl. 5:8]: "The king rules over all the land subject to him."

CHAPTER 3

WHETHER IT IS MORE EXPEDIENT FOR A CITY OR PROVINCE TO BE RULED BY ONE MAN OR BY MANY

[16] Having set forth these preliminary points we must now inquire what is better for a province or a city: whether to be ruled by one man or by many.

[17] This question may be considered first from the viewpoint of the purpose of government. The aim of any ruler should be directed towards securing the welfare of that which he undertakes to rule. The duty of the pilot, for instance, is to preserve his ship amidst the perils of the sea. and to bring it unharmed to the port of safety. Now the welfare and safety of a multitude formed into a society lies in the preservation of its unity, which is called peace. If this is removed, the benefit of social life is lost and, moreover, the multitude in its disagreement

becomes a burden to itself. The chief concern of the ruler of a multitude, therefore, is to procure the unity of peace. It is not even legitimate for him to deliberate whether he shall establish peace in the multitude subject to him, just as a physician does not deliberate whether he shall heal the sick man encharged to him, for no one should deliberate about an end which he is obliged to seek, but only about the means to attain that end. Wherefore the Apostle, having commended the unity of the faithful people, says: "Be ye careful to keep the unity of the spirit in the bond of peace." Thus, the more efficacious a. government is in keeping the unity of peace, the more useful it will be. For we call that more useful which leads more directly to the end. Now it is manifest that what is itself one can more efficaciously bring about unity than several—just as the most efficacious cause of heat is that which is by its nature hot. Therefore the rule of one man is more useful than the rule of many.

[18] Furthermore, it is evident that several persons could by no means preserve the stability of the community if they totally disagreed. For union is necessary among them if they are to rule at all: several men, for instance, could not pull a ship in one direction unless joined together in some fashion. Now several are said to be united according as they come closer to being one. So one man rules better than several who come near being one.

[19] Again, whatever is in accord with nature is best, for in all things nature does what is best. Now, every natural governance is governance by one. In the multitude of bodily members there is one which is the principal mover, namely, the heart; and among the powers of the soul one power presides as chief, namely, the reason. Among bees there is one king bee' and in the whole universe there is One God, Maker and Ruler of all things. And there is a reason for this. Every multitude is derived from unity. Wherefore, if artificial things are an imitation of natural things' and a work of art is better according as it attains a closer likeness to what is in nature, it follows that it is best for a human multitude to be ruled by one person.

[20] This is also evident from experience. For provinces or cities which are not ruled by one person are torn with dissensions and tossed about without peace, so that the complaint seems to be fulfilled which the Lord uttered through the Prophet [Jer 12:10]: "Many pastors have destroyed my vineyard." On the other hand, provinces and cities which are ruled under one king enjoy peace, flourish in justice, and delight in prosperity. Hence, the Lord by His prophets promises to His people as a great reward that He will give them one head and that "one Prince will be in the midst of them" [Ez 34:24, Jer 30:21].

CHAPTER 4

THAT THE DOMINION OF A TYRANT IS THE WORST

[21] Just as the government of a king is the best, so the government of a tyrant is the worst.

[22] For democracy stands in contrary opposition to polity, since both are governments carried on by many persons, as is clear from what has already been said; while oligarchy is the opposite of aristocracy, since both are governments carried on by a few persons; and kingship is the opposite of tyranny since both are carried on by one person. Now, as has been shown above, monarchy is the best government. If, therefore, "it is the contrary of the best that is worst." it follows that tyranny is the worst kind of government.

[23] Further, a united force is more efficacious in producing its effect than a force which is scattered or divided. Many persons together can pull a load which could not be pulled by each one taking his part separately and acting individually. Therefore, just as it is more useful for a force operating for a good to be more united, in order that it may work good more effectively, so a force operating for evil is more harmful when it is one than when it is divided. Now, the power of one who rules unjustly works to the detriment of the multitude, in that he diverts the common good of the multitude to his own benefit. Therefore, for the same reason that, in a just government, the government is better in proportion as the ruling power is one—thus monarchy is better than aristocracy, and aristocracy better than polity—so the contrary will be true of an unjust government, namely, that the ruling power will be more harmful in proportion as it is more unitary. Consequently, tyranny is more harmful than oligarchy; and oligarchy more harmful than democracy.

[24] Moreover, a government becomes unjust by the fact that the ruler, paying no heed to the common good, seeks his own private good. Wherefore the further he departs from the common good the more unjust will his government be. But there is a greater departure from the common good in an oligarchy, in which the advantage of a few is sought, than in a democracy, in which the advantage of many is sought; and there is a still greater departure from the common good in a tyranny, where the advantage of only one man is sought. For a large number is closer to the totality than a small number, and a small number than only one. Thus, the government of a tyrant is the most unjust.

[25] The same conclusion is made clear to those who consider the order of Divine Providence, which disposes everything in the best way. In all things, good ensues from one perfect cause, i.e. from the totality of the conditions favourable to the production of the effect, while evil results from any one partial defect. There is beauty in a body when all its members are fittingly disposed; ugliness, on the other hand, arises when any one member is not fittingly disposed. Thus ugliness

results in different ways from many causes; beauty in one way from one perfect cause. It is thus with all good and evil things, as if God so provided that good, arising from one cause, be stronger, and evil, arising from many causes, be weaker. It is expedient therefore that a just government be that of one man only in order that it may be stronger; however, if the government should turn away from justice, it is more expedient that it be a government by many, so that it may be weaker and the many may mutually hinder one another. Among unjust governments, therefore, democracy is the most tolerable, but the worst is tyranny.

[26] This same conclusion is also apparent if one considers the evils which come from tyrants. Since a tyrant, despising the common good, seeks his private interest, it follows that he will oppress his subjects in different ways according as he is dominated by different passions to acquire certain goods. The one who is enthralled by the passion of cupidity seizes the goods of his subjects; whence Solomon says [Prov 29:4]: "A just king sets up the land; a covetous man shall destroy it." If he is dominated by the passion of anger, he sheds blood for nothing; whence it is said by Ezekiel: ' "Her princes in the midst of her are like wolves ravening the prey to shed blood." Therefore this kind of government is to be avoided as the Wise man admonishes [Sirach 9:13]: "Keep far from the man who has the power to kill," because he kills not for justice' sake but by his power, for the lust of his will. Thus there can be no safety. Everything is uncertain when there is a departure from justice. Nobody will be able firmly to state: This thing is such and such, when it depends upon the will of another, not to say upon his caprice. Nor does the tyrant merely oppress his subjects in corporal things but he also hinders their spiritual good. Those who seek more to use, than to be of use to, their subjects prevent all progress, suspecting all excellence in their subjects to be prejudicial to their own evil domination. For tyrants hold the good in greater suspicion than the wicked, and to them the valour of others is always fraught with danger.

[27] So the above-mentioned tyrants strive to prevent those of their subjects who have become virtuous from acquiring valour and high spirit in order that they may not want to cast off their iniquitous domination. They also see to it that there be no friendly relations among these so that they may not enjoy the benefits resulting from being on good terms with one another, for as long as one has no confidence in the other, no plot will be set up against the tyrant's domination. Wherefore they sow discords among the people, foster any that have arisen, and forbid anything which furthers society and co-operation among men, such as marriage, company at table and anything of like character, through which familiarity and confidence are engendered among men. They moreover strive to prevent their subjects from becoming powerful and rich since, suspecting these to be as wicked as themselves, they fear their power and wealth; for the subjects might become harmful to them even as they are accustomed to use power and wealth to harm others. Whence in the Book of Job it is said of the tyrant [15:21]: "The sound of dread is always in his ears and when there is peace (that is, when there is no one to harm him), he always suspects treason."

[28] It thus results that when rulers, who ought to induce their subjects to virtue," are wickedly jealous of the virtue of their subjects and hinder it as much as they can, few virtuous men are found under the rule of tyrants. For, according to Aristotle's sentence [*Eth.* III, 11: 1116a 20], brave men are found where brave men are honoured. And as Tullius says [*Tuscul. Disp.* I, 2, 4]: "Those who are despised by everybody are disheartened and flourish but little." It is also natural that men, brought up in fear, should become mean of spirit and discouraged in the face of any strenuous and manly task. This is shown by experience in provinces that have long been under tyrants. Hence the Apostle says to the Colossians: "Fathers, provoke not your children to indignation, lest they be discouraged."

[29] So, considering these evil effects of tyranny King Solomon says [Prov 28:12]: "When the wicked reign, men are ruined" because, forsooth, through the wickedness of tyrants, subjects fall away from the perfection of virtue. And again he says [Prov 29:2]: "When the wicked rule the people shall mourn, as though led into slavery." And again [Prov 28:28]: "When the wicked rise up men shall hide themselves", that they may escape the cruelty of the tyrant. It is no wonder, for a man governing without reason, according to the lust of his soul, in no way differs from the beast. Whence Solomon says [Prov 28:15]: "As a roaring lion and a hungry bear, so is a wicked prince over the poor people." Therefore men hide from tyrants as from cruel beasts and it seems that to be subject to a tyrant is the same thing as to lie prostrate beneath a raging beast.

CHAPTER 5

WHY THE ROYAL DIGNITY IS RENDERED HATEFUL TO THE SUBJECTS

[30] Because both the best and the worst government are latent in monarchy, i.e. in the rule of one man, the royal dignity is rendered hateful to many people on account of the wickedness of tyrants. Some men, indeed, whilst they desire to be ruled by a king, fall under the cruelty of tyrants, and not a few rulers exercise tyranny under the cloak of royal dignity.

[31] A clear example of this is found in the Roman Republic. When the kings had been driven out by the Roman people, because they could not bear the royal, or rather tyrannical, arrogance, they instituted consuls and other magistrates by whom they began to be ruled and guided. They changed the kingdom into an aristocracy, and, as Sallust relates [*Bellum Catilinae* VI, 7]: "The Roman city, once liberty was won, waxed incredibly strong and great in a remarkably short time." For it frequently happens that men living under a king strive more sluggishly for the common good, inasmuch as they consider that what they devote to the common good, they do not confer upon themselves but upon another, under whose power they see the common goods to be. But when they see that the common good is not under the power of one man, they do not attend to it as if it belonged to another, but each one attends to it as if it were his own.

15

[32] Experience thus teaches that one city administered by rulers, changing annually, is sometimes able to do more than some kings having, perchance, two or three cities; and small services exacted by kings weigh more heavily than great burdens imposed by the community of citizens. This held good in the history of the Roman Republic. The plebs were enrolled in the army and were paid wages for military service. Then when the common treasury was failing, private riches came forth for public uses, to such an extent that not even the senators retained any gold for themselves save one ring and the one bulla (the insignia of their dignity).

[33] On the other hand, when the Romans were worn out by continual dissensions taking on the proportion of civil wars, and when by these wars the freedom for which they had greatly striven was snatched from their hands, they began to find themselves under the power of emperors who, from the beginning, were unwilling to be called kings, for the royal name was hateful to the Romans. Some emperors, it is true, faithfully cared for the common good in a kingly manner, and by their zeal the commonwealth was increased and preserved. But most of them became tyrants towards their subjects while indolent and vacillating before their enemies, and brought the Roman commonwealth to naught.

[34] A similar process took place, also, among the Hebrew people. At first, while they were ruled by judges, they were ravished by their enemies on every hand, for each one "did what was good in his sight" (1 Sam 3:18). Yet when, at their own pressing, God gave them kings, they departed from the worship of the one God and were finally led into bondage, on account of the wickedness of their kings.

[35] Danger thus lurks on either side. Either men are held by the fear of a tyrant and they miss the opportunity of having that very best government which is kingship; or, they want a king and the kingly power turns into tyrannical wickedness.

CHAPTER 6

THAT IT IS A LESSER EVIL WHEN A MONARCHY TURNS INTO TYRANNY THAN WHEN AN ARISTOCRACY BECOMES CORRUPT

[36] When a choice is to be made between two things, from both of which danger impends, surely that one should be chosen from which the lesser evil follows. Now, lesser evil follows from the corruption of a monarchy (which is tyranny) than from the corruption of an aristocracy.

[37] Group government [polyarchy] most frequently breeds dissension. This dissension runs counter to the good of peace which is the principal social good. A tyrant, on the other hand, does not destroy this good, rather he obstructs one or

the other individual interest of his subjects—unless, of course, there be an excess of tyranny and the tyrant rages against the whole community. Monarchy is therefore to be preferred to polyarchy, although either form of government might become dangerous.

[38] Further, that from which great dangers may follow more frequently is, it would seem, the more to be avoided. Now, considerable dangers to the multitude follow more frequently from polyarchy than from monarchy. There is a greater chance that, where there are many rulers, one of them will abandon the intention of the common good than that it will be abandoned when there is but one ruler. When any one among several rulers turns aside from the pursuit of the common good, danger of internal strife threatens the group because, when the chiefs quarrel, dissension will follow in the people. When, on the other hand, one man is in command, he more often keeps to governing for the sake of the common good. Should he not do so, it does not immediately follow that he also proceeds to the total oppression of his subjects. This, of course, would be the excess of tyranny and the worst wickedness in government, as has been shown above. The dangers, then, arising from a polyarchy are more to be guarded against than those arising from a monarchy.

[39] Moreover, in point of fact, a polyarchy deviates into tyranny not less but perhaps more frequently than a monarchy. When, on account of there being many rulers, dissensions arise in such a government, it often happens that the power of one preponderates and he then usurps the government of the multitude for himself. This indeed may be clearly seen from history. There has hardly ever been a polyarchy that did not end in tyranny. The best illustration of this fact is the history of the Roman Republic. It was for a long time administered by the magistrates but then animosities, dissensions and civil wars arose and it fell into the power of the most cruel tyrants. In general, if one carefully considers what has happened in the past and what is happening in the present, he will discover that more men have held tyrannical sway in lands previously ruled by many rulers than in those ruled by one.

[40] The strongest objection why monarchy, although it is "the best form of government", is not agreeable to the people is that, in fact, it may deviate into tyranny. Yet tyranny is wont to occur not less but more frequently on the basis of a polyarchy than on the basis of a monarchy. It follows that it is, in any case, more expedient to live under one king than under the rule of several men.

CHAPTER 7

HOW PROVISION MIGHT BE MADE THAT THE KING MAY NOT FALL INTO TYRANNY

[41] Therefore, since the rule of one man, which is the best, is to be preferred, and since it may happen that it be changed into a tyranny, which is the worst (all this is clear from what has been said), a scheme should be carefully worked out which would prevent the multitude ruled by a king from falling into the hands of a tyrant.

[42] First, it is necessary that the man who is raised up to be king by those whom it concerns should be of such condition that it is improbable that he should become a tyrant. Wherefore Daniel, commending the providence of God with respect to the institution of the king says [1 Sam 13:14]: "The Lord sought a man according to his own heart, and the Lord appointed him to be prince over his people." Then, once the king is established, the government of the kingdom must be so arranged that opportunity to tyrannize is removed. At the same time his power should be so tempered that he cannot easily fall into tyranny. How these things may be done we must consider in what follows.

[43] Finally, provision must be made for facing the situation should the king stray into tyranny.

[44] Indeed, if there be not an excess of tyranny it is more expedient to tolerate the milder tyranny for a while than, by acting against the tyrant, to become involved in many perils more grievous than the tyranny itself. For it may happen that those who act against the tyrant are unable to prevail and the tyrant then will rage the more. But should one be able to prevail against the tyrant, from this fact itself very grave dissensions among the people frequently ensue: the multitude may be broken up into factions either during their revolt against the tyrant, or in process of the organization of the government, after the tyrant has been overthrown. Moreover, it sometimes happens that while the multitude is driving out the tyrant by the help of some man, the latter, having received the power, thereupon seizes the tyranny. Then, fearing to suffer from another what he did to his predecessor, he oppresses his subjects with an even more grievous slavery. This is wont to happen in tyranny, namely, that the second becomes more grievous than the one preceding, inasmuch as, without abandoning the previous oppressions, he himself thinks up fresh ones from the malice of his heart. Whence in Syracuse, at a time when everyone desired the death of Dionysius, a certain old woman kept constantly praying that he might be unharmed and that he might survive her. When the tyrant learned this he asked why she did it. Then she said: "When I was a girl we had a harsh tyrant and I wished for his death; when he was killed, there succeeded him one who was a little harsher. I was very eager to see the end of his dominion also, and we began to have a third ruler still more harsh—that was you. So if you should be taken away, a worse would succeed in your place."

[45] If the excess of tyranny is unbearable, some have been of the opinion that it would be an act of virtue for strong men to slay the tyrant and to expose themselves to the danger of death in order to set the multitude free. An example of this occurs even in the Old Testament, for a certain Aioth slew Eglon, King of Moab, who was oppressing the people of God under harsh slavery, thrusting a dagger into his thigh; and he was made a judge of the people [Judges 3:14 ff].

[46] But this opinion is not in accord with apostolic teaching. For Peter admonishes us to be reverently subject to our masters, not only to the good and gentle but also the froward [1 Pet 2:18-19]: "For if one who suffers unjustly bear his trouble for conscience' sake, this is grace." Wherefore, when many emperors of the Romans tyrannically persecuted the faith of Christ, a great number both of the nobility and the common people were converted to the faith and were praised for patiently bearing death for Christ. They did not resist although they were armed, and this is plainly manifested in the case of the holy Theban legion." Aioth, then, must be considered rather as having slain a foe than assassinated a ruler, however tyrannical, of the people. Hence in the Old Testament we also read that they who killed Joas, the king of Juda, who had fallen away from the worship of God, were slain and their children spared according to the precept of the law" (2 Sam 14:5-6).

[47] Should private persons attempt on their own private presumption to kill the rulers, even though tyrants, this would be dangerous for the multitude as well as for their rulers. This is because the wicked usually expose themselves to dangers of this kind more than the good, for the rule of a king, no less than that of a tyrant, is burdensome to them since, according to the words of Solomon [Prov 20:26]: "A wise king scatters the wicked." Consequently, by presumption of this kind, danger to the people from the loss of a good king would be more probable than relief through the removal of a tyrant.

[48] Furthermore, it seems that to proceed against the cruelty of tyrants is an action to be undertaken, not through the private presumption of a few, but rather by public authority.

[49] If to provide itself with a king belongs to the right of a given multitude, it is not unjust that the king be deposed or have his power restricted by that same multitude if, becoming a tyrant, he abuses the royal power. It must not be thought that such a multitude is acting unfaithfully in deposing the tyrant, even though it had previously subjected itself to him in perpetuity, because he himself has deserved that the covenant with his subjects should not be kept, since, in ruling the multitude, he did not act faithfully as the office of a king demands. Thus did the Romans, who had accepted Tarquin the Proud as their king, cast him out from the kingship on account of his tyranny and the tyranny of his sons; and they set up in their place a lesser power, namely, the consular power. Similarly Domitian, who had succeeded those most moderate emperors, Vespasian, his father, and Titus, his brother, was slain by the Roman senate when he exercised tyranny, and all his wicked deeds were justly, and profitably declared null and void by a

19

decree of the senate. Thus it came about that Blessed John the Evangelist, the beloved disciple of God, who had been exiled to the island of Patmos by that very Domitian, was sent back to Ephesus by a decree of the senate.

[50] If, on the other hand, it pertains to the right of a higher authority to provide a king for a certain multitude, a remedy against the wickedness of a tyrant is to be looked for from him. Thus when Archelaus, who had already begun to reign in Judaea in the place of Herod his father, was imitating his father's wickedness, a complaint against him having been laid before Caesar Augustus by the Jews, his power was at first diminished by depriving him of his title of king and by dividing one-half of his kingdom between his two brothers. Later, since he was not restrained from tyranny even by this means, Tiberius Caesar sent him into exile to Lugdunum, a city in Gaul.

[51] Should no human aid whatsoever against a tyrant be forthcoming, recourse must be had to God, the King of all, Who is a helper in due time in tribulation. For it lies in his power to turn the cruel heart of the tyrant to mildness. According to Solomon [Prov 21:1]: "The heart of the king is in the hand of the Lord, withersoever He will He shall turn it." He it was who turned into mildness the cruelty of King Assuerus, who was preparing death for the Jews. He it was who so filled the cruel king Nabuchodonosor with piety that he became a proclaimer of the divine power. "Therefore," he said, "I, Nabuchodonosor do now praise and magnify and glorify the King of Heaven; because all His works are true and His ways judgments, and they that walk in pride He is able to abase" (Dan 4:34). Those tyrants, however, whom he deems unworthy of conversion, he is able to put out of the way or to degrade, according to the words of the Wise Man [Sirach 10:17]: "God has overturned the thrones of proud princes and has set up the meek in their stead." He it was who, seeing the affliction of his people in Egypt and hearing their cry, hurled Pharaoh, a tyrant over God's people, with all his army into the sea. He it was who not only banished from his kingly throne the above-mentioned Nabuchodonosor because of his former pride, but also cast him from the fellowship of men and changed him into the likeness of a beast. Indeed, his hand is not shortened that He cannot free His people from tyrants. For by Isaiah (14:3) He promised to give his people rest from their labours and lashings and harsh slavery in which they had formerly served; and by Ezekiel (34:10) He says: "I will deliver my flock from their mouth," i.e. from the mouth of shepherds who feed themselves.

[52] But to deserve to secure this benefit from God, the people must desist from sin, for it is by divine permission that wicked men receive power to rule as a punishment for sin, as the Lord says by the Prophet Hosea [13:11]: "I will give you a king in my wrath" and it is said in Job (34:30) that he "makes a man that is a hypocrite to reign for the sins of the people." Sin must therefore be done away with in order that the scourge of tyrants may cease.

CHAPTER 8

THAT MUNDANE HONOUR AND GLORY ARE NOT AN ADEQUATE REWARD FOR A KING

[53] Since, according to what has been said thus far, it is the king's duty to seek the good of the multitude, the task of a king may seem too burdensome unless some advantage to himself should result from it. It is fitting therefore to consider wherein a suitable reward for a good king is to be found.

[54] By some men this reward was considered to be nothing other than honour and glory. Whence Tullius says in the book On the Republic [*De Republica* V, 7, 9]: "The prince of the city should be nourished by glory," and Aristotle seems to assign the reason for this in his Book on *Ethics* [V, 10: 1134b 7]: "because the prince for whom honour and glory is not sufficient consequently turns into tyrant." For it is in the hearts of all men to seek their proper good. Therefore, if the prince is not content with glory and honour, he will seek pleasures an riches and so will resort to plundering and injuring his subjects.

[55] However, if we accept this opinion a great many incongruous results follow. In the first place, it would be costly to kings if so many labours and anxieties were to be endured for a reward so perishable, fo nothing, it seems, is more perishable among human things than the glory and honour of men's favour since it depends upon the report of men and their opinions, than which nothing in human life is more fickle. And this is why the Prophet Isaiah calls such glory "the flower of grass."

[56] Moreover, the desire for human glory takes away greatness of soul. For he who seeks the favour of men must serve their will in all he says and does, and thus, while striving to please all, he becomes a slave to each one. Wherefore the same Tullius says in his book *On Duties* [*De officiis*, I, 20, 68] that "the inordinate desire for glory is to be guarded against; it takes away freedom of soul, for the sake of which high-minded men should put forth all their efforts." Indeed there is nothing more becoming to a prince who has been set up for the doing of good works than greatness of soul. Thus, the reward of human glory is not enough for the services of a king.

[57] At the same time it also hurts the multitude if such a reward be set up for princes, for it is the duty of a good man to take no account of glory, just as he should take no account of other temporal goods. It is the mark of a virtuous and brave soul to despise glory as he despises life, for justice' sake: whence the strange thing results that glory ensues from virtuous acts, and out of virtue glory itself is despised: and therefore, through his very contempt for glory, a man is made glorious—according to the sentence of Fabius: "He who scorns glory shall have true glory," and as Sallust [*Bellum Catilinae* 54, 6] says of Cato: "The less he sought glory the more he achieved it." Even the disciples of Christ "exhibited themselves

as the ministers of God in honour and dishonour, in evil report and good report" (2 Cor 6:8). Glory is, therefore, not a fitting reward for a good man; good men spurn it. And, if it alone be set up as the reward for princes, it will follow that good men will not take upon themselves the chief office of the city, or if they take it, they will go unrewarded.

[58] Furthermore, dangerous evils come from the desire for glory. Many have been led unrestrainedly to seek glory in warfare, and have sent their armies and themselves to destruction, while the freedom of their country was turned into servitude under an enemy. Consider Torquatus, the Roman chief. In order to impress upon the people how imperative it is to avoid such danger, "he slew his own son who, being challenged by an enemy, had, through youthful impetuosity, fought and vanquished him. Yet he had done so contrary to orders given him by his father. Torquatus acted thus, lest more harm should accrue from the example of his son's presumption than advantage from the glory of slaying the enemy." [Cf. Augustine, *De civ. Dei*, V, 18.]

[59] Moreover, the desire for glory has another vice akin to it, namely hypocrisy. Since it is difficult to acquire true virtues, to which alone honour and glory are due, and it is therefore the lot of but a few to attain them, many who desire glory become simulators of virtue. On this account, as Sallust says [*Bellum Catilinae* 10, 5]: "Ambition drives many mortals to become false. They keep one thing shut up in their heart, another ready on the tongue, and they have more countenance than character." But our Saviour also calls those persons hypocrites, or simulators, who do good works that they may be seen by men. Therefore, just as there is danger for the multitude, if the prince seek pleasures and riches as his reward, that he become a plunderer and abusive, so there is danger, if glory be assigned to him as reward, that he become presumptuous and a hypocrite.

[60] Looking at what the above-mentioned wise men intended to say, they do not seem to have decided upon honour and glory as the reward of a prince because they judged that the king's intention should be principally directed to that object, but because it is more tolerable for him to seek glory than to desire money or pursue pleasure. For this vice is akin to virtue inasmuch as the glory which men desire, as Augustine says [*De civ. Dei* V, 12], is nothing else than the judgment of men who think well of men. So the desire for glory has some trace of virtue in it, at least so long as it seeks the approval of good men and is reluctant to displease them. Therefore, since few men reach true virtue, it seems more tolerable if one be set up to rule who, fearing the judgment of men, is restrained from manifest evils. For the man" who desires glory either endeavours to win the approval of men in the true way, by deeds of virtue, or at least strives for this by fraud and deceit. But if the one who desires to domineer lacks the desire for glory, he will have no fear of offending men of good judgment and will commonly strive to obtain what he chooses by the most open crimes. Thus he will surpass the beasts in the vices of cruelty and lust, as is evidenced in the case of the Emperor Nero, who was so effete, as Augustine says [*loc. cit.*], "that he despised everything virile, and yet so cruel that nobody would have thought him to be effeminate." Indeed all this is

quite clearly contained in what Aristotle says in his *Ethics*[IV, 7:1124a 16] regarding the magnanimous man: True, he does seek honour and glory, but not as something great which could be a sufficient reward of virtue. And beyond this he demands nothing more of men, for among all earthly goods the chief good, it seems, is this, that men bear testimony to the virtue of a man.

CHAPTER 9

THAT THE KING SHOULD LOOK TO GOD FOR ADEQUATE REWARD

[61] Therefore, since worldly honour and human glory are not a sufficient reward for royal cares, it remains to inquire what sort of reward is sufficient.

[62] It is proper that a king look to God for his reward, for a servant looks to his master for the reward of his service. The king is indeed the minister of God in governing the people, as the Apostle says: "All power is from the Lord God" (Rom 13:1) and God's minister is "an avenger to execute wrath upon him who does evil" (Rom 13:4). And in the Book of Wisdom (6:5), kings are described as being ministers of God. Consequently, kings ought to look to God for the reward of their ruling. Now God sometimes rewards kings for their service by temporal goods, but such rewards are common to both the good and the wicked. Wherefore the Lord says to Ezechiel (29:18): "Nabuchodonosor, king of Babylon, has made his army to undergo hard service against Tyre, and there has been no reward given him nor his army for Tyre, for the service he rendered Me against it," for that service namely, by which, according to the Apostle, power is "the minister of God and the avenger to execute wrath upon him who does evil." Afterwards He adds, regarding the reward: "Therefore, thus says the Lord God, 'I will set Nabuchodonosor the king of Babylon in the land of Egypt, and he shall rifle the spoils thereof, and it shall be wages for his army.'" Therefore, if God recompenses wicked kings who fight against the enemies of God, though not with the intention of serving Him but to execute their own hatred and cupidity, by giving them such great rewards as to yield them victory over their foes, subject kingdoms to their sway and grant them spoils to rifle, what will He do for kings who rule the people of God and assail His enemies from a holy motive? He promises them not an earthly reward indeed but an everlasting one and in none other than in Himself. As Peter says to the shepherds of the people (1 Pet 5:2,4): "Feed the flock of God that is among you and when the prince of pastors shall appear (i.e. the King of kings, Christ) you shall receive a never-fading crown of glory," concerning which Isaiah says (28:5): "The Lord shall be a crown of glory and a garland of joy to His people."

[63] This is also clearly shown by reason. It is implanted in the minds of all who have the use of reason that the reward of virtue is happiness. The virtue of anything whatsoever is explained to be that which makes its possessor good and renders his deed good. Moreover, everyone strives by working well to attain that

which is most deeply implanted in desire, namely, to be happy. This, no one is able not to wish. It is therefore fitting to expect as a reward for virtue that which makes man happy. Now, if to work well is a virtuous deed, and the king's work is to rule his people well, then that which makes him happy will be the king's reward. What this is has now to be considered." Happiness, we say, is the ultimate end of our desires. Now the movement of desire does not go on to infinity else natural desire would be vain, for infinity cannot be traversed. Since, then, the desire of an intellectual nature is for universal good, that good alone can make it truly happy which, when attained, leaves no further good to be desired. Whence happiness is called the perfect good inasmuch as it comprises in itself all things desirable. But no earthly good is such a good. They who have riches desire to have more, they who enjoy pleasure desire to enjoy more, and the like is clear for the rest: and if they do not seek more, they at least desire that those they have should abide or that others should follow in their stead. For nothing permanent is found in earthly things. Consequently there is nothing earthly which can calm desire. Thus, nothing earthly can make man happy, so that it may be a fitting reward for a king.

[64] Again, the last perfection and perfect good of anything one chooses depends upon something higher, for even bodily things are made better by the addition of better things and worse by being mixed with baser things. If gold is mingled with silver, the silver is made better, while by an admixture of lead it is rendered impure. Now it is manifest that all earthly things are beneath the human mind. But happiness is the last perfection and the perfect good of man, which all men desire to reach. Therefore there is no earthly thing which could make man happy, nor is any earthly thing a sufficient reward for a king. For, as Augustine" says, "we do not call Christian princes happy merely because they have reigned a long time, or because after a peaceful death they have left their sons to rule, or because they subdued the enemies of the state, or because they were able to guard against or to suppress citizens who rose up against them. Rather do we call them happy if they rule justly, if they prefer to rule their passions rather than nations, and if they do all things not for the love of vainglory but for the love of eternal happiness. Such Christian emperors we say are happy, now in hope, afterwards in very fact when that which we await shall come to pass. But neither is there any other created thing which would make a man happy and which could be set up as the reward for a king. For the desire of each thing tends towards its source, whence is the cause of its being. But the cause of the human soul is none other than God Who made it to His own image. Therefore it is God alone Who can still the desires of man and make him happy and be the fitting reward for a king.

[65] Furthermore, the human mind knows the universal good through the intellect, and desires it through the will: but the universal good is not found except in God. Therefore there is nothing which could make man happy, fulfilling his every desire, but God, of Whom it is said in the Psalm (102:5): "Who satisfies your desire with good things." In this, therefore, should the king place his reward. Wherefore, King David," with this in mind, said (Ps 72:25,28): "What have I in heaven? And besides You what do I desire upon earth?" and he

afterwards adds in answer to this question: "It is good for me to adhere to my God and to put my hope in the Lord God." For it is He Who gives salvation to kings, not merely temporal salvation by which He saves both men and beasts together, but also that salvation of which He says by the mouth of Isaiah (51:6): "But my salvation shall be for ever," that salvation by which He saves man and makes them equal to the angels.

[66] It can thus also be verified that the reward of the king is honour and glory. What worldly and frail honour can indeed be likened to this honour that a man be made a "citizen with the Saints and a kinsman of God" (Eph 2:19), numbered among the sons of God, and that he obtain the inheritance of the heavenly kingdom with Christ? This is the honour of which King David, in desire and wonder, says (Ps 138:17): "Your friends, O God, are made exceedingly honourable." And further, what glory of human praise can be compared to this, not uttered by the false tongue of flatterers nor the fallacious opinion of men, but issuing from the witness of our inmost conscience and confirmed by the testimony of God, Who promises to those who confess Him that He will confess them before the Angels of God in the glory of the Father? They who seek this glory will find it and they will win the glory of men which they do not seek: witness Solomon, who not only received from the Lord wisdom which he sought, but was made glorious above other kings.

CHAPTER 10

WHAT DEGREE OF HEAVENLY BEATITUDE THE KING MAY OBTAIN

[67] Now it remains further to consider that they who discharge the kingly office worthily and laudably will obtain an elevated and outstanding degree of heavenly happiness.

[68] For if happiness is the reward of virtue, it follows that a higher degree of happiness is due to greater virtue. Now, that indeed is signal virtue by which a man can guide not only himself but others, and the more persons he rules the greater his virtue. Similarly, in regard to bodily strength, a man is reputed to be more powerful the more adversaries he can beat or the more weights he can lift. Thus, greater virtue is required to rule a household than to rule one's self, and much greater to rule a city and a kingdom. To discharge well the office of a king is therefore a work of extraordinary virtue. To it, therefore, is due an extraordinary reward of happiness.

[69] Again, those who rule others well are more worthy of praise than those who act well under others' direction. This applies to the field of all arts and sciences. In the speculative sciences, for instance, it is nobler to impart truth to others by teaching than to be able to grasp what is taught by others. So, too, in matters of the crafts, an architect who plans a building is more highly esteemed and paid a

higher wage than is the builder who does the manual labour under his direction; also, in warfare the strategy of the general wins greater glory from victory than the bravery of the soldier. Now the ruler of a multitude stands in the same relation to the virtuous deeds performed by each individual as the teacher to the matters taught the architect to the buildings, and the general to the wars. Consequently, the king is worthy of a greater reward if he governs his subjects well than any of his subjects who act well under him.

[70] Further, if it is the part of virtue to render a man's work good, it is, it seems, from greater virtue that one does greater good. But the good of the multitude is greater and more divine than the good of one man. Wherefore the evil of one man is sometimes endured if it redounds to the good of the multitude, as when a robber is killed to bring peace to the multitude. God Himself would not allow evils to be in the world were it not for the fact that He brings good out of them for the advantage and beauty of the universe. Now it belongs to the office of the king to have zealous concern for the good of the multitude. Therefore a greater reward is due to the king for good ruling than to the subject for acting according to rule.

[71] This will become clearer if considered in greater detail. For a private person is praised by men, and his deed reckoned for reward by God, if he helps the needy, brings peace to those in discord, rescues one oppressed by a mightier; in a word, if in any way he gives to another assistance or advice for his welfare How much the more, then, is he to be praised by men and rewarded by God who makes a whole province rejoice in peace, who restrains violence, preserves justice and arranges by his laws and precepts what is to be done by men?

[72] The greatness of kingly virtue also appears in this, that he bears a special likeness to God, since he does in his kingdom what God does in the world; wherefore in Exodus (22:9) the judges of the people are called gods, and also among the Romans the emperors received the appellative *Divus*. Now the more a thing approaches to the likeness of God the more acceptable it is to Him. Hence, also, the Apostle urges (Eph 5:1): "Be therefore imitators of God as most dear children." But if according to the saying of the Wise Man (Sirach 13:9), every beast loves its like inasmuch as causes bear some likeness to the caused, it follows that good kings are most pleasing to God and are to be most highly rewarded by Him.

[73] Likewise, if I may use the words of Gregory [*Regula Pastoralis* I, 9]: "What else is it (for a king) to be at the pinnacle of power if not to find himself in a mental storm? When the sea is calm even an inexperienced man can steer a ship straight; when the sea is troubled by stormy waves, even an experienced sailor is bewildered. Whence it frequently happens that in the business of government the practice of good works is lost which in tranquil times was maintained." For, as Augustine says [*De civ. Dei* V, 24], it is very difficult for rulers "not to be puffed up amid flattering and honouring tongues and the obsequiousness of those who bow too humbly, but to remember that they are men." It is said also in Sirach (31:8,10): "Blessed is the rich man who has not gone after gold nor put his trust in money nor in treasures, who could have transgressed with impunity and did not

transgress, who could do evil and did not do it." Wherefore, having been tried in the work of virtue, he is found faithful and so, according to the proverb of Bias [Aristotle, *Eth. Nic.* V, 3: 1130a 1]: "Authority shows the man." For many who seemed virtuous while they were in lowly state fall from virtue when they reach the pinnacle of power. The very difficulty, then, of acting well, which besets kings, makes them more worthy of greater reward; and if through weakness they sometimes do amiss, they are rendered more excusable before men and more easily obtain forgiveness from God provided, as Augustine says (*De civ. Dei*, V, 24), they do not neglect to offer up to their true God the sacrifice of humility, mercy, and prayer for their sins. As an example of this, the Lord said to Elias concerning Achab, king of Israel, who had sinned a great deal: "Because he has humbled himself for My sake, I will not bring the evil in his days."

[74] That a very high reward is due to kings is not only demonstrated by reason but is also confirmed by divine authority. It is said in the prophecy of Zachariah (12:8) that, in that day of blessedness wherein God will be the protector of the inhabitants of Jerusalem (i.e. in the vision of eternal peace), the houses of others will be as the house of David, because all will then be kings and reign with Christ as the members with their head. But the house of David will be as the house of God, because just as he carried out the work of God among the people by ruling faithfully, so in his reward he will adhere more closely to God. Likewise, among the Gentiles this was dimly realized, as in a dream, for they thought to transform into gods the rulers and preservers of their cities.

CHAPTER 11

WHAT ADVANTAGES WHICH ARE RENDERED TO KINGS ARE LOST BY THE TYRANT

[75] Since such a magnificent reward in heavenly blessedness is in store for kings who have acted well in ruling, they ought to keep careful watch over themselves in order not to turn to tyranny. Nothing, indeed, can be more acceptable to them than to be transferred from the royal honour, to which they are raised on earth, into the glory of the heavenly kingdom. Tyrants, on the contrary, who desert justice for a few earthly advantages, are deprived of such a great reward which they could have obtained by ruling justly. How foolish it is to sacrifice the greatest and eternal goods for trifling, temporal goods is clear to everyone but a fool or an infidel.

[76] It is to be added further, however, that the very temporal advantages for which tyrants abandon justice work to the greater profit of kings when they observe justice.

[77] First of all, among all worldly things there is nothing which seems worthy to be preferred to friendship. Friendship unites good men and preserves and

promotes virtue. Friendship is needed by all men in whatsoever occupations they engage. In prosperity it does not thrust itself unwanted upon us, nor does it desert us in adversity. It is what brings with it the greatest delight, to such an extent that all that pleases is changed to weariness when friends are absent, and all difficult things are made easy and as nothing by love. There is no tyrant so cruel that friendship does not bring him pleasure. When Dionysius, sometime tyrant of Syracuse, wanted to kill one of two friends, Damon and Pythias, the one who was to be killed asked leave to go home and set his affairs in order, and the other friend surrendered himself to the tyrant as security for his return. When the appointed day was approaching and he had not yet returned, everyone said that his hostage was a fool, but he declared he had no fear whatever regarding his friend's loyalty. The very hour when he was to be put to death, his friend returned. Admiring the courage of both, the tyrant remitted the sentence on account of the loyalty of their friendship, and asked in addition that they should receive him as a third member in their bond of friendship. [Cf. Valerius Maximus IV, 7, Ext. 1; Vincent of Beauvais, *Specul. Doctrinale* V, 84.]

[78] Yet, although tyrants desire this very benefit of friendship, they cannot obtain it, for when they seek their own good instead of the common good there is little or no communion between them and their subjects. Now all friendship is concluded upon the basis of something common among those who are to be friends, for we see that those are united in friendship who have in common either their natural origin, or some similarity in habits of life, or any kind of social interests. Consequently there can be little or no friendship between tyrants and their subjects. When the latter are oppressed by tyrannical injustice and feel they are not loved but despised, they certainly do not conceive any love, for it is too great a virtue for the common man to love his enemies and to do good to his persecutors. Nor have tyrants any reason to complain of their subjects if they are not loved by them, since they do not act towards them in such a way that they ought to be loved by them. Good kings, on the contrary, are loved by many when they show that they love their subjects and are studiously intent on the common welfare, and when their subjects can see that they derive many benefits from this zealous care. For to hate their friends and return evil for good to their benefactors—this, surely, would be too great a malice to ascribe fittingly to the generality of men.

[79] The consequence of this love is that the government of good kings is stable, because their subjects do not refuse to expose themselves to any danger whatsoever on behalf of such kings. An example of this is to be seen in Julius Caesar who, as Suetonius relates [*Divus Iulius* 67], loved his soldiers to such an extent that when he heard that some of them were slaughtered, "he refused to cut either hair or beard until he had taken vengeance." In this way, he made his soldiers most loyal to himself as well as most valiant, so that many, on being taken prisoner, refused to accept their lives when offered them on the condition that they serve against Caesar. Octavianus Augustus, also, who was most moderate in his use of power, was so loved by his subjects that some of them "on their deathbeds provided in their wills a thank-offering to be paid by the

immolation of animals, so grateful were they that the emperor's life outlasted their own" [Suetonius, *Divus Augustus* 59]. Therefore it is no easy task to shake the government of a prince whom the people so unanimously love. This is why Solomon says (Prov 29:14): "The king that judgeth the poor in justice, his throne shall be established forever."

[80] The government of tyrants, on the other hand, cannot last long because it is hateful to the multitude, and what is against the wishes of the multitude cannot be long preserved. For a man can hardly pass through this present life without suffering some adversities, and in the time of his adversity occasion cannot be lacking to rise against the tyrant; and when there is an opportunity there will not be lacking at least one of the multitude to use it. Then the people will fervently favour the insurgent, and what is attempted with the sympathy of the multitude will not easily fail of its effects. It can thus scarcely come to pass that the government of a tyrant will endure for a long time.

[81] This is very clear, too, if we consider the means by which a tyrannical government is upheld. It is not upheld by love, since there is little or no bond of friendship between the subject multitude and the tyrant, as is evident from what we have said. On the other Aand, tyrants cannot rely on the loyalty of their subjects, for such a degree of virtue is not found among the generality of men, that they should be restrained by the virtue of fidelity from throwing off the yoke of unmerited servitude, if they are able to do so. Nor would it perhaps be a violation of fidelity at all, according to the opinion of many,' to frustrate the wickedness of tyrants by any means whatsoever. It remains, then, that the government of a tyrant is maintained by fear alone and consequently they strive with all their might to be feared by their subjects. Fear, however, is a weak support. Those who are kept down by fear will rise against their rulers if the opportunity ever occurs when they can hope to do it with impunity, and they will rebel against their rulers all the more furiously the more they have been kept in subjection against their will by fear alone, just as water confined under pressure flows with greater impetus when. it finds an outlet. That very fear itself is not without danger, because many become desperate from excessive fear, and despair of safety impels a man boldly to dare anything. Therefore the government of a tyrant cannot be of long duration.

[82] This appears clearly from examples no less than from reason. If we scan the history of antiquity and the events of modern times, we shall scarcely find one government of a tyrant which lasted a long time. So Aristotle, in his Politics [V, 12: 1315b 11-39], after enumerating many tyrants, shows that all their governments were of short duration; although some of them reigned a fairly long time because they were not very tyrannical but in many things imitated the moderation of kings.

[83] All this becomes still more evident if we consider the divine judgment, for, as we read in Job (24:30), "He makes a man who is a hypocrite to reign for the sins of the people." No one, indeed, can be more truly called a hypocrite than the man

29

who assumes the office of king and acts like a tyrant, for a hypocrite is one who mimics the person of another, as is done on the stage. Hence God permits tyrants to get into power to punish the sins of the subjects. In Holy Scripture it is customary to call such punishment the anger of God. Thus in Hosea (13:11) the Lord says: "I will give you a king in my wrath." Unhappy is a king who is given to the people in God's wrath, for his power cannot be stable, because "God does not forgets to show mercy nor does He shut up His mercies in His anger" (Ps 76:10). On the contrary, as we read in Joel (2:13): "He is patientand rich in mercy and ready to repent of the evil." So God does not permit tyrants to reign a long time, but after the storm brought on the people through these tyrants, He restores transquillity by casting them down. Therefore the Wise Man" says (Sirach 10:17): "God has overturned the thrones of proud princes and hath set up the meek in their stead."

[84] Experience further shows that kings acquire more wealth through justice than tyrants do through rapine. Because the government of tyrants is displeasing to the multitude subject to it, tyrants must have a great many satellites to safeguard themselves against their subjects. On these it is necessary to spend more than they can rob from their subjects. On the contrary, the government of kings, since it is pleasing to their subjects, has for its protection, instead of hirelings, all the subjects. And they demand no pay but, in time of need, freely give to their kings more than the tyrants can take. Thus the words of Solomon are fulfilled (Prov 11:24): "Some (namely, the kings) distribute their own goods (doing good to their subjects) and grow richer; others (namely, the tyrants) take away what is not their own and are always in want." In the same way it comes to pass, by the just judgment of God, that those who unjustly heap up riches, uselessly scatter them or are justly deprived of them. For, as Solomon says (Eccles. 5:9): "A covetous man shall not be satisfied with money and he who loves riches shall reap no fruit from them." Rather, we read in Proverbs (15:27): "He who is greedy of gain troubles his own house." But to kings who seek justice, God gives wealth, as He did to Solomon who, when he sought wisdom to do justice, received a promise of an abundance of wealth."

[85] It seems superfluous to speak about fame, for who can doubt that good kings live in a sense in the praises of men, not only in this life, but still more, after their death, and that men yearn for them? But the name of wicked kings straightway vanishes or, if they have been excessive in their wickedness, they are remembered with execration. Thus Solomon says (Prov 10:7): "The memory of the just is with praises, and the name of the wicked shall rot," either because it vanishes or it remains with stench.

CHAPTER 12

WHAT PUNISHMENTS ARE IN STORE FOR A TYRANT

[86] From the above arguments it is evident that stability of power, wealth, honour and fame come to fulfil the desires of kings rather than tyrants, and it is in seeking to acquire these things unduly that princes turn to tyranny. For no one falls away from justice except through a desire for some temporal advantage.

[87] The tyrant, moreover, loses the surpassing beatitude which is due as a reward to kings and, which is still more serious, brings upon himself great suffering as a punishment. For if the man who despoils a single man, or casts him into slavery, or kills him, deserves the greatest punishment (death in the judgment of men, and in the judgment of God eternal damnation), how much worse tortures must we consider a tyrant deserves, who on all sides robs everybody, works against the common liberty of all, and kills whom he will at his merest whim?

[88] Again, such men rarely repent; but puffed up by the wind of pride, deservedly abandoned by God for their sins, and besmirched by the flattery of men, they can rarely make worthy satisfaction. When will they ever restore all those things which they have received beyond their just due? Yet no one doubts that they are bound to restore those ill-gotten goods. When will they make amends to those whom they have oppressed and unjustly injured in their many ways?

[89] The malice of their impenitence is increased by the fact that they consider everything licit which they can do unresisted and with impunity. Hence they not only make no effort to repair the evil they have done but, taking their customary way of acting as their authority, they hand on their boldness in sinning to posterity. Consequently they are held guilty before God, not only for their own sins, but also for the crimes of those to whom they gave the occasion of sin.

[90] Their sin is made greater also from the dignity of the office they have assumed. Just as an earthly king inflicts a heavier punishment upon his ministers if he finds them traitors to him, so God will punish more severely those whom He made the executors and ministers of His government if they act wickedly, turning God's judgment into bitterness. Hence, in the Book of Wisdom (6:5-7), the following words are addressed to wicked kings: "Because being ministers of His kingdom, you have not judged rightly nor kept the law of justice nor walked according to the will of God, horribly and speedily will He appear to you, for a most severe judgment shall be for them that bear rule; for to him that is little, mercy is granted, but the mighty shall be mightily tormented." And to Nabuchodonosor it is said by Isaiah (14:15-16): "But you shall yet be brought down to hell, into the depth of the pit. They who see you shall turn toward you and gaze on you" as one more deeply buried in punishments.

[91] So, then, if to kings an abundance of temporal goods is given and an eminent degree of beatitude prepared for them by God, while tyrants are often prevented from obtaining even the temporal goods which they covet, subjected also to many dangers and, worse still, deprived of eternal happiness and destined for most grievous punishment, surely those who undertake the office of ruling must earnestly strive to act as kings towards their subjects, and not as tyrants.

[92] What has been said hitherto should suffice in order to show what a king is, and that it is good for the multitude to have a king, and also that it is expedient for a ruler to conduct himself towards the multitude of his subjects as a king, not as a tyrant.

CHAPTER 13

ON THE DUTIES OF A KING

[93] The next point to be Considered is what the kingly office is and what qualities the king should have. Since things which are in accordance with art are an imitation of the things which are in accordance with nature (from which we accept the rules to act according to reason), it seems best that we learn about the kingly office from the pattern of the regime of nature.

[94] In things of nature there is both a universal and a particular government. The former is God's government Whose rule embraces all things and Whose providence governs them all. The latter is found in man and it is much like the divine government. Hence man is called a microcosm. Indeed there is a similitude between both governments in regard to their form; for just as the universe of corporeal creatures and all spiritual powers come under the divine government, in like manner the members of the human body and all the powers of the soul are governed by reason. Thus, in a proportionate manner, reason is to man what God is to the world. Since, however, man is by nature a social animal living in a multitude, as we have pointed out above,' the analogy with the divine government is found in him not only in this way that one man governs himself by reason, but also in that the multitude of men is governed by the reason of one man. This is what first of all constitutes the office of a king. True, among certain animals that live socially there is a likeness to the king's rulership; so we say that there are kings among bees. Yet animals exercise rulership not through reason but through their natural instinct which is implanted in them by the Great Ruler the Author of nature.

[95] Therefore let the king recognize that such is the office which he undertakes, namely, that he is to be in the kingdom what the soul is in the body, and what God is in the world.' If he reflect seriously upon this, a zeal for justice will be enkindled in him when he contemplates that he has been appointed to this position in place of God, to exercise judgment in his kingdom; further, he will

acquire the gentleness of clemency and mildness when he considers as his own members those individuals who are subject to his rule.

CHAPTER 14

WHAT IT IS INCUMBENT UPON A KING TO DO AND HOW HE SHOULD GO ABOUT DOING IT

[96] Let us then examine what God does in the world, for in this way we shall be able to see what it is incumbent upon a king to do.

[97] Looking at the world as a whole, there are two works of God to be considered: the first is creation; the second, God's government of the things created. These two works are, in like manner, performed by the soul in the body since, first, by the virtue of the soul the body is formed, and then the latter is governed and moved by the soul.

[98] Of these works, the second more properly pertains to the office of kingship. Therefore government belongs to all kings (the very name rex is derived from the fact that they direct the government), while the first work does not fall to all kings, for not all kings establish the kingdom or city in which they rule but bestow their regal care upon a kingdom or city already established. We must remember, however, that if there were no one to establish the city or kingdom,' there would be no question of governing the kingdom. The very notion of kingly office, then, comprises the establishment of a city and kingdom, and some kings have indeed established cities in which to rule; for example, Ninus founded Ninevah, and Romulus, Rome. It pertains also to the governing office to preserve the things governed, and to use them for the purpose for which they were established. If, therefore, one does not know how a kingdom is established, one cannot fully understand the task of its government.

[99] Now, from the example of the creation of the world one may learn how a kingdom is established. In creation we may consider, first, the production of things; secondly, the orderly distinction of the parts of the world. Further, we observe that different species of things are distributed in different parts of the world: stars in the heavens, fowls in the air, fishes in the water, and animals on land. We notice further that, for each species, the things it needs are abundantly provided by the Divine Power. Moses has minutely and carefully set forth this plan of how the world was made. First of all, he sets forth the production of things in these words: "In the beginning God created the heavens and the earth" (Gen 1:1). Next, he declares that all things were distinguished from one another by God according to a suitable order: day from night, higher things from lower, the sea from the dry land. He next relates that the sky was adorned with luminaries, the air with birds, the sea with fishes, the earth with animals; finally,

dominion over earth and animals was given to men. He further states that, by Divine Providence, plants were made for the use of men and the other animals.

[100] Of course the founder of a city and kingdom cannot produce anew men, places in which to dwell, and the other necessities of life. He has to make use of those which already exist in nature, just as the other arts derive the material for their work from nature; as, for example, the smith takes iron, the builder wood and stone, to use in their respective arts. Therefore the founder of a city and kingdom must first choose a suitable place which will preserve the inhabitants by its healthfulness, provide the necessities of life by its fruitfulness, please them with its beauty, and render them safe from their enemies by its natural protection. If any of these advantages be lacking, the place will be more or less convenient in proportion as it offers more or less of the said advantages, or the more essential of them. Next, the founder of a city and kingdom must mark out the chosen place according to the exigencies of things necessary for the perfection of the city and kingdom. For example, when a kingdom is to be founded, he will have to determine which place is suitable for establishing cities, and which is best for villages and hamlets, where to locate the places of learning, the military training camps, the markets—and so on with other things which the perfection of the kingdom requires. And if it is a question of founding a city, he will have to determine what site is to be assigned to the churches, the law courts, and the various trades! Furthermore, he will have to gather together the men, who must be apportioned suitable locations according to their respective occupations. Finally, he must provide for each one what is necessary for his particular condition and state in life; otherwise, the kingdom or city could never endure.

[101] These are, briefly, the duties that pertain to the office of king in founding a city and kingdom, as derived from a comparison with the creation of the world.

CHAPTER 15

THAT THE OFFICE OF GOVERNING THE KINGDOM SHOULD BE LEARNED FROM THE DIVINE GOVERNMENT

[102] Just as the founding of a city or kingdom may suitably be learned from the way in which the world was created, so too the way to govern may be learned from the divine government of the world.

[103] Before going into that, however, we should consider that to govern is to lead the thmig governed in a suitable way towards its proper end. Thus a ship is said to be governed when, through the skill of the pilot, it is brought unharmed and by a direct route to harbour. Consequently, if a thing be directed to an end outside itself (as a ship to the harbour), it is the governor's duty, not only to preserve the thing unharmed, but further to guide it towards this end. If, on the contrary, there

be a thing whose end is not outside itself, then the governor's endeavours will merely tend to preserve the thing undamaged in its proper perfection.

[104] Nothing of this kind is to be found in reality, except God Himself, Who is the end of all. However, as concerns the thing which is directed to an end outside itself, care is exercised by different providers in different ways. One might have the task of preserving a thing in its being, another of bringing it to a further perfection. Such is clearly the case in the example of the ship; (the first meaning of the word gubernator [governor] is pilot.) It is the carpenter's business to repair anything which might be broken, while the pilot bears the responsibility of bringing the ship to port. It is the same with man. The doctor sees to it that a man's life is preserved; the tradesman supplies the, necessities of life; the teacher takes care that man may learn the truth; and the tutor sees that he lives according to reason.

[105] Now if man were not ordained to another end outside himself, the above-mentioned cares would be sufficient for him. But as long as man's mortal life endures there is an extrinsic good for him, namely, final beatitude which is looked for after death in the enjoyment of God, for as the Apostle' says (2 Cor 5:6): "As long as we are in the body we are far from the Lord." Consequently the Christian man, for whom that beatitude has been purchased by the blood of Christ, and who, in order to attain it, has received the earnest of the Holy Spirit, needs another and spiritual care to direct him to the harbour of eternal salvation, and this care is provided for the faithful by the ministers of the church of Christ.

[106] Now the same judgment is to be formed about the end of society as a whole as about the end of one man. If, therefore, the ultimate end of man were some good that existed in himself, then the ultimate end of the multitude to be governed would likewise be for the multitude to acquire such good, and persevere in its possession. If such an ultimate end either of an individual man or a multitude were a corporeal one, namely, life and health of body, to govern would then be a physician's charge. If that ultimate end were an abundance of wealth, then knowledge of economics would have the last word in the community's government. If the good of the knowledge of truth were of such a kind that the multitude might attain to it, the king would have to be a teacher. It is, however, clear that the end of a multitude gathered together is to live virtuously. For men form a group for the purpose of *living well* together, a thing which the individual man living alone could not attain, and *good life* is virtuous life. Therefore, virtuous life is the end for which men gather together. The evidence for this lies in the fact that only those who render mutual assistance to one another in living well form a genuine part of an assembled multitude. If men assembled merely to live, then animals and slaves would form a part of the civil community. Or, if men assembled only to accrue wealth, then all those who traded together would belong to one city. Yet we see that only such are regarded as forming one multitude as are directed by the same laws and the same government to live well.

[107] Yet through virtuous living man is further ordained to a higher end, which consists in the enjoyment of God, as we have said above. Consequently, since society must have the same end as the individual man, it is not the ultimate end of an assembled multitude to live virtuously, but through virtuous living to attain to the possession of God.

[108] If this end could be attained by the power of human nature, then the duty of a king would have to include the direction of men to it. We are supposing, of course, that he is called king to whom the supreme power of governing in human affairs is entrusted. Now the higher the end to which a government is ordained, the loftier that government is. Indeed, we always find that the one to whom it pertains to achieve the final end commands those who execute the things that are ordained to that end. For example, the captain, whose business it is to regulate navigation, tells the shipbuilder what kind of ship he must construct to be suitable for navigation; and the ruler of a city, who makes use of arms, tells the blacksmith what kind of arms to make. But because a man does not attain his end, which is the possession of God, by human power but by divine according to the words of the Apostle (Rom 6:23): "By the grace of God life everlasting" — therefore the task of leading him to that last end does not pertain to human but to divine government.

[109] Consequently, government of this kind pertains to that king who is not only a man, but also God, namely, our Lord Jesus Christ, Who by making men sons of God brought them to the glory of Heaven. This then is the government which has been delivered to Him and which "shall not be destroyed" (Dan 7:14), on account of which He is called, in Holy Writ, not Priest only, but King. As Jeremiah says (23:5): "The king shall reign and he shall be wise." Hence a royal priesthood is derived from Him, and what is more, all those who believe in Christ, in so far as they are His members, are called kings and priests.

[110] Thus, in order that spiritual things might be distinguished from earthly things, the ministry of this kingdom has been entrusted not to earthly kings but to priests, and most of all to the chief priest, the successor of St. Peter, the Vicar of Christ, the Roman Pontiff. To him all the kings of the Christian People are to be subject as to our Lord Jesus Christ Himself. For those to whom pertains the care of intermediate ends should be subject to him to whom pertains the care of the ultimate end, and be directed by his rule.

[111] Because the priesthood of the gentiles and the whole worship of their gods existed merely for the acquisition of temporal goods (which were all ordained to the common good of the multitude, whose care devolved upon the king), the priests of the gentiles were very properly subject to the kings. Similarly, since in the old law earthly goods were promised to the religious people (not indeed by demons but by the true God), the priests of the old law, we read, were also subject to the kings. But in the new law there is a higher priesthood by which men are guided to heavenly goods. Consequently, in the law of Christ, kings must be subject to priests.

[112] It was therefore also a marvellous disposition of Divine Providence that, in the city of Rome, which God had foreseen would be the principal seat of the Christian priesthood, the custom was gradually established that the rulers of the city should be subject to the priests, for as Valerius Maximus relates [*De Bello Gallico* VI, 13, 5]: "Our city has always considered that everything should yield precedence to religion, even those things in which it aimed to display the splendour of supreme majesty. We therefore unhesitatingly made the imperial dignity minister to religion, considering that the empire would thus hold control of human affairs if faithfully and constantly it were submissive to the divine power.

[113] And because it was to come to pass that the religion of the Christian priesthood should especially thrive in France, God provided that among the Gauls too their tribal priests, called Druids, should lay down the law of all Gaul, as Julius Caesar relates in the book which he wrote about the Gallic war.

CHAPTER 16

THAT REGAL GOVERNMENT SHOULD BE ORDAINED PRINCIPALLY TO ETERNAL BEATITUDE

[114] As the life by which men live well here on earth is ordained, as to its end, to that blessed life which we hope for in heaven, so too whatever particular goods are procured by man's agency — whether wealth, profits, health, eloquence, or learning — are ordained to the good life of the multitude. If, then, as we have said, the person who is charged with the care of our ultimate end ought to be over those who have charge of things ordained to that end, and to direct them by his rule, it clearly follows that, just as the king ought to be subject to the divine government administered by the office of priesthood, so he ought to preside over all human offices, and regulate them by the rule of his government.

[115] Now anyone on whom it devolves to do something which is ordained to another thing as to its end is bound to see that his work is suitable to that end; thus, for example, the armourer so fashions the sword that it is suitable for fighting, and the builder should so lay out the house that it is suitable for habitation. Therefore, since the beatitude of heaven is the end of that virtuous life which we live at present, it pertains to the king's office to promote the good life of the multitude in such a way as to make it suitable for the attainment of heavenly happiness, that is to say, he should command those things which lead to the happiness of Heaven and, as far as possible, forbid the contrary.

[116] What conduces to true beatitude and what hinders it are learned from the law of God, the teaching of which belongs to the office of the priest, according to the words of Malachi (2:7): "The lips of the priest shall guard knowledge and they shall seek the law from his mouth." Wherefore the Lord prescribes in the Book of

Deuteronomy (17:18-19) that "after he is raised to the throne of his kingdom, the king shall copy out to himself the Deutoronomy of this law, in a volume, taking the copy of the priests of the Levitical tribe, he shall have it with him and shall read it all the days of his life, that he may learn to fear the Lord his God, and keep his words and ceremonies which are commanded in the law." Thus the king, taught the law of God, should have for his principal concern the means by which the multitude subject to him may live well.

[117] This concern is threefold:, first of all, to establish a virtuous life in the multitude subject to him; second, to preserve it once established; and third, having preserved it, to promote its greater perfection.

[118] For an individual man to lead a good life two things are required. The first and most important is to act in a virtuous manner (for virtue is that by which one lives well); the second, which is secondary and instrumental, is a sufficiency of those bodily goods who se use is necessary for virtuous life. Yet the unity of man is brought about by nature, while the unity of multitude, which we call peace, must be procured through the efforts of the ruler. Therefore, to establish virtuous living in a multitude three things are necessary. First of all, that the multitude be established in the unity of peace. Second, that the multitude thus united in the bond of peace, be directed to acting well. For just as a man can do nothing well unless unity within his members be presupposed, so a multitude of men lacking the unity of peace will be hindered from virtuous action by the fact that it is fighting against itself. In the third place, it is necessary that there be at hand a sufficient supply of the things required for proper living, procured by the ruler's efforts.

[119] When virtuous living is set up in the multitude by the efforts of the king, it then remains for him to look to its conservation. Now there are three things which prevent the permanence of the public good. One of these arises from nature. The good of the multitude should not be established for one time only; it should be in a sense perpetual. Men, on the other hand, cannot abide forever, because they are mortal. Even while they are alive they do not always preserve the same vigour, for the life of man is subject to many changes, and thus a man is not equally suited to the performance of the same duties throughout the whole span of his life. A second impediment to the preservation of the public good, which comes from within, consists in the perversity of the wills of men, inasmuch as they are either too lazy to perform what the commonweal demands, or, still further, they are harmful to the peace of the multitude because, by transgressing justice, they disturb the peace of others. The third hindrance to the preservation of the commonweal comes from without, namely, when peace is destroyed through the attacks of enemies and, as it sometimes happens, the kingdom or city is completely blotted out.

[120] In regard to these three dangers, a triple charge is laid upon the king. First of all, he must take care of the appointment of men to succeed or replace others in charge of the various offices. Just as in regard to corruptible things (which cannot

remain the same forever) the government of God made provision that through generation one would take the place of another in order that, in this way, the integrity of the universe might be maintained, so too the good of the multitude subject to the king will be preserved through his care when he sets himself to attend to the appointment of new men to fill the place of those who drop out. In the second place, by his laws and orders, punishments and rewards, he should restrain the men subject to him from wickedness and induce them to virtuous deeds, following the example of God, Who gave His law to man and requites those who observe it with rewards, and those who transgress it with punishments. The king's third charge is to keep the multitude entrusted to him safe from the enemy, for it would be useless to prevent internal dangers if the multitude could not be defended against external dangers.

[121] Finally, for the proper direction of the multitude there remains the third duty of the kingly office, namely, that he be solicitous for its improvement. He performs this duty when, in each of the things we have mentioned, he corrects what is out of order and supplies what is lacking, and if any of them can be done better he tries to do so. This is why the Apostle exhorts the faithful to be "zealous for the better gifts" (1 Cor 12:31).

[122] These then are the duties of the kingly office, each of which must now be treated in greater detail.

TREATISE ON THE KINGSHIP

De Regiminie Principium

(De Regno)

BOOK TWO

Kolbe's Greatest Books
Volume Fourty Seven

By

Saint Thomas Aquinas

BOOK II

PART II

CHAPTER 1

THAT IT BELONGS TO THE OFFICE OF A KING TO FOUND THE CITY

[123] We must begin by explaining the duties of a king with regard to the founding of a city or kingdom. For, as Vegetius [*De Re Militari* IV, prol.] declares, "the mightiest nations and most commended kings thought it their greatest glory either to found new cities or have their names made part of, and in some way added to, the names of cities already founded by others." This, indeed, is in accord with Holy Scripture, for the Wise Man says in Sirach (40:19): "The building of a city shall establish a name." The name of Romulus, for instance, would be unknown today had he not founded the city of Rome.

[124] Now in founding a city or kingdom, the first step is the choice, if any be given, of its location. A temperate region should be chosen, for the inhabitants derive many advantages from a temperate climate. In the first place, it ensures them health of body and length of life; for, since good health consists in the right temperature of the vital fluids, it follows that health will be best preserved in a temperate clime, because like is preserved by like. Should, however, heat or cold be excessive, it needs must be that the condition of the body will be affected by the condition of the atmosphere; whence some animals instinctively migrate in cold weather to warmer regions, and in warm weather return to the colder places, in order to obtain, through the contrary dispositions of both locality and weather, the due temperature of their humours.

[125] Again, since it is warmth and moisture that preserve animal life, if the heat is intense the natural moisture of the body is dried up and life fails, just as a lantern is extinguished if the liquid poured into it be quickly consumed by too great a flame. Whence it is said that in certain very torrid parts of Ethiopia a man cannot live longer than thirty years. On the other hand, in extremely cold regions the natural moisture is easily frozen and the natural heat soon lost.

[126] Then, too, a temperate climate is most conducive to fitness for war, by which human society is kept in security. As Vegetius tells us [*De Re Militari* 1, 2], "all peoples that live near the sun and are dried up by the excessive heat have keener wits but less blood, so that they possess no constancy or self-reliance in hand-to-hand fighting; for, knowing they have but little blood, they have great fear of wounds. On the other hand, Northern tribes, far removed from the burning rays of the sun are more dull-witted indeed, but because they have an ample flow of blood, they are ever ready for war Those who dwell in temperate climes have, on the one hand, an abundance-of blood and thus make light of wounds or death,

and, on the other hand, no lack of prudence, which puts a proper restraint on them in camp and is of great advantage in war and peace as well.

[127] Finally, a temperate climate is of no little value for political life. As Aristotle says in his Politics [VII, 7: 1327b 23-32]: "Peoples that dwell in cold countries are full of spirit but have little intelligence and little skill. Consequently they maintain their liberty better but have no political life and (through lack of prudence) show no capacity for governing others. Those who live in hot regions are keen-witted and skilful in the things of the mind but possess little spirit, and so are in continuous subjection and servitude. But those who live between these extremes of climate are both spirited and intelligent; hence they are continuously free, their political life is very much developed, and they are capable of ruling others." Therefore, a temperate region should be chosen for the foundation of a city or a kingdom.

CHAPTER 2

THAT THE CITY SHOULD HAVE WHOLESOME AIR

[128] After deciding on the locality of the kingdom, the king must select a site suitable for building a city.

[129] Now the first requisite would seem to be wholesome air, for civil life presupposes natural life, whose health in turn depends on the wholesomeness of the air. According to Vitruvius [*De Architectura* I, 4], the most healthful spot is "a high place, troubled neither by mists nor frosts and facing neither the sultry nor the chilly parts of the sky. Also, it should not lie near marsh country." The altitude of the place contributes to the wholesomeness of the atmosphere because highlands are opento all the breezes which purify the air; besides, the vapours, which the strength of the sun's rays causes to rise from the earth and waters, are more dense in valleys and in low-lying places than in highlands, whence it is that the air on mountains is rarer. Now this rarified air, which is the best for easy and natural breathing, is vitiated by mists and frosts which are frequent in very damp places; as a consequence, such places are found to be inimical to health. Since marshy districts have an excess of humidity, the place chosen for the building of a city must be far from any marshes. "For when the morning breezes come at sunrise to such a place, and the mists that rise from the swamps join them, they will scatter through the town the breath of the poisonous beasts of the marshes mingled with the mist, and will render the site pestilential." "Should, however, the walls be built in marshes that lie along the coast and face the north (or thereabouts) and if these marshes be higher than the seashore, they would seem to be quite reasonably built, since, by digging ditches, a way will be opened to drain the water of the marshes into the sea, and when storms swell the sea it will flow back into the marshes and thus prevent the propagation of the animals there.

And if any animals come down from higher places, the unwonted saltiness of the water will destroy them."

[130] Further provision for the proper proportion of heat and cold must be made when laying out the city by having it face the correct part of the sky. "If the walls, particularly of a town built on the coast, face the south, it will not be healthy," since such a locality will be cold in the morning, for the rays of the sun do not reach it, but at noon will be baked in the full glare of the sun. As to places that face the west, at sunrise they are cool or even cold, at noon quite warm, and in the evening unpleasantly hot, both on account of the long-continued heat and the, exposure to the sun. On the other hand, if it has an eastern exposure, in the morning, with the sun directly opposite, it will be moderately warm, at noon it will not, be much warmer since the sun does not reach it, directly, but in the evening it will be cold as the rays of the sun will be entirely on the other side. And there will be the same or a similar proportion of heat and cold if the town faces the north. By experience we may learn that the change from cold to heat is unhealthy. "Animals which are transferred from cold to warm regions cannot endure but are dissolved," "since the heat sucks up their moisture and weakens their natural strength;" whence even in salubrious districts "all bodies become weak from the heat."

[131] Again, since suitable food is very helpful for preserving health, we must further judge of the salubrity of a place which has been chosen as a town-site by the condition of the food which grows upon its soil. The ancients were wont to explore this condition by examining the animals raised on the spot. For man, like other animals, finds nourishment in the products of the earth. Hence, if in a given place we kill some animals and find their entrails to be sound, the conclusion will be justified that man also will get good food in the same place. If, however, the members of these animals should be found diseased, we may reasonably infer that that country is no healthy place for men either.

[132] Just as a temperate climate must be sought, so good water must be made the object of investigation. For the body depends for its health on those things which men more frequently put to their use. With regard to the air it is clear that, breathing it continuously, we draw it down into our very vitals; as a result, purity of air is what conduces most to the preservation of men. But of all things put to use as nourishment, water is used most frequently both as drink and food. Nothing therefore, except good air, so much helps to make a district healthy as does pure water.

[133] There is still another means of judging the healthfulness of a place, i.e., by the ruddy complexion of the inhabitants, their sturdy, well-shaped limbs, the presence of many and vivacious children, and of many old people. On the other hand, there can be no doubt about the deadliness of a climate where people are misshapen and weak, their limbs either withering or swollen beyond proportion, where children are few and sickly, and old people rather scarce.

CHAPTER 3

THAT THE CITY SHOULD HAVE AN ABUNDANT SUPPLY OF FOOD

[134] It is not enough, however, that the place chosen for the site of a city be such as to preserve the health of the inhabitants; it must also be sufficiently fertile to provide food. A multitude of men cannot live where there is not a sufficient supply of food. Thus Vitruvius [I, 5] narrates that when Dinocrates, a brilliant architect, was explaining to Alexander of Macedon that a beautifully laid out city could be built upon a certain mountain, Alexander asked whether there were fields that could supply the city with sufficient grain. Finding out that there were not, he said that an architect who would build a city on such a site would be blameworthy. For "just as a newborn infant cannot be fed nor made to grow as it should, except on the nurse's milk, so a city cannot have a large population without a large supply of foodstuffs."

[135] Now there are two ways in which an abundance of foodstuffs can be supplied to a city. The first we have already mentioned, where the soil is so fertile that it amply provides for all the necessities of human life. The second is by trade, through which the necessaries of life are brought to the town in sufficient quantity from different places.

[136] It is quite clear that the first means is better. The more dignified a thing is, the more self-sufficient it is, since whatever needs another's help is by that fact proven to be deficient. Now the city which is supplied by the surrounding country with all its vital needs is more self-sufficient than another which must obtain those supplies by trade. A city therefore which has an abundance of food from its own territory is more dignified than one which is provisioned through trade.

[137] It seems that self-sufficiency is also safer, for the import of supplies and the access of merchants can easily be prevented whether owing to wars or to the many hazards of the sea, and thus the city may be overcome through lack of food.

[138] Moreover, this first method of supply is more conducive to the preservation of civic life. A city which must engage in much trade in order to supply its needs also has to put up with the continuous presence of foreigners. But intercourse with foreigners, according to Aristotle's *Politics* [V, 3: 1303a 27; VII, 6: 1327a 13-15], is particularly harmful to civic customs. For it is inevitable that strangers, brought up under other laws and customs, will in many cases act as the citizens are not wont to act and thus, since the citizens are drawn by their example to act likewise, their own civic life is upset.

[139] Again, if the citizens themselves devote their life to matters of trade, the way will be opened to many vices. Since the foremost tendency of tradesmen is to make money, greed is awakened in the hearts of the citizens through the pursuit

of trade. The result is that everything in the city will become venal; good faith will be destroyed and the way opened to all kinds of trickery; each one will work only for his own profit, despising the public good; the cultivation of virtue will fail since honour, virtue's reward, will be bestowed upon the rich. Thus, in such a city, civic life will necessarily be corrupted.

[140] The pursuit of trade is also very unfavourable to military activity.' Tradesmen, not being used to the open air and not doing any hard work but enjoying all pleasures, grow soft in spirit and their bodies are weakened and rendered unsuited to military labours. In accordance with this view, Civil Law" forbids soldiers to engage in business.

[141] Finally, that city enjoys a greater measure of peace whose people are more sparsely assembled together and dwell in smaller proportion within the walls of the town, for when men are crowded together it is an occasion for quarrels and all the elements for seditious plots are provided. Hence, according to Aristotle's doctrine, it is more profitable to have the people engaged outside the cities than for them to dwell constantly within the walls. But if a city is dependent on trade, it is of prime importance that the citizens stay within the town and there engage in trade. It is better, therefore, that the supplies of food be furnished to the city from its own fields than that it be wholly dependent on trade.

[142] Still, trade must not be entirely kept out of a city, since one cannot easily find any place so overflowing with the necessaries of life as not to need some commodities from other parts. Also, when there is an over-abundance of some commodities in one place, these goods would serve no purpose if they could not be carried elsewhere by professional traders. Consequently, the perfect city will make a moderate use of merchants.

CHAPTER 4

THAT THE CITY SHOULD HAVE A PLEASANT SITE

[143] A further requisite when choosing a site for the founding of a city is this, that it must charm the inhabitants by its beauty. A spot where life is pleasant will not easily be abandoned nor will men commonly be ready to flock to unpleasant places, since the life of man cannot endure without enjoyment. It belongs to the beauty of a place that it have a broad expanse of meadows, an abundant forest growth, mountains to be seen close at hand, pleasant groves and a copiousness of water.

[144] However, if a country is too beautiful, it will draw men to indulge in pleasures,' and this is most harmful to a city. In the first place, when men give themselves up to pleasure their senses are dulled, since this sweetness immerses the soul in the senses so that man cannot pass free judgment on the things which

cause delight. Whence, according to Aristotle's sentence [*Eth. Nic.* VI, 5: 1140b 11-21], the judgment of prudence is corrupted by pleasure.

[145] Again, indulgence in superfluous pleasure leads from the path of virtue, for nothing conduces more easily to immoderate increase which upsets the mean of virtue, than pleasure. Pleasure is, by its very nature, greedy, and thus on a slight occasion one is precipitated into the seductions of shameful pleasures just as a little spark is sufficient to kindle dry wood; moreover, indulgence does not satisfy the appetite for the first sip only makes the thirst all the keener. Consequently, it is part of virtue's task to lead men to refrain from pleasures. By thus avoiding any excess, the mean of virtue will be more easily attained.

[146] Also, they who give themselves up to pleasures grow soft in spirit and become weak-minded when it is a question of tackling some difficult enterprise, enduring toll, and facing dangers. Whence, too, indulgence in pleasures is detrimental to warfare, as Vegetius puts it in his *On the Art of Knighthood* (*De re militari* I, 3) "He fears death less who knows that he has had little pleasure in life."

[147] Finally, men who have become dissolute through pleasures usually grow lazy and, neglecting necessary matters and all the pursuits that duty lays upon them, devote themselves wholly to the quest of pleasure, on which they squander all that others had so carefully amassed. Thus, reduced to poverty and yet unable to deprive themselves of their wonted pleasures, they do not shrink from stealing and robbing in order to have the wherewithal to indulge their craving for pleasure.

[148] It is therefore harmful to a city to superabound in delightful things, whether it be on account of its situation or from whatever other cause. However, in human intercourse it is best to have a moderate share of pleasure as a spice of life, so to speak, wherein man's mind may find some recreation.

APPENDIX

SELECTED PARALLEL TEXTS

1. *Contra Impugnantes Dei Cultum et Religionem*, ch. 5

Avicenna says: Nature did not give covering to man (as she gave hair to other animals), nor means of defence (as the oxen received horns and the lions claws); nor did nature prepare man's food (except the mother's milk). Instead of all this man was endowed with reason to provide for these things, and with hands to execute the providence of reason, as the Philosopher says.

AVICENNA *De Anima* (*Sextus Naturalium*) V, 1: fol. 22rb: Man's actions possess certain properties which proceed from his soul and are not found in other animals. The first of these is that man's being in which he is created, could not last if he did not live in society. Man is not like other animals, each of which is self-sufficient for living with what it has by its nature. One man, on the contrary, if he were alone and left to rely on nothing but what he has by nature, would soon die, or at least his life would be miserable and certainly worse than it was meant to be. This is because of the nobility of man's nature and the ignobility of the nature of other beings... It is necessary for man to add certain things to what nature gives him: he must needs prepare his food and also his clothing; for raw food, not treated by art, is unbecoming to him: he would not be able to live well with it. Likewise does he have to treat certain materials and make them into garments, while other animals have their covering by nature. First of all, then, man needs the art of agriculture, and, in the second place, many other arts. Now, one man would be unable to acquire all these necessaries of life, if he were alone... He can do so, however, in society where one bakes the other's bread and the latter in turn weaves the former's clothes, and one man imports wares from far-away lands for which he receives remuneration from the produce of another man's country. These are the most evident among many other reasons why it is necessary for man to possess the natural ability to express to his fellowmen what is in his mind.... Thefirst and the easier means of doing this is through the voice... [the other, a more laborious one, being through gesture ...] Nature bestowed upon man's soul the faculty to compose out of sounds a sign which is capable of being understood by others. Other animals also utter sounds by which they are able to indicate their wants. Yet these sounds have but a natural and confused signification indicating only in a general way what is wanted or not wanted. Human sounds, on the contrary, may distinctly signify an infinite range of wants. Hence they in their turn are infinite in number. — Cf. Plato, *Republic* II, 11 ff. (369B ff); Aristotle, Politics III, 9: 1280a 25 ff.

2. *In Libros Ethicorum Aristotelis Expositio*, Lib. I, lect. 1

Man is by nature a social animal, since he stands in need of many vital things which he cannot come by through his own unaided effort (Avicenna). Hence he is naturally part of a group by which assistance is given him that he may live well. He needs this assistance with a view to life as well as to the good life. First, with a view to life, i.e., to having all those things which are necessary for life and without which this earthly lifecannot be lived. In this regard, assistance is given to man by the group called the household of which he is part. For everyone has from. his parents birth, nourishment and education. Also all the members of the household or family help one another in regard to the necessities of life. Assistance of another kind comes to man by another group of which he is part, assistance, that is, in view of the perfect fullness of life, in other words, that man may not only live but also live well, being equipped with all the things that make for the perfection of living. For this purpose, assistance comes to man from the civil group of which he is part. This assistance concerns not only man's corporal needs inasmuch as there are in a city many crafts which one household could not develop, but also his moral needs. Public power, indeed, by making itself feared, puts restraint upon those insolent youths who could not be corrected by paternal admonitions. [See *Summa* I-II, 95, 4.]

3. *In Libros Politicorum Aristotelis Expositio*, Lib. I, lect. 1. [*Pol.* I, 2; 1252b 12: The definition of the household.]

The Philosopher shows here for what purpose the community of the household is instituted. It is to be borne in mind that every human communication is built upon certain doings of men. Thereare some things which need to be done every clay, such as eating, seeking protection from the cold, and such like. Other things do not have to be done daily, such as trading, fighting the enemy, and such like. Now it is natural for men to communicate and to help one another in both these kinds of work. Therefore, Aristotle says, the household is a community naturally instituted for the life of every day, i.e., for those works which have to be done daily.

[*Ibid.* 1252b 15: The definition of the clan-village, called *vicus* in the mediaeval Latin translation.]

Here the Philosopher speaks about the [next] community, viz., the vicus. He calls vicus the first communication arising out of several households. It is the first communication after the household, since there is to follow another one, viz., the city. The vicus is not instituted for the life of every day, as was the household, but with a view to needs not recurring daily. The members of this community do not come together to communicate concerning those things which are to be done daily, such as eating, and sitting by the fire, and such like, but concerning external works transcending the daily round of necessities.

[*Ibid.* 1252b 16: The *vicus* appears to be most natural.]

The Philosopher says that the neighbourhood or vicinity of houses (which is the *vicus*) appears to be a most natural form of community; for nothing is more natural in the realm of live beings than the propagation of many from one: and this constitutes the cluster of homes (*vicinia domorum.*)

[Ibid. 1252b 27: The definition of the city.]

The Philosopher shows that in the nature of a city there are three essential characteristics. His first point is to determine what are the material elements of the city. Just as the *vicus* is composed of several households, so is the city composed of several *vici*. The second affirmation [concerns the formal characteristic of a city.] The city is the perfect community. This, Aristotle explains thus: Since every communication, whenever it is found among men, is ordained to something necessary for life, that community will be the perfect community which is ordained to the end that man may have the fullness of human life: and this is the city. For it is in the city that man finds the satisfaction of whatever needs human life may have in the circumstances in which it is lived (*sicut contingit esse*). Thus the city is composed of several vici in one of which the Smith's craft is exercised, in another the weaver's craft, and so on. It is clear then that the city is the perfect community. In the third place, the Philosopher shows to what end or purpose the city is instituted. Its origin, indeed, may be ascribed to the purpose of simply living, inasmuch as men find in it the things which make their life livable at all. But once it exists, it will provide men with the means not only to live but also to live well, inasmuch as, by the laws of the city, life is made to be virtuous life.

[*Ibid.* 1253a 7: The reason why man is a political animal.]

The Philosopher demonstrates from a consideration of man~s proper operation that man.is a civic animal (animal civile), even more so than bees or other gregarious animals. This is the reason: We say that nature makes nothing in vain, because she always works for a definite purpose. When, therefore, nature endows a being with something which, of itself, is ordained to an end, it is evident that this end is proposed to that being by nature. Now, we see that certain animals possess the faculty of making sounds, while man alone, above all other animals, has the faculty of language. Even when certain animals may utter the language of man, they do not speak in a proper sense, since they do not understand what they say but are merely trained to utter these sounds. Yet there is a difference between language and simple sound. A sound is the sign of grief and pleasure, and consequently of other passions, such as anger and fear which, as is said in the second book of the *Ethics* [3: 1104b 14] are all ordained to pleasure and grief. Therefore the faculty of sound is given to other animals, whose nature attains to the point at which they have the perceptions of pleasure and grief; and this is what they signify to one another by certain natural sounds, the lion by roaring and the dog by barking, instead of which we have our interjections. Human language, on the other hand, signifies what is advantageous and what is harmful. From this it follows that it signifies what is just and what is unjust. For justice and injustice consist in this, that several persons are adjusted, or not adjusted, to one another in respect of things advantageous or harmful. So language is proper to men, since it is a peculiarity of theirs in comparison with the rest of the animal world that they possess the knowledge of good and evil, of the just and the unjust, and of other similar relations.... In these things men communicate one with another naturally. Since, therefore, this communication constitutes the household and the city, man is naturally a domestic and a civic animal.

4. *In Libros Ethicorum Aristotelis Expositio*, Lib. VIII, lect. 10

[*Eth. Nic.* VIII, 10; 1160a 31-35: The classification of the constitutions.]

There are three species of constitutions and an equal number of corruptions or deviation-forms. The right constitutions are, first, kingship, i.e., the rule of one man; second, aristocracy, i.e., the rule of the best (this kind of civic order is indeed ruled by the virtuous men); thirdly, timocracy. Such a third species will have to be assumed, although not all agree to do so, as is said in the fifth (?) book of the *Politics* [IV, 3: 1290a 22]. Timocracy is fittingly called so from the [Greek] word *timae* which means remuneration (*pretium*); for under this constitution the poor are remunerated for attending, and the rich fined for not attending, the civic assemblies, as is said in the fourth book of the Politics. Others call this constitution by the generic name polity, since it is that of the rich and the poor alike; compare the fourth book of the *Politics*.

[*Ibid.* 35-36: Their respective value.]

Comparing these constitutions the Philosopher says that the best is kingship, since under this form of government one man, and the best of all, holds power. The least good is timocracy which is the ruling of the mediocre. Between these extremes lies aristocracy in which a few of the best are ruling but with less power of action than is invested in one man acting well and possessing the plenitude of power.

[*Ibid.* 1160a 36-b 12: On kingship and tyranny.]

...Tyranny is the deviation-form or corruption of kingship. [Thus these forms stand to each other in the opposition of contrariety.] In regard to this point, Aristotle shows, first, that both forms are of the same genus, for both are monarchies, i.e., one-man governments. Second, he brings out their differences, saying that they differ most widely, from which it appears that they are contraries. For contraries, being of the same genus, are most widely distant one from the other. What the difference is between tyranny and kingship, the Philosopher declares by saying that, in this regime, the tyrant looks to his own advantage, while the king has his eye on that of his subjects. This is further evidenced in what follows: The true king, Aristotle says, is sufficient for governing by his own resources and, therefore, should possess all good things: the goods of the soul, -those of the body, and external goods; and he should possess them in such abundance that he be worthy and, at the same time potent, to hold power. If he is such, he needs nothing further and so will not be tempted to care for his own advantage as do those who still are in need. The king will be the benefactor of his subjects, which is the attribute of those who have an overflowing abundance of good things. If a king is not such a man, he is rather a *clerotos*, as Aristotle says, which means he is king [not naturally but] by the decision of the lots. On the other hand, the tyrant, since he pursues his own interest, is the very contrary of the king. Hence it is clear that tyranny is the worst deviation-form. For it is the contrary of the best that is worst and a man passes over from kingship, i.e., the best form, to tyranny which is a de-o pravity of monarchy, i.e., one-nign rule; in other words, it is the bad king who becomes a tyrant. Tyranny, then, the Philosopher concludes, is the worst form of government.

[*Ibid.* 1260b 12-16: The corruption of aristocracy.]

Aristocracy, in its turn, passes over into oligarchy, i.e., the dominion of a few. This happens on account of the badness of the rulers who do not distribute according to worthiness the goods which belong to the city but snatch away either all or a great deal of them, for their own use and in order to enrich themselves and their friends. Thus it comes about that instead of the most worthy (who are the rulers in an aristocracy) there are now a few and bad man at the head of the city.

[*Ibid.* 16-22: The corruption of timocracy.]

Timocracy, according to the Philosopher, is corrupted into democracy, i.e., the power of the people. These forms are coterminous, i.e., close to each other. They are alike in two regards. First, timocracy (meaning the constitution characterized by a certain system of remunerations) as well as democracy are forms of government in which the many have power; second, in either constitution the criterion of estimating who are "the best people" is the same (*omnes qui sunt in honoribus constituti sunt aequales*). The difference between them consists in that timocracy keeps in view the common good of both the rich and the poor, while democracy knows only of the good of the poor. Hence democracy is the least bad of the deviation-forms. Its distance from timocracy which is a right constitution is very small indeed.

5. *In Libros Politicorum Aristotelis Expositio*, Lib. III, lect. 5-6.

[*Pol.* III, 6; 1279a 17-21: The distinction between right and wrong constitutions.]

The Philosopher propounds the distinction between right and unjust constitutions. Since don-Anion over free men is ordained to the interest of the subjects, it is clear that, when a constitution makes the holders of power aim at the common interest, it is a right constitution, judging by the standards of absolute justice. When, on the contrary, a constitution looks only to the interest of those who possess political power, it is a wrong constitution and a perversion of the right form. For there is, in this case, no absolute justice, i.e., justice for all, but only relative justice, namely, for those who are atthe top. They therefore exercise dominion over the city by using the citizens as slaves to the rulers' own advantage; and that is against justice, since the city is a community of freemen, the slaves not being citizens at all.

[*Ibid.* 7; 1279a 25-32: The classification of the constitutions.]

Here the Philosopher classifies the constitutions... A constitution, he says, is the ordering, in a city, of those who have power and those who are subjected (*ordo dominantium in civitate*). Therefore, the criterion for classifying the constitutions will be found in the diversity of those who possess the power. They are either One, or Few, or Many. Further, in each case, there are two different possibilities.

Power is held either for the common advantage, and in this case the constitution will be right; or for the advantage of the holders themselves, and in this case the constitution will be a perversion, no matter whether power is vested in one, or a few, or many. For this is the alternative: either the subjects are not citizens: [then they have no part in the common utility]; or they [are citizens and] have their share in the common good.

[*Ibid.* 1279a 32- b 4: The names of the right constitutions.]

Now the Philosopher proceeds to declarethe names of these constitutions. . . . If there is dominion of one man directed towards the common interest, the constitution is called monarchy, in the general use of language. If a few are holding the power and using it for the common good, this is an aristocracy, so-called because political power is held by the best, i.e., the virtuous men, or again because it is used for the best interest of the city and of all citizens. Finally, if many have power and exercise it with a view to the common interest, the constitution is commonly called polity which is the generic name of all constitutions. There is a good reason for this usage which gives to this form the generic name. It is easy to find in a city one man or a few who are of outstanding virtue. But it is very difficult indeed for there to be many who attain to the perfection of virtue. Most likely, however, one virtue will be common to a greater number of men, viz., military bravery. This is the reason why under this constitution warriors and those who carry arms are at the top.

[*Ibid.* 6-10: The names of the perverted constitutions.]

...They are as follows: The perversion of kingship is called tyranny; the perversion of aristocracy, oligarchy (which means: power of the few); finally democracy (meaning; power of the people, or rather the vulgar mass) is the perversion of that polity in which the many dominate but on the basis of at least one virtue, viz., military bravery. Hence, Aristotle concludes, tyranny is the dominion of one man aiming at his own interest; oligarchy is the dominion of a few aiming at the interest of the rich; democracy is the dominion of many aiming at the interest of the poor. None of these constitutions takes thought for the common good.

[*Ibid.* 8; 1279b 34-1280a 6: The criterion of number is not adequate.]

[After closer examination of these definitions] it appears that, in the case of democracy the large number of the holders of power is an accidental circumstance; and likewise, in the case of oligarchy the small number is merely accidental. For it is nothing but a fact that everywhere there are more poor than rich people. The above mentioned names, therefore, owe their origin [not to a universally valid reason but] simply to a fact which happens to be true in most of the cases. Since, however, a specific differentiation cannot be obtained on the basis of what is merely accidental, it follows that, per se, the distinction between oligarchies and democracies cannot be made in virtue of the larger or smaller number of the rulers. Rather their specific difference results from the difference between poverty and riches. If a regime is ordained to the increase of the possessions of the rich, its very species is determined by this end and it is for this reason that it differs specifically from a regime whose end is liberty, which regime is democracy. Hence, wherever the rich hold political power, no matter whether they are many or few, there will be oligarchy; and wherever the poor hold this power, there will be democracy; and that the latter are many and the former few is nothing but an accidental circumstance. For only a few have riches yet all partake of liberty. This is why both classes fight each other. The few want to dominate for the sake of their possessions and the many want to prevail upon the few since they believe that, by the criterion of liberty, they have just as good a right to political power as the rich.

6. *Scriptum Super Libros Sententiarum* II, dist. 44, q. II, a. 2.

[The problem is whether Christians are bound to obey secular powers, especially tyrants.]

The procedure in discussing this problem is this: It seems that they are not bound to this obedience... The fourth argument [in favour of this position) runs as follows: It is legitimate for anyone, who can do so, to re-take what has been taken away from him unjustly. Now many secular princes unjustly usurped the dominion of Christian lands. Since, therefore, in such cases rebellion is legitimate, Christians have no obligation to obey these princes. —The fifth argument: If it is a legitimate and even a praiseworthy deed to kill a person, then no obligation of obedience exists toward that person. Now in the *Book on Duties* [*De Officiis* I, 8, 26] Cicero justifies Julius Caesar's assassins. Although Caesar was a close friend of his, yet by usurping the empire he proved himself to be a tyrant. Therefore toward such powers there is no obligation of obedience.

On the other hand, however, there are the following arguments proving the contrary position: First, it is said: Servants, be in subjection to your masters (1 Pet. 2:18.) Second, it is also said: He who resists the power, withstands the ordinance of God (Rom. xiii, 2.) Now it is not legitimate to withstand the ordinance of God. Hence it is not legitimate either to withstand secular power.

Solution and determination. Obedience, by keeping a commandment, has for its [formal] object the obligation, involved in the cominandment, that it be kept. Now this obligation originates in that the commanding authority has the power to impose an obligation binding not only to external but also to internal and spiritual obedience—"for conscience sake", as the Apostle says (Rom. xiii, 5.) For power (authority) comes from God, as the Apostle implies in the same place. Hence, Christians are bound to obey the authorities inasmuch as they are from God; and they are not bound to obey inasmuch as the authority is not from God.

Now, this not being from God may be the case, first, as to the mode in which authority is acquired, and, second, as to the use which is made of authority.

Concerning the first case we must again distinguish two defects: There may be a defect of the person acquiring authority inasmuch as this person is unworthy of it. There may also be a defect in the mode of acquiring authority, namely, if it is obtained by violence, or simony, or other illegitimate means.

As to the first of these defects, we say that it does not constitute an obstacle against acquiring lawful authority. Since, then, as such, authority is always from God (and this is what causes the obligation of obedience), the subjects are bound to render obedience to these authorities, unworthy as they may be.

As to the second of those defects, we say that in such a case there is no lawful authority at all. He who seizes power by violence does not become a true holder of power. Hence, when it is possible to do so, anybody may repel this domination, unless, of course, the usurper should later on have become a true ruler by the consent of the subjects or by a recognition being extended to him by a higher authority.

The abuse of power might take on two forms. First, a commandment emanating from the authority might be contrary to the very end in view of which authority is instituted, i.e., to be an educator to, and a preserver of, virtue. Should therefore the authority command an act of sin contrary to virtue, we not only are not obliged to obey but we are also obliged not to obey, according to the example of the holy martyrs who preferred death to obeying those ungodly tyrants.

The second form of abusing power is for the authority to go beyond the bounds of its legal rights, for instance, when a master exacts duties which the servant is not bound to pay, or the like. In this case the subject is not obliged to obey, but neither is he obliged not to obey.

Consequently... to the fourth argument the answer is this: An authority acquired by violence is not a true authority, and there is no obligation of obedience, as we said above.

To the fifth argument the answer is that Cicero speaks of domination obtained by violence and ruse, the subjects being unwilling or even forced to accept it and there being no recourse open to a superior who might pronounce judgment upon the usurper. In this case he that kills the tyrant for the liberation of the country, is praised and rewarded.

7. *Contra Gentiles* IV, 76.

...It is evident that, although there are many different peoples in different dioceses and cities, yet there is one Christendom (*Populus Christianus*), just as there is one

Church. Therefore, just as there is one bishop appointed to one particular people in order to be the head of them all, so in the whole of Christendom one must be the head of the whole Church....

JOHN OF PARIS thought ftt to correct this text in the following way: It is evident that, although there are many different peoples in different dioceses and cities, in which the bishops hold authority in matters spiritual, yet there is one Church of all the Faithful and one Christendom. Therefore, just as there is one bishop in every diocese appointed to be the head of the particular church of that people, so in the whole Church and in the whole of Christendom, there is one supreme bishop, viz., the Pope. —*De Potestate Regia et Papali* (A.D. 1302), ch. III.

8. *Scriptum, Super Libros Sententiarum* II, dist. 44, Expositio textus.

[The problem is whether we should obey a superior authority more than an inferior one.]

If the position be taken that such is indeed our duty, this seems not to be true.... For [fourth argument] spiritual power is higher than secular power. If, then, it were true that we must obey more the superior power, the spiritual power would have the right always to release a man from his allegiance to a secular power, which is evidently not true.

Solution and determination. Two cases are to be considered in which we find the superior and the inferior authorities standing in different relations one to the other. First, the inferior authority originates totally from the superior authority. In this case, absolutely speaking and in all events, greater obedience is due to the superior power. An illustration of this is the order of natural causes: the first cause has a stronger impact upon the thing caused by a second cause than has this very second cause, as is said in the *Liber De Causis* [1]. In this position we find God's power in regard to every created power, or likewise the Emperor's power in regard to that of the Proconsul, or again the Pope's power in regard to every spiritual power in the Church, since by the Pope all degrees of different dignities in the Church are distributed and ordered. Whence papal authority is one of the foundations of the Church, as is evident from Matthew 16:18. So in all things, without any distinction, the Pope ought to be obeyed more than Bishops and Archbishops; (more also by the monk than is the abbot). —The second case to be considered is, that both the superior and the inferior powers originate from one supreme power. Their subordination, thus, depends on the latter who subordinates one to the other as he pleases. As to this case we say that here one power is superior to the other only in regard to those matters in view of which they have been so suborclinated one to the other by that supreme power. Hence in these matters alone greater obedience is due to the superior than to the inferior. An example of this is our relation to the authorities of a Bishop and an Archbishop, both of which descend from the papal authority.

The answer then... to the fourth argument is this. Spiritual as well as secular power comes from the divine power. Hence secular power is subjected to spiritual power in those matters concerning which the subjection has been specified and ordained by God, i.e., in matters belonging to the salvation of the soul. Hence in these we are to obey spiritual authority more than secular authority. On the other hand, more obedience is due to secular than to spiritual power in the things that belong to the civic good (*bonum civile*). For it is said Matthew 22:21: Render unto Caesar the things that are Caesar's. A special case occurs, however, when spiritual and secular power are so joined in one person as they are in the Pope, who holds the apex of both spiritual and secular powers. This has been so arranged by Him who is both Priest and King, Priest Eternal after the order of Melchisedech, King of Kings and Lord of Lords, Whose dominion shall not pass away, and his kingdom shall not be destroyed for ever and ever. Amen. [Conclusion of the second book of the *Scriptum*; this explains the doxological ending.]

TREATISE ON LAW FROM THE SUMMA THEOLOGIAE

Questions 90 - 108

Kolbe's Greatest Books
Volume Fourty Seven

By

Saint Thomas Aquinas

TREATISE ON LAW (Questions 90-108)
OF THE ESSENCE OF LAW (FOUR ARTICLES)

We have now to consider the extrinsic principles of acts. Now the extrinsic principle inclining to evil is the devil, of whose temptations we have spoken in the FP, Question [114]. But the extrinsic principle moving to good is God, Who both instructs us by means of His Law, and assists us by His Grace: wherefore in the first place we must speak of law; in the second place, of grace.

Concerning law, we must consider: (1) Law itself in general; (2) its parts. Concerning law in general three points offer themselves for our consideration: (1) Its essence; (2) The different kinds of law; (3) The effects of law.

Under the first head there are four points of inquiry:

(1) Whether law is something pertaining to reason?
(2) Concerning the end of law;
(3) Its cause;
(4) The promulgation of law.

Question 90 Article: 1

Whether law is something pertaining to reason?

Objection 1: It would seem that law is not something pertaining to reason. For the Apostle says (Rm. 7:23): "I see another law in my members," etc. But nothing pertaining to reason is in the members; since the reason does not make use of a bodily organ. Therefore law is not something pertaining to reason.

Objection 2: Further, in the reason there is nothing else but power, habit, and act. But law is not the power itself of reason. In like manner, neither is it a habit of reason: because the habits of reason are the intellectual virtues of which we have spoken above (Question [57]). Nor again is it an act of reason: because then law would cease, when the act of reason ceases, for instance, while we are asleep. Therefore law is nothing pertaining to reason.

Objection 3: Further, the law moves those who are subject to it to act aright. But it belongs properly to the will to move to act, as is evident from what has been said above (Question [9], Article [1]). Therefore law pertains, not to the reason, but to the will; according to the words of the Jurist (Lib. i, ff., De Const. Prin. leg. i): "Whatsoever pleaseth the sovereign, has force of law."

On the contrary, It belongs to the law to command and to forbid. But it belongs to reason to command, as stated above (Question [17], Article [1]). Therefore law is something pertaining to reason.

I answer that, Law is a rule and measure of acts, whereby man is induced to act or is restrained from acting: for "lex" [law] is derived from "ligare" [to bind], because it binds one to act. Now the rule and measure of human acts is the reason, which is the first principle of human acts, as is evident from what has been stated above (Question [1], Article [1], ad 3); since it belongs to the reason to direct to the end, which is the first principle in all matters of action, according to the Philosopher (Phys. ii). Now that which is the principle in any genus, is the rule and measure of that genus: for instance, unity in the genus of numbers, and the first movement in the genus of movements. Consequently it follows that law is something pertaining to reason.

Reply to Objection 1: Since law is a kind of rule and measure, it may be in something in two ways. First, as in that which measures and rules: and since this is proper to reason, it follows that, in this way, law is in the reason alone. Secondly, as in that which is measured and ruled. In this way, law is in all those things that are inclined to something by reason of some law: so that any inclination arising from a law, may be called a law, not essentially but by participation as it were. And thus the inclination of the members to concupiscence is called "the law of the members."

Reply to Objection 2: Just as, in external action, we may consider the work and the work done, for instance the work of building and the house built; so in the acts of reason, we may consider the act itself of reason, i.e. to understand and to reason, and something produced by this act. With regard to the speculative reason, this is first of all the definition; secondly, the proposition; thirdly, the syllogism or argument. And since also the practical reason makes use of a syllogism in respect of the work to be done, as stated above (Question [13], Article [3]; Question [76], Article [1]) and since as the Philosopher teaches (Ethic. vii, 3); hence we find in the practical reason something that holds the same position in regard to operations, as, in the speculative intellect, the proposition holds in regard to conclusions. Such like universal propositions of the practical intellect that are directed to actions have the nature of law. And these propositions are sometimes under our actual consideration, while sometimes they are retained in the reason by means of a habit.

Reply to Objection 3: Reason has its power of moving from the will, as stated above (Question [17], Article [1]): for it is due to the fact that one wills the end, that the reason issues its commands as regards things ordained to the end. But in order that the volition of what is commanded may have the nature of law, it needs to be in accord with some rule of reason. And in this sense is to be understood the saying that the will of the sovereign has the force of law; otherwise the sovereign's will would savor of lawlessness rather than of law.

Article: 2

Whether the law is always something directed to the common good?

Objection 1: It would seem that the law is not always directed to the common good as to its end. For it belongs to law to command and to forbid. But commands are directed to certain individual goods. Therefore the end of the law is not always the common good.

Objection 2: Further, the law directs man in his actions. But human actions are concerned with particular matters. Therefore the law is directed to some particular good.

Objection 3: Further, Isidore says (Etym. v, 3): "If the law is based on reason, whatever is based on reason will be a law." But reason is the foundation not only of what is ordained to the common good, but also of that which is directed private good. Therefore the law is not only directed to the good of all, but also to the private good of an individual.

On the contrary, Isidore says (Etym. v, 21) that "laws are enacted for no private profit, but for the common benefit of the citizens."

I answer that, As stated above (Article [1]), the law belongs to that which is a principle of human acts, because it is their rule and measure. Now as reason is a principle of human acts, so in reason itself there is something which is the principle in respect of all the rest: wherefore to this principle chiefly and mainly law must needs be referred. Now the first principle in practical matters, which are the object of the practical reason, is the last end: and the last end of human life is bliss or happiness, as stated above (Question [2], Article [7]; Question [3], Article [1]). Consequently the law must needs regard principally the relationship to happiness. Moreover, since every part is ordained to the whole, as imperfect to perfect; and since one man is a part of the perfect community, the law must needs regard properly the relationship to universal happiness. Wherefore the Philosopher, in the above definition of legal matters mentions both happiness and the body politic: for he says (Ethic. v, 1) that we call those legal matters "just, which are adapted to produce and preserve happiness and its parts for the body politic": since the state is a perfect community, as he says in Polit. i, 1.

Now in every genus, that which belongs to it chiefly is the principle of the others, and the others belong to that genus in subordination to that thing: thus fire, which is chief among hot things, is the cause of heat in mixed bodies, and these are said to be hot in so far as they have a share of fire. Consequently, since the law is chiefly ordained to the common good, any other precept in regard to some individual work, must needs be devoid of the nature of a law, save in so

60

far as it regards the common good. Therefore every law is ordained to the common good.

Reply to Objection 1: A command denotes an application of a law to matters regulated by the law. Now the order to the common good, at which the law aims, is applicable to particular ends. And in this way commands are given even concerning particular matters.

Reply to Objection 2: Actions are indeed concerned with particular matters: but those particular matters are referable to the common good, not as to a common genus or species, but as to a common final cause, according as the common good is said to be the common end.

Reply to Objection 3: Just as nothing stands firm with regard to the speculative reason except that which is traced back to the first indemonstrable principles, so nothing stands firm with regard to the practical reason, unless it be directed to the last end which is the common good: and whatever stands to reason in this sense, has the nature of a law.

Article: 3

Whether the reason of any man is competent to make laws?

Objection 1: It would seem that the reason of any man is competent to make laws. For the Apostle says (Rm. 2:14) that "when the Gentiles, who have not the law, do by nature those things that are of the law . . . they are a law to themselves." Now he says this of all in general. Therefore anyone can make a law for himself.

Objection 2: Further, as the Philosopher says (Ethic. ii, 1), "the intention of the lawgiver is to lead men to virtue." But every man can lead another to virtue. Therefore the reason of any man is competent to make laws.

Objection 3: Further, just as the sovereign of a state governs the state, so every father of a family governs his household. But the sovereign of a state can make laws for the state. Therefore every father of a family can make laws for his household.

On the contrary, Isidore says (Etym. v, 10): "A law is an ordinance of the people, whereby something is sanctioned by the Elders together with the Commonalty."

I answer that, A law, properly speaking, regards first and foremost the order to the common good. Now to order anything to the common good, belongs either to the whole people, or to someone who is the vicegerent of the whole people. And therefore the making of a law belongs either to the whole people or to a public personage who has care of the whole people: since in all other matters the directing of anything to the end concerns him to whom the end belongs.

Reply to Objection 1: As stated above (Article [1], ad 1), a law is in a person not only as in one that rules, but also by participation as in one that is ruled. In the latter way each one is a law to himself, in so far as he shares the direction that he receives from one who rules him. Hence the same text goes on: "Who show the work of the law written in their hearts."

Reply to Objection 2: A private person cannot lead another to virtue efficaciously: for he can only advise, and if his advice be not taken, it has no coercive power, such as the law should have, in order to prove an efficacious inducement to virtue, as the Philosopher says (Ethic. x, 9). But this coercive power is vested in the whole people or in some public personage, to whom it belongs to inflict penalties, as we shall state further on (Question [92], Article [2], ad 3; SS, Question [64], Article [3]). Wherefore the framing of laws belongs to him alone.

Reply to Objection 3: As one man is a part of the household, so a household is a part of the state: and the state is a perfect community, according to Polit. i, 1. And therefore, as the good of one man is not the last end, but is ordained to the common good; so too the good of one household is ordained to the good of a single state, which is a perfect community. Consequently he that governs a family, can indeed make certain commands or ordinances, but not such as to have properly the force of law.

Article: 4

Whether promulgation is essential to a law?

Objection 1: It would seem that promulgation is not essential to a law. For the natural law above all has the character of law. But the natural law needs no promulgation. Therefore it is not essential to a law that it be promulgated.

Objection 2: Further, it belongs properly to a law to bind one to do or not to do something. But the obligation of fulfilling a law touches not only those in whose presence it is promulgated, but also others. Therefore promulgation is not essential to a law.

Objection 3: Further, the binding force of a law extends even to the future, since "laws are binding in matters of the future," as the jurists say (Cod. 1, tit. De lege et constit. leg. vii). But promulgation concerns those who are present. Therefore it is not essential to a law.

On the contrary, It is laid down in the Decretals, dist. 4, that "laws are established when they are promulgated."

I answer that, As stated above (Article [1]), a law is imposed on others by way of a rule and measure. Now a rule or measure is imposed by being applied to those who are to be ruled and measured by it. Wherefore, in order that a law obtain the binding force which is proper to a law, it must needs be applied to the men who have to be ruled by it. Such application is made by its being notified to them by promulgation. Wherefore promulgation is necessary for the law to obtain its force.

Thus from the four preceding articles, the definition of law may be gathered; and it is nothing else than an ordinance of reason for the common good, made by him who has care of the community, and promulgated.

Reply to Objection 1: The natural law is promulgated by the very fact that God instilled it into man's mind so as to be known by him naturally.

Reply to Objection 2: Those who are not present when a law is promulgated, are bound to observe the law, in so far as it is notified or can be notified to them by others, after it has been promulgated.

Reply to Objection 3: The promulgation that takes place now, extends to future time by reason of the durability of written characters, by which means it is continually promulgated. Hence Isidore says (Etym. v, 3; ii, 10) that "lex [law] is derived from legere [to read] because it is written."

OF THE VARIOUS KINDS OF LAW (SIX ARTICLES)

We must now consider the various kinds of law: under which head there are six points of inquiry:

(1) Whether there is an eternal law?
(2) Whether there is a natural law?
(3) Whether there is a human law?
(4) Whether there is a Divine law?
(5) Whether there is one Divine law, or several?
(6) Whether there is a law of sin?

Question 91 Article: 1

Whether there is an eternal law?

Objection 1: It would seem that there is no eternal law. Because every law is imposed on someone. But there was not someone from eternity on whom a law could be imposed: since God alone was from eternity. Therefore no law is eternal.

Objection 2: Further, promulgation is essential to law. But promulgation could not be from eternity; because there was no one to whom it could be promulgated from eternity. Therefore no law can be eternal.

Objection 3: Further, a law implies order to an end. But nothing ordained to an end is eternal: for the last end alone is eternal. Therefore no law is eternal.

On the contrary, Augustine says (De Lib. Arb. i, 6): "That Law which is the Supreme Reason cannot be understood to be otherwise than unchangeable and eternal."

I answer that, As stated above (Question [90], Article [1], ad 2; Articles [3],4), a law is nothing else but a dictate of practical reason emanating from the ruler who governs a perfect community. Now it is evident, granted that the world is ruled by Divine Providence, as was stated in the FP, Question [22], Articles [1],2, that the whole community of the universe is governed by Divine Reason. Wherefore the very Idea of the government of things in God the Ruler of the universe, has the nature of a law. And since the Divine Reason's conception of things is not subject to time but is eternal, according to Prov. 8:23, therefore it is that this kind of law must be called eternal.

Reply to Objection 1: Those things that are not in themselves, exist with God, inasmuch as they are foreknown and preordained by Him, according to Rm.

4:17: "Who calls those things that are not, as those that are." Accordingly the eternal concept of the Divine law bears the character of an eternal law, in so far as it is ordained by God to the government of things foreknown by Him.

Reply to Objection 2: Promulgation is made by word of mouth or in writing; and in both ways the eternal law is promulgated: because both the Divine Word and the writing of the Book of Life are eternal. But the promulgation cannot be from eternity on the part of the creature that hears or reads.

Reply to Objection 3: The law implies order to the end actively, in so far as it directs certain things to the end; but not passively---that is to say, the law itself is not ordained to the end---except accidentally, in a governor whose end is extrinsic to him, and to which end his law must needs be ordained. But the end of the Divine government is God Himself, and His law is not distinct from Himself. Wherefore the eternal law is not ordained to another end.

Article: 2

Whether there is in us a natural law?

Objection 1: It would seem that there is no natural law in us. Because man is governed sufficiently by the eternal law: for Augustine says (De Lib. Arb. i) that "the eternal law is that by which it is right that all things should be most orderly." But nature does not abound in superfluities as neither does she fail in necessaries. Therefore no law is natural to man.

Objection 2: Further, by the law man is directed, in his acts, to the end, as stated above (Question [90], Article [2]). But the directing of human acts to their end is not a function of nature, as is the case in irrational creatures, which act for an end solely by their natural appetite; whereas man acts for an end by his reason and will. Therefore no law is natural to man.

Objection 3: Further, the more a man is free, the less is he under the law. But man is freer than all the animals, on account of his free-will, with which he is endowed above all other animals. Since therefore other animals are not subject to a natural law, neither is man subject to a natural law.

On the contrary, A gloss on Rm. 2:14: "When the Gentiles, who have not the law, do by nature those things that are of the law," comments as follows: "Although they have no written law, yet they have the natural law, whereby each one knows, and is conscious of, what is good and what is evil."

I answer that, As stated above (Question [90], Article [1], ad 1), law, being a rule and measure, can be in a person in two ways: in one way, as in him that rules and measures; in another way, as in that which is ruled and measured, since a thing is ruled and measured, in so far as it partakes of the rule or measure. Wherefore, since all things subject to Divine providence are ruled and measured by the eternal law, as was stated above (Article [1]); it is evident that all things partake somewhat of the eternal law, in so far as, namely, from its being imprinted on them, they derive their respective inclinations to their proper acts and ends. Now among all others, the rational creature is subject to Divine providence in the most excellent way, in so far as it partakes of a share of providence, by being provident both for itself and for others. Wherefore it has a share of the Eternal Reason, whereby it has a natural inclination to its proper act and end: and this participation of the eternal law in the rational creature is called the natural law. Hence the Psalmist after saying (Ps. 4:6): "Offer up the sacrifice of justice," as though someone asked what the works of justice are, adds: "Many say, Who showeth us good things?" in answer to which question he says: "The light of Thy countenance, O Lord, is signed upon us": thus implying that the light of natural reason, whereby we discern what is good and what is evil, which is the function of the natural law, is nothing else than an imprint on us of the Divine light. It is therefore evident that the natural law is nothing else than the rational creature's participation of the eternal law.

Reply to Objection 1: This argument would hold, if the natural law were something different from the eternal law: whereas it is nothing but a participation thereof, as stated above.

Reply to Objection 2: Every act of reason and will in us is based on that which is according to nature, as stated above (Question [10], Article [1]): for every act of reasoning is based on principles that are known naturally, and every act of appetite in respect of the means is derived from the natural appetite in respect of the last end. Accordingly the first direction of our acts to their end must needs be in virtue of the natural law.

Reply to Objection 3: Even irrational animals partake in their own way of the Eternal Reason, just as the rational creature does. But because the rational creature partakes thereof in an intellectual and rational manner, therefore the participation of the eternal law in the rational creature is properly called a law, since a law is something pertaining to reason, as stated above (Question [90], Article [1]). Irrational creatures, however, do not partake thereof in a rational manner, wherefore there is no participation of the eternal law in them, except by way of similitude.

Article: 3

Whether there is a human law?

Objection 1: It would seem that there is not a human law. For the natural law is a participation of the eternal law, as stated above (Article [2]). Now through the eternal law "all things are most orderly," as Augustine states (De Lib. Arb. i, 6). Therefore the natural law suffices for the ordering of all human affairs. Consequently there is no need for a human law.

Objection 2: Further, a law bears the character of a measure, as stated above (Question [90], Article [1]). But human reason is not a measure of things, but vice versa, as stated in Metaph. x, text. 5. Therefore no law can emanate from human reason.

Objection 3: Further, a measure should be most certain, as stated in Metaph. x, text. 3. But the dictates of human reason in matters of conduct are uncertain, according to Wis. 9:14: "The thoughts of mortal men are fearful, and our counsels uncertain." Therefore no law can emanate from human reason.

On the contrary, Augustine (De Lib. Arb. i, 6) distinguishes two kinds of law, the one eternal, the other temporal, which he calls human.

I answer that, As stated above (Question [90], Article [1], ad 2), a law is a dictate of the practical reason. Now it is to be observed that the same procedure takes place in the practical and in the speculative reason: for each proceeds from principles to conclusions, as stated above (De Lib. Arb. i, 6). Accordingly we conclude that just as, in the speculative reason, from naturally known indemonstrable principles, we draw the conclusions of the various sciences, the knowledge of which is not imparted to us by nature, but acquired by the efforts of reason, so too it is from the precepts of the natural law, as from general and indemonstrable principles, that the human reason needs to proceed to the more particular determination of certain matters. These particular determinations, devised by human reason, are called human laws, provided the other essential conditions of law be observed, as stated above (Question [90], Articles [2],3,4). Wherefore Tully says in his Rhetoric (De Invent. Rhet. ii) that "justice has its source in nature; thence certain things came into custom by reason of their utility; afterwards these things which emanated from nature and were approved by custom, were sanctioned by fear and reverence for the law."

Reply to Objection 1: The human reason cannot have a full participation of the dictate of the Divine Reason, but according to its own mode, and imperfectly. Consequently, as on the part of the speculative reason, by a natural participation of Divine Wisdom, there is in us the knowledge of certain general principles, but not proper knowledge of each single truth, such as that contained in the Divine Wisdom; so too, on the part of the practical reason, man has a natural participation of the eternal law, according to certain general principles, but not as regards the particular determinations of individual cases, which are, however, contained in the eternal law. Hence the need for human reason to proceed further to sanction them by law.

Reply to Objection 2: Human reason is not, of itself, the rule of things: but the principles impressed on it by nature, are general rules and measures of all things relating to human conduct, whereof the natural reason is the rule and measure, although it is not the measure of things that are from nature.

Reply to Objection 3: The practical reason is concerned with practical matters, which are singular and contingent: but not with necessary things, with which the speculative reason is concerned. Wherefore human laws cannot have that inerrancy that belongs to the demonstrated conclusions of sciences. Nor is it necessary for every measure to be altogether unerring and certain, but according as it is possible in its own particular genus.

Question 91 Article: 4

Whether there was any need for a Divine law?

Objection 1: It would seem that there was no need for a Divine law. Because, as stated above (Article [2]), the natural law is a participation in us of the eternal law. But the eternal law is a Divine law, as stated above (Article [1]). Therefore there was no need for a Divine law in addition to the natural law, and human laws derived therefrom.

Objection 2: Further, it is written (Ecclus. 15:14) that "God left man in the hand of his own counsel." Now counsel is an act of reason, as stated above (Question [14], Article [1]). Therefore man was left to the direction of his reason. But a dictate of human reason is a human law as stated above (Article [3]). Therefore there is no need for man to be governed also by a Divine law.

Objection 3: Further, human nature is more self-sufficing than irrational creatures. But irrational creatures have no Divine law besides the natural inclination impressed on them. Much less, therefore, should the rational creature have a Divine law in addition to the natural law.

On the contrary, David prayed God to set His law before him, saying (Ps. 118:33): "Set before me for a law the way of Thy justifications, O Lord."

I answer that, Besides the natural and the human law it was necessary for the directing of human conduct to have a Divine law. And this for four reasons. First, because it is by law that man is directed how to perform his proper acts in view of his last end. And indeed if man were ordained to no other end than that which is proportionate to his natural faculty, there would be no need for man to have any further direction of the part of his reason, besides the natural law and human law which is derived from it. But since man is ordained to an end of eternal happiness which is inproportionate to man's natural faculty, as stated above (Question [5], Article [5]), therefore it was necessary that, besides the

68

natural and the human law, man should be directed to his end by a law given by God.

Secondly, because, on account of the uncertainty of human judgment, especially on contingent and particular matters, different people form different judgments on human acts; whence also different and contrary laws result. In order, therefore, that man may know without any doubt what he ought to do and what he ought to avoid, it was necessary for man to be directed in his proper acts by a law given by God, for it is certain that such a law cannot err.

Thirdly, because man can make laws in those matters of which he is competent to judge. But man is not competent to judge of interior movements, that are hidden, but only of exterior acts which appear: and yet for the perfection of virtue it is necessary for man to conduct himself aright in both kinds of acts. Consequently human law could not sufficiently curb and direct interior acts; and it was necessary for this purpose that a Divine law should supervene.

Fourthly, because, as Augustine says (De Lib. Arb. i, 5,6), human law cannot punish or forbid all evil deeds: since while aiming at doing away with all evils, it would do away with many good things, and would hinder the advance of the common good, which is necessary for human intercourse. In order, therefore, that no evil might remain unforbidden and unpunished, it was necessary for the Divine law to supervene, whereby all sins are forbidden.

And these four causes are touched upon in Ps. 118:8, where it is said: "The law of the Lord is unspotted," i.e. allowing no foulness of sin; "converting souls," because it directs not only exterior, but also interior acts; "the testimony of the Lord is faithful," because of the certainty of what is true and right; "giving wisdom to little ones," by directing man to an end supernatural and Divine.

Reply to Objection 1: By the natural law the eternal law is participated proportionately to the capacity of human nature. But to his supernatural end man needs to be directed in a yet higher way. Hence the additional law given by God, whereby man shares more perfectly in the eternal law.

Reply to Objection 2: Counsel is a kind of inquiry: hence it must proceed from some principles. Nor is it enough for it to proceed from principles imparted by nature, which are the precepts of the natural law, for the reasons given above: but there is need for certain additional principles, namely, the precepts of the Divine law.

Reply to Objection 3: Irrational creatures are not ordained to an end higher than that which is proportionate to their natural powers: consequently the comparison fails.

Article: 5 Whether there is but one Divine law?

Objection 1: It would seem that there is but one Divine law. Because, where there is one king in one kingdom there is but one law. Now the whole of mankind is compared to God as to one king, according to Ps. 46:8: "God is the King of all the earth." Therefore there is but one Divine law.

Objection 2: Further, every law is directed to the end which the lawgiver intends for those for whom he makes the law. But God intends one and the same thing for all men; since according to 1 Tim. 2:4: "He will have all men to be saved, and to come to the knowledge of the truth." Therefore there is but one Divine law.

Objection 3: Further, the Divine law seems to be more akin to the eternal law, which is one, than the natural law, according as the revelation of grace is of a higher order than natural knowledge. Therefore much more is the Divine law but one.

On the contrary, The Apostle says (Heb. 7:12): "The priesthood being translated, it is necessary that a translation also be made of the law." But the priesthood is twofold, as stated in the same passage, viz. the levitical priesthood, and the priesthood of Christ. Therefore the Divine law is twofold, namely the Old Law and the New Law.

I answer that, As stated in the FP, Question [30], Article [3], distinction is the cause of number. Now things may be distinguished in two ways. First, as those things that are altogether specifically different, e.g. a horse and an ox. Secondly, as perfect and imperfect in the same species, e.g. a boy and a man: and in this way the Divine law is divided into Old and New. Hence the Apostle (Gal. 3:24,25) compares the state of man under the Old Law to that of a child "under a pedagogue"; but the state under the New Law, to that of a full grown man, who is "no longer under a pedagogue."

Now the perfection and imperfection of these two laws is to be taken in connection with the three conditions pertaining to law, as stated above. For, in the first place, it belongs to law to be directed to the common good as to its end, as stated above (Question [90], Article [2]). This good may be twofold. It may be a sensible and earthly good; and to this, man was directly ordained by the Old Law: wherefore, at the very outset of the law, the people were invited to the earthly kingdom of the Chananaeans (Ex. 3:8,17). Again it may be an intelligible and heavenly good: and to this, man is ordained by the New Law. Wherefore, at the very beginning of His preaching, Christ invited men to the kingdom of heaven, saying (Mt. 4:17): "Do penance, for the kingdom of heaven is at hand." Hence Augustine says (Contra Faust. iv) that "promises of temporal goods are contained in the Old Testament, for which reason it is called old; but the promise of eternal life belongs to the New Testament."

Secondly, it belongs to the law to direct human acts according to the order of righteousness (Article [4]): wherein also the New Law surpasses the Old Law, since it directs our internal acts, according to Mt. 5:20: "Unless your justice abound more than that of the Scribes and Pharisees, you shall not enter into the kingdom of heaven." Hence the saying that "the Old Law restrains the hand, but the New Law controls the mind" (Sentent. iii, D, xl).

Thirdly, it belongs to the law to induce men to observe its commandments. This the Old Law did by the fear of punishment: but the New Law, by love, which is poured into our hearts by the grace of Christ, bestowed in the New Law, but foreshadowed in the Old. Hence Augustine says (Contra Adimant. Manich. discip. xvii) that "there is little difference [*The 'little difference' refers to the Latin words 'timor' and 'amor'---'fear' and 'love.'] between the Law and the Gospel---fear and love."

Reply to Objection 1: As the father of a family issues different commands to the children and to the adults, so also the one King, God, in His one kingdom, gave one law to men, while they were yet imperfect, and another more perfect law, when, by the preceding law, they had been led to a greater capacity for Divine things.

Reply to Objection 2: The salvation of man could not be achieved otherwise than through Christ, according to Acts 4:12: "There is no other name . . . given to men, whereby we must be saved." Consequently the law that brings all to salvation could not be given until after the coming of Christ. But before His coming it was necessary to give to the people, of whom Christ was to be born, a law containing certain rudiments of righteousness unto salvation, in order to prepare them to receive Him.

Reply to Objection 3: The natural law directs man by way of certain general precepts, common to both the perfect and the imperfect: wherefore it is one and the same for all. But the Divine law directs man also in certain particular matters, to which the perfect and imperfect do not stand in the same relation. Hence the necessity for the Divine law to be twofold, as already explained.

Article: 6

Whether there is a law in the fomes of sin?

Objection 1: It would seem that there is no law of the "fomes" of sin. For Isidore says (Etym. v) that the "law is based on reason." But the "fomes" of sin is not

71

based on reason, but deviates from it. Therefore the "fomes" has not the nature of a law.

Objection 2: Further, every law is binding, so that those who do not obey it are called transgressors. But man is not called a transgressor, from not following the instigations of the "fomes"; but rather from his following them. Therefore the "fomes" has not the nature of a law.

Objection 3: Further, the law is ordained to the common good, as stated above (Question [90], Article [2]). But the "fomes" inclines us, not to the common, but to our own private good. Therefore the "fomes" has not the nature of sin.

On the contrary, The Apostle says (Rm. 7:23): "I see another law in my members, fighting against the law of my mind."

I answer that, As stated above (Article [2]; Question [90], Article [1], ad 1), the law, as to its essence, resides in him that rules and measures; but, by way of participation, in that which is ruled and measured; so that every inclination or ordination which may be found in things subject to the law, is called a law by participation, as stated above (Article [2]; Question [90], Article [1], ad 1). Now those who are subject to a law may receive a twofold inclination from the lawgiver. First, in so far as he directly inclines his subjects to something; sometimes indeed different subjects to different acts; in this way we may say that there is a military law and a mercantile law. Secondly, indirectly; thus by the very fact that a lawgiver deprives a subject of some dignity, the latter passes into another order, so as to be under another law, as it were: thus if a soldier be turned out of the army, he becomes a subject of rural or of mercantile legislation.

Accordingly under the Divine Lawgiver various creatures have various natural inclinations, so that what is, as it were, a law for one, is against the law for another: thus I might say that fierceness is, in a way, the law of a dog, but against the law of a sheep or another meek animal. And so the law of man, which, by the Divine ordinance, is allotted to him, according to his proper natural condition, is that he should act in accordance with reason: and this law was so effective in the primitive state, that nothing either beside or against reason could take man unawares. But when man turned his back on God, he fell under the influence of his sensual impulses: in fact this happens to each one individually, the more he deviates from the path of reason, so that, after a fashion, he is likened to the beasts that are led by the impulse of sensuality, according to Ps. 48:21: "Man, when he was in honor, did not understand: he hath been compared to senseless beasts, and made like to them."

So, then, this very inclination of sensuality which is called the "fomes," in other animals has simply the nature of a law (yet only in so far as a law may be said to be in such things), by reason of a direct inclination. But in man, it has not the nature of law in this way, rather is it a deviation from the law of reason. But since, by the just sentence of God, man is destitute of original justice, and his reason bereft of its vigor, this impulse of sensuality, whereby he is led, in so far as it is a penalty following from the Divine law depriving man of his proper dignity, has the nature of a law.

Reply to Objection 1: This argument considers the "fomes" in itself, as an incentive to evil. It is not thus that it has the nature of a law, as stated above, but according as it results from the justice of the Divine law: it is as though we were to say that the law allows a nobleman to be condemned to hard labor for some misdeed.

Reply to Objection 2: This argument considers law in the light of a rule or measure: for it is in this sense that those who deviate from the law become transgressors. But the "fomes" is not a law in this respect, but by a kind of participation, as stated above.

Reply to Objection 3: This argument considers the "fomes" as to its proper inclination, and not as to its origin. And yet if the inclination of sensuality be considered as it is in other animals, thus it is ordained to the common good, namely, to the preservation of nature in the species or in the individual. And this is in man also, in so far as sensuality is subject to reason. But it is called "fomes" in so far as it strays from the order of reason.

OF THE EFFECTS OF LAW (TWO ARTICLES)

We must now consider the effects of law; under which head there are two points of inquiry:

(1) Whether an effect of law is to make men good?

(2) Whether the effects of law are to command, to forbid, to permit, and to punish, as the Jurist states?

Question 92 Article: 1

Whether an effect of law is to make men good?

Objection 1: It seems that it is not an effect of law to make men good. For men are good through virtue, since virtue, as stated in Ethic. ii, 6 is "that which makes its subject good." But virtue is in man from God alone, because He it is Who "works it in us without us," as we stated above (Question [55], Article [4]) in giving the definition of virtue. Therefore the law does not make men good.

Objection 2: Further, Law does not profit a man unless he obeys it. But the very fact that a man obeys a law is due to his being good. Therefore in man goodness is presupposed to the law. Therefore the law does not make men good.

Objection 3: Further, Law is ordained to the common good, as stated above (Question [90], Article [2]). But some behave well in things regarding the community, who behave ill in things regarding themselves. Therefore it is not the business of the law to make men good.

Objection 4: Further, some laws are tyrannical, as the Philosopher says (Polit. iii, 6). But a tyrant does not intend the good of his subjects, but considers only his own profit. Therefore law does not make men good.

On the contrary, The Philosopher says (Ethic. ii, 1) that the "intention of every lawgiver is to make good citizens."

I answer that, as stated above (Question [90], Article [1], ad 2; Articles [3],4), a law is nothing else than a dictate of reason in the ruler by whom his subjects are governed. Now the virtue of any subordinate thing consists in its being well subordinated to that by which it is regulated: thus we see that the virtue of the irascible and concupiscible faculties consists in their being obedient to reason; and accordingly "the virtue of every subject consists in his being well subjected to his ruler," as the Philosopher says (Polit. i). But every law aims at being obeyed by those who are subject to it. Consequently it is evident that the proper effect of law is to lead its subjects to their proper virtue: and since virtue is "that which makes its subject good," it follows that the proper effect of law is to make those to whom it is given, good, either simply or in some particular respect. For if the intention of the lawgiver is fixed on true good, which is the common good regulated according to Divine justice, it follows that the effect of the law is to make men good simply. If, however, the intention of the lawgiver is fixed on that which is not simply good, but useful or pleasurable to himself, or in opposition to Divine justice; then the law does not make men good simply, but in respect to that particular government. In this way good is found even in things that are bad of themselves: thus a man is called a good robber, because he works in a way that is adapted to his end.

Reply to Objection 1: Virtue is twofold, as explained above (Question [63], Article [2]), viz. acquired and infused. Now the fact of being accustomed to an action contributes to both, but in different ways; for it causes the acquired virtue; while it disposes to infused virtue, and preserves and fosters it when it already exists. And since law is given for the purpose of directing human acts; as far as human acts conduce to virtue, so far does law make men good. Wherefore the Philosopher says in the second book of the Politics (Ethic. ii) that "lawgivers make men good by habituating them to good works."

Reply to Objection 2: It is not always through perfect goodness of virtue that one obeys the law, but sometimes it is through fear of punishment, and sometimes from the mere dictates of reason, which is a beginning of virtue, as stated above (Question [63], Article [1]).

Reply to Objection 3: The goodness of any part is considered in comparison with the whole; hence Augustine says (Confess. iii) that "unseemly is the part that harmonizes not with the whole." Since then every man is a part of the state, it is impossible that a man be good, unless he be well proportionate to the common good: nor can the whole be well consistent unless its parts be proportionate to it. Consequently the common good of the state cannot flourish, unless the citizens be virtuous, at least those whose business it is to govern. But it is enough for the good of the community, that the other citizens be so far virtuous that they obey the commands of their rulers. Hence the Philosopher says (Polit. ii, 2) that "the virtue of a sovereign is the same as that of a good man, but the virtue of any common citizen is not the same as that of a good man."

Reply to Objection 4: A tyrannical law, through not being according to reason, is not a law, absolutely speaking, but rather a perversion of law; and yet in so far as it is something in the nature of a law, it aims at the citizens' being good. For all it has in the nature of a law consists in its being an ordinance made by a superior to his subjects, and aims at being obeyed by them, which is to make them good, not simply, but with respect to that particular government.

Article: 2 Whether the acts of law are suitably assigned?

Objection 1: It would seem that the acts of law are not suitably assigned as consisting in "command," "prohibition," "permission" and "punishment." For "every law is a general precept," as the jurist states. But command and precept are the same. Therefore the other three are superfluous.

Objection 2: Further, the effect of a law is to induce its subjects to be good, as stated above (Article [1]). But counsel aims at a higher good than a command does. Therefore it belongs to law to counsel rather than to command.

Objection 3: Further, just as punishment stirs a man to good deeds, so does reward. Therefore if to punish is reckoned an effect of law, so also is to reward.

Objection 4: Further, the intention of a lawgiver is to make men good, as stated above (Article [1]). But he that obeys the law, merely through fear of being punished, is not good: because "although a good deed may be done through servile fear, i.e. fear of punishment, it is not done well," as Augustine says (Contra duas Epist. Pelag. ii). Therefore punishment is not a proper effect of law.

On the contrary, Isidore says (Etym. v, 19): "Every law either permits something, as: 'A brave man may demand his reward'": or forbids something, as: "No man may ask a consecrated virgin in marriage": or punishes, as: "Let him that commits a murder be put to death."

I answer that, Just as an assertion is a dictate of reason asserting something, so is a law a dictate of reason, commanding something. Now it is proper to reason to lead from one thing to another. Wherefore just as, in demonstrative sciences, the reason leads us from certain principles to assent to the conclusion, so it induces us by some means to assent to the precept of the law.

Now the precepts of law are concerned with human acts, in which the law directs, as stated above (Question [90], Articles [1],2; Question [91], Article [4]). Again there are three kinds of human acts: for, as stated above (Question [18], Article [8]), some acts are good generically, viz. acts of virtue; and in respect of these the act of the law is a precept or command, for "the law commands all acts of virtue" (Ethic. v, 1). Some acts are evil generically, viz. acts of vice, and in respect of these the law forbids. Some acts are generically indifferent, and in respect of these the law permits; and all acts that are either not distinctly good or not distinctly bad may be called indifferent. And it is the fear of punishment that law makes use of in order to ensure obedience: in which respect punishment is an effect of law.

Reply to Objection 1: Just as to cease from evil is a kind of good, so a prohibition is a kind of precept: and accordingly, taking precept in a wide sense, every law is a kind of precept.

Reply to Objection 2: To advise is not a proper act of law, but may be within the competency even of a private person, who cannot make a law. Wherefore too the Apostle, after giving a certain counsel (1 Cor. 7:12) says: "I speak, not the Lord." Consequently it is not reckoned as an effect of law.

Reply to Objection 3: To reward may also pertain to anyone: but to punish pertains to none but the framer of the law, by whose authority the pain is inflicted. Wherefore to reward is not reckoned an effect of law, but only to punish.

Reply to Objection 4: From becoming accustomed to avoid evil and fulfill what is good, through fear of punishment, one is sometimes led on to do so likewise, with delight and of one's own accord. Accordingly, law, even by punishing, leads men on to being good.

I. God = now

II. In respect to enfleshed things/beings w/ matter are subject to time/corruption

Scholastic - Katophatic — What can be said about God. Our speech about God corresponds to God's reality

Mysticism/Apophatic — Our speech about God falls infinitely short of his reality
⤷ Via Negativa

OF THE ETERNAL LAW (SIX ARTICLES)

We must now consider each law by itself; and (1) The eternal law; (2) The natural law; (3) The human law; (4) The old law; (5) The new law, which is the law of the Gospel. Of the sixth law which is the law of the "fomes," suffice what we have said when treating of original sin.

Concerning the first there are six points of inquiry:

(1) What is the eternal law?
(2) Whether it is known to all?
(3) Whether every law is derived from it?
(4) Whether necessary things are subject to the eternal law?
(5) Whether natural contingencies are subject to the eternal law?
(6) Whether all human things are subject to it?

Question 92 Article: 1

Whether the eternal law is a sovereign type [*Ratio] existing in God?

Objection 1: It would seem that the eternal law is not a sovereign type existing in God. For there is only one eternal law. But there are many types of things in the Divine mind; for Augustine says (Qq. lxxxiii, qu. 46) that God "made each thing according to its type." Therefore the eternal law does not seem to be a type existing in the Divine mind.

Objection 2: Further, it is essential to a law that it be promulgated by word, as stated above (Question [90], Article [4]). But Word is a Personal name in God, as stated in the FP, Question [34], Article [1]: whereas type refers to the Essence. Therefore the eternal law is not the same as a Divine type.

Objection 3: Further, Augustine says (De Vera Relig. xxx): "We see a law above our minds, which is called truth." But the law which is above our minds is the eternal law. Therefore truth is the eternal law. But the idea of truth is not the same as the idea of a type. Therefore the eternal law is not the same as the sovereign type.

On the contrary, Augustine says (De Lib. Arb. i, 6) that "the eternal law is the sovereign type, to which we must always conform."

I answer that, Just as in every artificer there pre-exists a type of the things that are made by his art, so too in every governor there must pre-exist the type of the order of those things that are to be done by those who are subject to his government. And just as the type of the things yet to be made by an art is called the art or exemplar of the products of that art, so too the type in him who governs the acts of his subjects, bears the character of a law, provided the other conditions be present which we have mentioned above (Question [90]). Now God, by His wisdom, is the Creator of all things in relation to which He stands as the artificer to the products of his art, as stated in the FP, Question [14], Article [8]. Moreover He governs all the acts and movements that are to be found in each single creature, as was also stated in the FP, Question [103], Article [5]. Wherefore as the type of the Divine Wisdom, inasmuch as by It all things are created, has the character of art, exemplar or idea; so the type of Divine Wisdom, as moving all things to their due end, bears the character of law. Accordingly the eternal law is nothing else than the type of Divine Wisdom, as directing all actions and movements.

Reply to Objection 1: Augustine is speaking in that passage of the ideal types which regard the proper nature of each single thing; and consequently in them there is a certain distinction and plurality, according to their different relations to things, as stated in the FP, Question [15], Article [2]. But law is said to direct human acts by ordaining them to the common good, as stated above (Question [90], Article [2]). And things, which are in themselves different, may be considered as one, according as they are ordained to one common thing. Wherefore the eternal law is one since it is the type of this order.

Reply to Objection 2: With regard to any sort of word, two points may be considered: viz. the word itself, and that which is expressed by the word. For the spoken word is something uttered by the mouth of man, and expresses that which is signified by the human word. The same applies to the human mental word, which is nothing else that something conceived by the mind, by which man expresses his thoughts mentally. So then in God the Word conceived by the intellect of the Father is the name of a Person: but all things that are in the Father's knowledge, whether they refer to the Essence or to the Persons, or to the works of God, are expressed by this Word, as Augustine declares (De Trin. xv, 14). And among other things expressed by this Word, the eternal law itself is expressed thereby. Nor does it follow that the eternal law is a Personal name in God: yet it is appropriated to the Son, on account of the kinship between type and word.

Reply to Objection 3: The types of the Divine intellect do not stand in the same relation to things, as the types of the human intellect. For the human intellect is measured by things, so that a human concept is not true by reason of itself, but by reason of its being consonant with things, since "an opinion is true or false according as it answers to the reality." But the Divine intellect is the measure of things: since each thing has so far truth in it, as it represents the Divine intellect, as was stated in the FP, Question [16], Article [1]. Consequently the Divine intellect is true in itself; and its type is truth itself.

Article: 2 Whether the eternal law is known to all?

Objection 1: It would seem that the eternal law is not known to all. Because, as the Apostle says (1 Cor. 2:11), "the things that are of God no man knoweth, but the Spirit of God." But the eternal law is a type existing in the Divine mind. Therefore it is unknown to all save God alone.

Objection 2: Further, as Augustine says (De Lib. Arb. i, 6) "the eternal law is that by which it is right that all things should be most orderly." But all do not know how all things are most orderly. Therefore all do not know the eternal law.

Objection 3: Further, Augustine says (De Vera Relig. xxxi) that "the eternal law is not subject to the judgment of man." But according to Ethic. i, "any man can judge well of what he knows." Therefore the eternal law is not known to us.

On the contrary, Augustine says (De Lib. Arb. i, 6) that "knowledge of the eternal law is imprinted on us."

I answer that, A thing may be known in two ways: first, in itself; secondly, in its effect, wherein some likeness of that thing is found: thus someone not seeing the sun in its substance, may know it by its rays. So then no one can know the eternal law, as it is in itself, except the blessed who see God in His Essence. But every rational creature knows it in its reflection, greater or less. For every knowledge of truth is a kind of reflection and participation of the eternal law, which is the unchangeable truth, as Augustine says (De Vera Relig. xxxi). Now all men know the truth to a certain extent, at least as to the common principles of the natural law: and as to the others, they partake of the knowledge of truth, some more, some less; and in this respect are more or less cognizant of the eternal law.

Reply to Objection 1: We cannot know the things that are of God, as they are in themselves; but they are made known to us in their effects, according to Rm. 1:20: "The invisible things of God . . . are clearly seen, being understood by the things that are made."

Reply to Objection 2: Although each one knows the eternal law according to his own capacity, in the way explained above, yet none can comprehend it: for it cannot be made perfectly known by its effects. Therefore it does not follow that anyone who knows the eternal law in the way aforesaid, knows also the whole order of things, whereby they are most orderly.

Reply to Objection 3: To judge a thing may be understood in two ways. First, as when a cognitive power judges of its proper object, according to Job 12:11: "Doth not the ear discern words, and the palate of him that eateth, the taste?" It is to this kind of judgment that the Philosopher alludes when he says that "anyone can judge well of what he knows," by judging, namely, whether what is put forward is true. In another way we speak of a superior judging of a subordinate by a kind of practical judgment, as to whether he should be such and such or not. And thus none can judge of the eternal law.

Article: 3

Whether every law is derived from the eternal law?

Objection 1: It would seem that not every law is derived from the eternal law. For there is a law of the "fomes," as stated above (Question [91], Article [6]), which is not derived from that Divine law which is the eternal law, since thereunto pertains the "prudence of the flesh," of which the Apostle says (Rm. 8:7), that "it cannot be subject to the law of God." Therefore not every law is derived from the eternal law.

Objection 2: Further, nothing unjust can be derived from the eternal law, because, as stated above (Article [2], Objection [2]), "the eternal law is that, according to which it is right that all things should be most orderly." But some laws are unjust, according to Is. 10:1: "Woe to them that make wicked laws." Therefore not every law is derived from the eternal law.

Objection 3: Further, Augustine says (De Lib. Arb. i, 5) that "the law which is framed for ruling the people, rightly permits many things which are punished by Divine providence." But the type of Divine providence is the eternal law, as stated above (Article [1]). Therefore not even every good law is derived from the eternal law.

On the contrary, Divine Wisdom says (Prov. 8:15): "By Me kings reign, and lawgivers decree just things." But the type of Divine Wisdom is the eternal law, as stated above (Article [1]). Therefore all laws proceed from the eternal law.

I answer that, As stated above (Question [90], Articles [1],2), the law denotes a kind of plan directing acts towards an end. Now wherever there are movers ordained to one another, the power of the second mover must needs be derived from the power of the first mover; since the second mover does not move except in so far as it is moved by the first. Wherefore we observe the same in all those who govern, so that the plan of government is derived by secondary governors from the governor in chief; thus the plan of what is to be done in a state flows from the king's command to his inferior administrators: and again in things of art the plan of whatever is to be done by art flows from the chief craftsman to the under-crafts-men, who work with their hands. Since then the eternal law is the plan of government in the Chief Governor, all the plans of government in the inferior governors must be derived from the eternal law. But these plans of inferior governors are all other laws besides the eternal law. Therefore all laws, in so far as they partake of right reason, are derived from the eternal law. Hence Augustine says (De Lib. Arb. i, 6) that "in temporal law there is nothing just and lawful, but what man has drawn from the eternal law."

Reply to Objection 1: The "fomes" has the nature of law in man, in so far as it is a punishment resulting from Divine justice; and in this respect it is evident that it is derived from the eternal law. But in so far as it denotes a proneness to sin, it is contrary to the Divine law, and has not the nature of law, as stated above (Question [91], Article [6]).

Reply to Objection 2: Human law has the nature of law in so far as it partakes of right reason; and it is clear that, in this respect, it is derived from the eternal law. But in so far as it deviates from reason, it is called an unjust law, and has the nature, not of law but of violence. Nevertheless even an unjust law, in so far as it retains some appearance of law, though being framed by one who is in power, is derived from the eternal law; since all power is from the Lord God, according to Rm. 13:1.

Reply to Objection 3: Human law is said to permit certain things, not as approving them, but as being unable to direct them. And many things are directed by the Divine law, which human law is unable to direct, because more things are subject to a higher than to a lower cause. Hence the very fact that human law does not meddle with matters it cannot direct, comes under the ordination of the eternal law. It would be different, were human law to sanction what the eternal law condemns. Consequently it does not follow that human law is not derived from the eternal law, but that it is not on a perfect equality with it.

Article: 4

Whether necessary and eternal things are subject to the eternal law?

Objection 1: It would seem that necessary and eternal things are subject to the eternal law. For whatever is reasonable is subject to reason. But the Divine will is reasonable, for it is just. Therefore it is subject to (the Divine) reason. But the eternal law is the Divine reason. Therefore God's will is subject to the eternal law. But God's will is eternal. Therefore eternal and necessary things are subject to the eternal law.

Objection 2: Further, whatever is subject to the King, is subject to the King's law. Now the Son, according to 1 Cor. 15:28,24, "shall be subject . . . to God and the Father . . . when He shall have delivered up the Kingdom to Him." Therefore the Son, Who is eternal, is subject to the eternal law.

Objection 3: Further, the eternal law is Divine providence as a type. But many necessary things are subject to Divine providence: for instance, the stability of incorporeal substances and of the heavenly bodies. Therefore even necessary things are subject to the eternal law.

On the contrary, Things that are necessary cannot be otherwise, and consequently need no restraining. But laws are imposed on men, in order to restrain them from evil, as explained above (Question [92], Article [2]). Therefore necessary things are not subject to the eternal law.

I answer that, As stated above (Article [1]), the eternal law is the type of the Divine government. Consequently whatever is subject to the Divine government, is subject to the eternal law: while if anything is not subject to the Divine government, neither is it subject to the eternal law. The application of this distinction may be gathered by looking around us. For those things are subject to human government, which can be done by man; but what pertains to the nature of man is not subject to human government; for instance, that he should have a soul, hands, or feet. Accordingly all that is in things created by God, whether it be contingent or necessary, is subject to the eternal law: while things pertaining to the Divine Nature or Essence are not subject to the eternal law, but are the eternal law itself.

Reply to Objection 1: We may speak of God's will in two ways. First, as to the will itself: and thus, since God's will is His very Essence, it is subject neither to the Divine government, nor to the eternal law, but is the same thing as the eternal law. Secondly, we may speak of God's will, as to the things themselves that God wills about creatures; which things are subject to the eternal law, in so far as they are planned by Divine Wisdom. In reference to these things God's will is said to be reasonable [rationalis]: though regarded in itself it should rather be called their type [ratio].

Reply to Objection 2: God the Son was not made by God, but was naturally born of God. Consequently He is not subject to Divine providence or to the eternal law: but rather is Himself the eternal law by a kind of appropriation, as Augustine explains (De Vera Relig. xxxi). But He is said to be subject to the Father by reason of His human nature, in respect of which also the Father is said to be greater than He.

The third objection we grant, because it deals with those necessary things that are created.

Reply to Objection 4: As the Philosopher says (Metaph. v, text. 6), some necessary things have a cause of their necessity: and thus they derive from something else the fact that they cannot be otherwise. And this is in itself a most effective restraint; for whatever is restrained, is said to be restrained in so far as it cannot do otherwise than it is allowed to.

Article: 5 Whether natural contingents are subject to the eternal law?

Objection 1: It would seem that natural contingents are not subject to the eternal law. Because promulgation is essential to law, as stated above (Question [90], Article [4]). But a law cannot be promulgated except to rational creatures, to whom it is possible to make an announcement. Therefore none but rational creatures are subject to the eternal law; and consequently natural contingents are not.

Objection 2: Further, "Whatever obeys reason partakes somewhat of reason," as stated in Ethic. i. But the eternal law, is the supreme type, as stated above (Article [1]). Since then natural contingents do not partake of reason in any way, but are altogether void of reason, it seems that they are not subject to the eternal law.

Objection 3: Further, the eternal law is most efficient. But in natural contingents defects occur. Therefore they are not subject to the eternal law.

On the contrary, It is written (Prov. 8:29): "When He compassed the sea with its bounds, and set a law to the waters, that they should not pass their limits."

I answer that, We must speak otherwise of the law of man, than of the eternal law which is the law of God. For the law of man extends only to rational creatures subject to man. The reason of this is because law directs the actions of those that are subject to the government of someone: wherefore, properly speaking, none imposes a law on his own actions. Now whatever is done regarding the use of irrational things subject to man, is done by the act of man himself moving those things, for these irrational creatures do not move themselves, but are moved by others, as stated above (Question [1], Article [2]). Consequently man cannot impose laws on irrational beings, however much they may be subject to him. But he can impose laws on rational beings subject to him, in so far as by his command or pronouncement of any kind, he imprints on their minds a rule which is a principle of action.

Now just as man, by such pronouncement, impresses a kind of inward principle of action on the man that is subject to him, so God imprints on the whole of nature the principles of its proper actions. And so, in this way, God is said to command the whole of nature, according to Ps. 148:6: "He hath made a decree, and it shall not pass away." And thus all actions and movements of the whole of nature are subject to the eternal law. Consequently irrational creatures are subject to the eternal law, through being moved by Divine providence; but not, as rational creatures are, through understanding the Divine commandment.

Reply to Objection 1: The impression of an inward active principle is to natural things, what the promulgation of law is to men: because law, by being promulgated, imprints on man a directive principle of human actions, as stated above.

Reply to Objection 2: Irrational creatures neither partake of nor are obedient to human reason: whereas they do partake of the Divine Reason by obeying it; because the power of Divine Reason extends over more things than human reason does. And as the members of the human body are moved at the command of reason, and yet do not partake of reason, since they have no apprehension subordinate to reason; so too irrational creatures are moved by God, without, on that account, being rational.

Reply to Objection 3: Although the defects which occur in natural things are outside the order of particular causes, they are not outside the order of universal causes, especially of the First Cause, i.e. God, from Whose providence nothing can escape, as stated in the FP, Question [22], Article [2]. And since the eternal law is the type of Divine providence, as stated above (Article [1]), hence the defects of natural things are subject to the eternal law.

Article: 6 Whether all human affairs are subject to the eternal law?

Objection 1: It would seem that not all human affairs are subject to the eternal law. For the Apostle says (Gal. 5:18): "If you are led by the spirit you are not under the law." But the righteous who are the sons of God by adoption, are led by the spirit of God, according to Rm. 8:14: "Whosoever are led by the spirit of God, they are the sons of God." Therefore not all men are under the eternal law.

Objection 2: Further, the Apostle says (Rm. 8:7): "The prudence [Vulg.: 'wisdom'] of the flesh is an enemy to God: for it is not subject to the law of God." But many are those in whom the prudence of the flesh dominates. Therefore all men are not subject to the eternal law which is the law of God.

Objection 3: Further, Augustine says (De Lib. Arb. i, 6) that "the eternal law is that by which the wicked deserve misery, the good, a life of blessedness." But those who are already blessed, and those who are already lost, are not in the state of merit. Therefore they are not under the eternal law.

On the contrary, Augustine says (De Civ. Dei xix, 12): "Nothing evades the laws of the most high Creator and Governor, for by Him the peace of the universe is administered."

I answer that, There are two ways in which a thing is subject to the eternal law, as explained above (Article [5]): first, by partaking of the eternal law by way of knowledge; secondly by way of action and passion, i.e. by partaking of the eternal law by way of an inward motive principle; and in this second way, irrational creatures are subject to the eternal law, as stated above (Article [5]). But since the rational nature, together with that which it has in common with all creatures, has something proper to itself inasmuch as it is rational, consequently it is subject to the eternal law in both ways; because while each rational creature has some knowledge of the eternal law, as stated above (Article [2]), it also has a natural inclination to that which is in harmony with the eternal law; for "we are naturally adapted to the recipients of virtue" (Ethic. ii, 1).

lesser in bad

greater in good

Both ways, however, are imperfect, and to a certain extent destroyed, in the wicked; because in them the natural inclination to virtue is corrupted by vicious habits, and, moreover, the natural knowledge of good is darkened by passions and habits of sin. But in the good both ways are found more perfect: because in them, besides the natural knowledge of good, there is the added knowledge of faith and wisdom; and again, besides the natural inclination to good, there is the added motive of grace and virtue.

Accordingly, the good are perfectly subject to the eternal law, as always acting according to it: whereas the wicked are subject to the eternal law, imperfectly as to their actions, indeed, since both their knowledge of good, and their inclination thereto, are imperfect; but this imperfection on the part of action is supplied on the part of passion, in so far as they suffer what the eternal law decrees concerning them, according as they fail to act in harmony with that law. Hence Augustine says (De Lib. Arb. i, 15): "I esteem that the righteous act according to the eternal law; and (De Catech. Rud. xviii): Out of the just misery of the souls which deserted Him, God knew how to furnish the inferior parts of His creation with most suitable laws."

Reply to Objection 1: This saying of the Apostle may be understood in two ways. First, so that a man is said to be under the law, through being pinned down thereby, against his will, as by a load. Hence, on the same passage a gloss says that "he is under the law, who refrains from evil deeds, through fear of punishment threatened by the law, and not from love of virtue." In this way the spiritual man is not under the law, because he fulfils the law willingly, through charity which is poured into his heart by the Holy Ghost. Secondly, it can be understood as meaning that the works of a man, who is led by the Holy Ghost, are the works of the Holy Ghost rather than his own. Therefore, since the Holy Ghost is not under the law, as neither is the Son, as stated above (Article [4], ad 2); it follows that such works, in so far as they are of the Holy Ghost, are not under the law. The Apostle witnesses to this when he says (2 Cor. 3:17): "Where the Spirit of the Lord is, there is liberty."

Reply to Objection 2: The prudence of the flesh cannot be subject to the law of God as regards action; since it inclines to actions contrary to the Divine law: yet it is subject to the law of God, as regards passion; since it deserves to suffer punishment according to the law of Divine justice. Nevertheless in no man does the prudence of the flesh dominate so far as to destroy the whole good of his nature: and consequently there remains in man the inclination to act in accordance with the eternal law. For we have seen above (Question [85], Article [2]) that sin does not destroy entirely the good of nature.

Reply to Objection 3: A thing is maintained in the end and moved towards the end by one and the same cause: thus gravity which makes a heavy body rest in the lower place is also the cause of its being moved thither. We therefore reply that as it is according to the eternal law that some deserve happiness, others unhappiness, so is it by the eternal law that some are maintained in a happy state, others in an unhappy state. Accordingly both the blessed and the damned are under the eternal law.

Irascible - resists attacks & hindrances to what is suitable

Concupiscible - seeks what is suitable to the senses & flees harm

Synderesis - [general] innate principle in the moral conscience steering to the good and away from evil

OF THE NATURAL LAW (SIX ARTICLES)

We must now consider the natural law; concerning which there are six points of inquiry:

(1) What is the natural law?
(2) What are the precepts of the natural law?
(3) Whether all acts of virtue are prescribed by the natural law?
(4) Whether the natural law is the same in all?
(5) Whether it is changeable?
(6) Whether it can be abolished from the heart of man?

Question 94 Article: 1

Whether the natural law is a habit?

Objection 1: It would seem that the natural law is a habit. Because, as the Philosopher says (Ethic. ii, 5), "there are three things in the soul: power, habit, and passion." But the natural law is not one of the soul's powers: nor is it one of the passions; as we may see by going through them one by one. Therefore the natural law is a habit.

Objection 2: Further, Basil [*Damascene, De Fide Orth. iv, 22] says that the conscience or "synderesis is the law of our mind"; which can only apply to the natural law. But the "synderesis" is a habit, as was shown in the FP, Question [79], Article [12]. Therefore the natural law is a habit.

Objection 3: Further, the natural law abides in man always, as will be shown further on (Article [6]). But man's reason, which the law regards, does not always think about the natural law. Therefore the natural law is not an act, but a habit.

On the contrary, Augustine says (De Bono Conjug. xxi) that "a habit is that whereby something is done when necessary." But such is not the natural law: since it is in infants and in the damned who cannot act by it. Therefore the natural law is not a habit.

I answer that, A thing may be called a habit in two ways. First, properly and essentially: and thus the natural law is not a habit. For it has been stated above (Question [90], Article [1], ad 2) that the natural law is something appointed by reason, just as a proposition is a work of reason. Now that which a man does is not the same as that whereby he does it: for he makes a becoming speech by the habit of grammar. Since then a habit is that by which we act, a law cannot be a habit properly and essentially.

Secondly, the term habit may be applied to that which we hold by a habit: thus faith may mean that which we hold by faith. And accordingly, since the precepts of the natural law are sometimes considered by reason actually, while sometimes they are in the reason only habitually in this way the natural law may be called a habit. Thus, in speculative matters, the indemonstrable principles are not the habit itself whereby we hold those principles, but are the principles the habit of which we possess.

Reply to Objection 1: The Philosopher proposes there to discover the genus of virtue; and since it is evident that virtue is a principle of action, he mentions only those things which are principles of human acts, viz. powers, habits and passions. But there are other things in the soul besides these three: there are acts; thus "to will" is in the one that wills; again, things known are in the knower; moreover its own natural properties are in the soul, such as immortality and the like.

Reply to Objection 2: "Synderesis" is said to be the law of our mind, because it is a habit containing the precepts of the natural law, which are the first principles of human actions.

Reply to Objection 3: This argument proves that the natural law is held habitually; and this is granted.

To the argument advanced in the contrary sense we reply that sometimes a man is unable to make use of that which is in him habitually, on account of some impediment: thus, on account of sleep, a man is unable to use the habit of science. In like manner, through the deficiency of his age, a child cannot use the habit of understanding of principles, or the natural law, which is in him habitually.

Article: 2

Whether the natural law contains several precepts, or only one?

Objection 1: It would seem that the natural law contains, not several precepts, but one only. For law is a kind of precept, as stated above (Question [92], Article [2]). If therefore there were many precepts of the natural law, it would follow that there are also many natural laws.

Objection 2: Further, the natural law is consequent to human nature. But human nature, as a whole, is one; though, as to its parts, it is manifold. Therefore, either there is but one precept of the law of nature, on account of the unity of nature as a whole; or there are many, by reason of the number of parts of human nature. The result would be that even things relating to the inclination of the concupiscible faculty belong to the natural law.

Objection 3: Further, law is something pertaining to reason, as stated above (Question [90], Article [1]). Now reason is but one in man. Therefore there is only one precept of the natural law.

On the contrary, The precepts of the natural law in man stand in relation to practical matters, as the first principles to matters of demonstration. But there are several first indemonstrable principles. Therefore there are also several precepts of the natural law.

I answer that, As stated above (Question [91], Article [3]), the precepts of the natural law are to the practical reason, what the first principles of demonstrations are to the speculative reason; because both are self-evident principles. Now a thing is said to be self-evident in two ways: first, in itself; secondly, in relation to us. Any proposition is said to be self-evident in itself, if its predicate is contained in the notion of the subject: although, to one who knows not the definition of the subject, it happens that such a proposition is not self-evident. For instance, this proposition, "Man is a rational being," is, in its very nature, self-evident, since who says "man," says "a rational being": and yet to one who knows not what a man is, this proposition is not self-evident. Hence it is that, as Boethius says (De Hebdom.), certain axioms or propositions are universally self-evident to all; and such are those propositions whose terms are known to all, as, "Every whole is greater than its part," and, "Things equal to one and the same are equal to one another." But some propositions are self-evident only to the wise, who understand the meaning of the terms of such propositions: thus to one who understands that an angel is not a body, it is self-evident that an angel is not circumscriptively in a place: but this is not evident to the unlearned, for they cannot grasp it.

Now a certain order is to be found in those things that are apprehended universally. For that which, before aught else, falls under apprehension, is "being," the notion of which is included in all things whatsoever a man apprehends. Wherefore the first indemonstrable principle is that "the same thing cannot be affirmed and denied at the same time," which is based on the notion of "being" and "not-being": and on this principle all others are based, as is stated in Metaph. iv, text. 9. Now as "being" is the first thing that falls under the apprehension simply, so "good" is the first thing that falls under the apprehension of the practical reason, which is directed to action: since every agent acts for an end under the aspect of good. Consequently the first principle of practical reason is one founded on the notion of good, viz. that "good is that which all things seek after." Hence this is the first precept of law, that "good is to be done and pursued, and evil is to be avoided." All other precepts of the natural law are based upon this: so that whatever the practical reason naturally apprehends as man's good (or evil) belongs to the precepts of the natural law as something to be done or avoided.

Since, however, good has the nature of an end, and evil, the nature of a contrary, hence it is that all those things to which man has a natural inclination, are naturally apprehended by reason as being good, and consequently as objects of pursuit, and their contraries as evil, and objects of avoidance. Wherefore according to the order of natural inclinations, is the order of the precepts of the natural law. Because in man there is first of all an inclination to good in accordance with the nature which he has in common with all substances: inasmuch as every substance seeks the preservation of its own being, according to its nature: and by reason of this inclination, whatever is a means of preserving human life, and of warding off its obstacles, belongs to the natural law. Secondly, there is in man an inclination to things that pertain to him more specially, according to that nature which he has in common with other animals: and in virtue of this inclination, those things are said to belong to the natural law, "which nature has taught to all animals" [*Pandect. Just. I, tit. i], such as sexual intercourse, education of offspring and so forth. Thirdly, there is in man an inclination to good, according to the nature of his reason, which nature is proper to him: thus man has a natural inclination to know the truth about God, and to live in society: and in this respect, whatever pertains to this inclination belongs to the natural law; for instance, to shun ignorance, to avoid offending those among whom one has to live, and other such things regarding the above inclination.

Reply to Objection 1: All these precepts of the law of nature have the character of one natural law, inasmuch as they flow from one first precept.

Reply to Objection 2: All the inclinations of any parts whatsoever of human nature, e.g. of the concupiscible and irascible parts, in so far as they are ruled by reason, belong to the natural law, and are reduced to one first precept, as stated above: so that the precepts of the natural law are many in themselves, but are based on one common foundation.

Reply to Objection 3: Although reason is one in itself, yet it directs all things regarding man; so that whatever can be ruled by reason, is contained under the law of reason.

Article: 3

Whether all acts of virtue are prescribed by the natural law?

Objection 1: It would seem that not all acts of virtue are prescribed by the natural law. Because, as stated above (Question [90], Article [2]) it is essential to a law that it be ordained to the common good. But some acts of virtue are ordained to the private good of the individual, as is evident especially in regards to acts of temperance. Therefore not all acts of virtue are the subject of natural law.

Objection 2: Further, every sin is opposed to some virtuous act. If therefore all acts of virtue are prescribed by the natural law, it seems to follow that all sins are against nature: whereas this applies to certain special sins.

Objection 3: Further, those things which are according to nature are common to all. But acts of virtue are not common to all: since a thing is virtuous in one, and vicious in another. Therefore not all acts of virtue are prescribed by the natural law.

On the contrary, Damascene says (De Fide Orth. iii, 4) that "virtues are natural." Therefore virtuous acts also are a subject of the natural law.

I answer that, We may speak of virtuous acts in two ways: first, under the aspect of virtuous; secondly, as such and such acts considered in their proper species. If then we speak of acts of virtue, considered as virtuous, thus all virtuous acts belong to the natural law. For it has been stated (Article [2]) that to the natural law belongs everything to which a man is inclined according to his nature. Now each thing is inclined naturally to an operation that is suitable to it according to its form: thus fire is inclined to give heat. Wherefore, since the rational soul is the proper form of man, there is in every man a natural inclination to act according to reason: and this is to act according to virtue. Consequently, considered thus, all acts of virtue are prescribed by the natural law: since each one's reason naturally dictates to him to act virtuously. But if we speak of virtuous acts, considered in themselves, i.e. in their proper species, thus not all virtuous acts are prescribed by the natural law: for many things are done virtuously, to which nature does not incline at first; but which, through the inquiry of reason, have been found by men to be conducive to well-living.

Reply to Objection 1: Temperance is about the natural concupiscences of food, drink and sexual matters, which are indeed ordained to the natural common good, just as other matters of law are ordained to the moral common good.

Reply to Objection 2: By human nature we may mean either that which is proper to man---and in this sense all sins, as being against reason, are also against nature, as Damascene states (De Fide Orth. ii, 30): or we may mean that nature which is common to man and other animals; and in this sense, certain special sins are said to be against nature; thus contrary to sexual intercourse, which is natural to all animals, is unisexual lust, which has received the special name of the unnatural crime.

Reply to Objection 3: This argument considers acts in themselves. For it is owing to the various conditions of men, that certain acts are virtuous for some, as being proportionate and becoming to them, while they are vicious for others, as being out of proportion to them.

Article: 4

Whether the natural law is the same in all men?

Objection 1: It would seem that the natural law is not the same in all. For it is stated in the Decretals (Dist. i) that "the natural law is that which is contained in the Law and the Gospel." But this is not common to all men; because, as it is written (Rm. 10:16), "all do not obey the gospel." Therefore the natural law is not the same in all men.

Objection 2: Further, "Things which are according to the law are said to be just," as stated in Ethic. v. But it is stated in the same book that nothing is so universally just as not to be subject to change in regard to some men. Therefore even the natural law is not the same in all men.

Objection 3: Further, as stated above (Articles [2],3), to the natural law belongs everything to which a man is inclined according to his nature. Now different men are naturally inclined to different things; some to the desire of pleasures, others to the desire of honors, and other men to other things. Therefore there is not one natural law for all.

On the contrary, Isidore says (Etym. v, 4): "The natural law is common to all nations."

I answer that, As stated above (Articles [2],3), to the natural law belongs those things to which a man is inclined naturally: and among these it is proper to man to be inclined to act according to reason. Now the process of reason is from the common to the proper, as stated in Phys. i. The speculative reason, however, is differently situated in this matter, from the practical reason. For, since the speculative reason is busied chiefly with the necessary things, which cannot be otherwise than they are, its proper conclusions, like the universal principles, contain the truth without fail. The practical reason, on the other hand, is busied with contingent matters, about which human actions are concerned: and consequently, although there is necessity in the general principles, the more we descend to matters of detail, the more frequently we encounter defects. Accordingly then in speculative matters truth is the same in all men, both as to principles and as to conclusions: although the truth is not known to all as regards the conclusions, but only as regards the principles which are called common notions. But in matters of action, truth or practical rectitude is not the same for all, as to matters of detail, but only as to the general principles: and where there is the same rectitude in matters of detail, it is not equally known to all.

It is therefore evident that, as regards the general principles whether of speculative or of practical reason, truth or rectitude is the same for all, and is equally known by all. As to the proper conclusions of the speculative reason, the truth is the same for all, but is not equally known to all: thus it is true for all that the three angles of a triangle are together equal to two right angles, although it is not known to all. But as to the proper conclusions of the practical reason, neither is the truth or rectitude the same for all, nor, where it is the same, is it equally known by all. Thus it is right and true for all to act according to reason: and from this principle it follows as a proper conclusion, that goods entrusted to another should be restored to their owner. Now this is true for the majority of cases: but it may happen in a particular case that it would be injurious, and therefore unreasonable, to restore goods held in trust; for instance, if they are claimed for the purpose of fighting against one's country. And this principle will be found to fail the more, according as we descend further into detail, e.g. if one were to say that goods held in trust should be restored with such and such a guarantee, or in such and such a way; because the greater the number of conditions added, the greater the number of ways in which the principle may fail, so that it be not right to restore or not to restore.

Consequently we must say that the natural law, as to general principles, is the same for all, both as to rectitude and as to knowledge. But as to certain matters of detail, which are conclusions, as it were, of those general principles, it is the same for all in the majority of cases, both as to rectitude and as to knowledge; and yet in some few cases it may fail, both as to rectitude, by reason of certain obstacles (just as natures subject to generation and corruption fail in some few cases on account of some obstacle), and as to knowledge, since in some the reason is perverted by passion, or evil habit, or an evil disposition of nature; thus formerly, theft, although it is expressly contrary to the natural law, was not considered wrong among the Germans, as Julius Caesar relates (De Bello Gall. vi).

Reply to Objection 1: The meaning of the sentence quoted is not that whatever is contained in the Law and the Gospel belongs to the natural law, since they contain many things that are above nature; but that whatever belongs to the natural law is fully contained in them. Wherefore Gratian, after saying that "the natural law is what is contained in the Law and the Gospel," adds at once, by way of example, "by which everyone is commanded to do to others as he would be done by."

Reply to Objection 2: The saying of the Philosopher is to be understood of things that are naturally just, not as general principles, but as conclusions drawn from them, having rectitude in the majority of cases, but failing in a few.

Reply to Objection 3: As, in man, reason rules and commands the other powers, so all the natural inclinations belonging to the other powers must needs be directed according to reason. Wherefore it is universally right for all men, that all their inclinations should be directed according to reason.

Article: 5 Whether the natural law can be changed?

Objection 1: It would seem that the natural law can be changed. Because on Ecclus. 17:9, "He gave them instructions, and the law of life," the gloss says: "He wished the law of the letter to be written, in order to correct the law of nature." But that which is corrected is changed. Therefore the natural law can be changed.

Objection 2: Further, the slaying of the innocent, adultery, and theft are against the natural law. But we find these things changed by God: as when God commanded Abraham to slay his innocent son (Gn. 22:2); and when he ordered the Jews to borrow and purloin the vessels of the Egyptians (Ex. 12:35); and when He commanded Osee to take to himself "a wife of fornications" (Osee 1:2). Therefore the natural law can be changed.

Objection 3: Further, Isidore says (Etym. 5:4) that "the possession of all things in common, and universal freedom, are matters of natural law." But these things are seen to be changed by human laws. Therefore it seems that the natural law is subject to change.

On the contrary, It is said in the Decretals (Dist. v): "The natural law dates from the creation of the rational creature. It does not vary according to time, but remains unchangeable."

I answer that, A change in the natural law may be understood in two ways. First, by way of addition. In this sense nothing hinders the natural law from being changed: since many things for the benefit of human life have been added over and above the natural law, both by the Divine law and by human laws.

Secondly, a change in the natural law may be understood by way of subtraction, so that what previously was according to the natural law, ceases to be so. In this sense, the natural law is altogether unchangeable in its first principles: but in its secondary principles, which, as we have said (Article [4]), are certain detailed proximate conclusions drawn from the first principles, the natural law is not changed so that what it prescribes be not right in most cases. But it may be changed in some particular cases of rare occurrence, through some special causes hindering the observance of such precepts, as stated above (Article [4]).

Reply to Objection 1: The written law is said to be given for the correction of the natural law, either because it supplies what was wanting to the natural law, or because the natural law was perverted in the hearts of some men, as to certain matters, so that they esteemed those things good which are naturally evil; which perversion stood in need of correction.

Reply to Objection 2: All men alike, both guilty and innocent, die the death of nature: which death of nature is inflicted by the power of God on account of original sin, according to 1 Kgs. 2:6: "The Lord killeth and maketh alive." Consequently, by the command of God, death can be inflicted on any man, guilty or innocent, without any injustice whatever. In like manner adultery is intercourse with another's wife; who is allotted to him by the law emanating from God. Consequently intercourse with any woman, by the command of God, is neither adultery nor fornication. The same applies to theft, which is the taking of another's property. For whatever is taken by the command of God, to Whom all things belong, is not taken against the will of its owner, whereas it is in this that theft consists. Nor is it only in human things, that whatever is commanded by God is right; but also in natural things, whatever is done by God, is, in some way, natural, as stated in the FP, Question [105], Article [6], ad 1.

 Reply to Objection 3: A thing is said to belong to the natural law in two ways. First, because nature inclines thereto: e.g. that one should not do harm to another. Secondly, because nature did not bring in the contrary: thus we might say that for man to be naked is of the natural law, because nature did not give him clothes, but art invented them. In this sense, "the possession of all things in common and universal freedom" are said to be of the natural law, because, to wit, the distinction of possessions and slavery were not brought in by nature, but devised by human reason for the benefit of human life. Accordingly the law of nature was not changed in this respect, except by addition.

Article: 6

Whether the law of nature can be abolished from the heart of man?

Objection 1: It would seem that the natural law can be abolished from the heart of man. Because on Rm. 2:14, "When the Gentiles who have not the law," etc. a gloss says that "the law of righteousness, which sin had blotted out, is graven on the heart of man when he is restored by grace." But the law of righteousness is the law of nature. Therefore the law of nature can be blotted out.

Objection 2: Further, the law of grace is more efficacious than the law of nature. But the law of grace is blotted out by sin. Much more therefore can the law of nature be blotted out.

Objection 3: Further, that which is established by law is made just. But many things are enacted by men, which are contrary to the law of nature. Therefore the law of nature can be abolished from the heart of man.

On the contrary, Augustine says (Confess. ii): "Thy law is written in the hearts of men, which iniquity itself effaces not." But the law which is written in men's hearts is the natural law. Therefore the natural law cannot be blotted out.

cannot

I answer that, As stated above (Articles [4],5), there belong to the natural law, first, certain most general precepts, that are known to all; and secondly, certain secondary and more detailed precepts, which are, as it were, conclusions following closely from first principles. As to those general principles, the natural law, in the abstract, can nowise be blotted out from men's hearts. But it is blotted out in the case of a particular action, in so far as reason is hindered from applying the general principle to a particular point of practice, on account of concupiscence or some other passion, as stated above (Question [77], Article [2]). But as to the other, i.e. the secondary precepts, the natural law can be blotted out from the human heart, either by evil persuasions, just as in speculative matters errors occur in respect of necessary conclusions; or by vicious customs and corrupt habits, as among some men, theft, and even unnatural vices, as the Apostle states (Rm. i), were not esteemed sinful.

Reply to Objection 1: Sin blots out the law of nature in particular cases, not universally, except perchance in regard to the secondary precepts of the natural law, in the way stated above.

Reply to Objection 2: Although grace is more efficacious than nature, yet nature is more essential to man, and therefore more enduring.

Reply to Objection 3: This argument is true of the secondary precepts of the natural law, against which some legislators have framed certain enactments which are unjust.

OF HUMAN LAW (FOUR ARTICLES)

We must now consider human law; and (1) this law considered in itself; (2) its power; (3) its mutability. Under the first head there are four points of inquiry:

(1) Its utility.
(2) Its origin.
(3) Its quality.
(4) Its division.

Question 95 Article: 1

Whether it was useful for laws to be framed by men?

Objection 1: It would seem that it was not useful for laws to be framed by men. Because the purpose of every law is that man be made good thereby, as stated above (Question [92], Article [1]). But men are more to be induced to be good willingly by means of admonitions, than against their will, by means of laws. Therefore there was no need to frame laws.

Objection 2: Further, As the Philosopher says (Ethic. v, 4), "men have recourse to a judge as to animate justice." But animate justice is better than inanimate justice, which contained in laws. Therefore it would have been better for the execution of justice to be entrusted to the decision of judges, than to frame laws in addition.

Objection 3: Further, every law is framed for the direction of human actions, as is evident from what has been stated above (Question [90], Articles [1],2). But since human actions are about singulars, which are infinite in number, matter pertaining to the direction of human actions cannot be taken into sufficient consideration except by a wise man, who looks into each one of them. Therefore it would have been better for human acts to be directed by the judgment of wise men, than by the framing of laws. Therefore there was no need of human laws.

On the contrary, Isidore says (Etym. v, 20): "Laws were made that in fear thereof human audacity might be held in check, that innocence might be safeguarded in the midst of wickedness, and that the dread of punishment might prevent the wicked from doing harm." But these things are most necessary to mankind. Therefore it was necessary that human laws should be made.

I answer that, As stated above (Question [63], Article [1]; Question [94], Article [3]), man has a natural aptitude for virtue; but the perfection of virtue must be acquired by man by means of some kind of training. Thus we observe that man is helped by industry in his necessities, for instance, in food and clothing. Certain beginnings of these he has from nature, viz. his reason and his hands; but he has not the full complement, as other animals have, to whom nature has given sufficiency of clothing and food. Now it is difficult to see how man could suffice for himself in the matter of this training: since the perfection of virtue consists chiefly in withdrawing man from undue pleasures, to which above all man is inclined, and especially the young, who are more capable of being trained. Consequently a man needs to receive this training from another, whereby to arrive at the perfection of virtue. And as to those young people who are inclined to acts of virtue, by their good natural disposition, or by custom, or rather by the gift of God, paternal training suffices, which is by admonitions. But since some are found to be depraved, and prone to vice, and not easily amenable to words, it was necessary for such to be restrained from evil by force and fear, in order that, at least, they might desist from evil-doing, and leave others in peace, and that they themselves, by being habituated in this way, might be brought to do willingly what hitherto they did from fear, and thus become virtuous. Now this kind of training, which compels through fear of punishment, is the discipline of laws. Therefore in order that man might have peace and virtue, it was necessary for laws to be framed: for, as the Philosopher says (Polit. i, 2), "as man is the most noble of animals if he be perfect in virtue, so is he the lowest of all, if he be severed from law and righteousness"; because man can use his reason to devise means of satisfying his lusts and evil passions, which other animals are unable to do.

Reply to Objection 1: Men who are well disposed are led willingly to virtue by being admonished better than by coercion: but men who are evilly disposed are not led to virtue unless they are compelled.

Reply to Objection 2: As the Philosopher says (Rhet. i, 1), "it is better that all things be regulated by law, than left to be decided by judges": and this for three reasons. First, because it is easier to find a few wise men competent to frame right laws, than to find the many who would be necessary to judge aright of each single case. Secondly, because those who make laws consider long beforehand what laws to make; whereas judgment on each single case has to be pronounced as soon as it arises: and it is easier for man to see what is right, by taking many instances into consideration, than by considering one solitary fact. Thirdly, because lawgivers judge in the abstract and of future events; whereas those who sit in judgment of things present, towards which they are affected by love, hatred, or some kind of cupidity; wherefore their judgment is perverted.

Since then the animated justice of the judge is not found in every man, and since it can be deflected, therefore it was necessary, whenever possible, for the law to determine how to judge, and for very few matters to be left to the decision of men.

Reply to Objection 3: Certain individual facts which cannot be covered by the law "have necessarily to be committed to judges," as the Philosopher says in the same passage: for instance, "concerning something that has happened or not happened," and the like.

Article: 2

Whether every human law is derived from the natural law?

Objection 1: It would seem that not every human law is derived from the natural law. For the Philosopher says (Ethic. v, 7) that "the legal just is that which originally was a matter of indifference." But those things which arise from the natural law are not matters of indifference. Therefore the enactments of human laws are not derived from the natural law.

Objection 2: Further, positive law is contrasted with natural law, as stated by Isidore (Etym. v, 4) and the Philosopher (Ethic. v, 7). But those things which flow as conclusions from the general principles of the natural law belong to the natural law, as stated above (Question [94], Article [4]). Therefore that which is established by human law does not belong to the natural law.

Objection 3: Further, the law of nature is the same for all; since the Philosopher says (Ethic. v, 7) that "the natural just is that which is equally valid everywhere." If therefore human laws were derived from the natural law, it would follow that they too are the same for all: which is clearly false.

Objection 4: Further, it is possible to give a reason for things which are derived from the natural law. But "it is not possible to give the reason for all the legal enactments of the lawgivers," as the jurist says [*Pandect. Justin. lib. i, ff, tit. iii, v; De Leg. et Senat.]. Therefore not all human laws are derived from the natural law.

On the contrary, Tully says (Rhet. ii): "Things which emanated from nature and were approved by custom, were sanctioned by fear and reverence for the laws."

I answer that, As Augustine says (De Lib. Arb. i, 5) "that which is not just seems to be no law at all": wherefore the force of a law depends on the extent of its justice. Now in human affairs a thing is said to be just, from being right, according to the rule of reason. But the first rule of reason is the law of nature, as is clear from what has been stated above (Question [91], Article [2], ad 2). Consequently every human law has just so much of the nature of law, as it is derived from the law of nature. But if in any point it deflects from the law of nature, it is no longer a law but a perversion of law.

But it must be noted that something may be derived from the natural law in two ways: first, as a conclusion from premises, secondly, by way of determination of certain generalities. The first way is like to that by which, in sciences, demonstrated conclusions are drawn from the principles: while the second mode is likened to that whereby, in the arts, general forms are particularized as to details: thus the craftsman needs to determine the general form of a house to some particular shape. Some things are therefore derived from the general principles of the natural law, by way of conclusions; e.g. that "one must not kill" may be derived as a conclusion from the principle that "one should do harm to no man": while some are derived therefrom by way of determination; e.g. the law of nature has it that the evil-doer should be punished; but that he be punished in this or that way, is a determination of the law of nature.

Accordingly both modes of derivation are found in the human law. But those things which are derived in the first way, are contained in human law not as emanating therefrom exclusively, but have some force from the natural law also. But those things which are derived in the second way, have no other force than that of human law.

Reply to Objection 1: The Philosopher is speaking of those enactments which are by way of determination or specification of the precepts of the natural law.

Reply to Objection 2: This argument avails for those things that are derived from the natural law, by way of conclusions.

Reply to Objection 3: The general principles of the natural law cannot be applied to all men in the same way on account of the great variety of human affairs: and hence arises the diversity of positive laws among various people.

Reply to Objection 4: These words of the Jurist are to be understood as referring to decisions of rulers in determining particular points of the natural law: on which determinations the judgment of expert and prudent men is based as on its principles; in so far, to wit, as they see at once what is the best thing to decide.

Hence the Philosopher says (Ethic. vi, 11) that in such matters, "we ought to pay as much attention to the undemonstrated sayings and opinions of persons who surpass us in experience, age and prudence, as to their demonstrations."

Article: 3

Whether Isidore's description of the quality of positive law is appropriate?

Objection 1: It would seem that Isidore's description of the quality of positive law is not appropriate, when he says (Etym. v, 21): "Law shall be virtuous, just,

101

Definition of Isidore possible to nature, according to the custom of the country, suitable to place and time, necessary, useful; clearly expressed, lest by its obscurity it lead to misunderstanding; framed for no private benefit, but for the common good." Because he had previously expressed the quality of law in three conditions, saying that "law is anything founded on reason, provided that it foster religion, be helpful to discipline, and further the common weal." Therefore it was needless to add any further conditions to these.

Objection 2: Further, Justice is included in honesty, as Tully says (De Offic. vii). Therefore after saying "honest" it was superfluous to add "just."

Objection 3: Further, written law is condivided with custom, according to Isidore (Etym. ii, 10). Therefore it should not be stated in the definition of law that it is "according to the custom of the country."

Objection 4: Further, a thing may be necessary in two ways. It may be necessary simply, because it cannot be otherwise: and that which is necessary in this way, is not subject to human judgment, wherefore human law is not concerned with necessity of this kind. Again a thing may be necessary for an end: and this necessity is the same as usefulness. Therefore it is superfluous to say both "necessary" and "useful."

On the contrary, stands the authority of Isidore.

I answer that, Whenever a thing is for an end, its form must be determined proportionately to that end; as the form of a saw is such as to be suitable for cutting (Phys. ii, text. 88). Again, everything that is ruled and measured must have a form proportionate to its rule and measure. Now both these conditions are verified of human law: since it is both something ordained to an end; and is a rule or measure ruled or measured by a higher measure. And this higher measure is twofold, viz. the Divine law and the natural law, as explained above (Article [2]; Question [93], Article [3]). Now the end of human law is to be useful to man, as the jurist states [*Pandect. Justin. lib. xxv, ff., tit. iii; De Leg. et Senat.].

3 conditions to Divine Law, Wherefore Isidore in determining the nature of law, lays down, at first, three conditions; viz. that it "foster religion," inasmuch as it is proportionate to the Divine law; that it be "helpful to discipline," inasmuch as it is proportionate to the nature law; and that it "further the common weal," inasmuch as it is proportionate to the utility of mankind.

All the other conditions mentioned by him are reduced to these three. For it is called virtuous because it fosters religion. And when he goes on to say that it should be "just, possible to nature, according to the customs of the country, adapted to place and time," he implies that it should be helpful to discipline. For human discipline depends on first on the order of reason, to which he refers by saying "just": secondly, it depends on the ability of the agent; because discipline should be adapted to each one according to his ability, taking also into account the ability of nature (for the same burdens should be not laid on children as adults); and should be according to human customs; since man cannot live alone in society, paying no heed to others: thirdly, it depends on certain circumstances, in respect of which he says, "adapted to place and time." The remaining words, "necessary, useful," etc. mean that law should further the common weal: so that "necessity" refers to the removal of evils; "usefulness" to the attainment of good; "clearness of expression," to the need of preventing any harm ensuing from the law itself. And since, as stated above (Question [90], Article [2]), law is ordained to the common good, this is expressed in the last part of the description.

This suffices for the Replies to the Objections.

Article: 4

Whether Isidore's division of human laws is appropriate?

Objection 1: It would seem that Isidore wrongly divided human statutes or human law (Etym. v, 4, seqq.). For under this law he includes the "law of nations," so called, because, as he says, "nearly all nations use it." But as he says, "natural law is that which is common to all nations." Therefore the law of nations is not contained under positive human law, but rather under natural law.

Objection 2: Further, those laws which have the same force, seem to differ not formally but only materially. But "statutes, decrees of the commonalty, senatorial decrees," and the like which he mentions (Etym. v, 9), all have the same force. Therefore they do not differ, except materially. But art takes no notice of such a distinction: since it may go on to infinity. Therefore this division of human laws is not appropriate.

Objection 3: Further, just as, in the state, there are princes, priests and soldiers, so are there other human offices. Therefore it seems that, as this division includes "military law," and "public law," referring to priests and magistrates; so also it should include other laws pertaining to other offices of the state.

Objection 4: Further, those things that are accidental should be passed over. But it is accidental to law that it be framed by this or that man. Therefore it is unreasonable to divide laws according to the names of lawgivers, so that one be called the "Cornelian" law, another the "Falcidian" law, etc.

On the contrary, The authority of Isidore (Objection [1]) suffices.

I answer that, A thing can of itself be divided in respect of something contained in the notion of that thing. Thus a soul either rational or irrational is contained in the notion of animal: and therefore animal is divided properly and of itself in respect of its being rational or irrational; but not in the point of its being white or black, which are entirely beside the notion of animal. Now, in the notion of human law, many things are contained, in respect of any of which human law can be divided properly and of itself. For in the first place it belongs to the notion of human law, to be derived from the law of nature, as explained above (Article [2]). In this respect positive law is divided into the "law of nations" and "civil law," according to the two ways in which something may be derived from the law of nature, as stated above (Article [2]). Because, to the law of nations belong those things which are derived from the law of nature, as conclusions from premises, e.g. just buyings and sellings, and the like, without which men cannot live together, which is a point of the law of nature, since man is by nature a social animal, as is proved in Polit. i, 2. But those things which are derived from the law of nature by way of particular determination, belong to the civil law, according as each state decides on what is best for itself.

Secondly, it belongs to the notion of human law, to be ordained to the common good of the state. In this respect human law may be divided according to the different kinds of men who work in a special way for the common good: e.g. priests, by praying to God for the people; princes, by governing the people; soldiers, by fighting for the safety of the people. Wherefore certain special kinds of law are adapted to these men.

Thirdly, it belongs to the notion of human law, to be framed by that one who governs the community of the state, as shown above (Question [90], Article [3]). In this respect, there are various human laws according to the various forms of government. Of these, according to the Philosopher (Polit. iii, 10) one is "monarchy," i.e. when the state is governed by one; and then we have "Royal Ordinances." Another form is "aristocracy," i.e. government by the best men or men of highest rank; and then we have the "Authoritative legal opinions" [Responsa Prudentum] and "Decrees of the Senate" [Senatus consulta]. Another form is "oligarchy," i.e. government by a few rich and powerful men; and then we have "Praetorian," also called "Honorary," law. Another form of government is that of the people, which is called "democracy," and there we have "Decrees of the commonalty" [Plebiscita]. There is also tyrannical government, which is altogether corrupt, which, therefore, has no corresponding law. Finally, there is a form of government made up of all these, and which is the best: and in this respect we have law sanctioned by the "Lords and Commons," as stated by Isidore (Etym. v, 4, seqq.).

Fourthly, it belongs to the notion of human law to direct human actions. In this respect, according to the various matters of which the law treats, there are various kinds of laws, which are sometimes named after their authors: thus we have the "Lex Julia" about adultery, the "Lex Cornelia" concerning assassins, and so on, differentiated in this way, not on account of the authors, but on account of the matters to which they refer.

Reply to Objection 1: The law of nations is indeed, in some way, natural to man, in so far as he is a reasonable being, because it is derived from the natural law by way of a conclusion that is not very remote from its premises. Wherefore men easily agreed thereto. Nevertheless it is distinct from the natural law, especially it is distinct from the natural law which is common to all animals.

The Replies to the other Objections are evident from what has been said.

OF THE POWER OF HUMAN LAW (SIX ARTICLES)

We must now consider the power of human law. Under this head there are six points of inquiry:

(1) Whether human law should be framed for the community?
(2) Whether human law should repress all vices?
(3) Whether human law is competent to direct all acts of virtue?
(4) Whether it binds man in conscience?
(5) Whether all men are subject to human law?
(6) Whether those who are under the law may act beside the letter of the law?

Question 96 Article: 1

Whether human law should be framed for the community rather than for the individual?

Objection 1: It would seem that human law should be framed not for the community, but rather for the individual. For the Philosopher says (Ethic. v, 7) that "the legal just . . . includes all particular acts of legislation . . . and all those matters which are the subject of decrees," which are also individual matters, since decrees are framed about individual actions. Therefore law is framed not only for the community, but also for the individual.

Objection 2: Further, law is the director of human acts, as stated above (Question [90], Articles [1],2). But human acts are about individual matters. Therefore human laws should be framed, not for the community, but rather for the individual.

Objection 3: Further, law is a rule and measure of human acts, as stated above (Question [90], Articles [1],2). But a measure should be most certain, as stated in Metaph. x. Since therefore in human acts no general proposition can be so certain as not to fail in some individual cases, it seems that laws should be framed not in general but for individual cases.

On the contrary, The jurist says (Pandect. Justin. lib. i, tit. iii, art. ii; De legibus, etc.) that "laws should be made to suit the majority of instances; and they are not framed according to what may possibly happen in an individual case."

I answer that, Whatever is for an end should be proportionate to that end. Now the end of law is the common good; because, as Isidore says (Etym. v, 21) that "law should be framed, not for any private benefit, but for the common good of all the citizens." Hence human laws should be proportionate to the common good. Now the common good comprises many things. Wherefore law should take account of many things, as to persons, as to matters, and as to times. Because the community of the state is composed of many persons; and its good is procured by many actions; nor is it established to endure for only a short time, but to last for all time by the citizens succeeding one another, as Augustine says (De Civ. Dei ii, 21; xxii, 6).

Reply to Objection 1: The Philosopher (Ethic. v, 7) divides the legal just, i.e. positive law, into three parts. For some things are laid down simply in a general way: and these are the general laws. Of these he says that "the legal is that which originally was a matter of indifference, but which, when enacted, is so no longer": as the fixing of the ransom of a captive. Some things affect the community in one respect, and individuals in another. These are called "privileges," i.e. "private laws," as it were, because they regard private persons, although their power extends to many matters; and in regard to these, he adds, "and further, all particular acts of legislation." Other matters are legal, not through being laws, but through being applications of general laws to particular cases: such are decrees which have the force of law; and in regard to these, he adds "all matters subject to decrees."

Reply to Objection 2: A principle of direction should be applicable to many; wherefore (Metaph. x, text. 4) the Philosopher says that all things belonging to one genus, are measured by one, which is the principle in that genus. For if there were as many rules or measures as there are things measured or ruled, they would cease to be of use, since their use consists in being applicable to many things. Hence law would be of no use, if it did not extend further than to one single act. Because the decrees than to one single act. Because the decrees of prudent men are made for the purpose of directing individual actions; whereas law is a general precept, as stated above (Question [92], Article [2], Objection [2]).

Reply to Objection 3: "We must not seek the same degree of certainty in all things" (Ethic. i, 3). Consequently in contingent matters, such as natural and human things, it is enough for a thing to be certain, as being true in the greater number of instances, though at times and less frequently it fail.

Article: 2

Whether it belongs to the human law to repress all vices?

Objection 1: It would seem that it belongs to human law to repress all vices. For Isidore says (Etym. v, 20) that "laws were made in order that, in fear thereof, man's audacity might be held in check." But it would not be held in check sufficiently, unless all evils were repressed by law. Therefore human laws should repress all evils.

Objection 2: Further, the intention of the lawgiver is to make the citizens virtuous. But a man cannot be virtuous unless he forbear from all kinds of vice. Therefore it belongs to human law to repress all vices.

Objection 3: Further, human law is derived from the natural law, as stated above (Question [95], Article [2]). But all vices are contrary to the law of nature. Therefore human law should repress all vices.

On the contrary, We read in De Lib. Arb. i, 5: "It seems to me that the law which is written for the governing of the people rightly permits these things, and that Divine providence punishes them." But Divine providence punishes nothing but vices. Therefore human law rightly allows some vices, by not repressing them.

I answer that, As stated above (Question [90], Articles [1],2), law is framed as a rule or measure of human acts. Now a measure should be homogeneous with that which it measures, as stated in Metaph. x, text. 3,4, since different things are measured by different measures. Wherefore laws imposed on men should also be in keeping with their condition, for, as Isidore says (Etym. v, 21), law should be "possible both according to nature, and according to the customs of the country." Now possibility or faculty of action is due to an interior habit or disposition: since the same thing is not possible to one who has not a virtuous habit, as is possible to one who has. Thus the same is not possible to a child as to a full-grown man: for which reason the law for children is not the same as for adults, since many things are permitted to children, which in an adult are punished by law or at any rate are open to blame. In like manner many things are permissible to men not perfect in virtue, which would be intolerable in a virtuous man.

Now human law is framed for a number of human beings, the majority of whom are not perfect in virtue. Wherefore human laws do not forbid all vices, from which the virtuous abstain, but only the more grievous vices, from which it is possible for the majority to abstain; and chiefly those that are to the hurt of others, without the prohibition of which human society could not be maintained: thus human law prohibits murder, theft and such like.

Reply to Objection 1: Audacity seems to refer to the assailing of others. Consequently it belongs to those sins chiefly whereby one's neighbor is injured: and these sins are forbidden by human law, as stated.

Reply to Objection 2: The purpose of human law is to lead men to virtue, not suddenly, but gradually. Wherefore it does not lay upon the multitude of imperfect men the burdens of those who are already virtuous, viz. that they should abstain from all evil. Otherwise these imperfect ones, being unable to bear such precepts, would break out into yet greater evils: thus it is written (Ps. 30:33): "He that violently bloweth his nose, bringeth out blood"; and (Mt. 9:17) that if "new wine," i.e. precepts of a perfect life, "is put into old bottles," i.e. into imperfect men, "the bottles break, and the wine runneth out," i.e. the precepts are despised, and those men, from contempt, break into evils worse still.

Reply to Objection 3: The natural law is a participation in us of the eternal law: while human law falls short of the eternal law. Now Augustine says (De Lib. Arb. i, 5): "The law which is framed for the government of states, allows and leaves unpunished many things that are punished by Divine providence. Nor, if this law does not attempt to do everything, is this a reason why it should be blamed for what it does." Wherefore, too, human law does not prohibit everything that is forbidden by the natural law.

Article: 3

Whether human law prescribes acts of all the virtues?

Objection 1: It would seem that human law does not prescribe acts of all the virtues. For vicious acts are contrary to acts of virtue. But human law does not prohibit all vices, as stated above (Article [2]). Therefore neither does it prescribe all acts of virtue.

Objection 2: Further, a virtuous act proceeds from a virtue. But virtue is the end of law; so that whatever is from a virtue, cannot come under a precept of law. Therefore human law does not prescribe all acts of virtue.

Objection 3: Further, law is ordained to the common good, as stated above (Question [90], Article [2]). But some acts of virtue are ordained, not to the common good, but to private good. Therefore the law does not prescribe all acts of virtue.

On the contrary, The Philosopher says (Ethic. v, 1) that the law "prescribes the performance of the acts of a brave man . . . and the acts of the temperate man . . . and the acts of the meek man: and in like manner as regards the other virtues and vices, prescribing the former, forbidding the latter."

I answer that, The species of virtues are distinguished by their objects, as explained above (Question [54], Article [2]; Question [60], Article [1]; Question [62], Article [2]). Now all the objects of virtues can be referred either to the private good of an individual, or to the common good of the multitude: thus matters of fortitude may be achieved either for the safety of the state, or for upholding the rights of a friend, and in like manner with the other virtues. But law, as stated above (Question [90], Article [2]) is ordained to the common good. Wherefore there is no virtue whose acts cannot be prescribed by the law. Nevertheless human law does not prescribe concerning all the acts of every virtue: but only in regard to those that are ordainable to the common good---

either immediately, as when certain things are done directly for the common good---or mediately, as when a lawgiver prescribes certain things pertaining to good order, whereby the citizens are directed in the upholding of the common good of justice and peace.

Reply to Objection 1: Human law does not forbid all vicious acts, by the obligation of a precept, as neither does it prescribe all acts of virtue. But it forbids certain acts of each vice, just as it prescribes some acts of each virtue.

Reply to Objection 2: An act is said to be an act of virtue in two ways. First, from the fact that a man does something virtuous; thus the act of justice is to do what is right, and an act of fortitude is to do brave things: and in this way law prescribes certain acts of virtue. Secondly an act of virtue is when a man does a virtuous thing in a way in which a virtuous man does it. Such an act always proceeds from virtue: and it does not come under a precept of law, but is the end at which every lawgiver aims.

Reply to Objection 3: There is no virtue whose act is not ordainable to the common good, as stated above, either mediately or immediately.

Article: 4

Whether human law binds a man in conscience?

Objection 1: It would seem that human law does not bind man in conscience. For an inferior power has no jurisdiction in a court of higher power. But the power of man, which frames human law, is beneath the Divine power. Therefore human law cannot impose its precept in a Divine court, such as is the court of conscience.

Objection 2: Further, the judgment of conscience depends chiefly on the commandments of God. But sometimes God's commandments are made void by human laws, according to Mt. 15:6: "You have made void the commandment of God for your tradition." Therefore human law does not bind a man in conscience.

Objection 3: Further, human laws often bring loss of character and injury on man, according to Is. 10:1 et seqq.: "Woe to them that make wicked laws, and when they write, write injustice; to oppress the poor in judgment, and do violence to the cause of the humble of My people." But it is lawful for anyone to avoid oppression and violence. Therefore human laws do not bind man in conscience.

On the contrary, It is written (1 Pt. 2:19): "This is thankworthy, if the conscience . . . a man endure sorrows, suffering wrongfully."

I answer that, Laws framed by man are either just or unjust. If they be just, they *Just* have the power of binding in conscience, from the eternal law whence they are *can* derived, according to Prov. 8:15: "By Me kings reign, and lawgivers decree just things." Now laws are said to be just, both from the end, when, to wit, they are ordained to the common good---and from their author, that is to say, when the law that is made does not exceed the power of the lawgiver---and from their form, when, to wit, burdens are laid on the subjects, according to an equality of proportion and with a view to the common good. For, since one man is a part of the community, each man in all that he is and has, belongs to the community; just as a part, in all that it is, belongs to the whole; wherefore nature inflicts a loss on the part, in order to save the whole: so that on this account, such laws as these, which impose proportionate burdens, are just and binding in conscience, and are legal laws.

On the other hand laws may be unjust in two ways; first, by being contrary to ① human good, through being opposed to the things mentioned above---either in respect of the end, as when an authority imposes on his subjects burdensome laws, conducive, not to the common good, but rather to his own cupidity or vainglory---or in respect of the author, as when a man makes a law that goes beyond the power committed to him---or in respect of the form, as when burdens are imposed unequally on the community, although with a view to the common good. The like are acts of violence rather than laws; because, as Augustine says *unjust* (De Lib. Arb. i, 5), "a law that is not just, seems to be no law at all." Wherefore *Can 4* such laws do not bind in conscience, except perhaps in order to avoid scandal or disturbance, for which cause a man should even yield his right, according to Mt. 5:40,41: "If a man . . . take away thy coat, let go thy cloak also unto him; and whosoever will force thee one mile, go with him other two."

Secondly, laws may be unjust through being opposed to the Divine good: such ② are the laws of tyrants inducing to idolatry, or to anything else contrary to the Divine law: and laws of this kind must nowise be observed, because, as stated in Acts 5:29, "we ought to obey God rather than man."

Reply to Objection 1: As the Apostle says (Rm. 13:1,2), all human power is from God . . . "therefore he that resisteth the power," in matters that are within its scope, "resisteth the ordinance of God"; so that he becomes guilty according to his conscience.

Reply to Objection 2: This argument is true of laws that are contrary to the commandments of God, which is beyond the scope of (human) power. Wherefore in such matters human law should not be obeyed.

Reply to Objection 3: This argument is true of a law that inflicts unjust hurt on its subjects. The power that man holds from God does not extend to this:

wherefore neither in such matters is man bound to obey the law, provided he avoid giving scandal or inflicting a more grievous hurt.

Article: 5

Whether all are subject to the law?

Objection 1: It would seem that not all are subject to the law. For those alone are subject to a law for whom a law is made. But the Apostle says (1 Tim. 1:9): "The law is not made for the just man." Therefore the just are not subject to the law.

Objection 2: Further, Pope Urban says [*Decretals. caus. xix, qu. 2]: "He that is guided by a private law need not for any reason be bound by the public law." Now all spiritual men are led by the private law of the Holy Ghost, for they are the sons of God, of whom it is said (Rm. 8:14): "Whosoever are led by the Spirit of God, they are the sons of God." Therefore not all men are subject to human law.

Objection 3: Further, the jurist says [*Pandect. Justin. i, ff., tit. 3, De Leg. et Senat.] that "the sovereign is exempt from the laws." But he that is exempt from the law is not bound thereby. Therefore not all are subject to the law.

On the contrary, The Apostle says (Rm. 13:1): "Let every soul be subject to the higher powers." But subjection to a power seems to imply subjection to the laws framed by that power. Therefore all men should be subject to human law.

I answer that, As stated above (Question [90], Articles [1],2; Article [3], ad 2), the notion of law contains two things: first, that it is a rule of human acts; secondly, that it has coercive power. Wherefore a man may be subject to law in two ways. First, as the regulated is subject to the regulator: and, in this way, whoever is subject to a power, is subject to the law framed by that power. But it may happen in two ways that one is not subject to a power. In one way, by being altogether free from its authority: hence the subjects of one city or kingdom are not bound by the laws of the sovereign of another city or kingdom, since they are not subject to his authority. In another way, by being under a yet higher law; thus the subject of a proconsul should be ruled by his command, but not in those matters in which the subject receives his orders from the emperor: for in these matters, he is not bound by the mandate of the lower authority, since he is directed by that of a higher. In this way, one who is simply subject to a law, may not be a subject thereto in certain matters, in respect of which he is ruled by a higher law.

Secondly, a man is said to be subject to a law as the coerced is subject to the coercer. In this way the virtuous and righteous are not subject to the law, but only the wicked. Because coercion and violence are contrary to the will: but the will of the good is in harmony with the law, whereas the will of the wicked is discordant from it. Wherefore in this sense the good are not subject to the law, but only the wicked.

Reply to Objection 1: This argument is true of subjection by way of coercion: for, in this way, "the law is not made for the just men": because "they are a law to themselves," since they "show the work of the law written in their hearts," as the Apostle says (Rm. 2:14,15). Consequently the law does not enforce itself upon them as it does on the wicked.

Reply to Objection 2: The law of the Holy Ghost is above all law framed by man: and therefore spiritual men, in so far as they are led by the law of the Holy Ghost, are not subject to the law in those matters that are inconsistent with the guidance of the Holy Ghost. Nevertheless the very fact that spiritual men are subject to law, is due to the leading of the Holy Ghost, according to 1 Pt. 2:13: "Be ye subject . . . to every human creature for God's sake."

Reply to Objection 3: The sovereign is said to be "exempt from the law," as to its coercive power; since, properly speaking, no man is coerced by himself, and law has no coercive power save from the authority of the sovereign. Thus then is the sovereign said to be exempt from the law, because none is competent to pass sentence on him, if he acts against the law. Wherefore on Ps. 50:6: "To Thee only have I sinned," a gloss says that "there is no man who can judge the deeds of a king." But as to the directive force of law, the sovereign is subject to the law by his own will, according to the statement (Extra, De Constit. cap. Cum omnes) that "whatever law a man makes for another, he should keep himself. And a wise authority [*Dionysius Cato, Dist. de Moribus] says: 'Obey the law that thou makest thyself.'" Moreover the Lord reproaches those who "say and do not"; and who "bind heavy burdens and lay them on men's shoulders, but with a finger of their own they will not move them" (Mt. 23:3,4). Hence, in the judgment of God, the sovereign is not exempt from the law, as to its directive force; but he should fulfil it to his own free-will and not of constraint. Again the sovereign is above the law, in so far as, when it is expedient, he can change the law, and dispense in it according to time and place.

Article: 6

Whether he who is under a law may act beside the letter of the law?

Objection 1: It seems that he who is subject to a law may not act beside the letter of the law. For Augustine says (De Vera Relig. 31): "Although men judge about temporal laws when they make them, yet when once they are made they must pass judgment not on them, but according to them." But if anyone disregard the letter of the law, saying that he observes the intention of the lawgiver, he seems to pass judgment on the law. Therefore it is not right for one who is under the law to disregard the letter of the law, in order to observe the intention of the lawgiver.

Objection 2: Further, he alone is competent to interpret the law who can make the law. But those who are subject to the law cannot make the law. Therefore they have no right to interpret the intention of the lawgiver, but should always act according to the letter of the law.

Objection 3: Further, every wise man knows how to explain his intention by words. But those who framed the laws should be reckoned wise: for Wisdom says (Prov. 8:15): "By Me kings reign, and lawgivers decree just things." Therefore we should not judge of the intention of the lawgiver otherwise than by the words of the law.

On the contrary, Hilary says (De Trin. iv): "The meaning of what is said is according to the motive for saying it: because things are not subject to speech, but speech to things." Therefore we should take account of the motive of the lawgiver, rather than of his very words.

I answer that, As stated above (Article [4]), every law is directed to the common weal of men, and derives the force and nature of law accordingly. Hence the jurist says [*Pandect. Justin. lib. i, ff., tit. 3, De Leg. et Senat.]: "By no reason of law, or favor of equity, is it allowable for us to interpret harshly, and render burdensome, those useful measures which have been enacted for the welfare of man." Now it happens often that the observance of some point of law conduces to the common weal in the majority of instances, and yet, in some cases, is very hurtful. Since then the lawgiver cannot have in view every single case, he shapes the law according to what happens most frequently, by directing his attention to the common good. Wherefore if a case arise wherein the observance of that law would be hurtful to the general welfare, it should not be observed. For instance, suppose that in a besieged city it be an established law that the gates of the city are to be kept closed, this is good for public welfare as a general rule: but, it were to happen that the enemy are in pursuit of certain citizens, who are defenders of the city, it would be a great loss to the city, if the gates were not opened to them: and so in that case the gates ought to be opened, contrary to the letter of the law, in order to maintain the common weal, which the lawgiver had in view.

Nevertheless it must be noted, that if the observance of the law according to the letter does not involve any sudden risk needing instant remedy, it is not competent for everyone to expound what is useful and what is not useful to the state: those alone can do this who are in authority, and who, on account of such like cases, have the power to dispense from the laws. If, however, the peril be so sudden as not to allow of the delay involved by referring the matter to authority, the mere necessity brings with it a dispensation, since necessity knows no law.

Reply to Objection 1: He who in a case of necessity acts beside the letter of the law, does not judge the law; but of a particular case in which he sees that the letter of the law is not to be observed.

Reply to Objection 2: He who follows the intention of the lawgiver, does not interpret the law simply; but in a case in which it is evident, by reason of the manifest harm, that the lawgiver intended otherwise. For if it be a matter of doubt, he must either act according to the letter of the law, or consult those in power.

Reply to Objection 3: No man is so wise as to be able to take account of every single case; wherefore he is not able sufficiently to express in words all those things that are suitable for the end he has in view. And even if a lawgiver were able to take all the cases into consideration, he ought not to mention them all, in order to avoid confusion: but should frame the law according to that which is of most common occurrence.

Justification vs. Sanctification

Justification — remove the sin that seperates us from God

at the Cross

Sanctification - the way in which souls or persons become holy

set apart // distinct

OF CHANGE IN LAWS (FOUR ARTICLES)

We must now consider change in laws: under which head there are four points of inquiry:

(1) Whether human law is changeable?
(2) Whether it should be always changed, whenever anything better occurs?
(3) Whether it is abolished by custom, and whether custom obtains the force of law?
(4) Whether the application of human law should be changed by dispensation of those in authority?

Question 97 Article: 1

Whether human law should be changed in any way?

Objection 1: It would seem that human law should not be changed in any way at all. Because human law is derived from the natural law, as stated above (Question [95], Article [2]). But the natural law endures unchangeably. Therefore human law should also remain without any change.

Objection 2: Further, as the Philosopher says (Ethic. v, 5), a measure should be absolutely stable. But human law is the measure of human acts, as stated above (Question [90], Articles [1],2). Therefore it should remain without change.

Objection 3: Further, it is of the essence of law to be just and right, as stated above (Question [95], Article [2]). But that which is right once is right always. Therefore that which is law once, should be always law.

On the contrary, Augustine says (De Lib. Arb. i, 6): "A temporal law, however just, may be justly changed in course of time."

I answer that, As stated above (Question [91], Article [3]), human law is a dictate of reason, whereby human acts are directed. Thus there may be two causes for the just change of human law: one on the part of reason; the other on the part of man whose acts are regulated by law. The cause on the part of reason is that it seems natural to human reason to advance gradually from the imperfect to the perfect. Hence, in speculative sciences, we see that the teaching of the early philosophers was imperfect, and that it was afterwards perfected by those who succeeded them. So also in practical matters: for those who first endeavored to discover something useful for the human community, not being able by themselves to take everything into consideration, set up certain institutions which were deficient in many ways; and these were changed by subsequent lawgivers who made institutions that might prove less frequently deficient in respect of the common weal.

On the part of man, whose acts are regulated by law, the law can be rightly changed on account of the changed condition of man, to whom different things are expedient according to the difference of his condition. An example is proposed by Augustine (De Lib. Arb. i, 6): "If the people have a sense of moderation and responsibility, and are most careful guardians of the common weal, it is right to enact a law allowing such a people to choose their own magistrates for the government of the commonwealth. But if, as time goes on, the same people become so corrupt as to sell their votes, and entrust the government to scoundrels and criminals; then the right of appointing their public officials is rightly forfeit to such a people, and the choice devolves to a few good men."

Reply to Objection 1: The natural law is a participation of the eternal law, as stated above (Question [91], Article [2]), and therefore endures without change, owing to the unchangeableness and perfection of the Divine Reason, the Author of nature. But the reason of man is changeable and imperfect: wherefore his law is subject to change. Moreover the natural law contains certain universal precepts, which are everlasting: whereas human law contains certain particular precepts, according to various emergencies.

Reply to Objection 2: A measure should be as enduring as possible. But nothing can be absolutely unchangeable in things that are subject to change. And therefore human law cannot be altogether unchangeable.

Reply to Objection 3: In corporal things, right is predicated absolutely: and therefore, as far as itself is concerned, always remains right. But right is predicated of law with reference to the common weal, to which one and the same thing is not always adapted, as stated above: wherefore rectitude of this kind is subject to change.

Article: 2

Whether human law should always be changed, whenever something better occurs?

Objection 1: It would seem that human law should be changed, whenever something better occurs. Because human laws are devised by human reason, like other arts. But in the other arts, the tenets of former times give place to others, if something better occurs. Therefore the same should apply to human laws.

Objection 2: Further, by taking note of the past we can provide for the future. Now unless human laws had been changed when it was found possible to improve them, considerable inconvenience would have ensued; because the laws

117

of old were crude in many points. Therefore it seems that laws should be changed, whenever anything better occurs to be enacted.

Objection 3: Further, human laws are enacted about single acts of man. But we cannot acquire perfect knowledge in singular matters, except by experience, which "requires time," as stated in Ethic. ii. Therefore it seems that as time goes on it is possible for something better to occur for legislation.

[handwritten margin note: something better comes]

On the contrary, It is stated in the Decretals (Dist. xii, 5): "It is absurd, and a detestable shame, that we should suffer those traditions to be changed which we have received from the fathers of old."

I answer that, As stated above (Article [1]), human law is rightly changed, in so far as such change is conducive to the common weal. But, to a certain extent, the mere change of law is of itself prejudicial to the common good: because custom avails much for the observance of laws, seeing that what is done contrary to general custom, even in slight matters, is looked upon as grave. Consequently, when a law is changed, the binding power of the law is diminished, in so far as custom is abolished. Wherefore human law should never be changed, unless, in some way or other, the common weal be compensated according to the extent of the harm done in this respect. Such compensation may arise either from some very great and every evident benefit conferred by the new enactment; or from the extreme urgency of the case, due to the fact that either the existing law is clearly unjust, or its observance extremely harmful. Wherefore the jurist says [*Pandect. Justin. lib. i, ff., tit. 4, De Constit. Princip.] that "in establishing new laws, there should be evidence of the benefit to be derived, before departing from a law which has long been considered just."

Reply to Objection 1: Rules of art derive their force from reason alone: and therefore whenever something better occurs, the rule followed hitherto should be changed. But "laws derive very great force from custom," as the Philosopher states (Polit. ii, 5): consequently they should not be quickly changed.

Reply to Objection 2: This argument proves that laws ought to be changed: not in view of any improvement, but for the sake of a great benefit or in a case of great urgency, as stated above. This answer applies also to the Third Objection.

Article: 3

Whether custom can obtain force of law?

Objection 1: It would seem that custom cannot obtain force of law, nor abolish a law. Because human law is derived from the natural law and from the Divine law, as stated above (Question [93], Article [3]; Question [95], Article [2]). But human custom cannot change either the law of nature or the Divine law. Therefore neither can it change human law.

Objection 2: Further, many evils cannot make one good. But he who first acted against the law, did evil. Therefore by multiplying such acts, nothing good is the result. Now a law is something good; since it is a rule of human acts. Therefore law is not abolished by custom, so that the mere custom should obtain force of law.

Objection 3: Further, the framing of laws belongs to those public men whose business it is to govern the community; wherefore private individuals cannot make laws. But custom grows by the acts of private individuals. Therefore custom cannot obtain force of law, so as to abolish the law.

On the contrary, Augustine says (Ep. ad Casulan. xxxvi): "The customs of God's people and the institutions of our ancestors are to be considered as laws. And those who throw contempt on the customs of the Church ought to be punished as those who disobey the law of God."

I answer that, All law proceeds from the reason and will of the lawgiver; the Divine and natural laws from the reasonable will of God; the human law from the will of man, regulated by reason. Now just as human reason and will, in practical matters, may be made manifest by speech, so may they be made known by deeds: since seemingly a man chooses as good that which he carries into execution. But it is evident that by human speech, law can be both changed and expounded, in so far as it manifests the interior movement and thought of human reason. Wherefore by actions also, especially if they be repeated, so as to make a custom, law can be changed and expounded; and also something can be established which obtains force of law, in so far as by repeated external actions, the inward movement of the will, and concepts of reason are most effectually declared; for when a thing is done again and again, it seems to proceed from a deliberate judgment of reason. Accordingly, custom has the force of a law, abolishes law, and is the interpreter of law.

Reply to Objection 1: The natural and Divine laws proceed from the Divine will, as stated above. Wherefore they cannot be changed by a custom proceeding from the will of man, but only by Divine authority. Hence it is that no custom can prevail over the Divine or natural laws: for Isidore says (Synon. ii, 16): "Let custom yield to authority: evil customs should be eradicated by law and reason."

Reply to Objection 2: As stated above (Question [96], Article [6]), human laws fail in some cases: wherefore it is possible sometimes to act beside the law; namely, in a case where the law fails; yet the act will not be evil. And when such cases are multiplied, by reason of some change in man, then custom shows that the law is no longer useful: just as it might be declared by the verbal promulgation of a law to the contrary. If, however, the same reason remains, for which the law was useful hitherto, then it is not the custom that prevails against the law, but the law that overcomes the custom: unless perhaps the sole reason for the law seeming useless, be that it is not "possible according to the custom of the country" [*Question [95], Article [3]], which has been stated to be one of the conditions of law. For it is not easy to set aside the custom of a whole people.

Reply to Objection 3: The people among whom a custom is introduced may be of two conditions. For if they are free, and able to make their own laws, the consent of the whole people expressed by a custom counts far more in favor of a particular observance, that does the authority of the sovereign, who has not the power to frame laws, except as representing the people. Wherefore although each individual cannot make laws, yet the whole people can. If however the people have not the free power to make their own laws, or to abolish a law made by a higher authority, nevertheless with such a people a prevailing custom obtains force of law, in so far as it is tolerated by those to whom it belongs to make laws for that people: because by the very fact that they tolerate it they seem to approve of that which is introduced by custom.

Article: 4

Whether the rulers of the people can dispense from human laws?

Objection 1: It would seem that the rulers of the people cannot dispense from human laws. For the law is established for the "common weal," as Isidore says (Etym. v, 21). But the common good should not be set aside for the private convenience of an individual: because, as the Philosopher says (Ethic. i, 2), "the good of the nation is more godlike than the good of one man." Therefore it seems that a man should not be dispensed from acting in compliance with the general law.

Objection 2: Further, those who are placed over others are commanded as follows (Dt. 1:17): "You shall hear the little as well as the great; neither shall you respect any man's person, because it is the judgment of God." But to allow one man to do that which is equally forbidden to all, seems to be respect of persons. Therefore the rulers of a community cannot grant such dispensations, since this is against a precept of the Divine law.

Objection 3: Further, human law, in order to be just, should accord with the natural and Divine laws: else it would not "foster religion," nor be "helpful to discipline," which is requisite to the nature of law, as laid down by Isidore (Etym. v, 3). But no man can dispense from the Divine and natural laws. Neither, therefore, can he dispense from the human law.

On the contrary, The Apostle says (1 Cor. 9:17): "A dispensation is committed to me."

I answer that, Dispensation, properly speaking, denotes a measuring out to individuals of some common goods: thus the head of a household is called a dispenser, because to each member of the household he distributes work and necessaries of life in due weight and measure. Accordingly in every community a man is said to dispense, from the very fact that he directs how some general precept is to be fulfilled by each individual. Now it happens at times that a precept, which is conducive to the common weal as a general rule, is not good for a particular individual, or in some particular case, either because it would hinder some greater good, or because it would be the occasion of some evil, as explained above (Question [96], Article [6]). But it would be dangerous to leave this to the discretion of each individual, except perhaps by reason of an evident and sudden emergency, as stated above (Question [96], Article [6]). Consequently he who is placed over a community is empowered to dispense in a human law that rests upon his authority, so that, when the law fails in its application to persons or circumstances, he may allow the precept of the law not to be observed. If however he grant this permission without any such reason, and of his mere will, he will be an unfaithful or an imprudent dispenser: unfaithful, if he has not the common good in view; imprudent, if he ignores the reasons for granting dispensations. Hence Our Lord says (Lk. 12:42): "Who, thinkest thou, is the faithful and wise dispenser [Douay: steward], whom his lord setteth over his family?"

Reply to Objection 1: When a person is dispensed from observing the general law, this should not be done to the prejudice of, but with the intention of benefiting, the common good.

Reply to Objection 2: It is not respect of persons if unequal measures are served out to those who are themselves unequal. Wherefore when the condition of any person requires that he should reasonably receive special treatment, it is not respect of persons if he be the object of special favor.

Reply to Objection 3: Natural law, so far as it contains general precepts, which never fail, does not allow of dispensations. In other precepts, however, which are as conclusions of the general precepts, man sometimes grants a dispensation: for instance, that a loan should not be paid back to the betrayer of his country, or something similar. But to the Divine law each man stands as a private person to the public law to which he is subject. Wherefore just as none can dispense from public human law, except the man from whom the law derives its authority, or his delegate; so, in the precepts of the Divine law, which are from God, none can dispense but God, or the man to whom He may give special power for that purpose.

OF THE OLD LAW (SIX ARTICLES)

In due sequence we must now consider the Old Law; and (1) The Law itself; (2) Its precepts. Under the first head there are six points of inquiry:

(1) Whether the Old Law was good?
(2) Whether it was from God?
(3) Whether it came from Him through the angels?
(4) Whether it was given to all?
(5) Whether it was binding on all?
(6) Whether it was given at a suitable time?

Question 98 Article:

Whether the Old Law was good?

Objection 1: It would seem that the Old Law was not good. For it is written (Ezech. 20:25): "I gave them statutes that were not good, and judgments in which they shall not live." But a law is not said to be good except on account of the goodness of the precepts that it contains. Therefore the Old Law was not good.

Objection 2: Further, it belongs to the goodness of a law that it conduce to the common welfare, as Isidore says (Etym. v, 3). But the Old Law was not salutary; rather was it deadly and hurtful. For the Apostle says (Rm. 7:8, seqq.): "Without the law sin was dead. And I lived some time without the law. But when the commandment came sin revived; and I died." Again he says (Rm. 5:20): "Law entered in that sin might abound." Therefore the Old Law was not good.

Objection 3: Further, it belongs to the goodness of the law that it should be possible to obey it, both according to nature, and according to human custom. But such the Old Law was not: since Peter said (Acts 15:10): "Why tempt you (God) to put a yoke on the necks of the disciples, which neither our fathers nor we have been able to bear?" Therefore it seems that the Old Law was not good.

On the contrary, The Apostle says (Rm. 7:12): "Wherefore the law indeed is holy, and the commandment holy, and just, and good."

I answer that, Without any doubt, the Old Law was good. For just as a doctrine is shown to be good by the fact that it accords with right reason, so is a law proved to be good if it accords with reason. Now the Old Law was in accordance with reason. Because it repressed concupiscence which is in conflict with reason, as evidenced by the commandment, "Thou shalt not covet thy neighbor's goods" (Ex. 20:17). Moreover the same law forbade all kinds of sin; and these too are contrary to reason. Consequently it is evident that it was a good law. The

Apostle argues in the same way (Rm. 7): "I am delighted," says he (verse 22), "with the law of God, according to the inward man": and again (verse 16): "I consent to the law, that is good."

But it must be noted that the good has various degrees, as Dionysius states (Div. Nom. iv): for there is a perfect good, and an imperfect good. In things ordained to an end, there is perfect goodness when a thing is such that it is sufficient in itself to conduce to the end: while there is imperfect goodness when a thing is of some assistance in attaining the end, but is not sufficient for the realization thereof. Thus a medicine is perfectly good, if it gives health to a man; but it is imperfect, if it helps to cure him, without being able to bring him back to health. Again it must be observed that the end of human law is different from the end of Divine law. For the end of human law is the temporal tranquillity of the state, which end law effects by directing external actions, as regards those evils which might disturb the peaceful condition of the state. On the other hand, the end of the Divine law is to bring man to that end which is everlasting happiness; which end is hindered by any sin, not only of external, but also of internal action. Consequently that which suffices for the perfection of human law, viz. the prohibition and punishment of sin, does not suffice for the perfection of the Divine law: but it is requisite that it should make man altogether fit to partake of everlasting happiness. Now this cannot be done save by the grace of the Holy Ghost, whereby "charity" which fulfilleth the law . . . "is spread abroad in our hearts" (Rm. 5:5): since "the grace of God is life everlasting" (Rm. 6:23). But the Old Law could not confer this grace, for this was reserved to Christ; because, as it is written (Jn. 1:17), the law was given "by Moses, grace and truth came by Jesus Christ." Consequently the Old Law was good indeed, but imperfect, according to Heb. 7:19: "The law brought nothing to perfection."

Reply to Objection 1: The Lord refers there to the ceremonial precepts; which are said not to be good, because they did not confer grace unto the remission of sins, although by fulfilling these precepts man confessed himself a sinner. Hence it is said pointedly, "and judgments in which they shall not live"; i.e. whereby they are unable to obtain life; and so the text goes on: "And I polluted them," i.e. showed them to be polluted, "in their own gifts, when they offered all that opened the womb, for their offenses."

Reply to Objection 2: The law is said to have been deadly, as being not the cause, but the occasion of death, on account of its imperfection: in so far as it did not confer grace enabling man to fulfil what is prescribed, and to avoid what it forbade. Hence this occasion was not given to men, but taken by them. Wherefore the Apostle says (Rm. 5:11): "Sin, taking occasion by the commandment, seduced me, and by it killed me." In the same sense when it is said that "the law entered in that sin might abound," the conjunction "that" must be taken as consecutive and not final: in so far as men, taking occasion from the law, sinned all the more, both because a sin became more grievous after law had

Pedagogue – teacher

123

forbidden it, and because concupiscence increased, since we desire a thing the more from its being forbidden.

Reply to Objection 3: The yoke of the law could not be borne without the help of grace, which the law did not confer: for it is written (Rm. 9:16): "It is not him that willeth, nor of him that runneth," viz. that he wills and runs in the commandments of God, "but of God that showeth mercy." Wherefore it is written (Ps. 118:32): "I have run the way of Thy commandments, when Thou didst enlarge my heart," i.e. by giving me grace and charity.

Article: 2

Whether the Old Law was from God?

Objection 1: It would seem that the Old Law was not from God. For it is written (Dt. 32:4): "The works of God are perfect." But the Law was imperfect, as stated above (Article [1]). Therefore the Old Law was not from God.

God is eternal, but law isn't Objection 2: Further, it is written (Eccles. 3:14): "I have learned that all the works which God hath made continue for ever." But the Old Law does not continue for ever: since the Apostle says (Heb. 7:18): "There is indeed a setting aside of the former commandment, because of the weakness and unprofitableness thereof." Therefore the Old Law was not from God.

Objection 3: Further, a wise lawgiver should remove, not only evil, but also the occasions of evil. But the Old Law was an occasion of sin, as stated above (Article [1], ad 2). Therefore the giving of such a law does not pertain to God, to Whom "none is like among the lawgivers" (Job 36:22).

Objection 4: Further, it is written (1 Tim. 2:4) that God "will have all men to be saved." But the Old Law did not suffice to save man, as stated above (Article [1]). Therefore the giving of such a law did not appertain to God. Therefore the Old Law was not from God.

On the contrary, Our Lord said (Mt. 15:6) while speaking to the Jews, to whom the Law was given: "You have made void the commandment of God for your tradition." And shortly before (verse 4) He had said: "Honor thy father and mother," which is contained expressly in the Old Law (Ex. 20:12; Dt. 5:16). Therefore the Old Law was from God.

I answer that, The Old Law was given by the good God, Who is the Father of Our Lord Jesus Christ. For the Old Law ordained men to Christ in two ways. First by bearing witness to Christ; wherefore He Himself says (Lk. 24:44): "All things must needs be fulfilled, which are written in the law . . . and in the prophets, and in the psalms, concerning Me": and (Jn. 5:46): "If you did believe

124

Moses, you would perhaps believe Me also; for he wrote of Me." Secondly, as a kind of disposition/ since by withdrawing men from idolatrous worship, it enclosed [concludebat] them in the worship of one God, by Whom the human race was to be saved through Christ. Wherefore the Apostle says (Gal. 3:23): "Before the faith came, we were kept under the law shut up [conclusi], unto that faith which was to be revealed." Now it is evident that the same thing it is, which gives a disposition to the end, and which brings to the end; and when I say "the same," I mean that it does so either by itself or through its subjects. For the devil would not make a law whereby men would be led to Christ, Who was to cast him out, according to Mt. 12:26: "If Satan cast out Satan, his kingdom is divided" [Vulg.: 'he is divided against himself']. Therefore the Old Law was given by the same God, from Whom came salvation to man, through the grace of Christ.

Reply to Objection 1: Nothing prevents a thing being not perfect simply, and yet perfect in respect of time: thus a boy is said to be perfect, not simply, but with regard to the condition of time. So, too, precepts that are given to children are perfect in comparison with the condition of those to whom they are given, although they are not perfect simply. Hence the Apostle says (Gal. 3:24): "The law was our pedagogue in Christ."

Reply to Objection 2: Those works of God endure for ever which God so made that they would endure for ever; and these are His perfect works. But the Old Law was set aside when there came the perfection of grace; not as though it were evil, but as being weak and useless for this time; because, as the Apostle goes on to say, "the law brought nothing to perfection": hence he says (Gal. 3:25): "After the faith is come, we are no longer under a pedagogue."

Reply to Objection 3: As stated above (Question [79], Article [4]), God sometimes permits certain ones to fall into sin, that they may thereby be humbled. So also did He wish to give such a law as men by their own forces could not fulfill, so that, while presuming on their own powers, they might find themselves to be sinners, and being humbled might have recourse to the help of grace.

Reply to Objection 4: Although the Old Law did not suffice to save man, yet another help from God besides the Law was available for man, viz. faith in the Mediator, by which the fathers of old were justified even as we were. Accordingly God did not fail man by giving him insufficient aids to salvation.

Article: 3

Whether the Old Law was given through the angels?

Objection 1: It seems that the Old Law was not given through the angels, but immediately by God. For an angel means a "messenger"; so that the word "angel" denotes ministry, not lordship, according to Ps. 102:20,21: "Bless the Lord, all ye His Angels . . . you ministers of His." But the Old Law is related to have been given by the Lord: for it is written (Ex. 20:1): "And the Lord spoke . . . these words," and further on: "I am the Lord Thy God." Moreover the same expression is often repeated in Exodus, and the later books of the Law. Therefore the Law was given by God immediately.

Objection 2: Further, according to Jn. 1:17, "the Law was given by Moses." But Moses received it from God immediately: for it is written (Ex. 33:11): "The Lord spoke to Moses face to face, as a man is wont to speak to his friend." Therefore the Old Law was given by God immediately.

Objection 3: Further, it belongs to the sovereign alone to make a law, as stated above (Question [90], Article [3]). But God alone is Sovereign as regards the salvation of souls: while the angels are the "ministering spirits," as stated in Heb. 1:14. Therefore it was not meet for the Law to be given through the angels, since it is ordained to the salvation of souls.

On the contrary, The Apostle said (Gal. 3:19) that the Law was "given [Vulg.: 'ordained'] by angels in the hand of a Mediator." And Stephen said (Acts 7:53): "(Who) have received the Law by the disposition of angels."

I answer that, The Law was given by God through the angels. And besides the general reason given by Dionysius (Coel. Hier. iv), viz. that "the gifts of God should be brought to men by means of the angels," there is a special reason why the Old Law should have been given through them. For it has been stated (Articles [1],2) that the Old Law was imperfect, and yet disposed man to that perfect salvation of the human race, which was to come through Christ. Now it is to be observed that wherever there is an order of powers or arts, he that holds the highest place, himself exercises the principal and perfect acts; while those things which dispose to the ultimate perfection are effected by him through his subordinates: thus the ship-builder himself rivets the planks together, but prepares the material by means of the workmen who assist him under his direction. Consequently it was fitting that the perfect law of the New Testament should be given by the incarnate God immediately; but that the Old Law should be given to men by the ministers of God, i.e. by the angels. It is thus that the Apostle at the beginning of his epistle to the Hebrews (1:2) proves the excellence of the New Law over the Old; because in the New Testament "God . . . hath spoken to us by His Son," whereas in the Old Testament "the word was spoken by angels" (Heb. 2:2).

Reply to Objection 1: As Gregory says at the beginning of his Morals (Praef. chap. i), "the angel who is described to have appeared to Moses, is sometimes mentioned as an angel, sometimes as the Lord: an angel, in truth, in respect of that which was subservient to the external delivery; and the Lord, because He was the Director within, Who supported the effectual power of speaking." Hence also it is that the angel spoke as personating the Lord.

Reply to Objection 2: As Augustine says (Gen. ad lit. xii, 27), it is stated in Exodus that "the Lord spoke to Moses face to face"; and shortly afterwards we read, "Show me Thy glory. Therefore He perceived what he saw and he desired what he saw not." Hence he did not see the very Essence of God; and consequently he was not taught by Him immediately. Accordingly when Scripture states that "He spoke to him face to face," this is to be understood as expressing the opinion of the people, who thought that Moses was speaking with God mouth to mouth, when God spoke and appeared to him, by means of a subordinate creature, i.e. an angel and a cloud. Again we may say that this vision "face to face" means some kind of sublime and familiar contemplation, inferior to the vision of the Divine Essence.

Reply to Objection 3: It is for the sovereign alone to make a law by his own authority; but sometimes after making a law, he promulgates it through others. Thus God made the Law by His own authority, but He promulgated it through the angels.

Article: 4

Whether the Old Law should have been given to the Jews alone?

Objection 1: It would seem that the Old Law should not have been given to the Jews alone. For the Old Law disposed men for the salvation which was to come through Christ, as stated above (Articles [2],3). But that salvation was to come not to the Jews alone but to all nations, according to Is. 49:6: "It is a small thing that thou shouldst be my servant to raise up the tribes of Jacob, and to convert the dregs of Israel. Behold I have given thee to be the light of the Gentiles, that thou mayest be My salvation, even to the farthest part of the earth." Therefore the Old Law should have been given to all nations, and not to one people only.

Objection 2: Further, according to Acts 10:34,35, "God is not a respecter of persons: but in every nation, he that feareth Him, and worketh justice, is acceptable to Him." Therefore the way of salvation should not have been opened to one people more than to another.

Objection 3: Further, the law was given through the angels, as stated above (Article [3]). But God always vouchsafed the ministrations of the angels not to the Jews alone, but to all nations: for it is written (Ecclus. 17:14): "Over every nation He set a ruler." Also on all nations He bestows temporal goods, which are of less account with God than spiritual goods. Therefore He should have given the Law also to all peoples.

On the contrary, It is written (Rm. 3:1,2): "What advantage then hath the Jew? . . . Much every way. First indeed, because the words of God were committed to them": and (Ps. 147:9): "He hath not done in like manner to every nation: and His judgments He hath not made manifest unto them."

I answer that, It might be assigned as a reason for the Law being given to the Jews rather than to other peoples, that the Jewish people alone remained faithful to the worship of one God, while the others turned away to idolatry; wherefore the latter were unworthy to receive the Law, lest a holy thing should be given to dogs.

But this reason does not seem fitting: because that people turned to idolatry, even after the Law had been made, which was more grievous, as is clear from Ex. 32 and from Amos 5:25,26: "Did you offer victims and sacrifices to Me in the desert for forty years, O house of Israel? But you carried a tabernacle for your Moloch, and the image of your idols, the star of your god, which you made to yourselves." Moreover it is stated expressly (Dt. 9:6): "Know therefore that the Lord thy God giveth thee not this excellent land in possession for thy justices, for thou art a very stiff-necked people": but the real reason is given in the preceding verse: "That the Lord might accomplish His word, which He promised by oath to thy fathers Abraham, Isaac, and Jacob."

What this promise was is shown by the Apostle, who says (Gal. 3:16) that "to Abraham were the promises made and to his seed. He saith not, 'And to his seeds,' as of many: but as of one, 'And to thy seed,' which is Christ." And so God vouchsafed both the Law and other special boons to that people, on account of the promised made to their fathers that Christ should be born of them. For it was fitting that the people, of whom Christ was to be born, should be signalized by a special sanctification, according to the words of Lev. 19:2: "Be ye holy, because I . . . am holy." Nor again was it on account of the merit of Abraham himself that this promise was made to him, viz. that Christ should be born of his seed: but of gratuitous election and vocation. Hence it is written (Is. 41:2): "Who hath raised up the just one form the east, hath called him to follow him?"

It is therefore evident that it was merely from gratuitous election that the patriarchs received the promise, and that the people sprung from them received the law; according to Dt. 4:36, 37: "Ye did [Vulg.: 'Thou didst'] hear His words out of the midst of the fire, because He loved thy fathers, and chose their seed after them." And if again it asked why He chose this people, and not another, that Christ might be born thereof; a fitting answer is given by Augustine (Tract. super Joan. xxvi): "Why He draweth one and draweth not another, seek not thou to judge, if thou wish not to err."

Reply to Objection 1: Although the salvation, which was to come through Christ, was prepared for all nations, yet it was necessary that Christ should be

✳ if you try to understand God, you will err. You cannot know

128

born of one people, which, for this reason, was privileged above other peoples; according to Rm. 9:4: "To whom," namely the Jews, "belongeth the adoption as of children (of God) . . . and the testament, and the giving of the Law . . . whose are the fathers, and of whom is Christ according to the flesh."

Reply to Objection 2: Respect of persons takes place in those things which are given according to due; but it has no place in those things which are bestowed gratuitously. Because he who, out of generosity, gives of his own to one and not to another, is not a respecter of persons: but if he were a dispenser of goods held in common, and were not to distribute them according to personal merits, he would be a respecter of persons. Now God bestows the benefits of salvation on the human race gratuitously: wherefore He is not a respecter of persons, if He gives them to some rather than to others. Hence Augustine says (De Praedest. Sanct. viii): "All whom God teaches, he teaches out of pity; but whom He teaches not, out of justice He teaches not": for this is due to the condemnation of the human race for the sin of the first parent.

Reply to Objection 3: The benefits of grace are forfeited by man on account of sin: but not the benefits of nature. Among the latter are the ministries of the angels, which the very order of various natures demands, viz. that the lowest beings be governed through the intermediate beings: and also bodily aids, which God vouchsafes not only to men, but also to beasts, according to Ps. 35:7: "Men and beasts Thou wilt preserve, O Lord."

Article: 5

Whether all men were bound to observe the Old Law?

Objection 1: It would seem that all men were bound to observe the Old Law. Because whoever is subject to the king, must needs be subject to his law. But the Old Law was given by God, Who is "King of all the earth" (Ps. 46:8). Therefore all the inhabitants of the earth were bound to observe the Law.

Objection 2: Further, the Jews could not be saved without observing the Old Law: for it is written (Dt. 27:26): "Cursed be he that abideth not in the words of this law, and fulfilleth them not in work." If therefore other men could be saved without the observance of the Old Law, the Jews would be in a worse plight than other men.

Objection 3: Further, the Gentiles were admitted to the Jewish ritual and to the observances of the Law: for it is written (Ex. 12:48): "If any stranger be willing to dwell among you, and to keep the Phase of the Lord, all his males shall first be circumcised, and then shall he celebrate it according to the manner; and he shall be as he that is born in the land." But it would have been useless to admit strangers to the legal observances according to Divine ordinance, if they could have been saved without the observance of the Law. Therefore none could be saved without observing the Law.

On the contrary, Dionysius says (Coel. Hier. ix) that many of the Gentiles were brought back to God by the angels. But it is clear that the Gentiles did not observe the Law. Therefore some could be saved without observing the Law.

I answer that, The Old Law showed forth the precepts of the natural law, and added certain precepts of its own. Accordingly, as to those precepts of the natural law contained in the Old Law, all were bound to observe the Old Law; not because they belonged to the Old Law, but because they belonged to the natural law. But as to those precepts which were added by the Old Law, they were not binding on save the Jewish people alone.

The reason of this is because the Old Law, as stated above (Article [4]), was given to the Jewish people, that it might receive a prerogative of holiness, in reverence for Christ Who was to be born of that people. Now whatever laws are enacted for the special sanctification of certain ones, are binding on them alone: thus clerics who are set aside for the service of God are bound to certain obligations to which the laity are not bound; likewise religious are bound by their profession to certain works of perfection, to which people living in the world are not bound. In like manner this people was bound to certain special observances, to which other peoples were not bound. Wherefore it is written (Dt. 18:13): "Thou shalt be perfect and without spot before the Lord thy God": and for this reason they used a kind of form of profession, as appears from Dt. 26:3: "I profess this day before the Lord thy God," etc.

Reply to Objection 1: Whoever are subject to a king, are bound to observe his law which he makes for all in general. But if he orders certain things to be observed by the servants of his household, others are not bound thereto.

Reply to Objection 2: The more a man is united to God, the better his state becomes: wherefore the more the Jewish people were bound to the worship of God, the greater their excellence over other peoples. Hence it is written (Dt. 4:8): "What other nation is there so renowned that hath ceremonies and just judgments, and all the law?" In like manner, from this point of view, the state of clerics is better than that of the laity, and the state of religious than that of folk living in the world.

Reply to Objection 3: The Gentiles obtained salvation more perfectly and more securely under the observances of the Law than under the mere natural law: and for this reason they were admitted to them. So too the laity are now admitted to the ranks of the clergy, and secular persons to those of the religious, although they can be saved without this.

Article: 6 Whether the Old Law was suitably given at the time of Moses?

Objection 1: It would seem that the Old Law was not suitably given at the time of Moses. Because the Old Law disposed man for the salvation which was to come through Christ, as stated above (Articles [2],3). But man needed this salutary remedy immediately after he had sinned. Therefore the Law should have been given immediately after sin.

Objection 2: Further, the Old Law was given for the sanctification of those from whom Christ was to be born. Now the promise concerning the "seed, which is Christ" (Gal. 3:16) was first made to Abraham, as related in Gn. 12:7. Therefore the Law should have been given at once at the time of Abraham.

Objection 3: Further, as Christ was born of those alone who descended from Noe through Abraham, to whom the promise was made; so was He born of no other of the descendants of Abraham but David, to whom the promise was renewed, according to 2 Kgs. 23:1: "The man to whom it was appointed concerning the Christ of the God of Jacob . . . said." Therefore the Old Law should have been given after David, just as it was given after Abraham.

On the contrary, The Apostle says (Gal. 3:19) that the Law "was set because of transgressions, until the seed should come, to whom He made the promise, being ordained by angels in the hand of a Mediator": ordained, i.e. "given in orderly fashion," as the gloss explains. Therefore it was fitting that the Old Law should be given in this order of time.

I answer that, It was most fitting for the Law to be given at the time of Moses. The reason for this may be taken from two things in respect of which every law is imposed on two kinds of men. Because it is imposed on some men who are hard-hearted and proud, whom the law restrains and tames: and it is imposed on good men, who, through being instructed by the law, are helped to fulfil what they desire to do. Hence it was fitting that the Law should be given at such a time as would be appropriate for the overcoming of man's pride. For man was proud of two things, viz. of knowledge and of power. He was proud of his knowledge, as though his natural reason could suffice him for salvation: and accordingly, in order that his pride might be overcome in this matter, man was left to the guidance of his reason without the help of a written law: and man was able to learn from experience that his reason was deficient, since about the time of Abraham man had fallen headlong into idolatry and the most shameful vices. Wherefore, after those times, it was necessary for a written law to be given as a remedy for human ignorance: because "by the Law is the knowledge of sin" (Rm. 3:20). But, after man had been instructed by the Law, his pride was convinced of his weakness, through his being unable to fulfil what he knew. Hence, as the Apostle concludes (Rm. 8:3,4), "what the Law could not do in that it was weak through the flesh, God sent [Vulg.: 'sending'] His own Son . . . that the justification of the Law might be fulfilled in us."

With regard to good men, the Law was given to them as a help; which was most needed by the people, at the time when the natural law began to be obscured on account of the exuberance of sin: for it was fitting that this help should be bestowed on men in an orderly manner, so that they might be led from imperfection to perfection; wherefore it was becoming that the Old Law should be given between the law of nature and the law of grace.

Reply to Objection 1: It was not fitting for the Old Law to be given at once after the sin of the first man: both because man was so confident in his own reason, that he did not acknowledge his need of the Old Law; because as yet the dictate of the natural law was not darkened by habitual sinning.

Reply to Objection 2: A law should not be given save to the people, since it is a general precept, as stated above (Question [90], Articles [2],3); wherefore at the time of Abraham God gave men certain familiar, and, as it were, household precepts: but when Abraham's descendants had multiplied, so as to form a people, and when they had been freed from slavery, it was fitting that they should be given a law; for "slaves are not that part of the people or state to which it is fitting for the law to be directed," as the Philosopher says (Polit. iii, 2,4,5).

Reply to Objection 3: Since the Law had to be given to the people, not only those, of whom Christ was born, received the Law, but the whole people, who were marked with the seal of circumcision, which was the sign of the promise made to Abraham, and in which he believed, according to Rm. 4:11: hence even before David, the Law had to be given to that people as soon as they were collected together.

OF THE PRECEPTS OF THE OLD LAW (SIX ARTICLES)

We must now consider the precepts of the Old Law; and (1) how they are distinguished from one another; (2) each kind of precept. Under the first head there are six points of inquiry:

(1) Whether the Old Law contains several precepts or only one?
(2) Whether the Old Law contains any moral precepts?
(3) Whether it contains ceremonial precepts in addition to the moral precepts?
(4) Whether besides these it contains judicial precepts?
(5) Whether it contains any others besides these?
(6) How the Old Law induced men to keep its precepts.

Questionj 99 Article: 1

Whether the Old Law contains only one precept?

Objection 1: It would seem that the Old Law contains but one precept. Because a law is nothing else than a precept, as stated above (Question [90], Articles [2],3). Now there is but one Old Law. Therefore it contains but one precept.

Objection 2: Further, the Apostle says (Rm. 13:9): "If there be any other commandment, it is comprised in this word: Thou shalt love thy neighbor as thyself." But this is only one commandment. Therefore the Old Law contained but one commandment.

Objection 3: Further, it is written (Mt. 7:12): "All things . . . whatsoever you would that men should do to you, do you also to them. For this is the Law and the prophets." But the whole of the Old Law is comprised in the Law and the prophets. Therefore the whole of the Old Law contains but one commandment.

On the contrary, The Apostle says (Eph. 2:15): "Making void the Law of commandments contained in decrees": where he is referring to the Old Law, as the gloss comments, on the passage. Therefore the Old Law comprises many commandments.

I answer that, Since a precept of law is binding, it is about something which must be done: and, that a thing must be done, arises from the necessity of some end. Hence it is evident that a precept implies, in its very idea, relation to an end, in so far as a thing is commanded as being necessary or expedient to an end. Now many things may happen to be necessary or expedient to an end; and, accordingly, precepts may be given about various things as being ordained to one end. Consequently we must say that all the precepts of the Old Law are one in respect of their relation to one end: and yet they are many in respect of the diversity of those things that are ordained to that end.

Reply to Objection 1: The Old Law is said to be one as being ordained to one end: yet it comprises various precepts, according to the diversity of the things which it directs to the end. Thus also the art of building is one according to the unity of its end, because it aims at the building of a house: and yet it contains various rules, according to the variety of acts ordained thereto.

Reply to Objection 2: As the Apostle says (1 Tim. 1:5), "the end of the commandment is charity"; since every law aims at establishing friendship, either between man and man, or between man and God. Wherefore the whole Law is comprised in this one commandment, "Thou shalt love thy neighbor as thyself," as expressing the end of all commandments: because love of one's neighbor includes love of God, when we love our neighbor for God's sake. Hence the Apostle put this commandment in place of the two which are about the love of God and of one's neighbor, and of which Our Lord said (Mt. 22:40): "On these two commandments dependeth the whole Law and the prophets."

Reply to Objection 3: As stated in Ethic. ix, 8, "friendship towards another arises from friendship towards oneself," in so far as man looks on another as on himself. Hence when it is said, "All things whatsoever you would that men should do to you, do you also to them," this is an explanation of the rule of neighborly love contained implicitly in the words, "Thou shalt love thy neighbor as thyself": so that it is an explanation of this commandment.

Article: 2

Whether the Old Law contains moral precepts?

Objection 1: It would seem that the Old Law contains no moral precepts. For the Old Law is distinct from the law of nature, as stated above (Question [91], Articles [4],5; Question [98], Article [5]). But the moral precepts belong to the law of nature. Therefore they do not belong to the Old Law.

Objection 2: Further, the Divine Law should have come to man's assistance where human reason fails him: as is evident in regard to things that are of faith, which are above reason. But man's reason seems to suffice for the moral precepts. Therefore the moral precepts do not belong to the Old Law, which is a Divine law.

Objection 3: Further, the Old Law is said to be "the letter that killeth" (2 Cor. 3:6). But the moral precepts do not kill, but quicken, according to Ps. 118:93: "Thy justifications I will never forget, for by them Thou hast given me life." Therefore the moral precepts do not belong to the Old Law.

On the contrary, It is written (Ecclus. 17:9): "Moreover, He gave them discipline [Douay: 'instructions'] and the law of life for an inheritance." Now discipline belongs to morals; for this gloss on Heb. 12:11: "Now all chastisement [disciplina]," etc., says: "Discipline is an exercise in morals by means of difficulties." Therefore the Law which was given by God comprised moral precepts.

I answer that, The Old Law contained some moral precepts; as is evident from Ex. 20:13,15: "Thou shalt not kill, Thou shalt not steal." This was reasonable: because, just as the principal intention of human law is to created friendship between man and man; so the chief intention of the Divine law is to establish man in friendship with God. Now since likeness is the reason of love, according to Ecclus. 13:19: "Every beast loveth its like"; there cannot possibly be any friendship of man to God, Who is supremely good, unless man become good: wherefore it is written (Lev. 19:2; 11:45): "You shall be holy, for I am holy." But the goodness of man is virtue, which "makes its possessor good" (Ethic. ii, 6). Therefore it was necessary for the Old Law to include precepts about acts of virtue: and these are the moral precepts of the Law.

Reply to Objection 1: The Old Law is distinct from the natural law, not as being altogether different from it, but as something added thereto. For just as grace presupposes nature, so must the Divine law presuppose the natural law.

Reply to Objection 2: It was fitting that the Divine law should come to man's assistance not only in those things for which reason is insufficient, but also in those things in which human reason may happen to be impeded. Now human reason could not go astray in the abstract, as to the universal principles of the natural law; but through being habituated to sin, it became obscured in the point of things to be done in detail. But with regard to the other moral precepts, which are like conclusions drawn from the universal principles of the natural law, the reason of many men went astray, to the extend of judging to be lawful, things that are evil in themselves. Hence there was need for the authority of the Divine law to rescue man from both these defects. Thus among the articles of faith not only are those things set forth to which reason cannot reach, such as the Trinity of the Godhead; but also those to which right reason can attain, such as the Unity of the Godhead; in order to remove the manifold errors to which reason is liable.

Reply to Objection 3: As Augustine proves (De Spiritu et Litera xiv), even the letter of the law is said to be the occasion of death, as to the moral precepts; in so far as, to wit, it prescribes what is good, without furnishing the aid of grace for its fulfilment.

Article: 3 Whether the Old Law comprises ceremonial, besides moral, precepts?

Objection 1: It would seem that the Old Law does not comprise ceremonial, besides moral, precepts. For every law that is given to man is for the purpose of directing human actions. Now human actions are called moral, as stated above (Question [1], Article [3]). Therefore it seems that the Old Law given to men should not comprise other than moral precepts.

Objection 2: Further, those precepts that are styled ceremonial seem to refer to the Divine worship. But Divine worship is the act of a virtue, viz. religion, which, as Tully says (De Invent. ii) "offers worship and ceremony to the Godhead." Since, then, the moral precepts are about acts of virtue, as stated above (Article [2]), it seems that the ceremonial precepts should not be distinct from the moral.

Objection 3: Further, the ceremonial precepts seem to be those which signify something figuratively. But, as Augustine observes (De Doctr. Christ. ii, 3,4), "of all signs employed by men words hold the first place." Therefore there is no need for the Law to contain ceremonial precepts about certain figurative actions.

On the contrary, It is written (Dt. 4:13,14): "Ten words . . . He wrote in two tables of stone; and He commanded me at that time that I should teach you the ceremonies and judgments which you shall do." But the ten commandments of the Law are moral precepts. Therefore besides the moral precepts there are others which are ceremonial.

I answer that, As stated above (Article [2]), the Divine law is instituted chiefly in order to direct men to God; while human law is instituted chiefly in order to direct men in relation to one another. Hence human laws have not concerned themselves with the institution of anything relating to Divine worship except as affecting the common good of mankind: and for this reason they have devised many institutions relating to Divine matters, according as it seemed expedient for the formation of human morals; as may be seen in the rites of the Gentiles. On the other hand the Divine law directed men to one another according to the demands of that order whereby man is directed to God, which order was the chief aim of that law. Now man is directed to God not only by the interior acts of the mind, which are faith, hope, and love, but also by certain external works, whereby man makes profession of his subjection to God: and it is these works that are said to belong to the Divine worship. This worship is called "ceremony" [the munia, i.e. gifts] of Ceres (who was the goddess of fruits), as some say: because, at first, offerings were made to God from the fruits: or because, as Valerius Maximus states [*Fact. et Dict. Memor. i, 1], the word "ceremony" was introduced among the Latins, to signify the Divine worship, being derived from a town near Rome called "Caere": since, when Rome was taken by the Gauls, the sacred chattels of the Romans were taken thither and most carefully preserved.

Accordingly those precepts of the Law which refer to the Divine worship are specially called ceremonial.

Reply to Objection 1: Human acts extend also to the Divine worship: and therefore the Old Law given to man contains precepts about these matters also.

Reply to Objection 2: As stated above (Question [91], Article [3]), the precepts of the natural law are general, and require to be determined: and they are determined both by human law and by Divine law. And just as these very determinations which are made by human law are said to be, not of natural, but of positive law; so the determinations of the precepts of the natural law, effected by the Divine law, are distinct from the moral precepts which belong to the natural law. Wherefore to worship God, since it is an act of virtue, belongs to a moral precept; but the determination of this precept, namely that He is to be worshipped by such and such sacrifices, and such and such offerings, belongs to the ceremonial precepts. Consequently the ceremonial precepts are distinct from the moral precepts.

Reply to Objection 3: As Dionysius says (Coel. Hier. i), the things of God cannot be manifested to men except by means of sensible similitudes. Now these similitudes move the soul more when they are not only expressed in words, but also offered to the senses. Wherefore the things of God are set forth in the Scriptures not only by similitudes expressed in words, as in the case of metaphorical expressions; but also by similitudes of things set before the eyes, which pertains to the ceremonial precepts.

Article: 4

Whether, besides the moral and ceremonial precepts, there are also judicial precepts?

Objection 1: It would seem that there are no judicial precepts in addition to the moral and ceremonial precepts in the Old Law. For Augustine says (Contra Faust. vi, 2) that in the Old Law there are "precepts concerning the life we have to lead, and precepts regarding the life that is foreshadowed." Now the precepts of the life we have to lead are moral precepts; and the precepts of the life that is foreshadowed are ceremonial. Therefore besides these two kinds of precepts we should not put any judicial precepts in the Law.

Objection 2: Further, a gloss on Ps. 118:102, "I have not declined from Thy judgments," says, i.e. "from the rule of life Thou hast set for me." But a rule of life belongs to the moral precepts. Therefore the judicial precepts should not be considered as distinct from the moral precepts.

Objection 3: Further, judgment seems to be an act of justice, according to Ps. 93:15: "Until justice be turned into judgment." But acts of justice, like the acts of other virtues, belong to the moral precepts. Therefore the moral precepts include the judicial precepts, and consequently should not be held as distinct from them.

On the contrary, It is written (Dt. 6:1): "These are the precepts and ceremonies, and judgments": where "precepts" stands for "moral precepts" antonomastically. Therefore there are judicial precepts besides moral and ceremonial precepts.

I answer that, As stated above (Articles [2],3), it belongs to the Divine law to direct men to one another and to God. Now each of these belongs in the abstract to the dictates of the natural law, to which dictates the moral precepts are to be referred: yet each of them has to be determined by Divine or human law, because naturally known principles are universal, both in speculative and in practical matters. Accordingly just as the determination of the universal principle about Divine worship is effected by the ceremonial precepts, so the determination of the general precepts of that justice which is to be observed among men is effected by the judicial precepts.

We must therefore distinguish three kinds of precept in the Old Law; viz. "moral" precepts, which are dictated by the natural law; "ceremonial" precepts, which are determinations of the Divine worship; and "judicial" precepts, which are determinations of the justice to be maintained among men. Wherefore the Apostle (Rm. 7:12) after saying that the "Law is holy," adds that "the commandment is just, and holy, and good": "just," in respect of the judicial precepts; "holy," with regard to the ceremonial precepts (since the word "sanctus"---"holy"---is applied to that which is consecrated to God); and "good," i.e. conducive to virtue, as to the moral precepts.

Reply to Objection 1: Both the moral and the judicial precepts aim at the ordering of human life: and consequently they are both comprised under one of the heads mentioned by Augustine, viz. under the precepts of the life we have to lead.

Reply to Objection 2: Judgment denotes execution of justice, by an application of the reason to individual cases in a determinate way. Hence the judicial precepts have something in common with the moral precepts, in that they are derived from reason; and something in common with the ceremonial precepts, in that they are determinations of general precepts. This explains why sometimes "judgments" comprise both judicial and moral precepts, as in Dt. 5:1: "Hear, O Israel, the ceremonies and judgments"; and sometimes judicial and ceremonial precepts, as in Lev. 18:4: "You shall do My judgments, and shall observe My precepts," where "precepts" denotes moral precepts, while "judgments" refers to judicial and ceremonial precepts.

Reply to Objection 3: The act of justice, in general, belongs to the moral precepts; but its determination to some special kind of act belongs to the judicial precepts.

Article: 5

Whether the Old Law contains any others besides the moral, judicial, and ceremonial precepts?

Objection 1: It would seem that the Old Law contains others besides the moral, judicial, and ceremonial precepts. Because the judicial precepts belong to the act of justice, which is between man and man; while the ceremonial precepts belong to the act of religion, whereby God is worshipped. Now besides these there are many other virtues, viz. temperance, fortitude, liberality, and several others, as stated above (Question [60], Article [5]). Therefore besides the aforesaid precepts, the Old Law should comprise others.

Objection 2: Further, it is written (Dt. 11:1): "Love the Lord thy God, and observe His precepts and ceremonies, His judgments and commandments." Now precepts concern moral matters, as stated above (Article [4]). Therefore besides the moral, judicial and ceremonial precepts, the Law contains others which are called "commandments." [*The "commandments" (mandata) spoken of here and in the body of this article are not to be confused with the Commandments (praecepta) in the ordinary acceptance of the word.]

Objection 3: Further, it is written (Dt. 6:17): "Keep the precepts of the Lord thy God, and the testimonies and ceremonies which I have [Vulg.: 'He hath'] commanded thee." Therefore in addition to the above, the Law comprises "testimonies."

Objection 4: Further, it is written (Ps. 118:93): "Thy justifications (i.e. "Thy Law," according to a gloss) I will never forget." Therefore in the Old Law there are not only moral, ceremonial and judicial precepts, but also others, called "justifications."

On the contrary, It is written (Dt. 6:1): "These are the precepts and ceremonies and judgments which the Lord your God commanded . . . you." And these words are placed at the beginning of the Law. Therefore all the precepts of the Law are included under them.

I answer that, Some things are included in the Law by way of precept; other things, as being ordained to the fulfilment of the precepts. Now the precepts refer to things which have to be done: and to their fulfilment man is induced by two considerations, viz. the authority of the lawgiver, and the benefit derived from the fulfilment, which benefit consists in the attainment of some good, useful, pleasurable or virtuous, or in the avoidance of some contrary evil. Hence it was necessary that in the Old Law certain things should be set forth to indicate the authority of God the lawgiver: e.g. Dt. 6:4: "Hear, O Israel, the Lord our God is one Lord"; and Gn. 1:1: "In the beginning God created heaven and earth": and these are called "testimonies." Again it was necessary that in the Law certain rewards should be appointed for those who observe the Law, and punishments for those who transgress; as it may be seen in Dt. 28: "If thou wilt hear the voice of the Lord thy God . . . He will make thee higher than all the nations," etc.: and these are called "justifications," according as God punishes or rewards certain ones justly.

The things that have to be done do not come under the precept except in so far as they have the character of a duty. Now a duty is twofold: one according to the rule of reason; the other according to the rule of a law which prescribes that duty: thus the Philosopher distinguishes a twofold just---moral and legal (Ethic. v, 7).

Moral duty is twofold: because reason dictates that something must be done, either as being so necessary that without it the order of virtue would be destroyed; or as being useful for the better maintaining of the order of virtue. And in this sense some of the moral precepts are expressed by way of absolute command or prohibition, as "Thou shalt not kill, Thou shalt not steal": and these are properly called "precepts." Other things are prescribed or forbidden, not as an absolute duty, but as something better to be done. These may be called "commandments"; because they are expressed by way of inducement and persuasion: an example whereof is seen in Ex. 22:26: "If thou take of thy neighbor a garment in pledge, thou shalt give it him again before sunset"; and in other like cases. Wherefore Jerome (Praefat. in Comment. super Marc.) says that "justice is in the precepts, charity in the commandments." Duty as fixed by the Law, belongs to the judicial precepts, as regards human affairs; to the "ceremonial" precepts, as regards Divine matters.

Nevertheless those ordinances also which refer to punishments and rewards may be called "testimonies," in so far as they testify to the Divine justice. Again all the precepts of the Law may be styled "justifications," as being executions of legal justice. Furthermore the commandments may be distinguished from the precepts, so that those things be called "precepts" which God Himself prescribed; and those things "commandments" which He enjoined [mandavit] through others, as the very word seems to denote.

From this it is clear that all the precepts of the Law are either moral, ceremonial, or judicial; and that other ordinances have not the character of a precept, but are directed to the observance of the precepts, as stated above.

Reply to Objection 1: Justice alone, of all the virtues, implies the notion of duty. Consequently moral matters are determinable by law in so far as they belong to justice: of which virtue religion is a part, as Tully says (De Invent. ii). Wherefore the legal just cannot be anything foreign to the ceremonial and judicial precepts.

The Replies to the other Objections are clear from what has been said.

Article: 6

Whether the Old Law should have induced men to the observance of its precepts, by means of temporal promises and threats?

Objection 1: It would seem that the Old Law should not have induced men to the observance of its precepts, by means of temporal promises and threats. For the purpose of the Divine law is to subject man to God by fear and love: hence it is written (Dt. 10:12): "And now, Israel, what doth the Lord thy God require of thee, but that thou fear the Lord thy God, and walk in His ways, and love Him?" But the desire for temporal goods leads man away from God: for Augustine says (Qq. lxxxiii, qu. 36), that "covetousness is the bane of charity." Therefore temporal promises and threats seem to be contrary to the intention of a lawgiver: and this makes a law worthy of rejection, as the Philosopher declares (Polit. ii, 6).

Objection 2: Further, the Divine law is more excellent than human law. Now, in sciences, we notice that the loftier the science, the higher the means of persuasion that it employs. Therefore, since human law employs temporal threats and promises, as means of persuading man, the Divine law should have used, not these, but more lofty means.

Objection 3: Further, the reward of righteousness and the punishment of guilt cannot be that which befalls equally the good and the wicked. But as stated in Eccles. 9:2, "all" temporal "things equally happen to the just and to the wicked, to the good and the evil, to the clean and to the unclean, to him that offereth victims, and to him that despiseth sacrifices." Therefore temporal goods or evils are not suitably set forth as punishments or rewards of the commandments of the Divine law.

On the contrary, It is written (Is. 1:19,20): "If you be willing, and will hearken to Me, you shall eat the good things of the land. But if you will not, and will provoke Me to wrath: the sword shall devour you."

I answer that, As in speculative sciences men are persuaded to assent to the conclusions by means of syllogistic arguments, so too in every law, men are persuaded to observe its precepts by means of punishments and rewards. Now it is to be observed that, in speculative sciences, the means of persuasion are adapted to the conditions of the pupil: wherefore the process of argument in sciences should be ordered becomingly, so that the instruction is based on principles more generally known. And thus also he who would persuade a man to the observance of any precepts, needs to move him at first by things for which he has an affection; just as children are induced to do something, by means of little childish gifts. Now it has been said above (Question [98], Articles [1],2,3) that the Old Law disposed men to (the coming of) Christ, as the imperfect in comparison disposes to the perfect, wherefore it was given to a people as yet imperfect in comparison to the perfection which was to result from Christ's coming: and for this reason, that people is compared to a child that is still under a pedagogue (Gal. 3:24). But the perfection of man consists in his despising temporal things and cleaving to things spiritual, as is clear from the words of the Apostle (Phil. 3:13,15): "Forgetting the things that are behind, I stretch [Vulg.: 'and stretching'] forth myself to those that are before . . . Let us therefore, as many as are perfect, be thus minded." Those who are yet imperfect desire temporal goods, albeit in subordination to God: whereas the perverse place their end in temporalities. It was therefore fitting that the Old Law should conduct men to God by means of temporal goods for which the imperfect have an affection.

Reply to Objection 1: Covetousness whereby man places his end in temporalities, is the bane of charity. But the attainment of temporal goods which man desires in subordination to God is a road leading the imperfect to the love of God, according to Ps. 48:19: "He will praise Thee, when Thou shalt do well to him."

Reply to Objection 2: Human law persuades men by means of temporal rewards or punishments to be inflicted by men: whereas the Divine law persuades men by meas of rewards or punishments to be received from God. In this respect it employs higher means.

Reply to Objection 3: As any one can see, who reads carefully the story of the Old Testament, the common weal of the people prospered under the Law as long as they obeyed it; and as soon as they departed from the precepts of the Law they were overtaken by many calamities. But certain individuals, although they observed the justice of the Law, met with misfortunes---either because they had already become spiritual (so that misfortune might withdraw them all the more from attachment to temporal things, and that their virtue might be tried)---or because, while outwardly fulfilling the works of the Law, their heart was altogether fixed on temporal goods, and far removed from God, according to Is. 29:13 (Mt. 15:8): "This people honoreth Me with their lips; but their hearts is far from Me."

OF THE MORAL PRECEPTS OF THE OLD LAW (TWELVE ARTICLES)

We must now consider each kind of precept of the Old Law: and (1) the moral precepts, (2) the ceremonial precepts, (3) the judicial precepts. Under the first head there are twelve points of inquiry:

(1) Whether all the moral precepts of the Old Law belong to the law of nature?
(2) Whether the moral precepts of the Old Law are about the acts of all the virtues?
(3) Whether all the moral precepts of the Old Law are reducible to the ten precepts of the decalogue?
(4) How the precepts of the decalogue are distinguished from one another?
(5) Their number;
(6) Their order;
(7) The manner in which they were given;
(8) Whether they are dispensable?
(9) Whether the mode of observing a virtue comes under the precept of the Law?
(10) Whether the mode of charity comes under the precept?
(11) The distinction of other moral precepts;
(12) Whether the moral precepts of the Old Law justified man?

Question 100 Article: 1

Whether all the moral precepts of the Old Law belong to the law of nature?

Objection 1: It would seem that not all the moral precepts belong to the law of nature. For it is written (Ecclus. 17:9): "Moreover He gave them instructions, and the law of life for an inheritance." But instruction is in contradistinction to the law of nature; since the law of nature is not learnt, but instilled by natural instinct. Therefore not all the moral precepts belong to the natural law.

Objection 2: Further, the Divine law is more perfect than human law. But human law adds certain things concerning good morals, to those that belong to the law of nature: as is evidenced by the fact that the natural law is the same in all men, while these moral institutions are various for various people. Much more reason therefore was there why the Divine law should add to the law of nature, ordinances pertaining to good morals.

Objection 3: Further, just as natural reason leads to good morals in certain matters, so does faith: hence it is written (Gal. 5:6) that faith "worketh by charity." But faith is not included in the law of nature; since that which is of faith is above nature. Therefore not all the moral precepts of the Divine law belong to the law of nature.

On the contrary, The Apostle says (Rm. 2:14) that "the Gentiles, who have not the Law, do by nature those things that are of the Law": which must be understood of things pertaining to good morals. Therefore all the moral precepts of the Law belong to the law of nature.

I answer that, The moral precepts, distinct from the ceremonial and judicial precepts, are about things pertaining of their very nature to good morals. Now since human morals depend on their relation to reason, which is the proper principle of human acts, those morals are called good which accord with reason, and those are called bad which are discordant from reason. And as every judgment of speculative reason proceeds from the natural knowledge of first principles, so every judgment of practical reason proceeds from principles known naturally, as stated above (Question [94], Articles [2],4): from which principles one may proceed in various ways to judge of various matters. For some matters connected with human actions are so evident, that after very little consideration one is able at once to approve or disapprove of them by means of these general first principles: while some matters cannot be the subject of judgment without much consideration of the various circumstances, which all are not competent to do carefully, but only those who are wise: just as it is not possible for all to consider the particular conclusions of sciences, but only for those who are versed in philosophy: and lastly there are some matters of which man cannot judge unless he be helped by Divine instruction; such as the articles of faith.

It is therefore evident that since the moral precepts are about matters which concern good morals; and since good morals are those which are in accord with reason; and since also every judgment of human reason must needs by derived in some way from natural reason; it follows, of necessity, that all the moral precepts belong to the law of nature; but not all in the same way. For there are certain things which the natural reason of every man, of its own accord and at once, judges to be done or not to be done: e.g. "Honor thy father and thy mother," and "Thou shalt not kill, Thou shalt not steal": and these belong to the law of nature absolutely. And there are certain things which, after a more careful consideration, wise men deem obligatory. Such belong to the law of nature, yet so that they need to be inculcated, the wiser teaching the less wise: e.g. "Rise up before the hoary head, and honor the person of the aged man," and the like. And there are some things, to judge of which, human reason needs Divine instruction, whereby we are taught about the things of God: e.g. "Thou shalt not make to thyself a graven thing, nor the likeness of anything; Thou shalt not take the name of the Lord thy God in vain."

This suffices for the Replies to the Objections.

Article: 2 Whether the moral precepts of the Law are about all the acts of virtue?

Objection 1: It would seem that the moral precepts of the Law are not about all the acts of virtue. For observance of the precepts of the Old Law is called justification, according to Ps. 118:8: "I will keep Thy justifications." But justification is the execution of justice. Therefore the moral precepts are only about acts of justice.

Objection 2: Further, that which comes under a precept has the character of a duty. But the character of duty belongs to justice alone and to none of the other virtues, for the proper act of justice consists in rendering to each one his due. Therefore the precepts of the moral law are not about the acts of the other virtues, but only about the acts of justice.

Objection 3: Further, every law is made for the common good, as Isidore says (Etym. v, 21). But of all the virtues justice alone regards the common good, as the Philosopher says (Ethic. v, 1). Therefore the moral precepts are only about the acts of justice.

On the contrary, Ambrose says (De Paradiso viii) that "a sin is a transgression of the Divine law, and a disobedience to the commandments of heaven." But there are sins contrary to all the acts of virtue. Therefore it belongs to Divine law to direct all the acts of virtue.

I answer that, Since the precepts of the Law are ordained to the common good, as stated above (Question [90], Article [2]), the precepts of the Law must needs be diversified according to the various kinds of community: hence the Philosopher (Polit. iv, 1) teaches that the laws which are made in a state which is ruled by a king must be different from the laws of a state which is ruled by the people, or by a few powerful men in the state. Now human law is ordained for one kind of community, and the Divine law for another kind. Because human law is ordained for the civil community, implying mutual duties of man and his fellows: and men are ordained to one another by outward acts, whereby men live in communion with one another. This life in common of man with man pertains to justice, whose proper function consists in directing the human community. Wherefore human law makes precepts only about acts of justice; and if it commands acts of other virtues, this is only in so far as they assume the nature of justice, as the Philosopher explains (Ethic. v, 1).

But the community for which the Divine law is ordained, is that of men in relation to God, either in this life or in the life to come. And therefore the Divine law proposes precepts about all those matters whereby men are well ordered in their relations to God. Now man is united to God by his reason or mind, in which is God's image. Wherefore the Divine law proposes precepts about all those matters whereby human reason is well ordered. But this is effected by the acts of all the virtues: since the intellectual virtues set in good order the acts of the reason in themselves: while the moral virtues set in good order the acts of the reason in reference to the interior passions and exterior actions. It is therefore evident that the Divine law fittingly proposes precepts about the acts of all the virtues: yet so that certain matters, without which the order of virtue, which is the order of reason, cannot even exist, come under an obligation of precept; while other matters, which pertain to the well-being of perfect virtue, come under an admonition of counsel.

Reply to Objection 1: The fulfilment of the commandments of the Law, even of those which are about the acts of the other virtues, has the character of justification, inasmuch as it is just that man should obey God: or again, inasmuch as it is just that all that belongs to man should be subject to reason.

Reply to Objection 2: Justice properly so called regards the duty of one man to another: but all the other virtues regard the duty of the lower powers to reason. It is in relation to this latter duty that the Philosopher speaks (Ethic. v, 11) of a kind of metaphorical justice.

The Reply to the Third Objection is clear from what has been said about the different kinds of community.

Article: 3

Whether all the moral precepts of the Old Law are reducible to the ten precepts of the decalogue?

Objection 1: It would seem that not all the moral precepts of the Old Law are reducible to the ten precepts of the decalogue. For the first and principal precepts of the Law are, "Thou shalt love the Lord thy God," and "Thou shalt love thy neighbor," as stated in Mt. 22:37,39. But these two are not contained in the precepts of the decalogue. Therefore not all the moral precepts are contained in the precepts of the decalogue.

Objection 2: Further, the moral precepts are not reducible to the ceremonial precepts, but rather vice versa. But among the precepts of the decalogue, one is ceremonial, viz. "Remember that thou keep holy the Sabbath-day." Therefore the moral precepts are not reducible to all the precepts of the decalogue.

Objection 3: Further, the moral precepts are about all the acts of virtue. But among the precepts of the decalogue are only such as regard acts of justice; as may be seen by going through them all. Therefore the precepts of the decalogue do not include all the moral precepts.

On the contrary, The gloss on Mt. 5:11: "Blessed are ye when they shall revile you," etc. says that "Moses, after propounding the ten precepts, set them out in detail." Therefore all the precepts of the Law are so many parts of the precepts of the decalogue.

I answer that, The precepts of the decalogue differ from the other precepts of the Law, in the fact that God Himself is said to have given the precepts of the decalogue; whereas He gave the other precepts to the people through Moses. Wherefore the decalogue includes those precepts the knowledge of which man has immediately from God. Such are those which with but slight reflection can be gathered at once from the first general principles: and those also which become known to man immediately through divinely infused faith. Consequently two kinds of precepts are not reckoned among the precepts of the decalogue: viz. first general principles, for they need no further promulgation after being once imprinted on the natural reason to which they are self-evident; as, for instance, that one should do evil to no man, and other similar principles: and again those which the careful reflection of wise men shows to be in accord with reason; since the people receive these principles from God, through being taught by wise men. Nevertheless both kinds of precepts are contained in the precepts of the decalogue; yet in different ways. For the first general principles are contained in them, as principles in their proximate conclusions; while those which are known through wise men are contained, conversely, as conclusions in their principles.

Reply to Objection 1: Those two principles are the first general principles of the natural law, and are self-evident to human reason, either through nature or through faith. Wherefore all the precepts of the decalogue are referred to these, as conclusions to general principles.

Reply to Objection 2: The precept of the Sabbath observance is moral in one respect, in so far as it commands man to give some time to the things of God, according to Ps. 45:11: "Be still and see that I am God." In this respect it is placed among the precepts of the decalogue: but not as to the fixing of the time, in which respect it is a ceremonial precept.

Reply to Objection 3: The notion of duty is not so patent in the other virtues as it is in justice. Hence the precepts about the acts of the other virtues are not so well known to the people as are the precepts about acts of justice. Wherefore the acts of justice especially come under the precepts of the decalogue, which are the primary elements of the Law.

Article: 4 Whether the precepts of the decalogue are suitably distinguished from one another?

Objection 1: It would seem that the precepts of the decalogue are unsuitably distinguished from one another. For worship is a virtue distinct from faith. Now the precepts are about acts of virtue. But that which is said at the beginning of the decalogue, "Thou shalt not have strange gods before Me," belongs to faith: and that which is added, "Thou shalt not make . . . any graven thing," etc. belongs to worship. Therefore these are not one precept, as Augustine asserts (Qq. in Exod. qu. lxxi), but two.

Objection 2: Further, the affirmative precepts in the Law are distinct from the negative precepts; e.g. "Honor thy father and thy mother," and, "Thou shalt not kill." But this, "I am the Lord thy God," is affirmative: and that which follows, "Thou shalt not have strange gods before Me," is negative. Therefore these are two precepts, and do not, as Augustine says (Qq. in Exod. qu. lxxi), make one.

Objection 3: Further, the Apostle says (Rm. 7:7): "I had not known concupiscence, if the Law did not say: 'Thou shalt not covet.'" Hence it seems that this precept, "Thou shalt not covet," is one precept; and, therefore, should not be divided into two.

On the contrary, stands the authority of Augustine who, in commenting on Exodus (Qq. in Exod. qu. lxxi) distinguishes three precepts as referring to God, and seven as referring to our neighbor.

I answer that, The precepts of the decalogue are differently divided by different authorities. For Hesychius commenting on Lev. 26:26, "Ten women shall bake your bread in one oven," says that the precept of the Sabbath-day observance is not one of the ten precepts, because its observance, in the letter, is not binding for all time. But he distinguishes four precepts pertaining to God, the first being, "I am the Lord thy God"; the second, "Thou shalt not have strange gods before Me," (thus also Jerome distinguishes these two precepts, in his commentary on Osee 10:10, "On thy" [Vulg.: "their"] "two iniquities"); the third precept according to him is, "Thou shalt not make to thyself any graven thing"; and the fourth, "Thou shalt not take the name of the Lord thy God in vain." He states that there are six precepts pertaining to our neighbor; the first, "Honor thy father and thy mother"; the second, "Thou shalt not kill"; the third, "Thou shalt not commit adultery"; the fourth, "Thou shalt not steal"; the fifth, "Thou shalt not bear false witness"; the sixth, "Thou shalt not covet."

But, in the first place, it seems unbecoming for the precept of the Sabbath-day observance to be put among the precepts of the decalogue, if it nowise belonged to the decalogue. Secondly, because, since it is written (Mt. 6:24), "No man can serve two masters," the two statements, "I am the Lord thy God," and, "Thou shalt not have strange gods before Me" seem to be of the same nature and to form one precept. Hence Origen (Hom. viii in Exod.) who also distinguishes four precepts as referring to God, unites these two under one precept; and reckons in the second place, "Thou shalt not make . . . any graven thing"; as third, "Thou shalt not take the name of the Lord thy God in vain"; and as fourth, "Remember that thou keep holy the Sabbath-day." The other six he reckons in the same way as Hesychius.

Since, however, the making of graven things or the likeness of anything is not forbidden except as to the point of their being worshipped as gods---for God commanded an image of the Seraphim [Vulg.: Cherubim] to be made and placed in the tabernacle, as related in Ex. 25:18---Augustine more fittingly unites these two, "Thou shalt not have strange gods before Me," and, "Thou shalt not make . . . any graven thing," into one precept. Likewise to covet another's wife, for the purpose of carnal knowledge, belongs to the concupiscence of the flesh; whereas, to covet other things, which are desired for the purpose of possession, belongs to the concupiscence of the eyes; wherefore Augustine reckons as distinct precepts, that which forbids the coveting of another's goods, and that which prohibits the coveting of another's wife. Thus he distinguishes three precepts as referring to God, and seven as referring to our neighbor. And this is better.

Reply to Objection 1: Worship is merely a declaration of faith: wherefore the precepts about worship should not be reckoned as distinct from those about faith. Nevertheless precepts should be given about worship rather than about faith, because the precept about faith is presupposed to the precepts of the decalogue, as is also the precept of charity. For just as the first general principles of the natural law are self-evident to a subject having natural reason, and need no promulgation; so also to believe in God is a first and self-evident principle to a subject possessed of faith: "for he that cometh to God, must believe that He is" (Heb. 11:6). Hence it needs no other promulgation that the infusion of faith.

Reply to Objection 2: The affirmative precepts are distinct from the negative, when one is not comprised in the other: thus that man should honor his parents does not include that he should not kill another man; nor does the latter include the former. But when an affirmative precept is included in a negative, or vice versa, we do not find that two distinct precepts are given: thus there is not one precept saying that "Thou shalt not steal," and another binding one to keep another's property intact, or to give it back to its owner. In the same way there are not different precepts about believing in God, and about not believing in strange gods.

Reply to Objection 3: All covetousness has one common ratio: and therefore the Apostle speaks of the commandment about covetousness as though it were one. But because there are various special kinds of covetousness, therefore Augustine distinguishes different prohibitions against coveting: for covetousness differs specifically in respect of the diversity of actions or things coveted, as the Philosopher says (Ethic. x, 5).

Article: 5

Whether the precepts of the decalogue are suitably set forth?

Objection 1: It would seem that the precepts of the decalogue are unsuitably set forth. Because sin, as stated by Ambrose (De Paradiso viii), is "a transgression of the Divine law and a disobedience to the commandments of heaven." But sins are distinguished according as man sins against God, or his neighbor, or himself. Since, then, the decalogue does not include any precepts directing man in his relations to himself, but only such as direct him in his relations to God and himself, it seems that the precepts of the decalogue are insufficiently enumerated.

Objection 2: Further, just as the Sabbath-day observance pertained to the worship of God, so also did the observance of other solemnities, and the offering of sacrifices. But the decalogue contains a precept about the Sabbath-day observance. Therefore it should contain others also, pertaining to the other solemnities, and to the sacrificial rite.

Objection 3: Further, as sins against God include the sin of perjury, so also do they include blasphemy, or other ways of lying against the teaching of God. But there is a precept forbidding perjury, "Thou shalt not take the name of the Lord thy God in vain." Therefore there should be also a precept of the decalogue forbidding blasphemy and false doctrine.

Objection 4: Further, just as man has a natural affection for his parents, so has he also for his children. Moreover the commandment of charity extends to all our neighbors. Now the precepts of the decalogue are ordained unto charity, according to 1 Tim. 1:5: "The end of the commandment is charity." Therefore as there is a precept referring to parents, so should there have been some precepts referring to children and other neighbors.

Objection 5: Further, in every kind of sin, it is possible to sin in thought or in deed. But in some kinds of sin, namely in theft and adultery, the prohibition of sins of deed, when it is said, "Thou shalt not commit adultery, Thou shalt not steal," is distinct from the prohibition of the sin of thought, when it is said, "Thou shalt not covet thy neighbor's goods," and, "Thou shalt not covet thy neighbor's wife." Therefore the same should have been done in regard to the sins of homicide and false witness.

Objection 6: Further, just as sin happens through disorder of the concupiscible faculty, so does it arise through disorder of the irascible part. But some precepts forbid inordinate concupiscence, when it is said, "Thou shalt not covet." Therefore the decalogue should have included some precepts forbidding the disorders of the irascible faculty. Therefore it seems that the ten precepts of the decalogue are unfittingly enumerated.

On the contrary, It is written (Dt. 4:13): "He shewed you His covenant, which He commanded you to do, and the ten words that He wrote in two tablets of stone."

I answer that, As stated above (Article [2]), just as the precepts of human law direct man in his relations to the human community, so the precepts of the Divine law direct man in his relations to a community or commonwealth of men under God. Now in order that any man may dwell aright in a community, two things are required: the first is that he behave well to the head of the community; the other is that he behave well to those who are his fellows and partners in the community. It is therefore necessary that the Divine law should contain in the first place precepts ordering man in his relations to God; and in the second place, other precepts ordering man in his relations to other men who are his neighbors and live with him under God.

Now man owes three things to the head of the community: first, fidelity; secondly, reverence; thirdly, service. Fidelity to his master consists in his not giving sovereign honor to another: and this is the sense of the first commandment, in the words "Thou shalt not have strange gods." Reverence to his master requires that he should do nothing injurious to him: and this is conveyed by the second commandment, "Thou shalt not take the name of the Lord thy God in vain." Service is due to the master in return for the benefits which his subjects receive from him: and to this belongs the third commandment of the sanctification of the Sabbath in memory of the creation of all things.

To his neighbors a man behaves himself well both in particular and in general. In particular, as to those to whom he is indebted, by paying his debts: and in this sense is to be taken the commandment about honoring one's parents. In general, as to all men, by doing harm to none, either by deed, or by word, or by thought. By deed, harm is done to one's neighbor---sometimes in his person, i.e. as to his personal existence; and this is forbidden by the words, "Thou shalt not kill": sometimes in a person united to him, as to the propagation of offspring; and this is prohibited by the words, "Thou shalt not commit adultery": sometimes in his possessions, which are directed to both the aforesaid; and with this regard to this it is said, "Thou shalt not steal." Harm done by word is forbidden when it is said, "Thou shalt not bear false witness against thy neighbor": harm done by thought is forbidden in the words, "Thou shalt not covet."

The three precepts that direct man in his behavior towards God may also be differentiated in this same way. For the first refers to deeds; wherefore it is said,

"Thou shalt not make . . . a graven thing": the second, to words; wherefore it is said, "Thou shalt not take the name of the Lord thy God in vain": the third, to thoughts; because the sanctification of the Sabbath, as the subject of a moral precept, requires repose of the heart in God. Or, according to Augustine (In Ps. 32: Conc. 1), by the first commandment we reverence the unity of the First Principle; by the second, the Divine truth; by the third, His goodness whereby we are sanctified, and wherein we rest as in our last end.

Reply to Objection 1: This objection may be answered in two ways. First, because the precepts of the decalogue can be reduced to the precepts of charity. Now there was need for man to receive a precept about loving God and his neighbor, because in this respect the natural law had become obscured on account of sin: but not about the duty of loving oneself, because in this respect the natural law retained its vigor: or again, because love of oneself is contained in the love of God and of one's neighbor: since true self-love consists in directing oneself to God. And for this reason the decalogue includes those precepts only which refer to our neighbor and to God.

Secondly, it may be answered that the precepts of the decalogue are those which the people received from God immediately; wherefore it is written (Dt. 10:4): "He wrote in the tables, according as He had written before, the ten words, which the Lord spoke to you." Hence the precepts of the decalogue need to be such as the people can understand at once. Now a precept implies the notion of duty. But it is easy for a man, especially for a believer, to understand that, of necessity, he owes certain duties to God and to his neighbor. But that, in matters which regard himself and not another, man has, of necessity, certain duties to himself, is not so evident: for, at the first glance, it seems that everyone is free in matters that concern himself. And therefore the precepts which prohibit disorders of a man with regard to himself, reach the people through the instruction of men who are versed through the instruction of men who are versed in such matters; and, consequently, they are not contained in the decalogue.

Reply to Objection 2: All the solemnities of the Old Law were instituted in celebration of some Divine favor, either in memory of past favors, or in sign of some favor to come: in like manner all the sacrifices were offered up with the same purpose. Now of all the Divine favors to be commemorated the chief was that of the Creation, which was called to mind by the sanctification of the Sabbath; wherefore the reason for this precept is given in Ex. 20:11: "In six days the Lord made heaven and earth," etc. And of all future blessings, the chief and final was the repose of the mind in God, either, in the present life, by grace, or, in the future life, by glory; which repose was also foreshadowed in the Sabbath-day observance: wherefore it is written (Is. 58:13): "If thou turn away thy foot from the Sabbath, from doing thy own will in My holy day, and call the Sabbath delightful, and the holy of the Lord glorious." Because these favors first and chiefly are borne in mind by men, especially by the faithful. But other solemnities were celebrated on account of certain particular favors temporal and transitory, such as the celebration of the Passover in memory of the past favor of the delivery from Egypt, and as a sign of the future Passion of Christ, which though temporal and transitory, brought us to the repose of the spiritual Sabbath. Consequently, the Sabbath alone, and none of the other solemnities and sacrifices, is mentioned in the precepts of the decalogue.

Reply to Objection 3: As the Apostle says (Heb. 6:16), "men swear by one greater than themselves; and an oath for confirmation is the end of all their controversy." Hence, since oaths are common to all, inordinate swearing is the matter of a special prohibition by a precept of the decalogue. According to one interpretation, however, the words, "Thou shalt not take the name of the Lord thy God in vain," are a prohibition of false doctrine, for one gloss expounds them thus: "Thou shalt not say that Christ is a creature."

Reply to Objection 4: That a man should not do harm to anyone is an immediate dictate of his natural reason: and therefore the precepts that forbid the doing of harm are binding on all men. But it is not an immediate dictate of natural reason that a man should do one thing in return for another, unless he happen to be indebted to someone. Now a son's debt to his father is so evident that one cannot get away from it by denying it: since the father is the principle of generation and being, and also of upbringing and teaching. Wherefore the decalogue does not prescribe deeds of kindness or service to be done to anyone except to one's parents. On the other hand parents do not seem to be indebted to their children for any favors received, but rather the reverse is the case. Again, a child is a part of his father; and "parents love their children as being a part of themselves," as the Philosopher states (Ethic. viii, 12). Hence, just as the decalogue contains no ordinance as to man's behavior towards himself, so, for the same reason, it includes no precept about loving one's children.

Reply to Objection 5: The pleasure of adultery and the usefulness of wealth, in so far as they have the character of pleasurable or useful good, are of themselves, objects of appetite: and for this reason they needed to be forbidden not only in the deed but also in the desire. But murder and falsehood are, of themselves, objects of repulsion (since it is natural for man to love his neighbor and the truth): and are desired only for the sake of something else. Consequently with regard to sins of murder and false witness, it was necessary to proscribe, not sins of thought, but only sins of deed.

Reply to Objection 6: As stated above (Question [25], Article [1]), all the passions of the irascible faculty arise from the passions of the concupiscible part. Hence, as the precepts of the decalogue are, as it were, the first elements of the Law, there was no need for mention of the irascible passions, but only of the concupiscible passions.

Article: 6 Whether the ten precepts of the decalogue are set in proper order?

Objection 1: It would seem that the ten precepts of the decalogue are not set in proper order. Because love of one's neighbor is seemingly previous to love of God, since our neighbor is better known to us than God is; according to 1 Jn. 4:20: "He that loveth not his brother, whom he seeth, how can he love God, Whom he seeth not?" But the first three precepts belong to the love of God, while the other seven pertain to the love of our neighbor. Therefore the precepts of the decalogue are not set in proper order.

Objection 2: Further, the acts of virtue are prescribed by the affirmative precepts, and acts of vice are forbidden by the negative precepts. But according to Boethius in his commentary on the Categories [*Lib. iv, cap. De Oppos.], vices should be uprooted before virtues are sown. Therefore among the precepts concerning our neighbor, the negative precepts should have preceded the affirmative.

Objection 3: Further, the precepts of the Law are about men's actions. But actions of thought precede actions of word or outward deed. Therefore the precepts about not coveting, which regard our thoughts, are unsuitably placed last in order.

On the contrary, The Apostle says (Rm. 13:1): "The things that are of God, are well ordered" [Vulg.: 'Those that are, are ordained of God']. But the precepts of the decalogue were given immediately by God, as stated above (Article [3]). Therefore they are arranged in becoming order.

I answer that, As stated above (Articles [3],5, ad 1), the precepts of the decalogue are such as the mind of man is ready to grasp at once. Now it is evident that a thing is so much the more easily grasped by the reason, as its contrary is more grievous and repugnant to reason. Moreover, it is clear, since the order of reason begins with the end, that, for a man to be inordinately disposed towards his end, is supremely contrary to reason. Now the end of human life and society is God. Consequently it was necessary for the precepts of the decalogue, first of all, to direct man to God; since the contrary to this is most grievous. Thus also, in an army, which is ordained to the commander as to its end, it is requisite first that the soldier should be subject to the commander, and the opposite of this is most grievous; and secondly it is requisite that he should be in coordination with the other soldiers.

Now among those things whereby we are ordained to God, the first is that man should be subjected to Him faithfully, by having nothing in common with His enemies. The second is that he should show Him reverence: the third that he should offer Him service. Thus, in an army, it is a greater sin for a soldier to act treacherously and make a compact with the foe, than to be insolent to his commander: and this last is more grievous than if he be found wanting in some point of service to him.

As to the precepts that direct man in his behavior towards his neighbor, it is evident that it is more repugnant to reason, and a more grievous sin, if man does not observe the due order as to those persons to whom he is most indebted. Consequently, among those precepts that direct man in his relations to his neighbor, the first place is given to that one which regards his parents. Among the other precepts we again find the order to be according to the gravity of sin. For it is more grave and more repugnant to reason, to sin by deed than by word; and by word than by thought. And among sins of deed, murder which destroys life in one already living is more grievous than adultery, which imperils the life of the unborn child; and adultery is more grave than theft, which regards external goods.

Reply to Objection 1: Although our neighbor is better known than God by the way of the senses, nevertheless the love of God is the reason for the love of our neighbor, as shall be declared later on (SS, Question [25], Article [1]; SS, Question [26], Article [2]). Hence the precepts ordaining man to God demanded precedence of the others.

Reply to Objection 2: Just as God is the universal principle of being in respect of all things, so is a father a principle of being in respect of his son. Therefore the precept regarding parents was fittingly placed after the precepts regarding God. This argument holds in respect of affirmative and negative precepts about the same kind of deed: although even then it is not altogether cogent. For although in the order of execution, vices should be uprooted before virtues are sown, according to Ps. 33:15: "Turn away from evil, and do good," and Is. 1:16,17: "Cease to do perversely; learn to do well"; yet, in the order of knowledge, virtue precedes vice, because "the crooked line is known by the straight" (De Anima i): and "by the law is the knowledge of sin" (Rm. 3:20). Wherefore the affirmation precept demanded the first place. However, this is not the reason for the order, but that which is given above. Because in the precepts regarding God, which belongs to the first table, an affirmative precept is placed last, since its transgression implies a less grievous sin.

Reply to Objection 3: Although sin of thought stands first in the order of execution, yet its prohibition holds a later position in the order of reason.

Article: 7

Whether the precepts of the decalogue are suitably formulated?

Objection 1: It would seem that the precepts of the decalogue are unsuitably formulated. Because the affirmative precepts direct man to acts of virtue, while the negative precepts withdraw him from acts of vice. But in every matter there are virtues and vices opposed to one another. Therefore in whatever matter there is an ordinance of a precept of the decalogue, there should have been an affirmative and a negative precept. Therefore it was unfitting that affirmative precepts should be framed in some matters, and negative precepts in others.

Objection 2: Further, Isidore says (Etym. ii, 10) that every law is based on reason. But all the precepts of the decalogue belong to the Divine law. Therefore the reason should have been pointed out in each precept, and not only in the first and third.

Objection 3: Further, by observing the precepts man deserves to be rewarded by God. But the Divine promises concern the rewards of the precepts. Therefore the promise should have been included in each precept, and not only in the second and fourth.

Objection 4: Further, the Old Law is called "the law of fear," in so far as it induced men to observe the precepts, by means of the threat of punishments. But all the precepts of the decalogue belong to the Old Law. Therefore a threat of punishment should have been included in each, and not only in the first and second.

Objection 5: Further, all the commandments of God should be retained in the memory: for it is written (Prov. 3:3): "Write them in the tables of thy heart." Therefore it was not fitting that mention of the memory should be made in the third commandment only. Consequently it seems that the precepts of the decalogue are unsuitably formulated.

On the contrary, It is written (Wis. 11:21) that "God made all things, in measure, number and weight." Much more therefore did He observe a suitable manner in formulating His Law.

I answer that, The highest wisdom is contained in the precepts of the Divine law: wherefore it is written (Dt. 4:6): "This is your wisdom and understanding in the sight of nations." Now it belongs to wisdom to arrange all things in due manner and order. Therefore it must be evident that the precepts of the Law are suitably set forth.

Reply to Objection 1: Affirmation of one thing always leads to the denial of its opposite: but the denial of one opposite does not always lead to the affirmation of the other. For it follows that if a thing is white, it is not black: but it does not follow that if it is not black, it is white: because negation extends further than affirmation. And hence too, that one ought not to do harm to another, which pertains to the negative precepts, extends to more persons, as a primary dictate of reason, than that one ought to do someone a service or kindness. Nevertheless it is a primary dictate of reason that man is a debtor in the point of rendering a service or kindness to those from whom he has received kindness, if he has not yet repaid the debt. Now there are two whose favors no man can sufficiently repay, viz. God and man's father, as stated in Ethic. viii, 14. Therefore it is that there are only two affirmative precepts; one about the honor due to parents, the other about the celebration of the Sabbath in memory of the Divine favor.

Reply to Objection 2: The reasons for the purely moral precepts are manifest; hence there was no need to add the reason. But some of the precepts include ceremonial matter, or a determination of a general moral precept; thus the first precept includes the determination, "Thou shalt not make a graven thing"; and in the third precept the Sabbath-day is fixed. Consequently there was need to state the reason in each case.

Reply to Objection 3: Generally speaking, men direct their actions to some point of utility. Consequently in those precepts in which it seemed that there would be no useful result, or that some utility might be hindered, it was necessary to add a promise of reward. And since parents are already on the way to depart from us, no benefit is expected from them: wherefore a promise of reward is added to the precept about honoring one's parents. The same applies to the precept forbidding idolatry: since thereby it seemed that men were hindered from receiving the apparent benefit which they think they can get by entering into a compact with the demons.

Reply to Objection 4: Punishments are necessary against those who are prone to evil, as stated in Ethic. x, 9. Wherefore a threat of punishment is only affixed to those precepts of the law which forbade evils to which men were prone. Now men were prone to idolatry by reason of the general custom of the nations. Likewise men are prone to perjury on account of the frequent use of oaths. Hence it is that a threat is affixed to the first two precepts.

Reply to Objection 5: The commandment about the Sabbath was made in memory of a past blessing. Wherefore special mention of the memory is made therein. Or again, the commandment about the Sabbath has a determination affixed to it that does not belong to the natural law, wherefore this precept needed a special admonition.

Article: 8

Whether the precepts of the decalogue are dispensable?

Objection 1: It would seem that the precepts of the decalogue are dispensable. For the precepts of the decalogue belong to the natural law. But the natural law fails in some cases and is changeable, like human nature, as the Philosopher says (Ethic. v, 7). Now the failure of law to apply in certain particular cases is a reason for dispensation, as stated above (Question [96], Article [6]; Question [97], Article [4]). Therefore a dispensation can be granted in the precepts of the decalogue.

Objection 2: Further, man stands in the same relation to human law as God does to Divine law. But man can dispense with the precepts of a law made by man. Therefore, since the precepts of the decalogue are ordained by God, it seems that God can dispense with them. Now our superiors are God's viceregents on earth; for the Apostle says (2 Cor. 2:10): "For what I have pardoned, if I have pardoned anything, for your sakes have I done it in the person of Christ." Therefore superiors can dispense with the precepts of the decalogue.

Objection 3: Further, among the precepts of the decalogue is one forbidding murder. But it seems that a dispensation is given by men in this precept: for instance, when according to the prescription of human law, such as evil-doers or enemies are lawfully slain. Therefore the precepts of the decalogue are dispensable.

Objection 4: Further, the observance of the Sabbath is ordained by a precept of the decalogue. But a dispensation was granted in this precept; for it is written (1 Macc. 2:4): "And they determined in that day, saying: Whosoever shall come up to fight against us on the Sabbath-day, we will fight against him." Therefore the precepts of the decalogue are dispensable.

On the contrary, are the words of Is. 24:5, where some are reproved for that "they have changed the ordinance, they have broken the everlasting covenant"; which, seemingly, apply principally to the precepts of the decalogue. Therefore the precepts of the decalogue cannot be changed by dispensation.

I answer that, As stated above (Question [96], Article [6]; Question [97], Article [4]), precepts admit of dispensation, when there occurs a particular case in which, if the letter of the law be observed, the intention of the lawgiver is frustrated. Now the intention of every lawgiver is directed first and chiefly to the common good; secondly, to the order of justice and virtue, whereby the common good is preserved and attained. If therefore there by any precepts which contain the very preservation of the common good, or the very order of justice and virtue, such precepts contain the intention of the lawgiver, and therefore are indispensable. For instance, if in some community a law were enacted, such as this---that no man should work for the destruction of the commonwealth, or betray the state to its enemies, or that no man should do anything unjust or evil, such precepts would not admit of dispensation. But if other precepts were enacted, subordinate to the above, and determining certain special modes of procedure, these latter precepts would admit of dispensation, in so far as the omission of these precepts in certain cases would not be prejudicial to the former precepts which contain the intention of the lawgiver. For instance if, for the safeguarding of the commonwealth, it were enacted in some city that from each ward some men should keep watch as sentries in case of siege, some might be dispensed from this on account of some greater utility.

Now the precepts of the decalogue contain the very intention of the lawgiver, who is God. For the precepts of the first table, which direct us to God, contain the very order to the common and final good, which is God; while the precepts of the second table contain the order of justice to be observed among men, that nothing undue be done to anyone, and that each one be given his due; for it is in this sense that we are to take the precepts of the decalogue. Consequently the precepts of the decalogue admit of no dispensation whatever.

Reply to Objection 1: The Philosopher is not speaking of the natural law which contains the very order of justice: for it is a never-failing principle that "justice should be preserved." But he is speaking in reference to certain fixed modes of observing justice, which fail to apply in certain cases.

Reply to Objection 2: As the Apostle says (2 Tim. 2:13), "God continueth faithful, He cannot deny Himself." But He would deny Himself if He were to do away with the very order of His own justice, since He is justice itself. Wherefore God cannot dispense a man so that it be lawful for him not to direct himself to God, or not to be subject to His justice, even in those matters in which men are directed to one another.

Reply to Objection 3: The slaying of a man is forbidden in the decalogue, in so far as it bears the character of something undue: for in this sense the precept contains the very essence of justice. Human law cannot make it lawful for a man to be slain unduly. But it is not undue for evil-doers or foes of the common weal to be slain: hence this is not contrary to the precept of the decalogue; and such a killing is no murder as forbidden by that precept, as Augustine observes (De Lib. Arb. i, 4). In like manner when a man's property is taken from him, if it be due that he should lose it, this is not theft or robbery as forbidden by the decalogue.

Consequently when the children of Israel, by God's command, took away the spoils of the Egyptians, this was not theft; since it was due to them by the sentence of God. Likewise when Abraham consented to slay his son, he did not consent to murder, because his son was due to be slain by the command of God, Who is Lord of life and death: for He it is Who inflicts the punishment of death on all men, both godly and ungodly, on account of the sin of our first parent, and if a man be the executor of that sentence by Divine authority, he will be no murderer any more than God would be. Again Osee, by taking unto himself a wife of fornications, or an adulterous woman, was not guilty either of adultery or of fornication: because he took unto himself one who was his by command of God, Who is the Author of the institution of marriage.

Accordingly, therefore, the precepts of the decalogue, as to the essence of justice which they contain, are unchangeable: but as to any determination by application to individual actions---for instance, that this or that be murder, theft or adultery, or not---in this point they admit of change; sometimes by Divine authority alone, namely, in such matters as are exclusively of Divine institution, as marriage and the like; sometimes also by human authority, namely in such matters as are subject to human jurisdiction: for in this respect men stand in the place of God: and yet not in all respects.

Reply to Objection 4: This determination was an interpretation rather than a dispensation. For a man is not taken to break the Sabbath, if he does something necessary for human welfare; as Our Lord proves (Mt. 12:3, seqq.).

Article: 9

Whether the mode of virtue falls under the precept of the law?

Objection 1: It would seem that the mode of virtue falls under the precept of the law. For the mode of virtue is that deeds of justice should be done justly, that deeds of fortitude should be done bravely, and in like manner as to the other virtues. But it is commanded (Dt. 26:20) that "thou shalt follow justly after that which is just." Therefore the mode of virtue falls under the precept.

Objection 2: Further, that which belongs to the intention of the lawgiver comes chiefly under the precept. But the intention of the lawgiver is directed chiefly to make men virtuous, as stated in Ethic. ii: and it belongs to a virtuous man to act virtuously. Therefore the mode of virtue falls under the precept.

Objection 3: Further, the mode of virtue seems to consist properly in working willingly and with pleasure. But this falls under a precept of the Divine law, for it is written (Ps. 99:2): "Serve ye the Lord with gladness"; and (2 Cor. 9:7): "Not with sadness or necessity: for God loveth a cheerful giver"; whereupon the gloss says: "Whatever ye do, do gladly; and then you will do it well; whereas if you do it sorrowfully, it is done in thee, not by thee." Therefore the mode of virtue falls under the precept of the law.

On the contrary, No man can act as a virtuous man acts unless he has the habit of virtue, as the Philosopher explains (Ethic. ii, 4; v, 8). Now whoever transgresses a precept of the law, deserves to be punished. Hence it would follow that a man who has not the habit of virtue, would deserve to be punished, whatever he does. But this is contrary to the intention of the law, which aims at leading man to virtue, by habituating him to good works. Therefore the mode of virtue does not fall under the precept.

I answer that, As stated above (Question [90], Article [3], ad 2), a precept of law has compulsory power. Hence that on which the compulsion of the law is brought to bear, falls directly under the precept of the law. Now the law compels through fear of punishment, as stated in Ethic. x, 9, because that properly falls under the precept of the law, for which the penalty of the law is inflicted. But Divine law and human law are differently situated as to the appointment of penalties; since the penalty of the law is inflicted only for those things which come under the judgment of the lawgiver; for the law punishes in accordance with the verdict given. Now man, the framer of human law, is competent to judge only of outward acts; because "man seeth those things that appear," according to 1 Kgs. 16:7: while God alone, the framer of the Divine law, is competent to judge of the inward movements of wills, according to Ps. 7:10: "The searcher of hearts and reins is God."

Accordingly, therefore, we must say that the mode of virtue is in some sort regarded both by human and by Divine law; in some respect it is regarded by the Divine, but not by the human law; and in another way, it is regarded neither by the human nor by the Divine law. Now the mode of virtue consists in three things, as the Philosopher states in Ethic. ii. The first is that man should act "knowingly": and this is subject to the judgment of both Divine and human law; because what a man does in ignorance, he does accidentally. Hence according to both human and Divine law, certain things are judged in respect of ignorance to be punishable or pardonable.

The second point is that a man should act "deliberately," i.e. "from choice, choosing that particular action for its own sake"; wherein a twofold internal movement is implied, of volition and of intention, about which we have spoken above (Questions [8], 12): and concerning these two, Divine law alone, and not human law, is competent to judge. For human law does not punish the man who wishes to slay, and slays not: whereas the Divine law does, according to Mt. 5:22: "Whosoever is angry with his brother, shall be in danger of the judgment."

The third point is that he should "act from a firm and immovable principle": which firmness belongs properly to a habit, and implies that the action proceeds from a rooted habit. In this respect, the mode of virtue does not fall under the precept either of Divine or of human law, since neither by man nor by God is he punished as breaking the law, who gives due honor to his parents and yet has not the habit of filial piety.

Reply to Objection 1: The mode of doing acts of justice, which falls under the precept, is that they be done in accordance with right; but not that they be done from the habit of justice.

Reply to Objection 2: The intention of the lawgiver is twofold. His aim, in the first place, is to lead men to something by the precepts of the law: and this is virtue. Secondly, his intention is brought to bear on the matter itself of the precept: and this is something leading or disposing to virtue, viz. an act of virtue. For the end of the precept and the matter of the precept are not the same: just as neither in other things is the end the same as that which conduces to the end.

Reply to Objection 3: That works of virtue should be done without sadness, falls under the precept of the Divine law; for whoever works with sadness works unwillingly. But to work with pleasure, i.e. joyfully or cheerfully, in one respect falls under the precept, viz. in so far as pleasure ensues from the love of God and one's neighbor (which love falls under the precept), and love causes pleasure: and in another respect does not fall under the precept, in so far as pleasure ensues from a habit; for "pleasure taken in a work proves the existence of a habit," as stated in Ethic. ii, 3. For an act may give pleasure either on account of its end, or through its proceeding from a becoming habit.

Article: 10

Whether the mode of charity falls under the precept of the Divine law?

Objection 1: It would seem that the mode of charity falls under the precept of the Divine law. For it is written (Mt. 19:17): "If thou wilt enter into life, keep the commandments": whence it seems to follow that the observance of the commandments suffices for entrance into life. But good works do not suffice for entrance into life, except they be done from charity: for it is written (1 Cor. 13:3): "If I should distribute all my goods to feed the poor, and if I should deliver my body to be burned, and have not charity, it profiteth me nothing." Therefore the mode of charity is included in the commandment.

Objection 2: Further, the mode of charity consists properly speaking in doing all things for God. But this falls under the precept; for the Apostle says (1 Cor. 10:31): "Do all to the glory of God." Therefore the mode of charity falls under the precept.

Objection 3: Further, if the mode of charity does not fall under the precept, it follows that one can fulfil the precepts of the law without having charity. Now what can be done without charity can be done without grace, which is always united to charity. Therefore one can fulfil the precepts of the law without grace. But this is the error of Pelagius, as Augustine declares (De Haeres. lxxxviii). Therefore the mode of charity is included in the commandment.

On the contrary, Whoever breaks a commandment sins mortally. If therefore the mode of charity falls under the precept, it follows that whoever acts otherwise than from charity sins mortally. But whoever has not charity, acts otherwise than from charity. Therefore it follows that whoever has not charity, sins mortally in whatever he does, however good this may be in itself: which is absurd.

I answer that, Opinions have been contrary on this question. For some have said absolutely that the mode of charity comes under the precept; and yet that it is possible for one not having charity to fulfil this precept: because he can dispose himself to receive charity from God. Nor (say they) does it follow that a man not having charity sins mortally whenever he does something good of its kind: because it is an affirmative precept that binds one to act from charity, and is binding not for all time, but only for such time as one is in a state of charity. On the other hand, some have said that the mode of charity is altogether outside the precept.

Both these opinions are true up to a certain point. Because the act of charity can be considered in two ways. First, as an act by itself: and thus it falls under the precept of the law which specially prescribes it, viz. "Thou shalt love the Lord thy God," and "Thou shalt love thy neighbor." In this sense, the first opinion is true. Because it is not impossible to observe this precept which regards the act of charity; since man can dispose himself to possess charity, and when he possesses it, he can use it. Secondly, the act of charity can be considered as being the mode of the acts of the other virtues, i.e. inasmuch as the acts of the other virtues are ordained to charity, which is "the end of the commandment," as stated in 1 Tim. i, 5: for it has been said above (Question [12], Article [4]) that the intention of the end is a formal mode of the act ordained to that end. In this sense the second opinion is true in saying that the mode of charity does not fall under the precept, that is to say that this commandment, "Honor thy father," does not mean that a man must honor his father from charity, but merely that he must honor him. Wherefore he that honors his father, yet has not charity, does not break this precept: although he does break the precept concerning the act of charity, for which reason he deserves to be punished.

Reply to Objection 1: Our Lord did not say, "If thou wilt enter into life, keep one commandment"; but "keep" all "the commandments": among which is included the commandment concerning the love of God and our neighbor.

Reply to Objection 2: The precept of charity contains the injunction that God should be loved from our whole heart, which means that all things would be referred to God. Consequently man cannot fulfil the precept of charity, unless he also refer all things to God. Wherefore he that honors his father and mother, is bound to honor them from charity, not in virtue of the precept, "Honor thy father and mother," but in virtue of the precept, "Thou shalt love the Lord thy God with thy whole heart." And since these are two affirmative precepts, not binding for all times, they can be binding, each one at a different time: so that it may happen that a man fulfils the precept of honoring his father and mother, without at the same time breaking the precept concerning the omission of the mode of charity.

Reply to Objection 3: Man cannot fulfil all the precepts of the law, unless he fulfil the precept of charity, which is impossible without charity. Consequently it is not possible, as Pelagius maintained, for man to fulfil the law without grace.

Article: 11

Whether it is right to distinguish other moral precepts of the law besides the decalogue?

Objection 1: It would seem that it is wrong to distinguish other moral precepts of the law besides the decalogue. Because, as Our Lord declared (Mt. 22:40), "on these two commandments" of charity "dependeth the whole law and the prophets." But these two commandments are explained by the ten commandments of the decalogue. Therefore there is no need for other moral precepts.

Objection 2: Further, the moral precepts are distinct from the judicial and ceremonial precepts, as stated above (Question [99], Articles [3],4). But the determinations of the general moral precepts belong to the judicial and ceremonial precepts: and the general moral precepts are contained in the decalogue, or are even presupposed to the decalogue, as stated above (Article [3]). Therefore it was unsuitable to lay down other moral precepts besides the decalogue.

Objection 3: Further, the moral precepts are about the acts of all the virtues, as stated above (Article [2]). Therefore, as the Law contains, besides the decalogue, moral precepts pertaining to religion, liberality, mercy, and chastity; so there should have been added some precepts pertaining to the other virtues, for instance, fortitude, sobriety, and so forth. And yet such is not the case. It is therefore unbecoming to distinguish other moral precepts in the Law besides those of the decalogue.

On the contrary, It is written (Ps. 18:8): "The law of the Lord is unspotted, converting souls." But man is preserved from the stain of sin, and his soul is converted to God by other moral precepts besides those of the decalogue. Therefore it was right for the Law to include other moral precepts.

I answer that, As is evident from what has been stated (Question [99], Articles [3],4), the judicial and ceremonial precepts derive their force from their institution alone: since before they were instituted, it seemed of no consequence whether things were done in this or that way. But the moral precepts derive their efficacy from the very dictate of natural reason, even if they were never included in the Law. Now of these there are three grades: for some are most certain, and so evident as to need no promulgation; such as the commandments of the love of God and our neighbor, and others like these, as stated above (Article [3]), which

164

are, as it were, the ends of the commandments; wherefore no man can have an erroneous judgment about them. Some precepts are more detailed, the reason of which even an uneducated man can easily grasp; and yet they need to be promulgated, because human judgment, in a few instances, happens to be led astray concerning them: these are the precepts of the decalogue. Again, there are some precepts the reason of which is not so evident to everyone, but only the wise; these are moral precepts added to the decalogue, and given to the people by God through Moses and Aaron.

But since the things that are evident are the principles whereby we know those that are not evident, these other moral precepts added to the decalogue are reducible to the precepts of the decalogue, as so many corollaries. Thus the first commandment of the decalogue forbids the worship of strange gods: and to this are added other precepts forbidding things relating to worship of idols: thus it is written (Dt. 18:10,11): "Neither let there be found among you anyone that shall expiate his son or daughter, making them to pass through the fire: . . . neither let there by any wizard nor charmer, nor anyone that consulteth pythonic spirits, or fortune-tellers, or that seeketh the truth from the dead." The second commandment forbids perjury. To this is added the prohibition of blasphemy (Lev. 24:15, seqq) and the prohibition of false doctrine (Dt. 13). To the third commandment are added all the ceremonial precepts. To the fourth commandment prescribing the honor due to parents, is added the precept about honoring the aged, according to Lev. 19:32: "Rise up before the hoary head, and honor the person of the aged man"; and likewise all the precepts prescribing the reverence to be observed towards our betters, or kindliness towards our equals or inferiors. To the fifth commandment, which forbids murder, is added the prohibition of hatred and of any kind of violence inflicted on our neighbor, according to Lev. 19:16: "Thou shalt not stand against the blood of thy neighbor": likewise the prohibition against hating one's brother (Lev. 19:17): "Thou shalt not hate thy brother in thy heart." To the sixth commandment which forbids adultery, is added the prohibition about whoredom, according to Dt. 23:17: "There shall be no whore among the daughters of Israel, nor whoremonger among the sons of Israel"; and the prohibition against unnatural sins, according to Lev. 28:22,23: "Thou shalt not lie with mankind . . . thou shalt not copulate with any beast." To the seventh commandment which prohibits theft, is added the precept forbidding usury, according to Dt. 23:19: "Thou shalt not lend to thy brother money to usury"; and the prohibition against fraud, according to Dt. 25:13: "Thou shalt not have divers weights in thy bag"; and universally all prohibitions relating to peculations and larceny. To the eighth commandment, forbidding false testimony, is added the prohibition against false judgment, according to Ex. 23:2: "Neither shalt thou yield in judgment, to the opinion of the most part, to stray from the truth"; and the prohibition against lying (Ex. 23:7): "Thou shalt fly lying," and the prohibition against detraction, according to Lev. 19:16: "Thou shalt not be a detractor, nor a whisperer among the people." To the other two commandments no further precepts are added, because thereby are forbidden all kinds of evil desires.

Reply to Objection 1: The precepts of the decalogue are ordained to the love of God and our neighbor as pertaining evidently to our duty towards them; but the other precepts are so ordained as pertaining thereto less evidently.

Reply to Objection 2: It is in virtue of their institution that the ceremonial and judicial precepts "are determinations of the precepts of the decalogue," not by reason of a natural instinct, as in the case of the superadded moral precepts.

Reply to Objection 3: The precepts of a law are ordained for the common good, as stated above (Question [90], Article [2]). And since those virtues which direct our conduct towards others pertain directly to the common good, as also does the virtue of chastity, in so far as the generative act conduces to the common good of the species; hence precepts bearing directly on these virtues are given, both in the decalogue and in addition thereto. As to the act of fortitude there are the order to be given by the commanders in the war, which is undertaken for the common good: as is clear from Dt. 20:3, where the priest is commanded (to speak thus): "Be not afraid, do not give back." In like manner the prohibition of acts of gluttony is left to paternal admonition, since it is contrary to the good of the household; hence it is said (Dt. 21:20) in the person of parents: "He slighteth hearing our admonitions, he giveth himself to revelling, and to debauchery and banquetings."

Article: 12

Whether the moral precepts of the Old Law justified man?

Objection 1: It would seem that the moral precepts of the Old Law justified man. Because the Apostle says (Rm. 2:13): "For not the hearers of the Law are justified before God, but the doers of the Law shall be justified." But the doers of the Law are those who fulfil the precepts of the Law. Therefore the fulfilling of the precepts of the Law was a cause of justification.

Objection 2: Further, it is written (Lev. 18:5): "Keep My laws and My judgments, which if a man do, he shall live in them." But the spiritual life of man is through justice. Therefore the fulfilling of the precepts of the Law was a cause of justification.

Objection 3: Further, the Divine law is more efficacious than human law. But human law justifies man; since there is a kind of justice consisting in fulfilling the precepts of law. Therefore the precepts of the Law justified man.

On the contrary, The Apostle says (2 Cor. 3:6): "The letter killeth": which, according to Augustine (De Spir. et Lit. xiv), refers even to the moral precepts. Therefore the moral precepts did not cause justice.

I answer that, Just as "healthy" is said properly and first of that which is possessed of health, and secondarily of that which is a sign or a safeguard of health; so justification means first and properly the causing of justice; while secondarily and improperly, as it were, it may denote a sign of justice or a disposition thereto. If justice be taken in the last two ways, it is evident that it was conferred by the precepts of the Law; in so far, to wit, as they disposed men to the justifying grace of Christ, which they also signified, because as Augustine says (Contra Faust. xxii, 24), "even the life of that people foretold and foreshadowed Christ."

But if we speak of justification properly so called, then we must notice that it can be considered as in the habit or as in the act: so that accordingly justification may be taken in two ways. First, according as man is made just, by becoming possessed of the habit of justice: secondly, according as he does works of justice, so that in this sense justification is nothing else than the execution of justice. Now justice, like the other virtues, may denote either the acquired or the infused virtue, as is clear from what has been stated (Question [63], Article [4]). The acquired virtue is caused by works; but the infused virtue is caused by God Himself through His grace. The latter is true justice, of which we are speaking now, and in this respect of which a man is said to be just before God, according to Rm. 4:2: "If Abraham were justified by works, he hath whereof to glory, but not before God." Hence this justice could not be caused by moral precepts, which are about human actions: wherefore the moral precepts could not justify man by causing justice.

If, on the other hand, by justification we understand the execution of justice, thus all the precepts of the Law justified man, but in various ways. Because the ceremonial precepts taken as a whole contained something just in itself, in so far as they aimed at offering worship to God; whereas taken individually they contained that which is just, not in itself, but by being a determination of the Divine law. Hence it is said of these precepts that they did not justify man save through the devotion and obedience of those who complied with them. On the other hand the moral and judicial precepts, either in general or also in particular, contained that which is just in itself: but the moral precepts contained that which is just in itself according to that "general justice" which is "every virtue" according to Ethic. v, 1: whereas the judicial precepts belonged to "special justice," which is about contracts connected with the human mode of life, between one man and another.

Reply to Objection 1: The Apostle takes justification for the execution of justice.

Reply to Objection 2: The man who fulfilled the precepts of the Law is said to live in them, because he did not incur the penalty of death, which the Law inflicted on its transgressors: in this sense the Apostle quotes this passage (Gal. 3:12).

Reply to Objection 3: The precepts of human law justify man by acquired justice: it is not about this that we are inquiring now, but only about that justice which is before God.

OF THE CEREMONIAL PRECEPTS IN THEMSELVES (FOUR ARTICLES)

We must now consider the ceremonial precepts: and first we must consider them in themselves; secondly, their cause; thirdly, their duration. Under the first head there are four points of inquiry:

(1) The nature of the ceremonial precepts;
(2) Whether they are figurative?
(3) Whether there should have been many of them?
(4) Of their various kinds.

Question 101 Article: 1

Whether the nature of the ceremonial precepts consists in their pertaining to the worship of God?

Objection 1: It would seem that the nature of the ceremonial precepts does not consist in their pertaining to the worship of God. Because, in the Old Law, the Jews were given certain precepts about abstinence from food (Lev. 11); and about refraining from certain kinds of clothes, e.g. (Lev. 19:19): "Thou shalt not wear a garment that is woven of two sorts"; and again (Num. 15:38): "To make to themselves fringes in the corners of their garments." But these are not moral precepts; since they do not remain in the New Law. Nor are they judicial precepts; since they do not pertain to the pronouncing of judgment between man and man. Therefore they are ceremonial precepts. Yet they seem in no way to pertain to the worship of God. Therefore the nature of the ceremonial precepts does not consist in their pertaining to Divine worship.

Objection 2: Further, some state that the ceremonial precepts are those which pertain to solemnities; as though they were so called from the "cerei" [candles] which are lit up on those occasions. But many other things besides solemnities pertain to the worship of God. Therefore it does not seem that the ceremonial precepts are so called from their pertaining to the Divine worship.

Objection 3: Further, some say that the ceremonial precepts are patterns, i.e. rules, of salvation: because the Greek {chaire} is the same as the Latin "salve." But all the precepts of the Law are rules of salvation, and not only those that pertain to the worship of God. Therefore not only those precepts which pertain to Divine worship are called ceremonial.

Objection 4: Further, Rabbi Moses says (Doct. Perplex. iii) that the ceremonial precepts are those for which there is no evident reason. But there is evident reason for many things pertaining to the worship of God; such as the observance of the Sabbath, the feasts of the Passover and of the Tabernacles, and many other things, the reason for which is set down in the Law. Therefore the ceremonial precepts are not those which pertain to the worship of God.

On the contrary, It is written (Ex. 18:19,20): "Be thou to the people in those things that pertain to God . . . and . . . shew the people the ceremonies and the manner of worshipping."

I answer that, As stated above (Question [99], Article [4]), the ceremonial precepts are determinations of the moral precepts whereby man is directed to God, just as the judicial precepts are determinations of the moral precepts whereby he is directed to his neighbor. Now man is directed to God by the worship due to Him. Wherefore those precepts are properly called ceremonial, which pertain to the Divine worship. The reason for their being so called was given above (Question [99], Article [3]), when we established the distinction between the ceremonial and the other precepts.

Reply to Objection 1: The Divine worship includes not only sacrifices and the like, which seem to be directed to God immediately, but also those things whereby His worshippers are duly prepared to worship Him: thus too in other matters, whatever is preparatory to the end comes under the science whose object is the end. Accordingly those precepts of the Law which regard the clothing and food of God's worshippers, and other such matters, pertain to a certain preparation of the ministers, with the view of fitting them for the Divine worship: just as those who administer to a king make use of certain special observances. Consequently such are contained under the ceremonial precepts.

Reply to Objection 2: The alleged explanation of the name does not seem very probable: especially as the Law does not contain many instances of the lighting of candles in solemnities; since, even the lamps of the Candlestick were furnished with "oil of olives," as stated in Lev. 24:2. Nevertheless we may say that all things pertaining to the Divine worship were more carefully observed on solemn festivals: so that all ceremonial precepts may be included under the observance of solemnities.

Reply to Objection 3: Neither does this explanation of the name appear to be very much to the point, since the word "ceremony" is not Greek but Latin. We may say, however, that, since man's salvation is from God, those precepts above all seem to be rules of salvation, which direct man to God: and accordingly those which refer to Divine worship are called ceremonial precepts.

Reply to Objection 4: This explanation of the ceremonial precepts has a certain amount of probability: not that they are called ceremonial precisely because there is no evident reason for them; this is a kind of consequence. For, since the precepts referring to the Divine worship must needs be figurative, as we shall state further on (Article [2]), the consequence is that the reason for them is not so very evident.

Article: 2

Whether the ceremonial precepts are figurative?

Objection 1: It would seem that the ceremonial precepts are not figurative. For it is the duty of every teacher to express himself in such a way as to be easily understood, as Augustine states (De Doctr. Christ. iv, 4,10) and this seems very necessary in the framing of a law: because precepts of law are proposed to the populace; for which reason a law should be manifest, as Isidore declares (Etym. v, 21). If therefore the precepts of the Law were given as figures of something, it seems unbecoming that Moses should have delivered these precepts without explaining what they signified.

Objection 2: Further, whatever is done for the worship of God, should be entirely free from unfittingness. But the performance of actions in representation of others, seems to savor of the theatre or of the drama: because formerly the actions performed in theatres were done to represent the actions of others. Therefore it seems that such things should not be done for the worship of God. But the ceremonial precepts are ordained to the Divine worship, as stated above (Article [1]). Therefore they should not be figurative.

Objection 3: Further, Augustine says (Enchiridion iii, iv) that "God is worshipped chiefly by faith, hope, and charity." But the precepts of faith, hope, and charity are not figurative. Therefore the ceremonial precepts should not be figurative.

Objection 4: Further, Our Lord said (Jn. 4:24): "God is a spirit, and they that adore Him, must adore Him in spirit and in truth." But a figure is not the very truth: in fact one is condivided with the other. Therefore the ceremonial precepts, which refer to the Divine worship, should not be figurative.

On the contrary, The Apostle says (Col. 2:16,17): "Let no man . . . judge you in meat or in drink, or in respect of a festival day, or of the new moon, or of the sabbaths, which are a shadow of things to come."

I answer that, As stated above (Article [1]; Question [99], Articles [3],4), the ceremonial precepts are those which refer to the worship of God. Now the Divine worship is twofold: internal, and external. For since man is composed of soul and body, each of these should be applied to the worship of God; the soul by an interior worship; the body by an outward worship: hence it is written (Ps. 83:3): "My heart and my flesh have rejoiced in the living God." And as the body is ordained to God through the soul, so the outward worship is ordained to the internal worship. Now interior worship consists in the soul being united to God by the intellect and affections. Wherefore according to the various ways in which the intellect and affections of the man who worships God are rightly united to God, his external actions are applied in various ways to the Divine worship.

For in the state of future bliss, the human intellect will gaze on the Divine Truth in Itself. Wherefore the external worship will not consist in anything figurative, but solely in the praise of God, proceeding from the inward knowledge and affection, according to Is. 51:3: "Joy and gladness shall be found therein, thanksgiving and the voice of praise."

But in the present state of life, we are unable to gaze on the Divine Truth in Itself, and we need the ray of Divine light to shine upon us under the form of certain sensible figures, as Dionysius states (Coel. Hier. i); in various ways, however, according to the various states of human knowledge. For under the Old Law, neither was the Divine Truth manifest in Itself, nor was the way leading to that manifestation as yet opened out, as the Apostle declares (Heb. 9:8). Hence the external worship of the Old Law needed to be figurative not only of the future truth to be manifested in our heavenly country, but also of Christ, Who is the way leading to that heavenly manifestation. But under the New Law this way is already revealed: and therefore it needs no longer to be foreshadowed as something future, but to be brought to our minds as something past or present: and the truth of the glory to come, which is not yet revealed, alone needs to be foreshadowed. This is what the Apostle says (Heb. 11:1): "The Law has [Vulg.: 'having'] a shadow of the good things to come, not the very image of the things": for a shadow is less than an image; so that the image belongs to the New Law, but the shadow to the Old.

Reply to Objection 1: The things of God are not to be revealed to man except in proportion to his capacity: else he would be in danger of downfall, were he to despise what he cannot grasp. Hence it was more beneficial that the Divine mysteries should be revealed to uncultured people under a veil of figures, that thus they might know them at least implicitly by using those figures to the honor of God.

Reply to Objection 2: Just as human reason fails to grasp poetical expressions on account of their being lacking in truth, so does it fail to grasp Divine things perfectly, on account of the sublimity of the truth they contain: and therefore in both cases there is need of signs by means of sensible figures.

Reply to Objection 3: Augustine is speaking there of internal worship; to which, however, external worship should be ordained, as stated above.

The same answer applies to the Fourth Objection: because men were taught by Him to practice more perfectly the spiritual worship of God.

Article: 3 Whether there should have been man ceremonial precepts?

Objection 1: It would seem that there should not have been many ceremonial precepts. For those things which conduce to an end should be proportionate to that end. But the ceremonial precepts, as stated above (Articles [1],2), are ordained to the worship of God, and to the foreshadowing of Christ. Now "there is but one God, of Whom are all things . . . and one Lord Jesus Christ, by Whom are all things" (1 Cor. 8:6). Therefore there should not have been many ceremonial precepts.

Objection 2: Further, the great number of the ceremonial precepts was an occasion of transgression, according to the words of Peter (Acts 15:10): "Why tempt you God, to put a yoke upon the necks of the disciples, which neither our fathers nor we have been able to bear?" Now the transgression of the Divine precepts is an obstacle to man's salvation. Since, therefore, every law should conduce to man's salvation, as Isidore says (Etym. v, 3), it seems that the ceremonial precepts should not have been given in great number.

Objection 3: Further, the ceremonial precepts referred to the outward and bodily worship of God, as stated above (Article [2]). But the Law should have lessened this bodily worship: since it directed men to Christ, Who taught them to worship God "in spirit and in truth," as stated in Jn. 4:23. Therefore there should not have been many ceremonial precepts.

On the contrary, (Osee 8:12): "I shall write to them [Vulg.: 'him'] My manifold laws"; and (Job 11:6): "That He might show thee the secrets of His wisdom, and that His Law is manifold."

I answer that, As stated above (Question [96], Article [1]), every law is given to a people. Now a people contains two kinds of men: some, prone to evil, who have to be coerced by the precepts of the law, as stated above (Question [95], Article [1]); some, inclined to good, either from nature or from custom, or rather from grace; and the like have to be taught and improved by means of the precepts of the law. Accordingly, with regard to both kinds of the law. Accordingly, with regard to both kinds of men it was expedient that the Old Law should contain many ceremonial precepts. For in that people there were many prone to idolatry; wherefore it was necessary to recall them by means of ceremonial precepts from the worship of idols to the worship of God. And since men served idols in many ways, it was necessary on the other hand to devise many means of repressing every single one: and again, to lay many obligations on such like men, in order that being burdened, as it were, by their duties to the Divine worship, they might have no time for the service of idols. As to those who were inclined to good, it was again necessary that there should be many ceremonial precepts; both because thus their mind turned to God in many ways, and more continually; and because the mystery of Christ, which was foreshadowed by these ceremonial precepts, brought many boons to the world, and afforded men many considerations, which needed to be signified by various ceremonies.

Reply to Objection 1: When that which conduces to an end is sufficient to conduce thereto, then one such thing suffices for one end: thus one remedy, if it be efficacious, suffices sometimes to restore men to health, and then the remedy needs not to be repeated. But when that which conduces to an end is weak and imperfect, it needs to be multiplied: thus many remedies are given to a sick man, when one is not enough to heal him. Now the ceremonies of the Old Law were weak and imperfect, both for representing the mystery of Christ, on account of its surpassing excellence; and for subjugating men's minds to God. Hence the Apostle says (Heb. 7:18,19): "There is a setting aside of the former commandment because of the weakness and unprofitableness thereof, for the law brought nothing to perfection." Consequently these ceremonies needed to be in great number.

Reply to Objection 2: A wise lawgiver should suffer lesser transgressions, that the greater may be avoided. And therefore, in order to avoid the sin of idolatry, and the pride which would arise in the hearts of the Jews, were they to fulfil all the precepts of the Law, the fact that they would in consequence find many occasions of disobedience did not prevent God from giving them many ceremonial precepts.

Reply to Objection 3: The Old Law lessened bodily worship in many ways. Thus it forbade sacrifices to be offered in every place and by any person. Many such like things did it enact for the lessening of bodily worship; as Rabbi Moses, the Egyptian testifies (Doct. Perplex. iii). Nevertheless it behooved not to attenuate the bodily worship of God so much as to allow men to fall away into the worship of idols.

Article: 4

Whether the ceremonies of the Old Law are suitably divided into sacrifices, sacred things, sacraments, and observances?

Objection 1: It would seem that the ceremonies of the Old Law are unsuitably divided into "sacrifices, sacred things, sacraments, and observances." For the ceremonies of the Old Law foreshadowed Christ. But this was done only by the sacrifices, which foreshadowed the sacrifice in which Christ "delivered Himself an oblation and a sacrifice to God" (Eph. 5:2). Therefore none but the sacrifices were ceremonies.

Objection 2: Further, the Old Law was ordained to the New. But in the New Law the sacrifice is the Sacrament of the Altar. Therefore in the Old Law there should be no distinction between "sacrifices" and "sacraments."

Objection 3: Further, a "sacred thing" is something dedicated to God: in which sense the tabernacle and its vessels were said to be consecrated. But all the ceremonial precepts were ordained to the worship of God, as stated above (Article [1]). Therefore all ceremonies were sacred things. Therefore "sacred things" should not be taken as a part of the ceremonies.

Objection 4: Further, "observances" are so called from having to be observed. But all the precepts of the Law had to be observed: for it is written (Dt. 8:11): "Observe [Douay: 'Take heed'] and beware lest at any time thou forget the Lord thy God, and neglect His commandments and judgments and ceremonies." Therefore the "observances" should not be considered as a part of the ceremonies.

Objection 5: Further, the solemn festivals are reckoned as part of the ceremonial: since they were a shadow of things to come (Col. 2:16,17): and the same may be said of the oblations and gifts, as appears from the words of the Apostle (Heb. 9:9): and yet these do not seem to be inclined in any of those mentioned above. Therefore the above division of ceremonies is unsuitable.

On the contrary, In the Old Law each of the above is called a ceremony. For the sacrifices are called ceremonies (Num. 15:24): "They shall offer a calf . . . and the sacrifices and libations thereof, as the ceremonies require." Of the sacrament of Order it is written (Lev. 7:35): "This is the anointing of Aaron and his sons in the ceremonies." Of sacred things also it is written (Ex. 38:21): "These are the instruments of the tabernacle of the testimony . . . in the ceremonies of the Levites." And again of the observances it is written (3 Kgs. 9:6): "If you . . . shall turn away from following Me, and will not observe [Douay: 'keep'] My . . . ceremonies which I have set before you."

I answer that, As stated above (Articles [1],2), the ceremonial precepts are ordained to the Divine worship. Now in this worship we may consider the worship itself, the worshippers, and the instruments of worship. The worship consists specially in "sacrifices," which are offered up in honor of God. The instruments of worship refer to the "sacred things," such as the tabernacle, the vessels and so forth. With regard to the worshippers two points may be considered. The first point is their preparation for Divine worship, which is effected by a sort of consecration either of the people or of the ministers; and to this the "sacraments" refer. The second point is their particular mode of life, whereby they are distinguished from those who do not worship God: and to this pertain the "observances," for instance, in matters of food, clothing, and so forth.

Reply to Objection 1: It was necessary for the sacrifices to be offered both in some certain place and by some certain men: and all this pertained to the worship of God. Wherefore just as their sacrifices signified Christ the victim, so too their sacraments and sacred things of the New Law; while their observances foreshadowed the mode of life of the people under the New Law: all of which things pertain to Christ.

Reply to Objection 2: The sacrifice of the New Law, viz. the Eucharist, contains Christ Himself, the Author of our Sanctification: for He sanctified "the people by His own blood" (Heb. 13:12). Hence this Sacrifice is also a sacrament. But the sacrifices of the Old Law did not contain Christ, but foreshadowed Him; hence they are not called sacraments. In order to signify this there were certain sacraments apart from the sacrifices of the Old Law, which sacraments were figures of the sanctification to come. Nevertheless to certain consecrations certain sacrifices were united.

Reply to Objection 3: The sacrifices and sacraments were of course sacred things. But certain things were sacred, through being dedicated to the Divine worship, and yet were not sacrifices or sacraments: wherefore they retained the common designation of sacred things.

Reply to Objection 4: Those things which pertained to the mode of life of the people who worshipped God, retained the common designation of observances, in so far as they fell short of the above. For they were not called sacred things, because they had no immediate connection with the worship of God, such as the tabernacle and its vessels had. But by a sort of consequence they were matters of ceremony, in so far as they affected the fitness of the people who worshipped God.

Reply to Objection 5: Just as the sacrifices were offered in a fixed place, so were they offered at fixed times: for which reason the solemn festivals seem to be reckoned among the sacred things. The oblations and gifts are counted together with the sacrifices; hence the Apostle says (Heb. 5:1): "Every high-priest taken from among men, is ordained for men in things that appertain to God, that he may offer up gifts and sacrifices."

OF THE CAUSES OF THE CEREMONIAL PRECEPTS (SIX ARTICLES)

We must now consider the causes of the ceremonial precepts: under which head there are six points of inquiry:

(1) Whether there was any cause for the ceremonial precepts?
(2) Whether the cause of the ceremonial precepts was literal or figurative?
(3) The causes of the sacrifices;
(4) The causes of the sacrifices;
(5) The causes of the sacred things;
(6) The causes of the observances.

Question 102 Article: 1

Whether there was any cause for the ceremonial precepts?

Objection 1: It would seem that there was no cause for the ceremonial precepts. Because on Eph. 2:15, "Making void the law of the commandments," the gloss says, (i.e.) "making void the Old Law as to the carnal observances, by substituting decrees, i.e. evangelical precepts, which are based on reason." But if the observances of the Old Law were based on reason, it would have been useless to void them by the reasonable decrees of the New Law. Therefore there was no reason for the ceremonial observances of the Old Law.

Objection 2: Further, the Old Law succeeded the law of nature. But in the law of nature there was a precept for which there was no reason save that man's obedience might be tested; as Augustine says (Gen. ad lit. viii, 6,13), concerning the prohibition about the tree of life. Therefore in the Old Law there should have been some precepts for the purpose of testing man's obedience, having no reason in themselves.

Objection 3: Further, man's works are called moral according as they proceed from reason. If therefore there is any reason for the ceremonial precepts, they would not differ from the moral precepts. It seems therefore that there was no cause for the ceremonial precepts: for the reason of a precept is taken from some cause.

On the contrary, It is written (Ps. 18:9): "The commandment of the Lord is lightsome, enlightening the eyes." But the ceremonial precepts are commandments of God. Therefore they are lightsome: and yet they would not be so, if they had no reasonable cause. Therefore the ceremonial precepts have a reasonable cause.

I answer that, Since, according to the Philosopher (Metaph. i, 2), it is the function of a "wise man to do everything in order," those things which proceed from the Divine wisdom must needs be well ordered, as the Apostle states (Rm. 13:1). Now there are two conditions required for things to be well ordered. First, that they be ordained to their due end, which is the principle of the whole order in matters of action: since those things that happen by chance outside the intention of the end, or which are not done seriously but for fun, are said to be inordinate. Secondly, that which is done in view of the end should be proportionate to the end. From this it follows that the reason for whatever conduces to the end is taken from the end: thus the reason for the disposition of a saw is taken from cutting, which is its end, as stated in Phys. ii, 9. Now it is evident that the ceremonial precepts, like all the other precepts of the Law, were institutions of Divine wisdom: hence it is written (Dt. 4:6): "This is your wisdom and understanding in the sight of nations." Consequently we must needs say that the ceremonial precepts were ordained to a certain end, wherefrom their reasonable causes can be gathered.

Reply to Objection 1: It may be said there was no reason for the observances of the Old Law, in the sense that there was no reason in the very nature of the thing done: for instance that a garment should not be made of wool and linen. But there could be a reason for them in relation to something else: namely, in so far as something was signified or excluded thereby. On the other hand, the decrees of the New Law, which refer chiefly to faith and the love of God, are reasonable from the very nature of the act.

Reply to Objection 2: The reason for the prohibition concerning the tree of knowledge of good and evil was not that this tree was naturally evil: and yet this prohibition was reasonable in its relation to something else, in as much as it signified something. And so also the ceremonial precepts of the Old Law were reasonable on account of their relation to something else.

Reply to Objection 3: The moral precepts in their very nature have reasonable causes: as for instance, "Thou shalt not kill, Thou shalt not steal." But the ceremonial precepts have a reasonable cause in their relation to something else, as stated above.

Article: 2

Whether the ceremonial precepts have a literal cause or merely a figurative cause?

Objection 1: It would seem that the ceremonial precepts have not a literal, but merely a figurative cause. For among the ceremonial precepts, the chief was circumcision and the sacrifice of the paschal lamb. But neither of these had any but a figurative cause: because each was given as a sign. For it is written (Gn.

17:11): "You shall circumcise the flesh of your foreskin, that it may be a sign of the covenant between Me and you": and of the celebration of the Passover it is written (Ex. 13:9): "It shall be as a sign in thy hand, and as a memorial before thy eyes." Therefore much more did the other ceremonial precepts have none but a figurative reason.

Objection 2: Further, an effect is proportionate to its cause. But all the ceremonial precepts are figurative, as stated above (Question [101], Article [2]). Therefore they have no other than a figurative cause.

Objection 3: Further, if it be a matter of indifference whether a certain thing, considered in itself, be done in a particular way or not, it seems that it has not a literal cause. Now there are certain points in the ceremonial precepts, which appear to be a matter of indifference, as to whether they be done in one way or in another: for instance, the number of animals to be offered, and other such particular circumstances. Therefore there is no literal cause for the precepts of the Old Law.

On the contrary, Just as the ceremonial precepts foreshadowed Christ, so did the stories of the Old Testament: for it is written (1 Cor. 10:11) that "all (these things) happened to them in figure." Now in the stories of the Old Testament, besides the mystical or figurative, there is the literal sense. Therefore the ceremonial precepts had also literal, besides their figurative causes.

I answer that, As stated above (Article [1]), the reason for whatever conduces to an end must be taken from that end. Now the end of the ceremonial precepts was twofold: for they were ordained to the Divine worship, for that particular time, and to the foreshadowing of Christ; just as the words of the prophets regarded the time being in such a way as to be utterances figurative of the time to come, as Jerome says on Osee 1:3. Accordingly the reasons for the ceremonial precepts of the Old Law can be taken in two ways. First, in respect of the Divine worship which was to be observed for that particular time: and these reasons are literal: whether they refer to the shunning of idolatry; or recall certain Divine benefits; or remind men of the Divine excellence; or point out the disposition of mind which was then required in those who worshipped God. Secondly, their reasons can be gathered from the point of view of their being ordained to foreshadow Christ: and thus their reasons are figurative and mystical: whether they be taken from Christ Himself and the Church, which pertains to the allegorical sense; or to the morals of the Christian people, which pertains to the moral sense; or to the state of future glory, in as much as we are brought thereto by Christ, which refers to the anagogical sense.

Reply to Objection 1: Just as the use of metaphorical expressions in Scripture belongs to the literal sense, because the words are employed in order to convey that particular meaning; so also the meaning of those legal ceremonies which commemorated certain Divine benefits, on account of which they were instituted, and of others similar which belonged to that time, does not go beyond the order of literal causes. Consequently when we assert that the cause of the celebration of the Passover was its signification of the delivery from Egypt, or that circumcision was a sign of God's covenant with Abraham, we assign the literal cause.

Reply to Objection 2: This argument would avail if the ceremonial precepts had been given merely as figures of things to come, and not for the purpose of worshipping God then and there.

Reply to Objection 3: As we have stated when speaking of human laws (Question [96], Articles [1],6), there is a reason for them in the abstract, but not in regard to particular conditions, which depend on the judgment of those who frame them; so also many particular determinations in the ceremonies of the Old Law have no literal cause, but only a figurative cause; whereas in the abstract they have a literal cause.

Article: 3

Whether a suitable cause can be assigned for the ceremonies which pertained to sacrifices?

Objection 1: It would seem that no suitable cause can be assigned for the ceremonies pertaining to sacrifices. For those things which were offered in sacrifice, are those which are necessary for sustaining human life: such as certain animals and certain loaves. But God needs no such sustenance; according to Ps. 49:13: "Shall I eat the flesh of bullocks? Or shall I drink the blood of goats?" Therefore such sacrifices were unfittingly offered to God.

Objection 2: Further, only three kinds of quadrupeds were offered in sacrifice to God, viz. oxen, sheep and goats; of birds, generally the turtledove and the dove; but specially, in the cleansing of a leper, an offering was made of sparrows. Now many other animals are more noble than these. Since therefore whatever is best should be offered to God, it seems that not only of these three should sacrifices have been offered to Him.

Objection 3: Further, just as man has received from God the dominion over birds and beasts, so also has he received dominion over fishes. Consequently it was unfitting for fishes to be excluded from the divine sacrifices.

Objection 4: Further, turtledoves and doves indifferently are commanded to be offered up. Since then the young of the dove are commanded to be offered, so also should the young of the turtledove.

Objection 5: Further, God is the Author of life, not only of men, but also of animals, as is clear from Gn. 1:20, seqq. Now death is opposed to life. Therefore it was fitting that living animals rather than slain animals should be offered to God, especially as the Apostle admonishes us (Rm. 12:1), to present our bodies "a living sacrifice, holy, pleasing unto God."

Objection 6: Further, if none but slain animals were offered in sacrifice to God, it seems that it mattered not how they were slain. Therefore it was unfitting that the manner of immolation should be determined, especially as regards birds (Lev. 1:15, seqq.).

Objection 7: Further, every defect in an animal is a step towards corruption and death. If therefore slain animals were offered to God, it was unreasonable to forbid the offering of an imperfect animal, e.g. a lame, or a blind, or otherwise defective animal.

Objection 8: Further, those who offer victims to God should partake thereof, according to the words of the Apostle (1 Cor. 10:18): "Are not they that eat of the sacrifices partakers of the altar?" It was therefore unbecoming for the offerers to be denied certain parts of the victims, namely, the blood, the fat, the breastbone and the right shoulder.

Objection 9: Further, just as holocausts were offered up in honor of God, so also were the peace-offerings and sin-offerings. But no female animals was offered up to God as a holocaust, although holocausts were offered of both quadrupeds and birds. Therefore it was inconsistent that female animals should be offered up in peace-offerings and sin-offerings, and that nevertheless birds should not be offered up in peace-offerings.

Objection 1:: Further, all the peace-offerings seem to be of one kind. Therefore it was unfitting to make a distinction among them, so that it was forbidden to eat the flesh of certain peace-offerings on the following day, while it was allowed to eat the flesh of other peace-offerings, as laid down in Lev. 7:15, seqq.

Objection 1:: Further, all sins agree in turning us from God. Therefore, in order to reconcile us to God, one kind of sacrifice should have been offered up for all sins.

Objection 1:: Further, all animals that were offered up in sacrifice, were offered up in one way, viz. slain. Therefore it does not seem to be suitable that products of the soil should be offered up in various ways; for sometimes an offering was made of ears of corn, sometimes of flour, sometimes of bread, this being baked sometimes in an oven, sometimes in a pan, sometimes on a gridiron.

Objection 1:: Further, whatever things are serviceable to us should be recognized as coming from God. It was therefore unbecoming that besides animals, nothing but bread, wine, oil, incense, and salt should be offered to God.

Objection 1:: Further, bodily sacrifices denote the inward sacrifice of the heart, whereby man offers his soul to God. But in the inward sacrifice, the sweetness, which is denoted by honey, surpasses the pungency which salt represents; for it is written (Ecclus. 24:27): "My spirit is sweet above honey." Therefore it was unbecoming that the use of honey, and of leaven which makes bread savory, should be forbidden in a sacrifice; while the use was prescribed, of salt which is pungent, and of incense which has a bitter taste. Consequently it seems that things pertaining to the ceremonies of the sacrifices have no reasonable cause.

On the contrary, It is written (Lev. 1:13): "The priest shall offer it all and burn it all upon the altar, for a holocaust, and most sweet savor to the Lord." Now according to Wis. 7:28, "God loveth none but him that dwelleth with wisdom": whence it seems to follow that whatever is acceptable to God is wisely done. Therefore these ceremonies of the sacrifices were wisely done, as having reasonable causes.

I answer that, As stated above (Article [2]), the ceremonies of the Old Law had a twofold cause, viz. a literal cause, according as they were intended for Divine worship; and a figurative or mystical cause, according as they were intended to foreshadow Christ: and on either hand the ceremonies pertaining to the sacrifices can be assigned to a fitting cause.

For, according as the ceremonies of the sacrifices were intended for the divine worship, the causes of the sacrifices can be taken in two ways. First, in so far as the sacrifice represented the directing of the mind to God, to which the offerer of the sacrifice was stimulated. Now in order to direct his mind to God aright, man must recognize that whatever he has is from God as from its first principle, and direct it to God as its last end. This was denoted in the offerings and sacrifices, by the fact that man offered some of his own belongings in honor of God, as though in recognition of his having received them from God, according to the saying of David (1 Paral. xxix, 14): "All things are Thine: and we have given Thee what we received of Thy hand." Wherefore in offering up sacrifices man made protestation that God is the first principle of the creation of all things, and their last end, to which all things must be directed. And since, for the human mind to be directed to God aright, it must recognize no first author of things other than God, nor place its end in any other; for this reason it was forbidden in the Law to offer sacrifice to any other but God, according to Ex. 22:20: "He that sacrificeth to gods, shall be put to death, save only to the Lord." Wherefore another reasonable cause may be assigned to the ceremonies of the sacrifices, from the fact that thereby men were withdrawn from offering sacrifices to idols. Hence too it is that the precepts about the sacrifices were not given to the Jewish people until after they had fallen into idolatry, by worshipping the molten calf: as though those sacrifices were instituted, that the people, being ready to offer sacrifices, might offer those sacrifices to God rather than to idols. Thus it is written (Jer. 7:22): "I spake not to your fathers and I commanded them not, in the day that I brought them out of the land of Egypt, concerning the matter of burnt-offerings and sacrifices."

Now of all the gifts which God vouchsafed to mankind after they had fallen away by sin, the chief is that He gave His Son; wherefore it is written (Jn. 3:16): "God so loved the world, as to give His only-begotten Son; that whosoever believeth in Him, may not perish, but may have life everlasting." Consequently the chief sacrifice is that whereby Christ Himself "delivered Himself . . . to God for an odor of sweetness" (Eph. 5:2). And for this reason all the other sacrifices of the Old Law were offered up in order to foreshadow this one individual and paramount sacrifice---the imperfect forecasting the perfect. Hence the Apostle says (Heb. 10:11) that the priest of the Old Law "often" offered "the same sacrifices, which can never take away sins: but" Christ offered "one sacrifice for sins, for ever." And since the reason of the figure is taken from that which the figure represents, therefore the reasons of the figurative sacrifices of the Old Law should be taken from the true sacrifice of Christ.

Reply to Objection 1: God did not wish these sacrifices to be offered to Him on account of the things themselves that were offered, as though He stood in need of them: wherefore it is written (Is. 1:11): "I desire not holocausts of rams, and fat of fatlings, and blood of calves and lambs and buckgoats." But, as stated above, He wished them to be offered to Him, in order to prevent idolatry; in order to signify the right ordering of man's mind to God; and in order to represent the mystery of the Redemption of man by Christ.

Reply to Objection 2: In all the respects mentioned above (ad 1), there was a suitable reason for these animals, rather than others, being offered in sacrifice to God. First, in order to prevent idolatry. Because idolaters offered all other animals to their gods, or made use of them in their sorceries: while the Egyptians (among whom the people had been dwelling) considered it abominable to slay these animals, wherefore they used not to offer them in sacrifice to their gods. Hence it is written (Ex. 8:26): "We shall sacrifice the abominations of the Egyptians to the Lord our God." For they worshipped the sheep; they reverenced the ram (because demons appeared under the form thereof); while they employed oxen for agriculture, which was reckoned by them as something sacred.

Secondly, this was suitable for the aforesaid right ordering of man's mind to God: and in two ways. First, because it is chiefly by means of these animals that human life is sustained: and moreover they are most clean, and partake of a most clean food: whereas other animals are either wild, and not deputed to ordinary use among men: or, if they be tame, they have unclean food, as pigs and geese: and nothing but what is clean should be offered to God. These birds especially were offered in sacrifice because there were plenty of them in the land of promise. Secondly, because the sacrificing of these animals represented purity of heart. Because as the gloss says on Lev. 1, "We offer a calf, when we overcome the pride of the flesh; a lamb, when we restrain our unreasonable motions; a goat, when we conquer wantonness; a turtledove, when we keep chaste; unleavened bread, when we feast on the unleavened bread of sincerity." And it is evident that the dove denotes charity and simplicity of heart.

Thirdly, it was fitting that these animals should be offered, that they might foreshadow Christ. Because, as the gloss observes, "Christ is offered in the calf, to denote the strength of the cross; in the lamb, to signify His innocence; in the ram, to foreshadow His headship; and in the goat, to signify the likeness of 'sinful flesh' [*An allusion to Col. 2:11 (Textus Receptus)]. The turtledove and dove denoted the union of the two natures"; or else the turtledove signified chastity; while the dove was a figure of charity. "The wheat-flour foreshadowed the sprinkling of believers with the water of Baptism."

Reply to Objection 3: Fish through living in water are further removed from man than other animals, which, like man, live in the air. Again, fish die as soon as they are taken out of water; hence they could not be offered in the temple like other animals.

Reply to Objection 4: Among turtledoves the older ones are better than the young; while with doves the case is the reverse. Wherefore, as Rabbi Moses observes (Doct. Perplex. iii), turtledoves and young doves are commanded to be offered, because nothing should be offered to God but what is best.

Reply to Objection 5: The animals which were offered in sacrifice were slain, because it is by being killed that they become useful to man, forasmuch as God gave them to man for food. Wherefore also they were burnt with fire: because it is by being cooked that they are made fit for human consumption. Moreover the slaying of the animals signified the destruction of sins: and also that man deserved death on account of his sins; as though those animals were slain in man's stead, in order to betoken the expiation of sins. Again the slaying of these animals signified the slaying of Christ.

Reply to Objection 6: The Law fixed the special manner of slaying the sacrificial animals in order to exclude other ways of killing, whereby idolaters sacrificed animals to idols. Or again, as Rabbi Moses says (Doct. Perplex. iii), "the Law chose that manner of slaying which was least painful to the slain animal." This excluded cruelty on the part of the offerers, and any mangling of the animals slain.

Reply to Objection 7: It is because unclean animals are wont to be held in contempt among men, that it was forbidden to offer them in sacrifice to God: and for this reason too they were forbidden (Dt. 23:18) to offer "the hire of a strumpet or the price of a dog in the house of . . . God." For the same reason they did not offer animals before the seventh day, because such were abortive as it were, the flesh being not yet firm on account of its exceeding softness.

Reply to Objection 8: There were three kinds of sacrifices. There was one in which the victim was entirely consumed by fire: this was called "a holocaust, i.e. all burnt." For this kind of sacrifice was offered to God specially to show reverence to His majesty, and love of His goodness: and typified the state of perfection as regards the fulfilment of the counsels. Wherefore the whole was burnt up: so that as the whole animal by being dissolved into vapor soared aloft, so it might denote that the whole man, and whatever belongs to him, are subject to the authority of God, and should be offered to Him.

Another sacrifice was the "sin-offering," which was offered to God on account of man's need for the forgiveness of sin: and this typifies the state of penitents in satisfying for sins. It was divided into two parts: for one part was burnt; while the other was granted to the use of the priests to signify that remission of sins is granted by God through the ministry of His priests. When, however, this sacrifice was offered for the sins of the whole people, or specially for the sin of the priest, the whole victim was burnt up. For it was not fitting that the priests should have the use of that which was offered for their own sins, to signify that nothing sinful should remain in them. Moreover, this would not be satisfaction for sin: for if the offering were granted to the use of those for whose sins it was offered, it would seem to be the same as if it had not been offered.

The third kind of sacrifice was called the "peace-offering," which was offered to God, either in thanksgiving, or for the welfare and prosperity of the offerers, in acknowledgment of benefits already received or yet to be received: and this typifies the state of those who are proficient in the observance of the commandments. These sacrifices were divided into three parts: for one part was burnt in honor of God; another part was allotted to the use of the priests; and the third part to the use of the offerers; in order to signify that man's salvation is from God, by the direction of God's ministers, and through the cooperation of those who are saved.

But it was the universal rule that the blood and fat were not allotted to the use either of the priests or of the offerers: the blood being poured out at the foot of the altar, in honor of God, while the fat was burnt upon the altar (Lev. 9:9,10). The reason for this was, first, in order to prevent idolatry: because idolaters used to drink the blood and eat the fat of the victims, according to Dt. 32:38: "Of whose victims they eat the fat, and drank the wine of their drink-offerings." Secondly, in order to form them to a right way of living. For they were forbidden the use of the blood that they might abhor the shedding of human blood; wherefore it is written (Gn. 9:4,5): "Flesh with blood you shall not eat: for I will require the blood of your lives": and they were forbidden to eat the fat, in order

185

to withdraw them from lasciviousness; hence it is written (Ezech. 34:3): "You have killed that which was fat." Thirdly, on account of the reverence due to God: because blood is most necessary for life, for which reason "life" is said to be "in the blood" (Lev. 17:11,14): while fat is a sign of abundant nourishment. Wherefore, in order to show that to God we owe both life and a sufficiency of all good things, the blood was poured out, and the fat burnt up in His honor. Fourthly, in order to foreshadow the shedding of Christ's blood, and the abundance of His charity, whereby He offered Himself to God for us.

In the peace-offerings, the breast-bone and the right shoulder were allotted to the use of the priest, in order to prevent a certain kind of divination which is known as "spatulamantia," so called because it was customary in divining to use the shoulder-blade [spatula], and the breast-bone of the animals offered in sacrifice; wherefore these things were taken away from the offerers. This is also denoted the priest's need of wisdom in the heart, to instruct the people---this was signified by the breast-bone, which covers the heart; and his need of fortitude, in order to bear with human frailty---and this was signified by the right shoulder.

Reply to Objection 9: Because the holocaust was the most perfect kind of sacrifice, therefore none but a male was offered for a holocaust: because the female is an imperfect animal. The offering of turtledoves and doves was on account of the poverty of the offerers, who were unable to offer bigger animals. And since peace-victims were offered freely, and no one was bound to offer them against his will, hence these birds were offered not among the peace-victims, but among the holocausts and victims for sin, which man was obliged to offer at times. Moreover these birds, on account of their lofty flight, while befitting the perfection of the holocausts: and were suitable for sin-offerings because their song is doleful.

Reply to Objection 1:: The holocaust was the chief of all the sacrifices: because all were burnt in honor of God, and nothing of it was eaten. The second place in holiness, belongs to the sacrifice for sins, which was eaten in the court only, and on the very day of the sacrifice (Lev. 7:6,15). The third place must be given to the peace-offerings of thanksgiving, which were eaten on the same day, but anywhere in Jerusalem. Fourth in order were the "ex-voto" peace-offerings, the flesh of which could be eaten even on the morrow. The reason for this order is that man is bound to God, chiefly on account of His majesty; secondly, on account of the sins he has committed; thirdly, because of the benefits he has already received from Him; fourthly, by reason of the benefits he hopes to receive from Him.

Reply to Objection 1:: Sins are more grievous by reason of the state of the sinner, as stated above (Question [73], Article [10]): wherefore different victims are commanded to be offered for the sin of a priest, or of a prince, or of some other private individual. "But," as Rabbi Moses says (Doct. Perplex. iii), "we must take note that the more grievous the sin, the lower the species of animals offered for it. Wherefore the goat, which is a very base animal, was offered for idolatry; while a calf was offered for a priest's ignorance, and a ram for the negligence of a prince."

Reply to Objection 1:: In the matter of sacrifices the Law had in view the poverty of the offerers; so that those who could not have a four-footed animal at their disposal, might at least offer a bird; and that he who could not have a bird might at least offer bread; and that if a man had not even bread he might offer flour or ears of corn.

The figurative cause is that the bread signifies Christ Who is the "living bread" (Jn. 6:41,51). He was indeed an ear of corn, as it were, during the state of the law of nature, in the faith of the patriarchs; He was like flour in the doctrine of the Law of the prophets; and He was like perfect bread after He had taken human nature; baked in the fire, i.e. formed by the Holy Ghost in the oven of the virginal womb; baked again in a pan by the toils which He suffered in the world; and consumed by fire on the cross as on a gridiron.

Reply to Objection 1:: The products of the soil are useful to man, either as food, and of these bread was offered; or as drink, and of these wine was offered; or as seasoning, and of these oil and salt were offered; or as healing, and of these they offered incense, which both smells sweetly and binds easily together.

Now the bread foreshadowed the flesh of Christ; and the wine, His blood, whereby we were redeemed; oil betokens the grace of Christ; salt, His knowledge; incense, His prayer.

Reply to Objection 1:: Honey was not offered in the sacrifices to God, both because it was wont to be offered in the sacrifices to idols; and in order to denote the absence of all carnal sweetness and pleasure from those who intend to sacrifice to God. Leaven was not offered, to denote the exclusion of corruption. Perhaps too, it was wont to be offered in the sacrifices to idols.

Salt, however, was offered, because it wards off the corruption of putrefaction: for sacrifices offered to God should be incorrupt. Moreover, salt signifies the discretion of wisdom, or again, mortification of the flesh.

Incense was offered to denote devotion of the heart, which is necessary in the offerer; and again, to signify the odor of a good name: for incense is composed of matter, both rich and fragrant. And since the sacrifice "of jealousy" did not proceed from devotion, but rather from suspicion, therefore incense was not offered therein (Num. 5:15).

Article: 4

Whether sufficient reason can be assigned for the ceremonies pertaining to holy things?

Objection 1: It would seem that no sufficient reason can be assigned for the ceremonies of the Old Law that pertain to holy things. For Paul said (Acts 17:24): "God Who made the world and all things therein; He being Lord of heaven and earth, dwelleth not in temples made by hands." It was therefore unfitting that in the Old Law a tabernacle or temple should be set up for the worship of God.

Objection 2: Further, the state of the Old Law was not changed except by Christ. But the tabernacle denoted the state of the Old Law. Therefore it should not have been changed by the building of a temple.

Objection 3: Further, the Divine Law, more than any other indeed, should lead man to the worship of God. But an increase of divine worship requires multiplication of altars and temples; as is evident in regard to the New Law. Therefore it seems that also under the Old Law there should have been not only one tabernacle or temple, but many.

Objection 4: Further, the tabernacle or temple was ordained to the worship of God. But in God we should worship above all His unity and simplicity. Therefore it seems unbecoming for the tabernacle or temple to be divided by means of veils.

Objection 5: Further, the power of the First Mover, i.e. God, appears first of all in the east, for it is in that quarter that the first movement begins. But the tabernacle was set up for the worship of God. Therefore it should have been built so as to point to the east rather than the west.

Objection 6: Further, the Lord commanded (Ex. 20:4) that they should "not make . . . a graven thing, nor the likeness of anything." It was therefore unfitting for graven images of the cherubim to be set up in the tabernacle or temple. In like manner, the ark, the propitiatory, the candlestick, the table, the two altars, seem to have been placed there without reasonable cause.

Objection 7: Further, the Lord commanded (Ex. 20:24): "You shall make an altar of earth unto Me": and again (Ex. 20:26): "Thou shalt not go up by steps unto My altar." It was therefore unfitting that subsequently they should be commanded to make an altar of wood laid over with gold or brass; and of such a height that it was impossible to go up to it except by steps. For it is written (Ex. 27:1,2): "Thou shalt make also an altar of setim wood, which shall be five cubits long, and as many broad . . . and three cubits high . . . and thou shalt cover it with brass": and

(Ex. 30:1,3): "Thou shalt make . . . an altar to burn incense, of setim wood . . . and thou shalt overlay it with the purest gold."

Objection 8: Further, in God's works nothing should be superfluous; for not even in the works of nature is anything superfluous to be found. But one cover suffices for one tabernacle or house. Therefore it was unbecoming to furnish the tabernacle with many coverings, viz. curtains, curtains of goats' hair, rams' skins dyed red, and violet-colored skins (Ex. 26).

Objection 9: Further, exterior consecration signifies interior holiness, the subject of which is the soul. It was therefore unsuitable for the tabernacle and its vessels to be consecrated, since they were inanimate things.

Objection 1:: Further, it is written (Ps. 33:2): "I will bless the Lord at all times, His praise shall always be in my mouth." But the solemn festivals were instituted for the praise of God. Therefore it was not fitting that certain days should be fixed for keeping solemn festivals; so that it seems that there was no suitable cause for the ceremonies relating to holy things.

On the contrary, The Apostle says (Heb. 8:4) that those who "offer gifts according to the law . . . serve unto the example and shadow of heavenly things. As it was answered to Moses, when he was to finish the tabernacle: See, says He, that thou make all things according to the pattern which was shown thee on the mount." But that is most reasonable, which presents a likeness to heavenly things. Therefore the ceremonies relating to holy things had a reasonable cause.

I answer that, The chief purpose of the whole external worship is that man may give worship to God. Now man's tendency is to reverence less those things which are common, and indistinct from other things; whereas he admires and reveres those things which are distinct from others in some point of excellence. Hence too it is customary among men for kings and princes, who ought to be reverenced by their subjects, to be clothed in more precious garments, and to possess vaster and more beautiful abodes. And for this reason it behooved special times, a special abode, special vessels, and special ministers to be appointed for the divine worship, so that thereby the soul of man might be brought to greater reverence for God.

In like manner the state of the Old Law, as observed above (Article [2]; Question [100], Article [12]; 2, Article [2]), was instituted that it might foreshadow the mystery of Christ. Now that which foreshadows something should be determinate, so that it may present some likeness thereto. Consequently, certain special points had to be observed in matters pertaining to the worship of God.

Reply to Objection 1: The divine worship regards two things: namely, God Who is worshipped; and men, who worship Him. Accordingly God, Who is worshipped, is confined to no bodily place: wherefore there was no need, on His part, for a tabernacle or temple to be set up. But men, who worship Him, are corporeal beings: and for their sake there was need for a special tabernacle or temple to be set up for the worship of God, for two reasons. First, that through coming together with the thought that the place was set aside for the worship of God, they might approach thither with greater reverence. Secondly, that certain things relating to the excellence of Christ's Divine or human nature might be signified by the arrangement of various details in such temple or tabernacle.

To this Solomon refers (3 Kgs. 8:27) when he says: "If heaven and the heavens of heavens cannot contain Thee, how much less this house which I have built" for Thee? And further on (3 Kgs. 8:29,20) he adds: "That Thy eyes may be open upon this house . . . of which Thou hast said: My name shall be there; . . . that Thou mayest hearken to the supplication of Thy servant and of Thy people Israel." From this it is evident that the house of the sanctuary was set up, not in order to contain God, as abiding therein locally, but that God might be made known there by means of things done and said there; and that those who prayed there might, through reverence for the place, pray more devoutly, so as to be heard more readily.

Reply to Objection 2: Before the coming of Christ, the state of the Old Law was not changed as regards the fulfilment of the Law, which was effected in Christ alone: but it was changed as regards the condition of the people that were under the Law. Because, at first, the people were in the desert, having no fixed abode: afterwards they were engaged in various wars with the neighboring nations; and lastly, at the time of David and Solomon, the state of that people was one of great peace. And then for the first time the temple was built in the place which Abraham, instructed by God, had chosen for the purpose of sacrifice. For it is written (Gn. 22:2) that the Lord commanded Abraham to "offer" his son "for a holocaust upon one of the mountains which I will show thee": and it is related further on (Gn. 22:14) that "he calleth the name of that place, The Lord seeth," as though, according to the Divine prevision, that place were chosen for the worship of God. Hence it is written (Dt. 12:5,6): "You shall come to the place which the Lord your God shall choose . . . and you shall offer . . . your holocausts and victims."

Now it was not meet for that place to be pointed out by the building of the temple before the aforesaid time; for three reasons assigned by Rabbi Moses. First, lest the Gentiles might seize hold of that place. Secondly, lest the Gentiles might destroy it. The third reason is lest each tribe might wish that place to fall to their lot, and strifes and quarrels be the result. Hence the temple was not built until they had a king who would be able to quell such quarrels. Until that time a portable tabernacle was employed for divine worship, no place being as yet fixed for the worship of God. This is the literal reason for the distinction between the tabernacle and the temple.

The figurative reason may be assigned to the fact that they signify a twofold state. For the tabernacle, which was changeable, signifies the state of the present changeable life: whereas the temple, which was fixed and stable, signifies the state of future life which is altogether unchangeable. For this reason it is said that in the building of the temple no sound was heard of hammer or saw, to signify that all movements of disturbance will be far removed from the future state. Or else the tabernacle signifies the state of the Old Law; while the temple built by Solomon betokens the state of the New Law. Hence the Jews alone worked at the building of the tabernacle; whereas the temple was built with the cooperation of the Gentiles, viz. the Tyrians and Sidonians.

Reply to Objection 3: The reason for the unity of the temple or tabernacle may be either literal or figurative. The literal reason was the exclusion of idolatry. For the Gentiles put up various times to various gods: and so, to strengthen in the minds of men their belief in the unity of the Godhead, God wished sacrifices to be offered to Him in one place only. Another reason was in order to show that bodily worship is not acceptable of itself: and so they restrained from offering sacrifices anywhere and everywhere. But the worship of the New Law, in the sacrifice whereof spiritual grace is contained, is of itself acceptable to God; and consequently the multiplication of altars and temples is permitted in the New Law.

As to those matters that regarded the spiritual worship of God, consisting in the teaching of the Law and the Prophets, there were, even under the Old Law, various places, called synagogues, appointed for the people to gather together for the praise of God; just as now there are places called churches in which the Christian people gather together for the divine worship. Thus our church takes the place of both temple and synagogue: since the very sacrifice of the Church is spiritual; wherefore with us the place of sacrifice is not distinct from the place of teaching. The figurative reason may be that hereby is signified the unity of the Church, whether militant or triumphant.

Reply to Objection 4: Just as the unity of the temple or tabernacle betokened the unity of God, or the unity of the Church, so also the division of the tabernacle or temple signified the distinction of those things that are subject to God, and from which we arise to the worship of God. Now the tabernacle was divided into two parts: one was called the "Holy of Holies," and was placed to the west; the other was called the "Holy Place" [*Or 'Sanctuary'. The Douay version uses both expressions], which was situated to the east. Moreover there was a court facing the tabernacle. Accordingly there are two reasons for this distinction. One is in respect of the tabernacle being ordained to the worship of God. Because the different parts of the world are thus betokened by the division of the tabernacle. For that part which was called the Holy of Holies signified the higher world, which is that of spiritual substances: while that part which is called the Holy Place signified the corporeal world. Hence the Holy Place was separated from the Holy of Holies by a veil, which was of four different colors (denoting the four elements), viz. of linen, signifying earth, because linen, i.e. flax, grows out of the earth; purple, signifying water, because the purple tint was made from certain shells found in the sea; violet, signifying air, because it has the color of the air; and scarlet twice dyed, signifying fire: and this because matter composed of the four elements is a veil between us and incorporeal substances. Hence the high-priest alone, and that once a year, entered into the inner tabernacle, i.e. the Holy of Holies: whereby we are taught that man's final perfection consists in his entering into that (higher) world: whereas into the outward tabernacle, i.e. the Holy Place, the priests entered every day: whereas the people were only admitted to the court; because the people were able to perceived material things, the inner nature of which only wise men by dint of study are able to discover.

But regard to the figurative reason, the outward tabernacle, which was called the Holy Place, betokened the state of the Old Law, as the Apostle says (Heb. 9:6, seqq.): because into that tabernacle "the priests always entered accomplishing the offices of sacrifices." But the inner tabernacle, which was called the Holy of Holies, signified either the glory of heaven or the spiritual state of the New Law to come. To the latter state Christ brought us; and this was signified by the high-priest entering alone, once a year, into the Holy of Holies. The veil betokened the concealing of the spiritual sacrifices under the sacrifices of old. This veil was adorned with four colors: viz. that of linen, to designate purity of the flesh; purple, to denote the sufferings which the saints underwent for God; scarlet twice dyed, signifying the twofold love of God and our neighbor; and violet, in token of heavenly contemplation. With regard to the state of the Old Law the people and the priests were situated differently from one another. For the people saw the mere corporeal sacrifices which were offered in the court: whereas the priests were intent on the inner meaning of the sacrifices, because their faith in the mysteries of Christ was more explicit. Hence they entered into the outer tabernacle. This outer tabernacle was divided from the court by a veil; because some matters relating to the mystery of Christ were hidden from the people, while they were known to the priests: though they were not fully revealed to them, as they were subsequently in the New Testament (cf. Eph. 3:5).

Reply to Objection 5: Worship towards the west was introduced in the Law to the exclusion of idolatry: because all the Gentiles, in reverence to the sun, worshipped towards the east; hence it is written (Ezech. 8:16) that certain men "had their backs towards the temple of the Lord, and their faces to the east, and they adored towards the rising of the sun." Accordingly, in order to prevent this, the tabernacle had the Holy of Holies to westward, that they might adore toward the west. A figurative reason may also be found in the fact that the whole state of the first tabernacle was ordained to foreshadow the death of Christ, which is signified by the west, according to Ps. 67:5: "Who ascendeth unto the west; the Lord is His name."

Reply to Objection 6: Both literal and figurative reasons may be assigned for the things contained in the tabernacle. The literal reason is in connection with the divine worship. And because, as already observed (ad 4), the inner tabernacle, called the Holy of Holies, signified the higher world of spiritual substances, hence that tabernacle contained three things, viz. "the ark of the testament in which was a golden pot that had manna, and the rod of Aaron that had blossomed, and the tables" (Heb. 9:4) on which were written the ten commandments of the Law. Now the ark stood between two "cherubim" that looked one towards the other: and over the ark was a table, called the "propitiatory," raised above the wings of the cherubim, as though it were held up by them; and appearing, to the imagination, to be the very seat of God. For this reason it was called the "propitiatory," as though the people received propitiation thence at the prayers of the high-priest. And so it was held up, so to speak, by the cherubim, in obedience, as it were, to God: while the ark of the testament was like the foot-stool to Him that sat on the propitiatory. These three things denote three things in that higher world: namely, God Who is above all, and incomprehensible to any creature. Hence no likeness of Him was set up; to denote His invisibility. But there was something to represent his seat; since, to wit, the creature, which is beneath God, as the seat under the sitter, is comprehensible. Again in that higher world there are spiritual substances called angels. These are signified by the two cherubim, looking one towards the other, to show that they are at peace with one another, according to Job 25:2: "Who maketh peace in . . . high places." For this reason, too, there was more than one cherub, to betoken the multitude of heavenly spirits, and to prevent their receiving worship from those who had been commanded to worship but one God. Moreover there are, enclosed as it were in that spiritual world, the intelligible types of whatsoever takes place in this world, just as in every cause are enclosed the types of its effects, and in the craftsman the types of the works of his craft. This was betokened by the ark, which represented, by means of the three things it contained, the three things of greatest import in human affairs. These are wisdom, signified by the tables of the testament; the power of governing, betokened by the rod of Aaron; and life, betokened by the manna which was the means of sustenance. Or else these three things signified the three Divine attributes, viz. wisdom, in the tables; power, in the rod; goodness, in the manna---both by reason of its sweetness, and because it was through the goodness of God that it was granted to man, wherefore it was preserved as a memorial of the Divine mercy. Again, these three things were represented in Isaias' vision. For he "saw the Lord sitting upon a throne high and elevated"; and the seraphim standing by; and that the house was filled with the glory of the Lord; wherefrom the seraphim cried out: "All the earth is full of His glory" (Is. 6:1,3). And so the images of the seraphim were set up, not to be worshipped, for this was forbidden by the first commandment; but as a sign of their function, as stated above.

The outer tabernacle, which denotes this present world, also contained three things, viz. the "altar of incense," which was directly opposite the ark; the "table of proposition," with the twelve loaves of proposition on it, which stood on the northern side; and the "candlestick," which was placed towards the south. These three things seem to correspond to the three which were enclosed in the ark; and they represented the same things as the latter, but more clearly: because, in order that wise men, denoted by the priests entering the temple, might grasp the meaning of these types, it was necessary to express them more manifestly than they are in the Divine or angelic mind. Accordingly the candlestick betokened, as a sensible sign thereof, the wisdom which was expressed on the tables (of the Law) in intelligible words. The altar of incense signified the office of the priest, whose duty it was to bring the people to God: and this was signified also by the rod: because on that altar the sweet-smelling incense was burnt, signifying the holiness of the people acceptable to God: for it is written (Apoc. 8:3) that the smoke of the sweet-smelling spices signifies the "justifications of the saints" (cf. Apoc. 19:8). Moreover it was fitting that the dignity of the priesthood should be denoted, in the ark, by the rod, and, in the outer tabernacle, by the altar of incense: because the priest is the mediator between God and the people, governing the people by Divine power, denoted by the rod; and offering to God the fruit of His government, i.e. the holiness of the people, on the altar of incense, so to speak. The table signified the sustenance of life, just as the manna did: but the former, a more general and a coarser kind of nourishment; the latter, a sweeter and more delicate. Again, the candlestick was fittingly placed on the southern side, while the table was placed to the north: because the south is the right-hand side of the world, while the north is the left-hand side, as stated in De Coelo et Mundo ii; and wisdom, like other spiritual goods, belongs to the right hand, while temporal nourishment belongs on the left, according to Prov. 3:16: "In her left hand (are) riches and glory." And the priestly power is midway between temporal goods and spiritual wisdom; because thereby both spiritual wisdom and temporal goods are dispensed.

Another literal signification may be assigned. For the ark contained the tables of the Law, in order to prevent forgetfulness of the Law, wherefore it is written (Ex. 24:12): "I will give thee two tables of stone, and the Law, and the commandments which I have written: that thou mayest teach them" to the children of Israel. The rod of Aaron was placed there to restrain the people from insubordination to the priesthood of Aaron; wherefore it is written (Num. 17:10): "Carry back the rod of Aaron into the tabernacle of the testimony, that it may be kept there for a token of the rebellious children of Israel." The manna was kept in the ark to remind them of the benefit conferred by God on the children of Israel in the desert; wherefore it is written (Ex. 16:32): "Fill a gomor of it, and let it be kept unto generations to come hereafter, that they may know the bread wherewith I fed you in the wilderness." The candlestick was set up to enhance the beauty of the temple, for the magnificence of a house depends on its being well lighted. Now the candlestick had seven branches, as Josephus observes (Antiquit. iii, 7,8), to signify the seven planets, wherewith the whole world is illuminated. Hence the candlestick was placed towards the south; because for us the course of the planets is from that quarter. The altar of incense was instituted that there might always be in the tabernacle a sweet-smelling smoke; both through respect for the tabernacle, and as a remedy for the stenches arising from the shedding of blood and the slaying of animals. For men despise evil-smelling things as being vile, whereas sweet-smelling things are much appreciated. The table was place there to signify that the priests who served the temple should take their food in the temple: wherefore, as stated in Mt. 12:4, it was lawful for none but the priests to eat the twelve loaves which were put on the table in memory of the twelve tribes. And the table was not placed in the middle directly in front of the propitiatory, in order to exclude an idolatrous rite: for the Gentiles, on the feasts of the moon, set up a table in front of the idol of the moon, wherefore it is written (Jer. 7:18): "The women knead the dough, to make cakes to the queen of heaven."

In the court outside the tabernacle was the altar of holocausts, on which sacrifices of those things which the people possessed were offered to God: and consequently the people who offered these sacrifices to God by the hands of the priest could be present in the court. But the priests alone, whose function it was to offer the people to God, could approach the inner altar, whereon the very devotion and holiness of the people was offered to God. And this altar was put up outside the tabernacle and in the court, to the exclusion of idolatrous worship: for the Gentiles placed altars inside the temples to offer up sacrifices thereon to idols.

The figurative reason for all these things may be taken from the relation of the tabernacle to Christ, who was foreshadowed therein. Now it must be observed that to show the imperfection of the figures of the Law, various figures were instituted in the temple to betoken Christ. For He was foreshadowed by the "propitiatory," since He is "a propitiation for our sins" (1 Jn. 2:2). This propitiatory was fittingly carried by cherubim, since of Him it is written (Heb. 1:6): "Let all the angels of God adore Him." He is also signified by the ark: because just as the ark was made of setim-wood, so was Christ's body composed of most pure members. More over it was gilded: for Christ was full of wisdom and charity, which are betokened by gold. And in the ark was a golden pot, i.e. His holy soul, having manna, i.e. "all the fulness of the Godhead" (Col. 2:9). Also there was a rod in the ark, i.e. His priestly power: for "He was made a . . . priest for ever" (Heb. 6:20). And therein were the tables of the Testament, to denote that Christ Himself is a lawgiver. Again, Christ was signified by the candlestick, for He said Himself (Jn. 8:12): "I am the Light of the world"; while the seven lamps denoted the seven gifts of the Holy Ghost. He is also betokened in the table, because He is our spiritual food, according to Jn. 6:41,51: "I am the living bread": and the twelve loaves signified the twelve apostles, or their teaching. Or again, the candlestick and table may signify the Church's teaching, and faith, which also enlightens and refreshes. Again, Christ is signified by the two altars of holocausts and incense. Because all works of virtue must be offered to us to God through Him; both those whereby we afflict the body, which are offered, as it were, on the altar of holocausts; and those which, with greater perfection of

195

mind, are offered to God in Christ, by the spiritual desires of the perfect, on the altar of incense, as it were, according to Heb. 13:15: "By Him therefore let us offer the sacrifice of praise always to God."

Reply to Objection 7: The Lord commanded an altar to be made for the offering of sacrifices and gifts, in honor of God, and for the upkeep of the ministers who served the tabernacle. Now concerning the construction of the altar the Lord issued a twofold precept. One was at the beginning of the Law (Ex. 20:24, seqq.) when the Lord commanded them to make "an altar of earth," or at least "not of hewn stones"; and again, not to make the altar high, so as to make it necessary to "go up" to it "by steps." This was in detestation of idolatrous worship: for the Gentiles made their altars ornate and high, thinking that there was something holy and divine in such things. For this reason, too, the Lord commanded (Dt. 16:21): "Thou shalt plant no grove, nor any tree near the altar of the Lord thy God": since idolaters were wont to offer sacrifices beneath trees, on account of the pleasantness and shade afforded by them. There was also a figurative reason for these precepts. Because we must confess that in Christ, Who is our altar, there is the true nature of flesh, as regards His humanity---and this is to make an altar of earth; and again, in regard to His Godhead, we must confess His equality with the Father---and this is "not to go up" to the altar by steps. Moreover we should not couple the doctrine of Christ to that of the Gentiles, which provokes men to lewdness.

But when once the tabernacle had been constructed to the honor of God, there was no longer reason to fear these occasions of idolatry. Wherefore the Lord commanded the altar of holocausts to be made of brass, and to be conspicuous to all the people; and the altar of incense, which was visible to none but the priests. Nor was brass so precious as to give the people an occasion for idolatry.

Since, however, the reason for the precept, "Thou shalt not go up by steps unto My altar" (Ex. 20:26) is stated to have been "lest thy nakedness be discovered," it should be observed that this too was instituted with the purpose of preventing idolatry, for in the feasts of Priapus the Gentiles uncovered their nakedness before the people. But later on the priests were prescribed the use of loin-cloths for the sake of decency: so that without any danger the altar could be placed so high that the priests when offering sacrifices would go up by steps of wood, not fixed but movable.

Reply to Objection 8: The body of the tabernacle consisted of boards placed on end, and covered on the inside with curtains of four different colors, viz. twisted linen, violet, purple, and scarlet twice dyed. These curtains, however, covered the sides only of the tabernacle; and the roof of the tabernacle was covered with violet-colored skins; and over this there was another covering of rams' skins dyed red; and over this there was a third curtain made of goats' hair, which covered not only the roof of the tabernacle, but also reached to the ground and covered the boards of the tabernacle on the outside. The literal reason of these coverings taken altogether was the adornment and protection of the tabernacle, that it might be an object of respect. Taken singly, according to some, the curtains denoted the starry heaven, which is adorned with various stars; the curtain (of goats' skin) signified the waters which are above the firmament; the skins dyed red denoted the empyrean heaven, where the angels are; the violet skins, the heaven of the Blessed Trinity.

The figurative meaning of these things is that the boards of which the tabernacle was constructed signify the faithful of Christ, who compose the Church. The boards were covered on the inner side by curtains of four colors: because the faithful are inwardly adorned with the four virtues: for "the twisted linen," as the gloss observes, "signifies the flesh refulgent with purity; violet signifies the mind desirous of heavenly things; purple denotes the flesh subject to passions; the twice dyed scarlet betokens the mind in the midst of the passions enlightened by the love of God and our neighbor." The coverings of the building designate prelates and doctors, who ought to be conspicuous for their heavenly manner of life, signified by the violet colored skins: and who should also be ready to suffer martyrdom, denoted by the skins dyed red; and austere of life and patient in adversity, betokened by the curtains of goats' hair, which were exposed to wind and rain, as the gloss observes.

Reply to Objection 9: The literal reason for the sanctification of the tabernacle and vessels was that they might be treated with greater reverence, being deputed, as it were, to the divine worship by this consecration. The figurative reason is that this sanctification signified the sanctification of the living tabernacle, i.e. the faithful of whom the Church of Christ is composed.

Reply to Objection 1:: Under the Old Law there were seven temporal solemnities, and one continual solemnity, as may be gathered from Num. 28,29. There was a continual feast, since the lamb was sacrificed every day, morning and evening: and this continual feast of an abiding sacrifice signified the perpetuity of Divine bliss. Of the temporal feasts the first was that which was repeated every week. This was the solemnity of the "Sabbath," celebrated in memory of the work of the creation of the universe. Another solemnity, viz. the "New Moon," was repeated every month, and was observed in memory of the work of the Divine government. For the things of this lower world owe their variety chiefly to the movement of the moon; wherefore this feast was kept at the new moon: and not at the full moon, to avoid the worship of idolaters who used to offer sacrifices to the moon at that particular time. And these two blessings are bestowed in common on the whole human race; and hence they were repeated more frequently.

The other five feasts were celebrated once a year: and they commemorated the benefits which had been conferred especially on that people. For there was the feast of the "Passover" in the first month to commemorate the blessing of being delivered out of Egypt. The feast of "Pentecost" was celebrated fifty days later, to recall the blessing of the giving of the Law. The other three feasts were kept in the seventh month, nearly the whole of which was solemnized by them, just as the seventh day. For on the first of the seventh month was the feast of "Trumpets," in memory of the delivery of Isaac, when Abraham found the ram caught by its horns, which they represented by the horns which they blew. The feast of Trumpets was a kind of invitation whereby they prepared themselves to keep the following feast which was kept on the tenth day. This was the feast of "Expiation," in memory of the blessing whereby, at the prayer of Moses, God forgave the people's sin of worshipping the calf. After this was the feast of "Scenopegia" or of "Tents," which was kept for seven days, to commemorate the blessing of being protected and led by God through the desert, where they lived in tents. Hence during this feast they had to take "the fruits of the fairest tree," i.e. the citron, "and the trees of dense foliage" [*Douay and A. V. and R. V. read: 'Boughs of thick trees'], i.e. the myrtle, which is fragrant, "and the branches of palm-trees, and willows of the brook," which retain their greenness a long time; and these are to be found in the Land of promise; to signify that God had brought them through the arid land of the wilderness to a land of delights. On the eighth day another feast was observed, of "Assembly and Congregation," on which the people collected the expenses necessary for the divine worship: and it signified the uniting of the people and the peace granted to them in the Land of promise.

The figurative reason for these feasts was that the continual sacrifice of the lamb foreshadowed the perpetuity of Christ, Who is the "Lamb of God," according to Heb. 13:8: "Jesus Christ yesterday and today, and the same for ever." The Sabbath signified the spiritual rest bestowed by Christ, as stated in Heb. 4. The Neomenia, which is the beginning of the new moon, signified the enlightening of the primitive Church by Christ's preaching and miracles. The feast of Pentecost signified the Descent of the Holy Ghost on the apostles. The feast of Trumpets signified the preaching of the apostles. The feast of Expiation signified the cleansing of the Christian people from sins: and the feast of Tabernacles signified their pilgrimage in this world, wherein they walk by advancing in virtue. The feast of Assembly or Congregation foreshadowed the assembly of the faithful in the kingdom of heaven: wherefore this feast is described as "most holy" (Lev. 23:36). These three feasts followed immediately on one another, because those who expiate their vices should advance in virtue, until they come to see God, as stated in Ps. 83:8.

Article: 5

Whether there can be any suitable cause for the sacraments of the Old Law?

Objection 1: It would seem that there can be no suitable cause for the sacraments of the Old Law. Because those things that are done for the purpose of divine worship should not be like the observances of idolaters: since it is written

(Dt. 12:31): "Thou shalt not do in like manner to the Lord thy God: for they have done to their gods all the abominations which the Lord abhorreth." Now worshippers of idols used to knive themselves to the shedding of blood: for it is related (3 Kgs. 18:28) that they "cut themselves after their manner with knives and lancets, till they were all covered with blood." For this reason the Lord commanded (Dt. 14:1): "You shall not cut yourselves nor make any baldness for the dead." Therefore it was unfitting for circumcision to be prescribed by the Law (Lev. 12:3).

Objection 2: Further, those things which are done for the worship of God should be marked with decorum and gravity; according to Ps. 34:18: "I will praise Thee in a grave [Douay: 'strong'] people." But it seems to savor of levity for a man to eat with haste. Therefore it was unfittingly commanded (Ex. 12:11) that they should eat the Paschal lamb "in haste." Other things too relative to the eating of the lamb were prescribed, which seem altogether unreasonable.

Objection 3: Further, the sacraments of the Old Law were figures of the sacraments of the New Law. Now the Paschal lamb signified the sacrament of the Eucharist, according to 1 Cor. 5:7: "Christ our Pasch is sacrificed." Therefore there should also have been some sacraments of the Old Law to foreshadow the other sacraments of the New Law, such as Confirmation, Extreme Unction, and Matrimony, and so forth.

Objection 4: Further, purification can scarcely be done except by removing something impure. But as far as God is concerned, no bodily thing is reputed impure, because all bodies are God's creatures; and "every creature of God is good, and nothing to be rejected that is received with thanksgiving" (1 Tim. 4:4). It was therefore unfitting for them to be purified after contact with a corpse, or any similar corporeal infection.

Objection 5: Further, it is written (Ecclus. 34:4): "What can be made clean by the unclean?" But the ashes of the red heifer [*Cf. Heb. 9:13] which was burnt, were unclean, since they made a man unclean: for it is stated (Num. 19:7, seqq.) that the priest who immolated her was rendered unclean "until the evening"; likewise he that burnt her; and he that gathered up her ashes. Therefore it was unfittingly prescribed there that the unclean should be purified by being sprinkled with those cinders.

Objection 6: Further, sins are not something corporeal that can be carried from one place to another: nor can man be cleansed from sin by means of something unclean. It was therefore unfitting for the purpose of expiating the sins of the people that the priest should confess the sins of the children of Israel on one of the buck-goats, that it might carry them away into the wilderness: while they were rendered unclean by the other, which they used for the purpose of purification, by burning it together with the calf outside the camp; so that they had to wash their clothes and their bodies with water (Lev. 16).

Objection 7: Further, what is already cleansed should not be cleansed again. It was therefore unfitting to apply a second purification to a man cleansed from leprosy, or to a house; as laid down in Lev. 14.

Objection 8: Further, spiritual uncleanness cannot be cleansed by material water or by shaving the hair. Therefore it seems unreasonable that the Lord ordered (Ex. 30:18, seqq.) the making of a brazen laver with its foot, that the priests might wash their hands and feet before entering the temple; and that He commanded (Num. 8:7) the Levites to be sprinkled with the water of purification, and to shave all the hairs of their flesh.

Objection 9: Further, that which is greater cannot be cleansed by that which is less. Therefore it was unfitting that, in the Law, the higher and lower priests, as stated in Lev. 8 [*Cf. Ex. 29], and the Levites, according to Num. 8, should be consecrated with any bodily anointing, bodily sacrifices, and bodily oblations.

Objection 1:: Further, as stated in 1 Kgs. 16:7, "Man seeth those things that appear, but the Lord beholdeth the heart." But those things that appear outwardly in man are the dispositions of his body and his clothes. Therefore it was unfitting for certain special garments to be appointed to the higher and lower priests, as related in Ex. 28 [*Cf. Lev. 8:7, seqq.]. It seems, moreover, unreasonable that anyone should be debarred from the priesthood on account of defects in the body, as stated in Lev. 21:17, seqq.: "Whosoever of thy seed throughout their families, hath a blemish, he shall not offer bread to his God . . . if he be blind, if he be lame," etc. It seems, therefore, that the sacraments of the Old Law were unreasonable.

On the contrary, It is written (Lev. 20:8): "I am the Lord that sanctify you." But nothing unreasonable is done by God, for it is written (Ps. 103:24): "Thou hast made all things in wisdom." Therefore there was nothing without a reasonable cause in the sacraments of the Old Law, which were ordained to the sanctification of man.

I answer that, As stated above (Question [101], Article [4]), the sacraments are, properly speaking, things applied to the worshippers of God for their consecration so as, in some way, to depute them to the worship of God. Now the worship of God belonged in a general way to the whole people; but in a special way, it belonged to the priests and Levites, who were the ministers of divine worship. Consequently, in these sacraments of the Old Law, certain things concerned the whole people in general; while others belonged to the ministers.

In regard to both, three things were necessary. The first was to be established in the state of worshipping God: and this institution was brought about---for all in general, by circumcision, without which no one was admitted to any of the legal observances---and for the priests, by their consecration. The second thing required was the use of those things that pertain to divine worship. And thus, as to the people, there was the partaking of the paschal banquet, to which no uncircumcised man was admitted, as is clear from Ex. 12:43, seqq.: and, as to the priests, the offering of the victims, and the eating of the loaves of proposition and of other things that were allotted to the use of the priests. The third thing required was the removal of all impediments to divine worship, viz. of uncleannesses. And then, as to the people, certain purifications were instituted for the removal of certain external uncleannesses; and also expiations from sins; while, as to the priests and Levites, the washing of hands and feet and the shaving of the hair were instituted.

And all these things had reasonable causes, both literal, in so far as they were ordained to the worship of God for the time being, and figurative, in so far as they were ordained to foreshadow Christ: as we shall see by taking them one by one.

Reply to Objection 1: The chief literal reason for circumcision was in order that man might profess his belief in one God. And because Abraham was the first to sever himself from the infidels, by going out from his house and kindred, for this reason he was the first to receive circumcision. This reason is set forth by the Apostle (Rm. 4:9, seqq.) thus: "He received the sign of circumcision, a seal of the justice of the faith which he had, being uncircumcised"; because, to wit, we are told that "unto Abraham faith was reputed to justice," for the reason that "against hope he believed in hope," i.e. against the hope that is of nature he believed in the hope that is of grace, "that he might be made the father of many nations," when he was an old man, and his wife an old and barren woman. And in order that this declaration, and imitation of Abraham's faith, might be fixed firmly in the hearts of the Jews, they received in their flesh such a sign as they could not forget, wherefore it is written (Gn. 17:13): "My covenant shall be in your flesh for a perpetual covenant." This was done on the eighth day, because until then a child is very tender, and so might be seriously injured; and is considered as something not yet consolidated: wherefore neither are animals offered before the eighth day. And it was not delayed after that time, lest some might refuse the sign of circumcision on account of the pain: and also lest the parents, whose love for their children increases as they become used to their presence and as they grow older, should withdraw their children from circumcision. A second reason may have been the weakening of concupiscence in that member. A third motive may have been to revile the worship of Venus and Priapus, which gave honor to that part of the body. The Lord's prohibition extended only to the cutting of oneself in honor of idols: and such was not the circumcision of which we have been speaking.

The figurative reason for circumcision was that it foreshadowed the removal of corruption, which was to be brought about by Christ, and will be perfectly fulfilled in the eighth age, which is the age of those who rise from the dead. And since all corruption of guilt and punishment comes to us through our carnal origin, from the sin of our first parent, therefore circumcision was applied to the generative member. Hence the Apostle says (Col. 2:11): "You are circumcised" in Christ "with circumcision not made by hand in despoiling of the body of the flesh, but in the circumcision of" Our Lord Jesus "Christ."

Reply to Objection 2: The literal reason of the paschal banquet was to commemorate the blessing of being led by God out of Egypt. Hence by celebrating this banquet they declared that they belonged to that people which God had taken to Himself out of Egypt. For when they were delivered from Egypt, they were commanded to sprinkle the lamb's blood on the transoms of their house doors, as though declaring that they were averse to the rites of the Egyptians who worshipped the ram. Wherefore they were delivered by the sprinkling or rubbing of the blood of the lamb on the door-posts, from the danger of extermination which threatened the Egyptians.

Now two things are to be observed in their departure from Egypt: namely, their haste in going, for the Egyptians pressed them to go forth speedily, as related in Ex. 12:33; and there was danger that anyone who did not hasten to go with the crowd might be slain by the Egyptians. Their haste was shown in two ways. First by what they ate. For they were commanded to eat unleavened bread, as a sign "that it could not be leavened, the Egyptians pressing them to depart"; and to eat roast meat, for this took less time to prepare; and that they should not break a bone thereof, because in their haste there was no time to break bones. Secondly, as to the manner of eating. For it is written: "You shall gird your reins, and you shall have shoes on your feet, holding staves in your hands, and you shall eat in haste": which clearly designates men at the point of starting on a journey. To this also is to be referred the command: "In one house shall it be eaten, neither shall you carry forth of the flesh thereof out of the house": because, to wit, on account of their haste, they could not send any gifts of it.

The stress they suffered while in Egypt was denoted by the wild lettuces. The figurative reason is evident, because the sacrifice of the paschal lamb signified the sacrifice of Christ according to 1 Cor. 5:7: "Christ our pasch is sacrificed." The blood of the lamb, which ensured deliverance from the destroyer, by being sprinkled on the transoms, signified faith in Christ's Passion, in the hearts and on the lips of the faithful, by which same Passion we are delivered from sin and death, according to 1 Pt. 1:18: "You were . . . redeemed . . . with the precious blood . . . of a lamb unspotted." The partaking of its flesh signified the eating of Christ's body in the Sacrament; and the flesh was roasted at the fire to signify Christ's Passion or charity. And it was eaten with unleavened bread to signify the blameless life of the faithful who partake of Christ's body, according to 1 Cor.

5:8: "Let us feast . . . with the unleavened bread of sincerity and truth." The wild
lettuces were added to denote repentance for sins, which is required of those
who receive the body of Christ. Their loins were girt in sign of chastity: and the
shoes of their feet are the examples of our dead ancestors. The staves they were
to hold in their hands denoted pastoral authority: and it was commanded that
the paschal lamb should be eaten in one house, i.e. in a catholic church, and not
in the conventicles of heretics.

Reply to Objection 3: Some of the sacraments of the New Law had
corresponding figurative sacraments in the Old Law. For Baptism, which is the
sacrament of Faith, corresponds to circumcision. Hence it is written (Col.
2:11,12): "You are circumcised . . . in the circumcision of" Our Lord Jesus "Christ:
buried with Him in Baptism." In the New Law the sacrament of the Eucharist
corresponds to the banquet of the paschal lamb. The sacrament of Penance in the
New Law corresponds to all the purifications of the Old Law. The sacrament of
Orders corresponds to the consecration of the pontiff and of the priests. To the
sacrament of Confirmation, which is the sacrament of the fulness of grace, there
would be no corresponding sacrament of the Old Law, because the time of
fulness had not yet come, since "the Law brought no man [Vulg.: 'nothing'] to
perfection" (Heb. 7:19). The same applies to the sacrament of Extreme Unction,
which is an immediate preparation for entrance into glory, to which the way was
not yet opened out in the Old Law, since the price had not yet been paid.
Matrimony did indeed exist under the Old Law, as a function of nature, but not
as the sacrament of the union of Christ with the Church, for that union was not
as yet brought about. Hence under the Old Law it was allowable to give a bill of
divorce, which is contrary to the nature of the sacrament.

Reply to Objection 4: As already stated, the purifications of the Old Law were
ordained for the removal of impediments to the divine worship: which worship
is twofold; viz. spiritual, consisting in devotion of the mind to God; and corporal,
consisting in sacrifices, oblations, and so forth. Now men are hindered in the
spiritual worship by sins, whereby men were said to be polluted, for instance, by
idolatry, murder, adultery, or incest. From such pollutions men were purified by
certain sacrifices, offered either for the whole community in general, or also for
the sins of individuals; not that those carnal sacrifices had of themselves the
power of expiating sin; but that they signified that expiation of sins which was to
be effected by Christ, and of which those of old became partakers by protesting
their faith in the Redeemer, while taking part in the figurative sacrifices.

The impediments to external worship consisted in certain bodily
uncleannesses; which were considered in the first place as existing in man, and
consequently in other animals also, and in man's clothes, dwelling-place, and
vessels. In man himself uncleanness was considered as arising partly from
himself and partly from contact with unclean things. Anything proceeding from
man was reputed unclean that was already subject to corruption, or exposed
thereto: and consequently since death is a kind of corruption, the human corpse

was considered unclean. In like manner, since leprosy arises from corruption of the humors, which break out externally and infect other persons, therefore were lepers also considered unclean; and, again, women suffering from a flow of blood, whether from weakness, or from nature (either at the monthly course or at the time of conception); and, for the same reason, men were reputed unclean if they suffered from a flow of seed, whether due to weakness, to nocturnal pollution, or to sexual intercourse. Because every humor issuing from man in the aforesaid ways involves some unclean infection. Again, man contracted uncleanness by touching any unclean thing whatever.

Now there was both a literal and a figurative reason for these uncleannesses. The literal reason was taken from the reverence due to those things that belong to the divine worship: both because men are not wont, when unclean, to touch precious things: and in order that by rarely approaching sacred things they might have greater respect for them. For since man could seldom avoid all the aforesaid uncleannesses, the result was that men could seldom approach to touch things belonging to the worship of God, so that when they did approach, they did so with greater reverence and humility. Moreover, in some of these the literal reason was that men should not be kept away from worshipping God through fear of coming in contact with lepers and others similarly afflicted with loathsome and contagious diseases. In others, again, the reason was to avoid idolatrous worship: because in their sacrificial rites the Gentiles sometimes employed human blood and seed. All these bodily uncleannesses were purified either by the mere sprinkling of water, or, in the case of those which were more grievous, by some sacrifice of expiation for the sin which was the occasion of the uncleanness in question.

The figurative reason for these uncleannesses was that they were figures of various sins. For the uncleanness of any corpse signifies the uncleanness of sin, which is the death of the soul. The uncleanness of leprosy betokened the uncleanness of heretical doctrine: both because heretical doctrine is contagious just as leprosy is, and because no doctrine is so false as not to have some truth mingled with error, just as on the surface of a leprous body one may distinguish the healthy parts from those that are infected. The uncleanness of a woman suffering from a flow of blood denotes the uncleanness of idolatry, on account of the blood which is offered up. The uncleanness of the man who has suffered seminal loss signifies the uncleanness of empty words, for "the seed is the word of God." The uncleanness of sexual intercourse and of the woman in child-birth signifies the uncleanness of original sin. The uncleanness of the woman in her periods signifies the uncleanness of a mind that is sensualized by pleasure. Speaking generally, the uncleanness contracted by touching an unclean thing denotes the uncleanness arising from consent in another's sin, according to 2 Cor. 6:17: "Go out from among them, and be ye separate . . . and touch not the unclean thing."

Moreover, this uncleanness arising from the touch was contracted even by inanimate objects; for whatever was touched in any way by an unclean man, became itself unclean. Wherein the Law attenuated the superstition of the Gentiles, who held that uncleanness was contracted not only by touch, but also by speech or looks, as Rabbi Moses states (Doct. Perplex. iii) of a woman in her periods. The mystical sense of this was that "to God the wicked and his wickedness are hateful alike" (Wis. 14:9).

There was also an uncleanness of inanimate things considered in themselves, such as the uncleanness of leprosy in a house or in clothes. For just as leprosy occurs in men through a corrupt humor causing putrefaction and corruption in the flesh; so, too, through some corruption and excess of humidity or dryness, there arises sometimes a kind of corruption in the stones with which a house is built, or in clothes. Hence the Law called this corruption by the name of leprosy, whereby a house or a garment was deemed to be unclean: both because all corruption savored of uncleanness, as stated above, and because the Gentiles worshipped their household gods as a preservative against this corruption. Hence the Law prescribed such houses, where this kind of corruption was of a lasting nature, to be destroyed; and such garments to be burnt, in order to avoid all occasion of idolatry. There was also an uncleanness of vessels, of which it is written (Num. 19:15): "The vessel that hath no cover, and binding over it, shall be unclean." The cause of this uncleanness was that anything unclean might easily drop into such vessels, so as to render them unclean. Moreover, this command aimed at the prevention of idolatry. For idolaters believed that if mice, lizards, or the like, which they used to sacrifice to the idols, fell into the vessels or into the water, these became more pleasing to the gods. Even now some women let down uncovered vessels in honor of the nocturnal deities which they call "Janae."

The figurative reason of these uncleannesses is that the leprosy of a house signified the uncleanness of the assembly of heretics; the leprosy of a linen garment signified an evil life arising from bitterness of mind; the leprosy of a woolen garment denoted the wickedness of flatterers; leprosy in the warp signified the vices of the soul; leprosy on the woof denoted sins of the flesh, for as the warp is in the woof, so is the soul in the body. The vessel that has neither cover nor binding, betokens a man who lacks the veil of taciturnity, and who is unrestrained by any severity of discipline.

Reply to Objection 5: As stated above (ad 4), there was a twofold uncleanness in the Law; one by way of corruption in the mind or in the body; and this was the graver uncleanness; the other was by mere contact with an unclean thing, and this was less grave, and was more easily expiated. Because the former uncleanness was expiated by sacrifices for sins, since all corruption is due to sin, and signifies sin: whereas the latter uncleanness was expiated by the mere sprinkling of a certain water, of which water we read in Num. 19. For there God commanded them to take a red cow in memory of the sin they had committed in worshipping a calf. And a cow is mentioned rather than a calf, because it was thus that the Lord was wont to designate the synagogue, according to Osee 4:16: "Israel hath gone astray like a wanton heifer": and this was, perhaps, because they worshipped heifers after the custom of Egypt, according to Osee 10:5: "(They) have worshipped the kine of Bethaven." And in detestation of the sin of idolatry it was sacrificed outside the camp; in fact, whenever sacrifice was offered up in expiation of the multitude of sins, it was all burnt outside the camp. Moreover, in order to show that this sacrifice cleansed the people from all their sins, "the priest" dipped "his finger in her blood," and sprinkled "it over against the door of the tabernacle seven times"; for the number seven signified universality. Further, the very sprinkling of blood pertained to the detestation of idolatry, in which the blood that was offered up was not poured out, but was collected together, and men gathered round it to eat in honor of the idols. Likewise it was burnt by fire, either because God appeared to Moses in a fire, and the Law was given from the midst of fire; or to denote that idolatry, together with all that was connected therewith, was to be extirpated altogether; just as the cow was burnt "with her skin and her flesh, her blood and dung being delivered to the flames." To this burning were added "cedar-wood, and hyssop, and scarlet twice dyed," to signify that just as cedar-wood is not liable to putrefaction, and scarlet twice dyed does not easily lose its color, and hyssop retains its odor after it has been dried; so also was this sacrifice for the preservation of the whole people, and for their good behavior and devotion. Hence it is said of the ashes of the cow: "That they may be reserved for the multitude of the children of Israel." Or, according to Josephus (Antiq. iii, 8,9,10), the four elements are indicated here: for "cedar-wood" was added to the fire, to signify the earth, on account of its earthiness; "hyssop," to signify the air, on account of its smell; "scarlet twice dyed," to signify water, for the same reason as purple, on account of the dyes which are taken out of the water: thus denoting the fact that this sacrifice was offered to the Creator of the four elements. And since this sacrifice was offered for the sin of idolatry, both "he that burned her," and "he that gathered up the ashes," and "he that sprinkled the water" in which the ashes were placed, were deemed unclean in detestation of that sin, in order to show that whatever was in any way connected with idolatry should be cast aside as being unclean. From this uncleanness they were purified by the mere washing of their clothes; nor did they need to be sprinkled with the water on account of this kind of uncleanness, because otherwise the process would have been unending, since he that sprinkled the water became unclean, so that if he were to sprinkle himself he would remain unclean; and if another were to sprinkle him, that one would have become unclean, and in like manner, whoever might sprinkle him, and so on indefinitely.

The figurative reason of this sacrifice was that the red cow signified Christ in respect his assumed weakness, denoted by the female sex; while the color of the cow designated the blood of His Passion. And the "red cow was of full age," because all Christ's works are perfect, "in which there" was "no blemish"; "and which" had "not carried the yoke," because Christ was innocent, nor did He carry the yoke of sin. It was commanded to be taken to Moses, because they blamed

Him for transgressing the law of Moses by breaking the Sabbath. And it was commanded to be delivered "to Eleazar the priest," because Christ was delivered into the hands of the priests to be slain. It was immolated "without the camp," because Christ "suffered outside the gate" (Heb. 13:12). And the priest dipped "his finger in her blood," because the mystery of Christ's Passion should be considered and imitated.

It was sprinkled "over against . . . the tabernacle," which denotes the synagogue, to signify either the condemnation of the unbelieving Jews, or the purification of believers; and this "seven times," in token either of the seven gifts of the Holy Ghost, or of the seven days wherein all time is comprised. Again, all things that pertain to the Incarnation of Christ should be burnt with fire, i.e. they should be understood spiritually; for the "skin" and "flesh" signified Christ's outward works; the "blood" denoted the subtle inward force which quickened His external deeds; the "dung" betokened His weariness, His thirst, and all such like things pertaining to His weakness. Three things were added, viz. "cedar-wood," which denotes the height of hope or contemplation; "hyssop," in token of humility or faith; "scarlet twice dyed," which denotes twofold charity; for it is by these three that we should cling to Christ suffering. The ashes of this burning were gathered by "a man that is clean," because the relics of the Passion came into the possession of the Gentiles, who were not guilty of Christ's death. The ashes were put into water for the purpose of expiation, because Baptism receives from Christ's Passion the power of washing away sins. The priest who immolated and burned the cow, and he who burned, and he who gathered together the ashes, were unclean, as also he that sprinkled the water: either because the Jews became unclean through putting Christ to death, whereby our sins are expiated; and this, until the evening, i.e. until the end of the world, when the remnants of Israel will be converted; or else because they who handle sacred things with a view to the cleansing of others contract certain uncleannesses, as Gregory says (Pastor. ii, 5); and this until the evening, i.e. until the end of this life.

Reply to Objection 6: As stated above (ad 5), an uncleanness which was caused by corruption either of mind or of body was expiated by sin-offerings. Now special sacrifices were wont to be offered for the sins of individuals: but since some were neglectful about expiating such sins and uncleannesses; or, through ignorance, failed to offer this expiation; it was laid down that once a year, on the tenth day of the seventh month, a sacrifice of expiation should be offered for the whole people. And because, as the Apostle says (Heb. 7:28), "the Law maketh men priests, who have infirmity," it behooved the priest first of all to offer a calf for his own sins, in memory of Aaron's sin in fashioning the molten calf; and besides, to offer a ram for a holocaust, which signified that the priestly sovereignty denoted by the ram, who is the head of the flock, was to be ordained to the glory of God. Then he offered two he-goats for the people: one of which was offered in expiation of the sins of the multitude. For the he-goat is an evil-smelling animal; and from its skin clothes are made having a pungent odor; to signify the stench, uncleanness and the sting of sin. After this he-goat had been immolated, its blood was taken, together with the blood of the calf, into the Holy of Holies, and the entire sanctuary was sprinkled with it; to signify that the tabernacle was cleansed from the uncleanness of the children of Israel. But the corpses of the he-goat and calf which had been offered up for sin had to be burnt, to denote the destruction of sins. They were not, however, burnt on the altar: since none but holocausts were burnt thereon; but it was prescribed that they should be burnt without the camp, in detestation of sin: for this was done whenever sacrifice was offered for a grievous sin, or for the multitude of sins. The other goat was let loose into the wilderness: not indeed to offer it to the demons, whom the Gentiles worshipped in desert places, because it was unlawful to offer aught to them; but in order to point out the effect of the sacrifice which had been offered up. Hence the priest put his hand on its head, while confessing the sins of the children of Israel: as though that goat were to carry them away into the wilderness, where it would be devoured by wild beasts, because it bore the punishment of the people's sins. And it was said to bear the sins of the people, either because the forgiveness of the people's sins was signified by its being let loose, or because on its head written lists of sins were fastened.

The figurative reason of these things was that Christ was foreshadowed both by the calf, on account of His power; and by the ram, because He is the Head of the faithful; and by the he-goat, on account of "the likeness of sinful flesh" (Rm. 8:3). Moreover, Christ was sacrificed for the sins of both priests and people: since both those of high and those of low degree are cleansed from sin by His Passion. The blood of the calf and of the goat was brought into the Holies by the priest, because the entrance to the kingdom of heaven was opened to us by the blood of Christ's Passion. Their bodies were burnt without the camp, because "Christ suffered without the gate," as the Apostle declares (Heb. 13:12). The scape-goat may denote either Christ's Godhead Which went away into solitude when the Man Christ suffered, not by going to another place, but by restraining His power: or it may signify the base concupiscence which we ought to cast away from ourselves, while we offer up to Our Lord acts of virtue.

With regard to the uncleanness contracted by those who burnt these sacrifices, the reason is the same as that which we assigned (ad 5) to the sacrifice of the red heifer.

Reply to Objection 7: The legal rite did not cleanse the leper of his deformity, but declared him to be cleansed. This is shown by the words of Lev. 14:3, seqq., where it was said that the priest, "when he shall find that the leprosy is cleansed," shall command "him that is to be purified": consequently, the leper was already healed: but he was said to be purified in so far as the verdict of the priest restored him to the society of men and to the worship of God. It happened sometimes, however, that bodily leprosy was miraculously cured by the legal rite, when the priest erred in his judgment.

Now this purification of a leper was twofold: for, in the first place, he was declared to be clean; and, secondly, he was restored, as clean, to the society of men and to the worship of God, to wit, after seven days. At the first purification the leper who sought to be cleansed offered for himself "two living sparrows . . . cedar-wood, and scarlet, and hyssop," in such wise that a sparrow and the hyssop should be tied to the cedar-wood with a scarlet thread, so that the cedar-wood was like the handle of an aspersory: while the hyssop and sparrow were that part of the aspersory which was dipped into the blood of the other sparrow which was "immolated . . . over living waters." These things he offered as an antidote to the four defects of leprosy: for cedar-wood, which is not subject to putrefaction, was offered against the putrefaction; hyssop, which is a sweet-smelling herb, was offered up against the stench; a living sparrow was offered up against numbness; and scarlet, which has a vivid color, was offered up against the repulsive color of leprosy. The living sparrow was let loose to fly away into the plain, because the leper was restored to his former liberty.

On the eighth day he was admitted to divine worship, and was restored to the society of men; but only after having shaved all the hair of his body, and washed his clothes, because leprosy rots the hair, infects the clothes, and gives them an evil smell. Afterwards a sacrifice was offered for his sin, since leprosy was frequently a result of sin: and some of the blood of the sacrifice was put on the tip of the ear of the man that was to be cleansed, "and on the thumb of his right hand, and the great toe of his right foot"; because it is in these parts that leprosy is first diagnosed and felt. In this rite, moreover, three liquids were employed: viz. blood, against the corruption of the blood; oil, to denote the healing of the disease; and living waters, to wash away the filth.

The figurative reason was that the Divine and human natures in Christ were denoted by the two sparrows, one of which, in likeness of His human nature, was offered up in an earthen vessel over living waters, because the waters of Baptism are sanctified by Christ's Passion. The other sparrow, in token of His impassible Godhead, remained living, because the Godhead cannot die: hence it flew away, for the Godhead could not be encompassed by the Passion. Now this living sparrow, together with the cedar-wood and scarlet or cochineal, and hyssop, i.e. faith, hope and charity, as stated above (ad 5), was put into the water for the purpose of sprinkling, because we are baptized in the faith of the God-Man. By the waters of Baptism or of his tears man washes his clothes, i.e. his works, and all his hair, i.e. his thoughts. The tip of the right ear of the man to be cleansed is moistened with some the blood and oil, in order to strengthen his hearing against harmful words; and the thumb and toe of his right hand and foot are moistened that his deeds may be holy. Other matters pertaining to this purification, or to that also of any other uncleannesses, call for no special remark, beyond what applies to other sacrifices, whether for sins or for trespasses.

Reply to Objection 8:and 9: Just as the people were initiated by circumcision to the divine worship, so were the ministers by some special purification or consecration: wherefore they are commanded to be separated from other men, as being specially deputed, rather than others, to the ministry of the divine worship. And all that was done touching them in their consecration or institution, was with a view to show that they were in possession of a prerogative of purity, power and dignity. Hence three things were done in the institution of ministers: for first, they were purified; secondly, they were adorned [*'Ornabantur.' Some editions have 'ordinabantur'---'were ordained': the former reading is a reference to Lev. 8:7-9] and consecrated; thirdly, they were employed in the ministry. All in general used to be purified by washing in water, and by certain sacrifices; but the Levites in particular shaved all the hair of their bodies, as stated in Lev. 8 (cf. Num. 8).

With regard to the high-priests and priests the consecration was performed as follows. First, when they had been washed, they were clothed with certain special garments in designation of their dignity. In particular, the high-priest was anointed on the head with the oil of unction: to denote that the power of consecration was poured forth by him on to others, just as oil flows from the head on to the lower parts of the body; according to Ps. 132:2: "Like the precious ointment on the head that ran down upon the beard, the beard of Aaron." But the Levites received no other consecration besides being offered to the Lord by the children of Israel through the hands of the high-priest, who prayed for them. The lesser priests were consecrated on the hands only, which were to be employed in the sacrifices. The tip of their right ear and the thumb of their right hand, and the great toe of their right foot were tinged with the blood of the sacrificial animal, to denote that they should be obedient to God's law in offering the sacrifices (this is denoted by touching their right ear); and that they should be careful and ready in performing the sacrifices (this is signified by the moistening of the right foot and hand). They themselves and their garments were sprinkled with the blood of the animal that had been sacrificed, in memory of the blood of the lamb by which they had been delivered in Egypt. At their consecration the following sacrifices were offered: a calf, for sin, in memory of Aaron's sin in fashioning the molten calf; a ram, for a holocaust, in memory of the sacrifice of Abraham, whose obedience it behooved the high-priest to imitate; again, a ram of consecration, which was a peace-offering, in memory of the delivery form Egypt through the blood of the lamb; and a basket of bread, in memory of the manna vouchsafed to the people.

In reference to their being destined to the ministry, the fat of the ram, one roll of bread, and the right shoulder were placed on their hands, to show that they received the power of offering these things to the Lord: while the Levites were initiated to the ministry by being brought into the tabernacle of the covenant, as being destined to the ministry touching the vessels of the sanctuary.

The figurative reason of these things was that those who are to be consecrated to the spiritual ministry of Christ, should be first of all purified by the waters of Baptism, and by the waters of tears, in their faith in Christ's Passion, which is a sacrifice both of expiation and of purification. They have also to shave all the hair of their body, i.e. all evil thoughts. They should, moreover, be decked with virtues, and be consecrated with the oil of the Holy Ghost, and with the sprinkling of Christ's blood. And thus they should be intent on the fulfilment of their spiritual ministry.

Reply to Objection 1:: As already stated (Article [4]), the purpose of the Law was to induce men to have reverence for the divine worship: and this in two ways; first, by excluding from the worship of God whatever might be an object of contempt; secondly, by introducing into the divine worship all that seemed to savor of reverence. And, indeed, if this was observed in regard to the tabernacle and its vessels, and in the animals to be sacrificed, much more was it to be observed in the very ministers. Wherefore, in order to obviate contempt for the ministers, it was prescribed that they should have no bodily stain or defect: since men so deformed are wont to be despised by others. For the same reason it was also commanded that the choice of those who were to be destined to the service of God was not to be made in a broadcast manner from any family, but according to their descent from one particular stock, thus giving them distinction and nobility.

In order that they might be revered, special ornate vestments were appointed for their use, and a special form of consecration. This indeed is the general reason of ornate garments. But the high-priest in particular had eight vestments. First, he had a linen tunic. Secondly, he had a purple tunic; round the bottom of which were placed "little bells" and "pomegranates of violet, and purple, and scarlet twice dyed." Thirdly, he had the ephod, which covered his shoulders and his breast down to the girdle; and it was made of gold, and violet and purple, and scarlet twice dyed and twisted linen: and on his shoulders he bore two onyx stones, on which were graven the names of the children of Israel. Fourthly, he had the rational, made of the same material; it was square in shape, and was worn on the breast, and was fastened to the ephod. On this rational there were twelve precious stones set in four rows, on which also were graven the names of the children of Israel, in token that the priest bore the burden of the whole people, since he bore their names on his shoulders; and that it was his duty ever to think of their welfare, since he wore them on his breast, bearing them in his heart, so to speak. And the Lord commanded the "Doctrine and Truth" to be put in the rational: for certain matters regarding moral and dogmatic truth were written on it. The Jews indeed pretend that on the rational was placed a stone which changed color according to the various things which were about to happen to the children of Israel: and this they call the "Truth and Doctrine." Fifthly, he wore a belt or girdle made of the four colors mentioned above. Sixthly, there was the tiara or mitre which was made of linen. Seventhly, there was the golden plate which hung over his forehead; on it was inscribed the Lord's name. Eighthly, there were "the linen breeches to cover the flesh of their nakedness," when they went up to the sanctuary or altar. Of these eight vestments the lesser priests had four, viz. the linen tunic and breeches, the belt and the tiara.

According to some, the literal reason for these vestments was that they denoted the disposition of the terrestrial globe; as though the high-priest confessed himself to be the minister of the Creator of the world, wherefore it is written (Wis. 18:24): "In the robe" of Aaron "was the whole world" described. For the linen breeches signified the earth out of which the flax grows. The surrounding belt signified the ocean which surrounds the earth. The violet tunic denoted the air by its color: its little bells betoken the thunder; the pomegranates, the lightning. The ephod, by its many colors, signified the starry heaven; the two onyx stones denoted the two hemispheres, or the sun and moon. The twelve precious stones on the breast are the twelve signs of the zodiac: and they are said to have been placed on the rational because in heaven, are the types [rationes] of earthly things, according to Job 38:33: "Dost thou know the order of heaven, and canst thou set down the reason [rationem] thereof on the earth?" The turban or tiara signified the empyrean: the golden plate was a token of God, the governor of the universe.

The figurative reason is evident. Because bodily stains or defects wherefrom the priests had to be immune, signify the various vices and sins from which they should be free. Thus it is forbidden that he should be blind, i.e. he ought not to be ignorant: he must not be lame, i.e. vacillating and uncertain of purpose: that he must have "a little, or a great, or a crooked nose," i.e. that he should not, from lack of discretion, exceed in one direction or in another, or even exercise some base occupation: for the nose signifies discretion, because it discerns odors. It is forbidden that he should have "a broken foot" or "hand," i.e. he should not lose the power of doing good works or of advancing in virtue. He is rejected, too, if he have a swelling either in front or behind [Vulg.: 'if he be crook-backed']: by which is signified too much love of earthly things: if he be blear-eyed, i.e. if his mind is darkened by carnal affections: for running of the eyes is caused by a flow of matter. He is also rejected if he had "a pearl in his eye," i.e. if he presumes in his own estimation that he is clothed in the white robe of righteousness. Again, he is rejected "if he have a continued scab," i.e. lustfulness of the flesh: also, if he have "a dry scurf," which covers the body without giving pain, and is a blemish on the comeliness of the members; which denotes avarice. Lastly, he is rejected "if he have a rupture" or hernia; through baseness rending his heart, though it appear not in his deeds.

The vestments denote the virtues of God's ministers. Now there are four things that are necessary to all His ministers, viz. chastity denoted by the breeches; a pure life, signified by the linen tunic; the moderation of discretion, betokened by the girdle; and rectitude of purpose, denoted by the mitre covering the head. But the high-priests needed four other things in addition to these. First, a continual recollection of God in their thoughts; and this was signified by the golden plate worn over the forehead, with the name of God engraved thereon. Secondly, they had to bear with the shortcomings of the people: this was denoted by the ephod which they bore on their shoulders. Thirdly, they had to carry the people in their mind and heart by the solicitude of charity, in token of which they wore the rational. Fourthly, they had to lead a godly life by performing works of perfection; and this was signified by the violet tunic. Hence little golden bells were fixed to the bottom of the violet tunic, which bells signified the teaching of divine things united in the high-priest to his godly mode of life. In addition to these were the pomegranates, signifying unity of faith and concord in good morals: because his doctrine should hold together in such a way that it should not rend asunder the unity of faith and peace.

Article: 6

Whether there was any reasonable cause for the ceremonial observances?

Objection 1: It would seem that there was no reasonable cause for the ceremonial observances. Because, as the Apostle says (1 Tim. 4:4), "every creature of God is good, and nothing to be rejected that is received with thanksgiving." It was therefore unfitting that they should be forbidden to eat certain foods, as being unclean according to Lev. 11 [*Cf. Dt. 14].

Objection 2: Further, just as animals are given to man for food, so also are herbs: wherefore it is written (Gn. 9:3): "As the green herbs have I delivered all" flesh "to you." But the Law did not distinguish any herbs from the rest as being unclean, although some are most harmful, for instance, those that are poisonous. Therefore it seems that neither should any animals have been prohibited as being unclean.

Objection 3: Further, if the matter from which a thing is generated be unclean, it seems that likewise the thing generated therefrom is unclean. But flesh is generated from blood. Since therefore all flesh was not prohibited as unclean, it seems that in like manner neither should blood have been forbidden as unclean; nor the fat which is engendered from blood.

Objection 4: Further, Our Lord said (Mt. 10:28; cf. Lk. 12:4), that those should not be feared "that kill the body," since after death they "have no more that they can do": which would not be true if after death harm might come to man through anything done with his body. Much less therefore does it matter to an animal already dead how its flesh be cooked. Consequently there seems to be no reason in what is said, Ex. 23:19: "Thou shalt not boil a kid in the milk of its dam."

Objection 5: Further, all that is first brought forth of man and beast, as being most perfect, is commanded to be offered to the Lord (Ex. 13). Therefore it is an unfitting command that is set forth in Lev. 19:23: "when you shall be come into the land, and shall have planted in it fruit trees, you shall take away the uncircumcision [*'Praeputia,' which Douay version renders 'first fruits'] of them," i.e. the first crops, and they "shall be unclean to you, neither shall you eat of them."

Objection 6: Further, clothing is something extraneous to man's body. Therefore certain kinds of garments should not have been forbidden to the Jews: for instance (Lev. 19:19): "Thou shalt not wear a garment that is woven of two sorts": and (Dt. 22:5): "A woman shall not be clothed with man's apparel, neither shall a man use woman's apparel": and further on (Dt. 22:11): "Thou shalt not wear a garment that is woven of woolen and linen together."

Objection 7: Further, to be mindful of God's commandments concerns not the body but the heart. Therefore it is unsuitably prescribed (Dt. 6:8, seqq.) that they should "bind" the commandments of God "as a sign" on their hands; and that they should "write them in the entry"; and (Num. 15:38, seqq.) that they should "make to themselves fringes in the corners of their garments, putting in them ribands of blue . . . they may remember . . . the commandments of the Lord."

Objection 8: Further, the Apostle says (1 Cor. 9:9) that God does not "take care for oxen," and, therefore, neither of other irrational animals. Therefore without reason is it commanded (Dt. 22:6): "If thou find, as thou walkest by the way, a bird's nest in a tree . . . thou shalt not take the dam with her young"; and (Dt. 25:4): "Thou shalt not muzzle the ox that treadeth out thy corn"; and (Lev. 19:19): "Thou shalt not make thy cattle to gender with beasts of any other kind."

Objection 9: Further, no distinction was made between clean and unclean plants. Much less therefore should any distinction have been made about the cultivation of plants. Therefore it was unfittingly prescribed (Lev. 19:19): "Thou shalt not sow thy field with different seeds"; and (Dt. 22:9, seqq.): "Thou shalt sow thy vineyard with divers seeds"; and: "Thou shalt not plough with an ox and an ass together."

Objection 1:: Further, it is apparent that inanimate things are most of all subject to the power of man. Therefore it was unfitting to debar man from taking silver and gold of which idols were made, or anything they found in the houses of idols, as expressed in the commandment of the Law (Dt. 7:25, seqq.). It also seems an absurd commandment set forth in Dt. 23:13, that they should "dig round about and . . . cover with earth that which they were eased of."

Objection 1:: Further, piety is required especially in priests. But it seems to be an act of piety to assist at the burial of one's friends: wherefore Tobias is commended for so doing (Tob. 1:20, seqq.). In like manner it is sometimes an act of piety to marry a loose woman, because she is thereby delivered from sin and infamy. Therefore it seems inconsistent for these things to be forbidden to priests (Lev. 21).

On the contrary, It is written (Dt. 18:14): "But thou art otherwise instructed by the Lord thy God": from which words we may gather that these observances were instituted by God to be a special prerogative of that people. Therefore they are not without reason or cause.

I answer that, The Jewish people, as stated above (Article [5]), were specially chosen for the worship of God, and among them the priests themselves were specially set apart for that purpose. And just as other things that are applied to the divine worship, need to be marked in some particular way so that they be worthy of the worship of God; so too in that people's, and especially the priests', mode of life, there needed to be certain special things befitting the divine worship, whether spiritual or corporal. Now the worship prescribed by the Law foreshadowed the mystery of Christ: so that whatever they did was a figure of things pertaining to Christ, according to 1 Cor. 10:11: "All these things happened to them in figures." Consequently the reasons for these observances may be taken in two ways, first according to their fittingness to the worship of God; secondly, according as they foreshadow something touching the Christian mode of life.

Reply to Objection 1: As stated above (Article [5], ad 4,5), the Law distinguished a twofold pollution or uncleanness; one, that of sin, whereby the soul was defiled; and another consisting in some kind of corruption, whereby the body was in some way infected. Speaking then of the first-mentioned uncleanness, no kind of food is unclean, or can defile a man, by reason of its nature; wherefore we read (Mt. 15:11): "Not that which goeth into the mouth defileth a man; but what cometh out of the mouth, this defileth a man": which words are explained (Mt. 15:17) as referring to sins. Yet certain foods can defile the soul accidentally; in so far as man partakes of them against obedience or a vow, or from excessive concupiscence; or through their being an incentive to lust, for which reason some refrain from wine and flesh-meat.

If, however, we speak of bodily uncleanness, consisting in some kind of corruption, the flesh of certain animals is unclean, either because like the pig they feed on unclean things; or because their life is among unclean surroundings: thus certain animals, like moles and mice and such like, live underground, whence they contract a certain unpleasant smell; or because their flesh, through being too moist or too dry, engenders corrupt humors in the human body. Hence they were forbidden to eat the flesh of flat-footed animals, i.e. animals having an uncloven hoof, on account of their earthiness; and in like manner they were forbidden to eat the flesh of animals that have many clefts in their feet, because such are very fierce and their flesh is very dry, such as the flesh of lions and the like. For the same reason they were forbidden to eat certain birds of prey the flesh of which is very dry, and certain water-fowl on account of their exceeding humidity. In like manner certain fish lacking fins and scales were prohibited on account of their excessive moisture; such as eels and the like. They were, however, allowed to eat ruminants and animals with a divided hoof, because in such animals the humors are well absorbed, and their nature well balanced: for neither are they too moist, as is indicated by the hoof; nor are they too earthly, which is shown by their having not a flat but a cloven hoof. Of fishes they were allowed to partake of the drier kinds, of which the fins and scales are an indication, because thereby the moist nature of the fish is tempered. Of birds they were allowed to eat the tamer kinds, such as hens, partridges, and the like. Another reason was detestation of idolatry: because the Gentiles, and especially the Egyptians, among whom they had grown up, offered up these forbidden animals to their idols, or employed them for the purpose of sorcery: whereas they did not eat those animals which the Jews were allowed to eat, but worshipped them as gods, or abstained, for some other motive, from eating them, as stated above (Article [3], ad 2). The third reason was to prevent excessive care about food: wherefore they were allowed to eat those animals which could be procured easily and promptly.

With regard to blood and fat, they were forbidden to partake of those of any animals whatever without exception. Blood was forbidden, both in order to avoid cruelty, that they might abhor the shedding of human blood, as stated above (Article [3], ad 8); and in order to shun idolatrous rite whereby it was customary for men to collect the blood and to gather together around it for a banquet in honor of the idols, to whom they held the blood to be most acceptable. Hence the Lord commanded the blood to be poured out and to be covered with earth (Lev. 17:13). For the same reason they were forbidden to eat animals that had been suffocated or strangled: because the blood of these animals would not be separated from the body: or because this form of death is very painful to the victim; and the Lord wished to withdraw them from cruelty even in regard to irrational animals, so as to be less inclined to be cruel to other men, through being used to be kind to beasts. They were forbidden to eat the fat: both because idolaters ate it in honor of their gods; and because it used to be burnt in honor of God; and, again, because blood and fat are not nutritious, which is the cause assigned by Rabbi Moses (Doct. Perplex. iii). The reason why they were forbidden to eat the sinews is given in Gn. 32:32, where it is stated that "the children of Israel . . . eat not the sinew . . . because he touched the sinew of" Jacob's "thing and it shrank."

The figurative reason for these things is that all these animals signified certain sins, in token of which those animals were prohibited. Hence Augustine says (Contra Faustum iv, 7): "If the swine and lamb be called in question, both are clean by nature, because all God's creatures are good: yet the lamb is clean, and the pig is unclean in a certain signification. Thus if you speak of a foolish, and of a wise man, each of these expressions is clean considered in the nature of the sound, letters and syllables of which it is composed: but in signification, the one is clean, the other unclean." The animal that chews the cud and has a divided hoof, is clean in signification. Because division of the hoof is a figure of the two Testaments: or of the Father and Son: or of the two natures in Christ: of the distinction of good and evil. While chewing the cud signifies meditation on the

Scriptures and a sound understanding thereof; and whoever lacks either of these is spiritually unclean. In like manner those fish that have scales and fins are clean in signification. Because fins signify the heavenly or contemplative life; while scales signify a life of trials, each of which is required for spiritual cleanness. Of birds certain kinds were forbidden. In the eagle which flies at a great height, pride is forbidden: in the griffon which is hostile to horses and men, cruelty of powerful men is prohibited. The osprey, which feeds on very small birds, signifies those who oppress the poor. The kite, which is full of cunning, denotes those who are fraudulent in their dealings. The vulture, which follows an army, expecting to feed on the carcases of the slain, signifies those who like others to die or to fight among themselves that they may gain thereby. Birds of the raven kind signify those who are blackened by their lusts; or those who lack kindly feelings, for the raven did not return when once it had been let loose from the ark. The ostrich which, though a bird, cannot fly, and is always on the ground, signifies those who fight God's cause, and at the same time are taken up with worldly business. The owl, which sees clearly at night, but cannot see in the daytime, denotes those who are clever in temporal affairs, but dull in spiritual matters. The gull, which flies both in the air and swims in the water, signifies those who are partial both to Circumcision and to Baptism: or else it denotes those who would fly by contemplation, yet dwell in the waters of sensual delights. The hawk, which helps men to seize the prey, is a figure of those who assist the strong to prey on the poor. The screech-owl, which seeks its food by night but hides by day, signifies the lustful man who seeks to lie hidden in his deeds of darkness. The cormorant, so constituted that it can stay a long time under water, denotes the glutton who plunges into the waters of pleasure. The ibis is an African bird with a long beak, and feeds on snakes; and perhaps it is the same as the stork: it signifies the envious man, who refreshes himself with the ills of others, as with snakes. The swan is bright in color, and by the aid of its long neck extracts its food from deep places on land or water: it may denote those who seek earthly profit though an external brightness of virtue. The bittern is a bird of the East: it has a long beak, and its jaws are furnished with follicules, wherein it stores its food at first, after a time proceeding to digest it: it is a figure of the miser, who is excessively careful in hoarding up the necessaries of life. The coot [*Douay: 'porphyrion.' St. Thomas' description tallies with the coot or moorhen: though of course he is mistaken about the feet differing from one another.] has this peculiarity apart from other birds, that it has a webbed foot for swimming, and a cloven foot for walking: for it swims like a duck in the water, and walks like a partridge on land: it drinks only when it bites, since it dips all its food in water: it is a figure of a man who will not take advice, and does nothing but what is soaked in the water of his own will. The heron [*Vulg.: 'herodionem'], commonly called a falcon, signifies those whose "feet are swift to shed blood" (Ps. 13:3). The plover [*Here, again, the Douay translators transcribed from the Vulgate: 'charadrion'; 'charadrius' is the generic name for all plovers.], which is a garrulous bird, signifies the gossip. The hoopoe, which builds its nest on dung, feeds on foetid ordure, and whose song is like a groan, denotes worldly grief which works death in those who are unclean. The bat, which flies near the ground, signifies those who being gifted with worldly knowledge, seek none but earthly things. Of fowls and quadrupeds those alone were permitted which have the hind-legs longer than the forelegs, so that they can leap: whereas those were forbidden which cling rather to the earth: because those who abuse the doctrine of the four Evangelists, so that they are not lifted up thereby, are reputed unclean. By the prohibition of blood, fat and nerves, we are to understand the forbidding of cruelty, lust, and bravery in committing sin.

Reply to Objection 2: Men were wont to eat plants and other products of the soil even before the deluge: but the eating of flesh seems to have been introduced after the deluge; for it is written (Gn. 9:3): "Even as the green herbs have I delivered . . . all" flesh "to you." The reason for this was that the eating of the products of the soil savors rather of a simple life; whereas the eating of flesh savors of delicate and over-careful living. For the soil gives birth to the herb of its own accord; and such like products of the earth may be had in great quantities with very little effort: whereas no small trouble is necessary either to rear or to catch an animal. Consequently God being wishful to bring His people back to a more simple way of living, forbade them to eat many kinds of animals, but not those things that are produced by the soil. Another reason may be that animals were offered to idols, while the products of the soil were not.

The Reply to the Third Objection is clear from what has been said (ad 1).

Reply to Objection 4: Although the kid that is slain has no perception of the manner in which its flesh is cooked, yet it would seem to savor of heartlessness if the dam's milk, which was intended for the nourishment of her offspring, were served up on the same dish. It might also be said that the Gentiles in celebrating the feasts of their idols prepared the flesh of kids in this manner, for the purpose of sacrifice or banquet: hence (Ex. 23) after the solemnities to be celebrated under the Law had been foretold, it is added: "Thou shalt not boil a kid in the milk of its dam." The figurative reason for this prohibition is this: the kid, signifying Christ, on account of "the likeness of sinful flesh" (Rm. 8:3), was not to be seethed, i.e. slain, by the Jews, "in the milk of its dam," i.e. during His infancy. Or else it signifies that the kid, i.e. the sinner, should not be boiled in the milk of its dam, i.e. should not be cajoled by flattery.

Reply to Objection 5: The Gentiles offered their gods the first-fruits, which they held to bring them good luck: or they burnt them for the purpose of secrecy. Consequently (the Israelites) were commanded to look upon the fruits of the first three years as unclean: for in that country nearly all the trees bear fruit in three years' time; those trees, to wit, that are cultivated either from seed, or from a graft, or from a cutting: but it seldom happens that the fruit-stones or seeds encased in a pod are sown: since it would take a longer time for these to bear fruit: and the Law considered what happened most frequently. The fruits, however, of the fourth year, as being the firstlings of clean fruits, were offered to God: and from the fifth year onward they were eaten.

The figurative reason was that this foreshadowed the fact that after the three states of the Law (the first lasting from Abraham to David, the second, until they were carried away to Babylon, the third until the time of Christ), the Fruit of the Law, i.e. Christ, was to be offered to God. Or again, that we must mistrust our first efforts, on account of their imperfection.

Reply to Objection 6: It is said of a man in Ecclus. 19:27, that "the attire of the body . . . " shows "what he is." Hence the Lord wished His people to be distinguished from other nations, not only by the sign of the circumcision, which was in the flesh, but also by a certain difference of attire. Wherefore they were forbidden to wear garments woven of woolen and linen together, and for a woman to be clothed with man's apparel, or vice versa, for two reasons. First, to avoid idolatrous worship. Because the Gentiles, in their religious rites, used garments of this sort, made of various materials. Moreover in the worship of Mars, women put on men's armor; while, conversely, in the worship of Venus men donned women's attire. The second reason was to preserve them from lust: because the employment of various materials in the making of garments signified inordinate union of sexes, while the use of male attire by a woman, or vice versa, has an incentive to evil desires, and offers an occasion of lust. The figurative reason is that the prohibition of wearing a garment woven of woolen and linen signified that it was forbidden to unite the simplicity of innocence, denoted by wool, with the duplicity of malice, betokened by linen. It also signifies that woman is forbidden to presume to teach, or perform other duties of men: or that man should not adopt the effeminate manners of a woman.

Reply to Objection 7: As Jerome says on Mt. 23:6, "the Lord commanded them to make violet-colored fringes in the four corners of their garments, so that the Israelites might be distinguished from other nations." Hence, in this way, they professed to be Jews: and consequently the very sight of this sign reminded them of their law.

When we read: "Thou shalt bind them on thy hand, and they shall be ever before thy eyes [Vulg.: 'they shall be and shall move between thy eyes'], the Pharisees gave a false interpretation to these words, and wrote the decalogue of Moses on a parchment, and tied it on their foreheads like a wreath, so that it moved in front of their eyes": whereas the intention of the Lord in giving this commandment was that they should be bound in their hands, i.e. in their works; and that they should be before their eyes, i.e. in their thoughts. The violet-colored fillets which were inserted in their cloaks signify the godly intention which should accompany our every deed. It may, however, be said that, because they were a carnal-minded and stiff-necked people, it was necessary for them to be stirred by these sensible things to the observance of the Law.

Reply to Objection 8: Affection in man is twofold: it may be an affection of reason, or it may be an affection of passion. If a man's affection be one of reason, it matters not how man behaves to animals, because God has subjected all things to man's power, according to Ps. 8:8: "Thou hast subjected all things under his feet": and it is in this sense that the Apostle says that "God has no care for oxen"; because God does not ask of man what he does with oxen or other animals.

But if man's affection be one of passion, then it is moved also in regard to other animals: for since the passion of pity is caused by the afflictions of others; and since it happens that even irrational animals are sensible to pain, it is possible for the affection of pity to arise in a man with regard to the sufferings of animals. Now it is evident that if a man practice a pitiful affection for animals, he is all the more disposed to take pity on his fellow-men: wherefore it is written (Prov. 11:10): "The just regardeth the lives of his beasts: but the bowels of the wicked are cruel." Consequently the Lord, in order to inculcate pity to the Jewish people, who were prone to cruelty, wished them to practice pity even with regard to dumb animals, and forbade them to do certain things savoring of cruelty to animals. Hence He prohibited them to "boil a kid in the milk of its dam"; and to "muzzle the ox that treadeth out the corn"; and to slay "the dam with her young." It may, nevertheless, be also said that these prohibitions were made in hatred of idolatry. For the Egyptians held it to be wicked to allow the ox to eat of the grain while threshing the corn. Moreover certain sorcerers were wont to ensnare the mother bird with her young during incubation, and to employ them for the purpose of securing fruitfulness and good luck in bringing up children: also because it was held to be a good omen to find the mother sitting on her young.

As to the mingling of animals of divers species, the literal reason may have been threefold. The first was to show detestation for the idolatry of the Egyptians, who employed various mixtures in worshipping the planets, which produce various effects, and on various kinds of things according to their various conjunctions. The second reason was in condemnation of unnatural sins. The third reason was the entire removal of all occasions of concupiscence. Because animals of different species do not easily breed, unless this be brought about by man; and movements of lust are aroused by seeing such things. Wherefore in the Jewish traditions we find it prescribed as stated by Rabbi Moses that men shall turn away their eyes from such sights.

The figurative reason for these things is that the necessities of life should not be withdrawn from the ox that treadeth the corn, i.e. from the preacher bearing the sheaves of doctrine, as the Apostle states (1 Cor. 9:4, seqq.). Again, we should not take the dam with her young: because in certain things we have to keep the spiritual senses, i.e. the offspring, and set aside the observance of the letter, i.e. the mother, for instance, in all the ceremonies of the Law. It is also forbidden that beast of burden, i.e. any of the common people, should be allowed to engender, i.e. to have any connection, with animals of another kind, i.e. with Gentiles or Jews.

Reply to Objection 9: All these minglings were forbidden in agriculture; literally, in detestation of idolatry. For the Egyptians in worshipping the stars employed various combinations of seeds, animals and garments, in order to represent the various connections of the stars. Or else all these minglings were forbidden in detestation of the unnatural vice.

They have, however, a figurative reason. For the prohibition: "Thou shalt not sow thy field with different seeds," is to be understood, in the spiritual sense, of the prohibition to sow strange doctrine in the Church, which is a spiritual vineyard. Likewise "the field," i.e. the Church, must not be sown "with different seeds," i.e. with Catholic and heretical doctrines. Neither is it allowed to plough "with an ox and an ass together"; thus a fool should not accompany a wise man in preaching, for one would hinder the other.

Reply to Objection 1:: [*The Reply to the Tenth Objection is lacking in the codices. The solution given here is found in some editions, and was supplied by Nicolai.] Silver and gold were reasonably forbidden (Dt. 7) not as though they were not subject to the power of man, but because, like the idols themselves, all materials out of which idols were made, were anathematized as hateful in God's sight. This is clear from the same chapter, where we read further on (Dt. 7:26): "Neither shalt thou bring anything of the idol into thy house, lest thou become an anathema like it." Another reason was lest, by taking silver and gold, they should be led by avarice into idolatry to which the Jews were inclined. The other precept (Dt. 23) about covering up excretions, was just and becoming, both for the sake of bodily cleanliness; and in order to keep the air wholesome; and by reason of the respect due to the tabernacle of the covenant which stood in the midst of the camp, wherein the Lord was said to dwell; as is clearly set forth in the same passage, where after expressing the command, the reason thereof is at once added, to wit: "For the Lord thy God walketh in the midst of thy camp, to deliver thee, and to give up thy enemies to thee, and let thy camp be holy [i.e. clean], and let no uncleanness appear therein." The figurative reason for this precept, according to Gregory (Moral. xxxi), is that sins which are the fetid excretions of the mind should be covered over by repentance, that we may become acceptable to God, according to Ps. 31:1: "Blessed are they whose iniquities are forgiven, and whose sins are covered." Or else according to a gloss, that we should recognize the unhappy condition of human nature, and humbly cover and purify the stains of a puffed-up and proud spirit in the deep furrow of self-examination.

Reply to Objection 1:: Sorcerers and idolatrous priests made use, in their rites, of the bones and flesh of dead men. Wherefore, in order to extirpate the customs of idolatrous worship, the Lord commanded that the priests of inferior degree, who at fixed times served in the temple, should not "incur an uncleanness at the death" of anyone except of those who were closely related to them, viz. their father or mother, and others thus near of kin to them. But the high-priest had always to be ready for the service of the sanctuary; wherefore he was absolutely forbidden to approach the dead, however nearly related to him. They were also forbidden to marry a "harlot" or "one that has been put away," or any other than a virgin: both on account of the reverence due to the priesthood, the honor of which would seem to be tarnished by such a marriage: and for the sake of the children who would be disgraced by the mother's shame: which was most of all to be avoided when the priestly dignity was passed on from father to son. Again, they were commanded to shave neither head nor beard, and not to make incisions in their flesh, in order to exclude the rites of idolatry. For the priests of the Gentiles shaved both head and beard, wherefore it is written (Bar 6:30): "Priests sit in their temples having their garments rent, and their heads and beards shaven." Moreover, in worshipping their idols "they cut themselves with knives and lancets" (3 Kgs. 18:28). For this reason the priests of the Old Law were commanded to do the contrary.

The spiritual reason for these things is that priests should be entirely free from dead works, i.e. sins. And they should not shave their heads, i.e. set wisdom aside; nor should they shave their beards, i.e. set aside the perfection of wisdom; nor rend their garments or cut their flesh, i.e. they should not incur the sin of schism.

OF THE DURATION OF THE CEREMONIAL PRECEPTS (FOUR ARTICLES)

We must now consider the duration of the ceremonial precepts: under which head there are four points of inquiry:

(1) Whether the ceremonial precepts were in existence before the Law?
(2) Whether at the time of the Law the ceremonies of the Old Law had any power of justification?
(3) Whether they ceased at the coming of Christ?
(4) Whether it is a mortal sin to observe them after the coming of Christ?

Question 103 Article: 1

Whether the ceremonies of the Law were in existence before the Law?

Objection 1: It would seem that the ceremonies of the Law were in existence before the Law. For sacrifices and holocausts were ceremonies of the Old Law, as stated above (Question [101], Article [4]). But sacrifices and holocausts preceded the Law: for it is written (Gn. 4:3,4) that "Cain offered, of the fruits of the earth, gifts to the Lord," and that "Abel offered of the firstlings of his flock, and of their fat." Noe also "offered holocausts" to the Lord (Gn. 18:20), and Abraham did in like manner (Gn. 22:13). Therefore the ceremonies of the Old Law preceded the Law.

Objection 2: Further, the erecting and consecrating of the altar were part of the ceremonies relating to holy things. But these preceded the Law. For we read (Gn. 13:18) that "Abraham . . . built . . . an altar to the Lord"; and (Gn. 28:18) that "Jacob . . . took the stone . . . and set it up for a title, pouring oil upon the top of it." Therefore the legal ceremonies preceded the Law.

Objection 3: Further, the first of the legal sacraments seems to have been circumcision. But circumcision preceded the Law, as appears from Gn. 17. In like manner the priesthood preceded the Law; for it is written (Gn. 14:18) that "Melchisedech . . . was the priest of the most high God." Therefore the sacramental ceremonies preceded the Law.

Objection 4: Further, the distinction of clean from unclean animals belongs to the ceremonies of observances, as stated above (Question [100], 2, Article [6], ad 1). But this distinction preceded the Law; for it is written (Gn. 7:2,3): "Of all clean beasts take seven and seven . . . but of the beasts that are unclean, two and two." Therefore the legal ceremonies preceded the Law.

On the contrary, It is written (Dt. 6:1): "These are the precepts and ceremonies . . . which the Lord your God commanded that I should teach you." But they would not have needed to be taught about these things, if the aforesaid ceremonies had been already in existence. Therefore the legal ceremonies did not precede the Law.

I answer that, As is clear from what has been said (Question [101], Article [2]; Question [102], Article [2]), the legal ceremonies were ordained for a double purpose; the worship of God, and the foreshadowing of Christ. Now whoever worships God must needs worship Him by means of certain fixed things pertaining to external worship. But the fixing of the divine worship belongs to the ceremonies; just as the determining of our relations with our neighbor is a matter determined by the judicial precepts, as stated above (Question [99], Article [4]). Consequently, as among men in general there were certain judicial precepts, not indeed established by Divine authority, but ordained by human reason; so also there were some ceremonies fixed, not by the authority of any law, but according to the will and devotion of those that worship God. Since, however, even before the Law some of the leading men were gifted with the spirit of prophecy, it is to be believed that a heavenly instinct, like a private law, prompted them to worship God in a certain definite way, which would be both in keeping with the interior worship, and a suitable token of Christ's mysteries, which were foreshadowed also by other things that they did, according to 1 Cor. 10:11: "All . . . things happened to them in figure." Therefore there were some ceremonies before the Law, but they were not legal ceremonies, because they were not as yet established by legislation.

Reply to Objection 1: The patriarchs offered up these oblations, sacrifices and holocausts previously to the Law, out of a certain devotion of their own will, according as it seemed proper to them to offer up in honor of God those things which they had received from Him, and thus to testify that they worshipped God Who is the beginning and end of all.

Reply to Objection 2: They also established certain sacred things, because they thought that the honor due to God demanded that certain places should be set apart from others for the purpose of divine worship.

Reply to Objection 3: The sacrament of circumcision was established by command of God before the Law. Hence it cannot be called a sacrament of the Law as though it were an institution of the Law, but only as an observance included in the Law. Hence Our Lord said (Jn. 7:20) that circumcision was "not of Moses, but of his fathers." Again, among those who worshipped God, the priesthood was in existence before the Law by human appointment, for the Law allotted the priestly dignity to the firstborn.

Reply to Objection 4: The distinction of clean from unclean animals was in vogue before the Law, not with regard to eating them, since it is written (Gn. 9:3): "Everything that moveth and liveth shall be meat for you": but only as to the offering of sacrifices because they used only certain animals for that purpose. If, however, they did make any distinction in regard to eating; it was not that it was considered illegal to eat such animals, since this was not forbidden by any law, but from dislike or custom: thus even now we see that certain foods are looked upon with disgust in some countries, while people partake of them in others.

Article: 2

Whether, at the time of the Law, the ceremonies of the Old Law had any power of justification?

Objection 1: It would seem that the ceremonies of the Old Law had the power of justification at the time of the Law. Because expiation from sin and consecration pertains to justification. But it is written (Ex. 39:21) that the priests and their apparel were consecrated by the sprinkling of blood and the anointing of oil; and (Lev. 16:16) that, by sprinkling the blood of the calf, the priest expiated "the sanctuary from the uncleanness of the children of Israel, and from their transgressions and . . . their sins." Therefore the ceremonies of the Old Law had the power of justification.

Objection 2: Further, that by which man pleases God pertains to justification, according to Ps. 10:8: "The Lord is just and hath loved justice." But some pleased God by means of ceremonies, according to Lev. 10:19: "How could I . . . please the Lord in the ceremonies, having a sorrowful heart?" Therefore the ceremonies of the Old Law had the power of justification.

Objection 3: Further, things relating to the divine worship regard the soul rather than the body, according to Ps. 18:8: "The Law of the Lord is unspotted, converting souls." But the leper was cleansed by means of the ceremonies of the Old Law, as stated in Lev. 14. Much more therefore could the ceremonies of the Old Law cleanse the soul by justifying it.

On the contrary, The Apostle says (Gal. 2) [*The first words of the quotation are from 3:21: St. Thomas probably quoting from memory, substituted them for 2:21, which runs thus: 'If justice be by the Law, then Christ died in vain.']: "If there had been a law given which could justify [Vulg.: 'give life'], Christ died in vain," i.e. without cause. But this is inadmissible. Therefore the ceremonies of the Old Law did not confer justice.

I answer that, As stated above (Question [102], Article [5], ad 4), a twofold uncleanness was distinguished in the Old Law. One was spiritual and is the uncleanness of sin. The other was corporal, which rendered a man unfit for divine worship; thus a leper, or anyone that touched carrion, was said to be unclean: and thus uncleanness was nothing but a kind of irregularity. From this uncleanness, then, the ceremonies of the Old Law had the power to cleanse:

because they were ordered by the Law to be employed as remedies for the removal of the aforesaid uncleannesses which were contracted in consequence of the prescription of the Law. Hence the Apostle says (Heb. 9:13) that "the blood of goats and of oxen, and the ashes of a heifer, being sprinkled, sanctify such as are defiled, to the cleansing of the flesh." And just as this uncleanness which was washed away by such like ceremonies, affected the flesh rather than the soul, so also the ceremonies themselves are called by the Apostle shortly before (Heb. 9:10) justices of the flesh: "justices of the flesh," says he, "being laid on them until the time of correction."

On the other hand, they had no power of cleansing from uncleanness of the soul, i.e. from the uncleanness of sin. The reason of this was that at no time could there be expiation from sin, except through Christ, "Who taketh away the sins [Vulg.: 'sin'] of the world" (Jn. 1:29). And since the mystery of Christ's Incarnation and Passion had not yet really taken place, those ceremonies of the Old Law could not really contain in themselves a power flowing from Christ already incarnate and crucified, such as the sacraments of the New Law contain. Consequently they could not cleanse from sin: thus the Apostle says (Heb. 10:4) that "it is impossible that with the blood of oxen and goats sin should be taken away"; and for this reason he calls them (Gal. 4:9) "weak and needy elements": weak indeed, because they cannot take away sin; but this weakness results from their being needy, i.e. from the fact that they do not contain grace within themselves.

However, it was possible at the time of the Law, for the minds of the faithful, to be united by faith to Christ incarnate and crucified; so that they were justified by faith in Christ: of which faith the observance of these ceremonies was a sort of profession, inasmuch as they foreshadowed Christ. Hence in the Old Law certain sacrifices were offered up for sins, not as though the sacrifices themselves washed sins away, but because they were professions of faith which cleansed from sin. In fact, the Law itself implies this in the terms employed: for it is written (Lev. 4:26; 5:16) that in offering the sacrifice for sin "the priest shall pray for him . . . and it shall be forgiven him," as though the sin were forgiven, not in virtue of the sacrifices, but through the faith and devotion of those who offered them. It must be observed, however, that the very fact that the ceremonies of the Old Law washed away uncleanness of the body, was a figure of that expiation from sins which was effected by Christ.

It is therefore evident that under the state of the Old Law the ceremonies had no power of justification.

Reply to Objection 1: That sanctification of priests and their sons, and of their apparel or of anything else belonging to them, by sprinkling them with blood, had no other effect but to appoint them to the divine worship, and to remove impediments from them, "to the cleansing of the flesh," as the Apostle states (Heb. 9:13) in token of that sanctification whereby "Jesus" sanctified "the people by His own blood" (Heb. 13:12). Moreover, the expiation must be understood as referring to the removal of these bodily uncleannesses, not to the forgiveness of sin. Hence even the sanctuary which could not be the subject of sin is stated to be expiated.

Reply to Objection 2: The priests pleased God in the ceremonies by their obedience and devotion, and by their faith in the reality foreshadowed; not by reason of the things considered in themselves.

Reply to Objection 3: Those ceremonies which were prescribed in the cleansing of a leper, were not ordained for the purpose of taking away the defilement of leprosy. This is clear from the fact that these ceremonies were not applied to a man until he was already healed: hence it is written (Lev. 14:3,4) that the priest, "going out of the camp, when he shall find that the leprosy is cleansed, shall command him that is to be purified to offer," etc.; whence it is evident that the priest was appointed the judge of leprosy, not before, but after cleansing. But these ceremonies were employed for the purpose of taking away the uncleanness of irregularity. They do say, however, that if a priest were to err in his judgment, the leper would be cleansed miraculously by the power of God, but not in virtue of the sacrifice. Thus also it was by miracle that the thigh of the adulterous woman rotted, when she had drunk the water "on which" the priest had "heaped curses," as stated in Num. 5:19-27.

Article: 3

Whether the ceremonies of the Old Law ceased at the coming of Christ?

Objection 1: It would seem that the ceremonies of the Old Law did not cease at the coming of Christ. For it is written (Bar 4:1): "This is the book of the commandments of God, and the law that is for ever." But the legal ceremonies were part of the Law. Therefore the legal ceremonies were to last for ever.

Objection 2: Further, the offering made by a leper after being cleansed was a ceremony of the Law. But the Gospel commands the leper, who has been cleansed, to make this offering (Mt. 8:4). Therefore the ceremonies of the Old Law did not cease at Christ's coming.

Objection 3: Further, as long as the cause remains, the effect remains. But the ceremonies of the Old Law had certain reasonable causes, inasmuch as they were ordained to the worship of God, besides the fact that they were intended to be figures of Christ. Therefore the ceremonies of the Old Law should not have ceased.

Objection 4: Further, circumcision was instituted as a sign of Abraham's faith: the observance of the sabbath, to recall the blessing of creation: and other solemnities, in memory of other Divine favors, as state above (Question [102], Article [4], ad 10; Article [5], ad 1). But Abraham's faith is ever to be imitated even by us: and the blessing of creation and other Divine favors should never be forgotten. Therefore at least circumcision and the other legal solemnities should not have ceased.

On the contrary, The Apostle says (Col. 2:16,17): "Let no man . . . judge you in meat or in drink, or in respect of a festival day, or of the new moon, or of the sabbaths, which are a shadow of things to come": and (Heb. 8:13): "In saying a new (testament), he hath made the former old: and that which decayeth and groweth old, is near its end."

I answer that, All the ceremonial precepts of the Old Law were ordained to the worship of God as stated above (Question [101], Articles [1],2). Now external worship should be in proportion to the internal worship, which consists in faith, hope and charity. Consequently exterior worship had to be subject to variations according to the variations in the internal worship, in which a threefold state may be distinguished. One state was in respect of faith and hope, both in heavenly goods, and in the means of obtaining them---in both of these considered as things to come. Such was the state of faith and hope in the Old Law. Another state of interior worship is that in which we have faith and hope in heavenly goods as things to come; but in the means of obtaining heavenly goods, as in things present or past. Such is the state of the New Law. The third state is that in which both are possessed as present; wherein nothing is believed in as lacking, nothing hoped for as being yet to come. Such is the state of the Blessed.

In this state of the Blessed, then, nothing in regard to worship of God will be figurative; there will be naught but "thanksgiving and voice of praise" (Is. 51:3). Hence it is written concerning the city of the Blessed (Apoc. 21:22): "I saw no temple therein: for the Lord God Almighty is the temple thereof, and the Lamb." Proportionately, therefore, the ceremonies of the first-mentioned state which foreshadowed the second and third states, had need to cease at the advent of the second state; and other ceremonies had to be introduced which would be in keeping with the state of divine worship for that particular time, wherein heavenly goods are a thing of the future, but the Divine favors whereby we obtain the heavenly boons are a thing of the present.

Reply to Objection 1: The Old Law is said to be "for ever" simply and absolutely, as regards its moral precepts; but as regards the ceremonial precepts it lasts for even in respect of the reality which those ceremonies foreshadowed.

Reply to Objection 2: The mystery of the redemption of the human race was fulfilled in Christ's Passion: hence Our Lord said then: "It is consummated" (Jn. 19:30). Consequently the prescriptions of the Law must have ceased then altogether through their reality being fulfilled. As a sign of this, we read that at the Passion of Christ "the veil of the temple was rent" (Mt. 27:51). Hence, before Christ's Passion, while Christ was preaching and working miracles, the Law and the Gospel were concurrent, since the mystery of Christ had already begun, but was not as yet consummated. And for this reason Our Lord, before His Passion, commanded the leper to observe the legal ceremonies.

Reply to Objection 3: The literal reasons already given (Question [102]) for the ceremonies refer to the divine worship, which was founded on faith in that which was to come. Hence, at the advent of Him Who was to come, both that worship ceased, and all the reasons referring thereto.

Reply to Objection 4: The faith of Abraham was commended in that he believed in God's promise concerning his seed to come, in which all nations were to blessed. Wherefore, as long as this seed was yet to come, it was necessary to make profession of Abraham's faith by means of circumcision. But now that it is consummated, the same thing needs to be declared by means of another sign, viz. Baptism, which, in this respect, took the place of circumcision, according to the saying of the Apostle (Col. 2:11, 12): "You are circumcised with circumcision not made by hand, in despoiling of the body of the flesh, but in the circumcision of Christ, buried with Him in Baptism."

As to the sabbath, which was a sign recalling the first creation, its place is taken by the "Lord's Day," which recalls the beginning of the new creature in the Resurrection of Christ. In like manner other solemnities of the Old Law are supplanted by new solemnities: because the blessings vouchsafed to that people, foreshadowed the favors granted us by Christ. Hence the feast of the Passover gave place to the feast of Christ's Passion and Resurrection: the feast of Pentecost when the Old Law was given, to the feast of Pentecost on which was given the Law of the living spirit: the feast of the New Moon, to Lady Day, when appeared the first rays of the sun, i.e. Christ, by the fulness of grace: the feast of Trumpets, to the feasts of the Apostles: the feast of Expiation, to the feasts of Martyrs and Confessors: the feast of Tabernacles, to the feast of the Church Dedication: the feast of the Assembly and Collection, to feast of the Angels, or else to the feast of All Hallows.

Article: 4

Whether since Christ's Passion the legal ceremonies can be observed without committing mortal sin?

Objection 1: It would seem that since Christ's Passion the legal ceremonies can be observed without committing mortal sin. For we must not believe that the apostles committed mortal sin after receiving the Holy Ghost: since by His fulness they were "endued with power from on high" (Lk. 24:49). But the apostles observed the legal ceremonies after the coming of the Holy Ghost: for it is stated

(Acts 16:3) that Paul circumcised Timothy: and (Acts 21:26) that Paul, at the advice of James, "took the men, and . . . being purified with them, entered into the temple, giving notice of the accomplishment of the days of purification, until an oblation should be offered for every one of them." Therefore the legal ceremonies can be observed since the Passion of Christ without mortal sin.

Objection 2: Further, one of the legal ceremonies consisted in shunning the fellowship of Gentiles. But the first Pastor of the Church complied with this observance; for it is stated (Gal. 2:12) that, "when" certain men "had come" to Antioch, Peter "withdrew and separated himself" from the Gentiles. Therefore the legal ceremonies can be observed since Christ's Passion without committing mortal sin.

Objection 3: Further, the commands of the apostles did not lead men into sin. But it was commanded by apostolic decree that the Gentiles should observe certain ceremonies of the Law: for it is written (Acts 15:28,29): "It hath seemed good to the Holy Ghost and to us, to lay no further burden upon you than these necessary things: that you abstain from things sacrificed to idols, and from blood, and from things strangled, and from fornication." Therefore the legal ceremonies can be observed since Christ's Passion without committing mortal sin.

On the contrary, The Apostle says (Gal. 5:2): "If you be circumcised, Christ shall profit you nothing." But nothing save mortal sin hinders us from receiving Christ's fruit. Therefore since Christ's Passion it is a mortal sin to be circumcised, or to observe the other legal ceremonies.

I answer that, All ceremonies are professions of faith, in which the interior worship of God consists. Now man can make profession of his inward faith, by deeds as well as by words: and in either profession, if he make a false declaration, he sins mortally. Now, though our faith in Christ is the same as that of the fathers of old; yet, since they came before Christ, whereas we come after Him, the same faith is expressed in different words, by us and by them. For by them was it said: "Behold a virgin shall conceive and bear a son," where the verbs are in the future tense: whereas we express the same by means of verbs in the past tense, and say that she "conceived and bore." In like manner the ceremonies of the Old Law betokened Christ as having yet to be born and to suffer: whereas our sacraments signify Him as already born and having suffered. Consequently, just as it would be a mortal sin now for anyone, in making a profession of faith, to say that Christ is yet to be born, which the fathers of old said devoutly and truthfully; so too it would be a mortal sin now to observe those ceremonies which the fathers of old fulfilled with devotion and fidelity. Such is the teaching Augustine (Contra Faust. xix, 16), who says: "It is no longer promised that He shall be born, shall suffer and rise again, truths of which their sacraments were a kind of image: but it is declared that He is already born, has suffered and risen again; of which our sacraments, in which Christians share, are the actual representation."

Reply to Objection 1: On this point there seems to have been a difference of opinion between Jerome and Augustine. For Jerome (Super Galat. ii, 11, seqq.) distinguished two periods of time. One was the time previous to Christ's Passion, during which the legal ceremonies were neither dead, since they were obligatory, and did expiate in their own fashion; nor deadly, because it was not sinful to observe them. But immediately after Christ's Passion they began to be not only dead, so as no longer to be either effectual or binding; but also deadly, so that whoever observed them was guilty of mortal sin. Hence he maintained that after the Passion the apostles never observed the legal ceremonies in real earnest; but only by a kind of pious pretense, lest, to wit, they should scandalize the Jews and hinder their conversion. This pretense, however, is to be understood, not as though they did not in reality perform those actions, but in the sense that they performed them without the mind to observe the ceremonies of the Law: thus a man might cut away his foreskin for health's sake, not with the intention of observing legal circumcision.

But since it seems unbecoming that the apostles, in order to avoid scandal, should have hidden things pertaining to the truth of life and doctrine, and that they should have made use of pretense, in things pertaining to the salvation of the faithful; therefore Augustine (Epist. lxxxii) more fittingly distinguished three periods of time. One was the time that preceded the Passion of Christ, during which the legal ceremonies were neither deadly nor dead: another period was after the publication of the Gospel, during which the legal ceremonies are both dead and deadly. The third is a middle period, viz. from the Passion of Christ until the publication of the Gospel, during which the legal ceremonies were dead indeed, because they had neither effect nor binding force; but were not deadly, because it was lawful for the Jewish converts to Christianity to observe them, provided they did not put their trust in them so as to hold them to be necessary unto salvation, as though faith in Christ could not justify without the legal observances. On the other hand, there was no reason why those who were converted from heathendom to Christianity should observe them. Hence Paul circumcised Timothy, who was born of a Jewish mother; but was unwilling to circumcise Titus, who was of heathen nationality.

The reason why the Holy Ghost did not wish the converted Jews to be debarred at once from observing the legal ceremonies, while converted heathens were forbidden to observe the rites of heathendom, was in order to show that there is a difference between these rites. For heathenish ceremonial was rejected as absolutely unlawful, and as prohibited by God for all time; whereas the legal ceremonial ceased as being fulfilled through Christ's Passion, being instituted by God as a figure of Christ.

Reply to Objection 2: According to Jerome, Peter withdrew himself from the Gentiles by pretense, in order to avoid giving scandal to the Jews, of whom he was the Apostle. Hence he did not sin at all in acting thus. On the other hand, Paul in like manner made a pretense of blaming him, in order to avoid scandalizing the Gentiles, whose Apostle he was. But Augustine disapproves of this solution: because in the canonical Scripture (viz. Gal. 2:11), wherein we must not hold anything to be false, Paul says that Peter "was to be blamed." Consequently it is true that Peter was at fault: and Paul blamed him in very truth and not with pretense. Peter, however, did not sin, by observing the legal ceremonial for the time being; because this was lawful for him who was a converted Jew. But he did sin by excessive minuteness in the observance of the legal rites lest he should scandalize the Jews, the result being that he gave scandal to the Gentiles.

Reply to Objection 3: Some have held that this prohibition of the apostles is not to be taken literally, but spiritually: namely, that the prohibition of blood signifies the prohibition of murder; the prohibition of things strangled, that of violence and rapine; the prohibition of things offered to idols, that of idolatry; while fornication is forbidden as being evil in itself: which opinion they gathered from certain glosses, which expound these prohibitions in a mystical sense. Since, however, murder and rapine were held to be unlawful even by the Gentiles, there would have been no need to give this special commandment to those who were converted to Christ from heathendom. Hence others maintain that those foods were forbidden literally, not to prevent the observance of legal ceremonies, but in order to prevent gluttony. Thus Jerome says on Ezech. 44:31 ("The priest shall not eat of anything that is dead"): "He condemns those priests who from gluttony did not keep these precepts."

But since certain foods are more delicate than these and more conducive to gluttony, there seems no reason why these should have been forbidden more than the others.

We must therefore follow the third opinion, and hold that these foods were forbidden literally, not with the purpose of enforcing compliance with the legal ceremonies, but in order to further the union of Gentiles and Jews living side by side. Because blood and things strangled were loathsome to the Jews by ancient custom; while the Jews might have suspected the Gentiles of relapse into idolatry if the latter had partaken of things offered to idols. Hence these things were prohibited for the time being, during which the Gentiles and Jews were to become united together. But as time went on, with the lapse of the cause, the effect lapsed also, when the truth of the Gospel teaching was divulged, wherein Our Lord taught that "not that which entereth into the mouth defileth a man" (Mt. 15:11); and that "nothing is to be rejected that is received with thanksgiving" (1 Tim. 4:4). With regard to fornication a special prohibition was made, because the Gentiles did not hold it to be sinful.

OF THE JUDICIAL PRECEPTS (FOUR ARTICLES)

We must now consider the judicial precepts: and first of all we shall consider them in general; in the second place we shall consider their reasons. Under the first head there are four points of inquiry:

(1) What is meant by the judicial precepts?
(2) Whether they are figurative?
(3) Their duration;
(4) Their division.

Question 104 Article: 1

Whether the judicial precepts were those which directed man in relation to his neighbor?

Objection 1: It would seem that the judicial precepts were not those which directed man in his relations to his neighbor. For judicial precepts take their name from "judgment." But there are many things that direct man as to his neighbor, which are not subordinate to judgment. Therefore the judicial precepts were not those which directed man in his relations to his neighbor.

Objection 2: Further, the judicial precepts are distinct from the moral precepts, as stated above (Question [99], Article [4]). But there are many moral precepts which direct man as to his neighbor: as is evidently the case with the seven precepts of the second table. Therefore the judicial precepts are not so called from directing man as to his neighbor.

Objection 3: Further, as the ceremonial precepts relate to God, so do the judicial precepts relate to one's neighbor, as stated above (Question [99], Article [4]; Question [101], Article [1]). But among the ceremonial precepts there are some which concern man himself, such as observances in matter of food and apparel, of which we have already spoken (Question [102], Article [6], ad 1,6). Therefore the judicial precepts are not so called from directing man as to his neighbor.

On the contrary, It is reckoned (Ezech. 18:8) among other works of a good and just man, that "he hath executed true judgment between man and man." But judicial precepts are so called from "judgment." Therefore it seems that the judicial precepts were those which directed the relations between man and man.

I answer that, As is evident from what we have stated above (Question [95], Article [2]; Question [99], Article [4]), in every law, some precepts derive their binding force from the dictate of reason itself, because natural reason dictates that something ought to be done or to be avoided. These are called "moral" precepts: since human morals are based on reason. At the same time there are other precepts which derive their binding force, not from the very dictate of reason (because, considered in themselves, they do not imply an obligation of something due or undue); but from some institution, Divine or human: and such are certain determinations of the moral precepts. When therefore the moral precepts are fixed by Divine institution in matters relating to man's subordination to God, they are called "ceremonial" precepts: but when they refer to man's relations to other men, they are called "judicial" precepts. Hence there are two conditions attached to the judicial precepts: viz. first, that they refer to man's relations to other men; secondly, that they derive their binding force not from reason alone, but in virtue of their institution.

Reply to Objection 1: Judgments emanate through the official pronouncement of certain men who are at the head of affairs, and in whom the judicial power is vested. Now it belongs to those who are at the head of affairs to regulate not only litigious matters, but also voluntary contracts which are concluded between man and man, and whatever matters concern the community at large and the government thereof. Consequently the judicial precepts are not only those which concern actions at law; but also all those that are directed to the ordering of one man in relation to another, which ordering is subject to the direction of the sovereign as supreme judge.

Reply to Objection 2: This argument holds in respect of those precepts which direct man in his relations to his neighbor, and derive their binding force from the mere dictate of reason.

Reply to Objection 3: Even in those precepts which direct us to God, some are moral precepts, which the reason itself dictates when it is quickened by faith; such as that God is to be loved and worshipped. There are also ceremonial precepts, which have no binding force except in virtue of their Divine institution. Now God is concerned not only with the sacrifices that are offered to Him, but also with whatever relates to the fitness of those who offer sacrifices to Him and worship Him. Because men are ordained to God as to their end; wherefore it concerns God and, consequently, is a matter of ceremonial precept, that man should show some fitness for the divine worship. On the other hand, man is not ordained to his neighbor as to his end, so as to need to be disposed in himself with regard to his neighbor, for such is the relationship of a slave to his master, since a slave "is his master's in all that he is," as the Philosopher says (Polit. i, 2). Hence there are no judicial precepts ordaining man in himself; all such precepts are moral: because the reason, which is the principal in moral matters, holds the same position, in man, with regard to things that concern him, as a prince or judge holds in the state. Nevertheless we must take note that, since the relations of man to his neighbor are more subject to reason than the relations of man to God, there are more precepts whereby man is directed in his relations to his neighbor, than whereby he is directed to God. For the same reason there had to be more ceremonial than judicial precepts in the Law.

Article: 2

Whether the judicial precepts were figurative?

Objection 1: It would seem that the judicial precepts were not figurative. Because it seems proper to the ceremonial precepts to be instituted as figures of something else. Therefore, if the judicial precepts are figurative, there will be no difference between the judicial and ceremonial precepts.

Objection 2: Further, just as certain judicial precepts were given to the Jewish people, so also were some given to other heathen peoples. But the judicial precepts given to other peoples were not figurative, but stated what had to be done. Therefore it seems that neither were the judicial precepts of the Old Law figures of anything.

Objection 3: Further, those things which relate to the divine worship had to be taught under certain figures, because the things of God are above our reason, as stated above (Question [101], Article [2], ad 2). But things concerning our neighbor are not above our reason. Therefore the judicial precepts which direct us in relation to our neighbor should not have been figurative.

On the contrary, The judicial precepts are expounded both in the allegorical and in the moral sense (Ex. 21).

I answer that, A precept may be figurative in two ways. First, primarily and in itself: because, to wit, it is instituted principally that it may be the figure of something. In this way the ceremonial precepts are figurative; since they were instituted for the very purpose that they might foreshadow something relating to the worship of God and the mystery of Christ. But some precepts are figurative, not primarily and in themselves, but consequently. In this way the judicial precepts of the Old Law are figurative. For they were not instituted for the purpose of being figurative, but in order that they might regulate the state of that people according to justice and equity. Nevertheless they did foreshadow something consequently: since, to wit, the entire state of that people, who were directed by these precepts, was figurative, according to 1 Cor. 10:11: "All . . . things happened to them in figure."

Reply to Objection 1: The ceremonial precepts are not figurative in the same way as the judicial precepts, as explained above.

Reply to Objection 2: The Jewish people were chosen by God that Christ might be born of them. Consequently the entire state of that people had to be prophetic and figurative, as Augustine states (Contra Faust. xxii, 24). For this reason even the judicial precepts that were given to this people were more figurative that those which were given to other nations. Thus, too, the wars and deeds of this people are expounded in the mystical sense: but not the wars and deeds of the Assyrians or Romans, although the latter are more famous in the eyes of men.

Reply to Objection 3: In this people the direction of man in regard to his neighbor, considered in itself, was subject to reason. But in so far as it was referred to the worship of God, it was above reason: and in this respect it was figurative.

Article: 3

Whether the judicial precepts of the Old Law bind for ever?

Objection 1: It would seem that the judicial precepts of the Old Law bind for ever. Because the judicial precepts relate to the virtue of justice: since a judgment is an execution of the virtue of justice. Now "justice is perpetual and immortal" (Wis. 1:15). Therefore the judicial precepts bind for ever.

Objection 2: Further, Divine institutions are more enduring than human institutions. But the judicial precepts of human laws bind for ever. Therefore much more do the judicial precepts of the Divine Law.

Objection 3: Further, the Apostle says (Heb. 7:18) that "there is a setting aside of the former commandment, because of the weakness and unprofitableness thereof." Now this is true of the ceremonial precept, which "could [Vulg.: 'can'] not, as to the conscience, make him perfect that serveth only in meats and in drinks, and divers washings and justices of the flesh," as the Apostle declares (Heb. 9:9,10). On the other hand, the judicial precepts were useful and efficacious in respect of the purpose for which they were instituted, viz. to establish justice and equity among men. Therefore the judicial precepts of the Old Law are not set aside, but still retain their efficacy.

On the contrary, The Apostle says (Heb. 7:12) that "the priesthood being translated it is necessary that a translation also be made of the Law." But the priesthood was transferred from Aaron to Christ. Therefore the entire Law was also transferred. Therefore the judicial precepts are no longer in force.

I answer that, The judicial precepts did not bind for ever, but were annulled by the coming of Christ: yet not in the same way as the ceremonial precepts. For the ceremonial precepts were annulled so far as to be not only "dead," but also deadly to those who observe them since the coming of Christ, especially since the promulgation of the Gospel. On the other hand, the judicial precepts are dead indeed, because they have no binding force: but they are not deadly. For if a sovereign were to order these judicial precepts to be observed in his kingdom, he would not sin: unless perchance they were observed, or ordered to be observed, as though they derived their binding force through being institutions of the Old Law: for it would be a deadly sin to intend to observe them thus.

The reason for this difference may be gathered from what has been said above (Article [2]). For it has been stated that the ceremonial precepts are figurative primarily and in themselves, as being instituted chiefly for the purpose of foreshadowing the mysteries of Christ to come. On the other hand, the judicial precepts were not instituted that they might be figures, but that they might shape the state of that people who were directed to Christ. Consequently, when the state of that people changed with the coming of Christ, the judicial precepts lost their binding force: for the Law was a pedagogue, leading men to Christ, as stated in Gal. 3:24. Since, however, these judicial precepts are instituted, not for the purpose of being figures, but for the performance of certain deeds, the observance thereof is not prejudicial to the truth of faith. But the intention of observing them, as though one were bound by the Law, is prejudicial to the truth of faith: because it would follow that the former state of the people still lasts, and that Christ has not yet come.

Reply to Objection 1: The obligation of observing justice is indeed perpetual. But the determination of those things that are just, according to human or Divine institution, must needs be different, according to the different states of mankind.

Reply to Objection 2: The judicial precepts established by men retain their binding force for ever, so long as the state of government remains the same. But if the state or nation pass to another form of government, the laws must needs be changed. For democracy, which is government by the people, demands different laws from those of oligarchy, which is government by the rich, as the Philosopher shows (Polit. iv, 1). Consequently when the state of that people changed, the judicial precepts had to be changed also.

Reply to Objection 3: Those judicial precepts directed the people to justice and equity, in keeping with the demands of that state. But after the coming of Christ, there had to be a change in the state of that people, so that in Christ there was no distinction between Gentile and Jew, as there had been before. For this reason the judicial precepts needed to be changed also.

Article: 4

Whether it is possible to assign a distinct division of the judicial precepts?

Objection 1: It would seem that it is impossible to assign a distinct division of the judicial precepts. Because the judicial precepts direct men in their relations to one another. But those things which need to be directed, as pertaining to the relationship between man and man, and which are made use of by men, are not subject to division, since they are infinite in number. Therefore it is not possible to assign a distinct division of the judicial precepts.

Objection 2: Further, the judicial precepts are decisions on moral matters. But moral precepts do not seem to be capable of division, except in so far as they are reducible to the precepts of the decalogue. Therefore there is no distinct division of the judicial precepts.

Objection 3: Further, because there is a distinct division of the ceremonial precepts, the Law alludes to this division, by describing some as "sacrifices," others as "observances." But the Law contains no allusion to a division of the judicial precepts. Therefore it seems that they have no distinct division.

On the contrary, Wherever there is order there must needs be division. But the notion of order is chiefly applicable to the judicial precepts, since thereby that people was ordained. Therefore it is most necessary that they should have a distinct division.

I answer that, Since law is the art, as it were, of directing or ordering the life of man, as in every art there is a distinct division in the rules of art, so, in every law, there must be a distinct division of precepts: else the law would be rendered useless by confusion. We must therefore say that the judicial precepts of the Old Law, whereby men were directed in their relations to one another, are subject to division according to the divers ways in which man is directed.

Now in every people a fourfold order is to be found: one, of the people's sovereign to his subjects; a second of the subjects among themselves; a third, of the citizens to foreigners; a fourth, of members of the same household, such as the order of the father to his son; of the wife to her husband; of the master to his servant: and according to these four orders we may distinguish different kinds of judicial precepts in the Old Law. For certain precepts are laid down concerning the institution of the sovereign and relating to his office, and about the respect due to him: this is one part of the judicial precepts. Again, certain precepts are given in respect of a man to his fellow citizens: for instance, about buying and selling, judgments and penalties: this is the second part of the judicial precepts. Again, certain precepts are enjoined with regard to foreigners: for instance, about wars waged against their foes, and about the way to receive travelers and strangers: this is the third part of the judicial precepts. Lastly, certain precepts are given relating to home life: for instance, about servants, wives and children: this is the fourth part of the judicial precepts.

Reply to Objection 1: Things pertaining to the ordering of relations between one man and another are indeed infinite in number: yet they are reducible to certain distinct heads, according to the different relations in which one man stands to another, as stated above.

Reply to Objection 2: The precepts of the decalogue held the first place in the moral order, as stated above (Question [100], Article [3]): and consequently it is fitting that other moral precepts should be distinguished in relation to them. But the judicial and ceremonial precepts have a different binding force, derived, not from natural reason, but from their institution alone. Hence there is a distinct reason for distinguishing them.

Reply to Objection 3: The Law alludes to the division of the judicial precepts in the very things themselves which are prescribed by the judicial precepts of the Law.

OF THE REASON FOR THE JUDICIAL PRECEPTS (FOUR ARTICLES)

We must now consider the reason for the judicial precepts: under which head there are four points of inquiry:

(1) Concerning the reason for the judicial precepts relating to the rulers;
(2) Concerning the fellowship of one man with another;
(3) Concerning matters relating to foreigners;
(4) Concerning things relating to domestic matters.

Question 105 Article: 1

Whether the Old Law enjoined fitting precepts concerning rulers?

Objection 1: It would seem that the Old Law made unfitting precepts concerning rulers. Because, as the Philosopher says (Polit. iii, 4), "the ordering of the people depends mostly on the chief ruler." But the Law contains no precept relating to the institution of the chief ruler; and yet we find therein prescriptions concerning the inferior rulers: firstly (Ex. 18:21): "Provide out of all the people wise [Vulg.: 'able'] men," etc.; again (Num. 11:16): "Gather unto Me seventy men of the ancients of Israel"; and again (Dt. 1:13): "Let Me have from among you wise and understanding men," etc. Therefore the Law provided insufficiently in regard to the rulers of the people.

Objection 2: Further, "The best gives of the best," as Plato states (Tim. ii). Now the best ordering of a state or of any nation is to be ruled by a king: because this kind of government approaches nearest in resemblance to the Divine government, whereby God rules the world from the beginning. Therefore the Law should have set a king over the people, and they should not have been allowed a choice in the matter, as indeed they were allowed (Dt. 17:14,15): "When thou . . . shalt say: I will set a king over me . . . thou shalt set him," etc.

Objection 3: Further, according to Mt. 12:25: "Every kingdom divided against itself shall be made desolate": a saying which was verified in the Jewish people, whose destruction was brought about by the division of the kingdom. But the Law should aim chiefly at things pertaining to the general well-being of the people. Therefore it should have forbidden the kingdom to be divided under two kings: nor should this have been introduced even by Divine authority; as we read of its being introduced by the authority of the prophet Ahias the Silonite (3 Kgs. 11:29, seqq.).

Objection 4: Further, just as priests are instituted for the benefit of the people in things concerning God, as stated in Heb. 5:1; so are rulers set up for the benefit of the people in human affairs. But certain things were allotted as a means of livelihood for the priests and Levites of the Law: such as the tithes and first-fruits, and many like things. Therefore in like manner certain things should have been determined for the livelihood of the rulers of the people: the more that they were forbidden to accept presents, as is clearly stated in Ex. 23:8: "You shall not [Vulg.: 'Neither shalt thou'] take bribes, which even blind the wise, and pervert the words of the just."

Objection 5: Further, as a kingdom is the best form of government, so is tyranny the most corrupt. But when the Lord appointed the king, He established a tyrannical law; for it is written (1 Kgs. 8:11): "This will be the right of the king, that shall reign over you: He will take your sons," etc. Therefore the Law made unfitting provision with regard to the institution of rulers.

On the contrary, The people of Israel is commended for the beauty of its order (Num. 24:5): "How beautiful are thy tabernacles, O Jacob, and thy tents." But the beautiful ordering of a people depends on the right establishment of its rulers. Therefore the Law made right provision for the people with regard to its rulers.

I answer that, Two points are to be observed concerning the right ordering of rulers in a state or nation. One is that all should take some share in the government: for this form of constitution ensures peace among the people, commends itself to all, and is most enduring, as stated in Polit. ii, 6. The other point is to be observed in respect of the kinds of government, or the different ways in which the constitutions are established. For whereas these differ in kind, as the Philosopher states (Polit. iii, 5), nevertheless the first place is held by the "kingdom," where the power of government is vested in one; and "aristocracy," which signifies government by the best, where the power of government is vested in a few. Accordingly, the best form of government is in a state or kingdom, where one is given the power to preside over all; while under him are others having governing powers: and yet a government of this kind is shared by all, both because all are eligible to govern, and because the rules are chosen by all. For this is the best form of polity, being partly kingdom, since there is one at the head of all; partly aristocracy, in so far as a number of persons are set in authority; partly democracy, i.e. government by the people, in so far as the rulers can be chosen from the people, and the people have the right to choose their rulers.

Such was the form of government established by the Divine Law. For Moses and his successors governed the people in such a way that each of them was ruler over all; so that there was a kind of kingdom. Moreover, seventy-two men were chosen, who were elders in virtue: for it is written (Dt. 1:15): "I took out of your tribes wise and honorable, and appointed them rulers": so that there was an element of aristocracy. But it was a democratical government in so far as the rulers were chosen from all the people; for it is written (Ex. 18:21): "Provide out of all the people wise [Vulg.: 'able'] men," etc.; and, again, in so far as they were chosen by the people; wherefore it is written (Dt. 1:13): "Let me have from among you wise [Vulg.: 'able'] men," etc. Consequently it is evident that the ordering of the rulers was well provided for by the Law.

Reply to Objection 1: This people was governed under the special care of God: wherefore it is written (Dt. 7:6): "The Lord thy God hath chosen thee to be His peculiar people": and this is why the Lord reserved to Himself the institution of the chief ruler. For this too did Moses pray (Num. 27:16): "May the Lord the God of the spirits of all the flesh provide a man, that may be over this multitude." Thus by God's orders Josue was set at the head in place of Moses; and we read about each of the judges who succeeded Josue that God "raised . . . up a saviour" for the people, and that "the spirit of the Lord was" in them (Jgs 3:9,10,15). Hence the Lord did not leave the choice of a king to the people; but reserved this to Himself, as appears from Dt. 17:15: "Thou shalt set him whom the Lord thy God shall choose."

Reply to Objection 2: A kingdom is the best form of government of the people, so long as it is not corrupt. But since the power granted to a king is so great, it easily degenerates into tyranny, unless he to whom this power is given be a very virtuous man: for it is only the virtuous man that conducts himself well in the midst of prosperity, as the Philosopher observes (Ethic. iv, 3). Now perfect virtue is to be found in few: and especially were the Jews inclined to cruelty and avarice, which vices above all turn men into tyrants. Hence from the very first the Lord did not set up the kingly authority with full power, but gave them judges and governors to rule them. But afterwards when the people asked Him to do so, being indignant with them, so to speak, He granted them a king, as is clear from His words to Samuel (1 Kgs. 8:7): "They have not rejected thee, but Me, that I should not reign over them."

Nevertheless, as regards the appointment of a king, He did establish the manner of election from the very beginning (Dt. 17:14, seqq.): and then He determined two points: first, that in choosing a king they should wait for the Lord's decision; and that they should not make a man of another nation king, because such kings are wont to take little interest in the people they are set over, and consequently to have no care for their welfare: secondly, He prescribed how the king after his appointment should behave, in regard to himself; namely, that he should not accumulate chariots and horses, nor wives, nor immense wealth: because through craving for such things princes become tyrants and forsake justice. He also appointed the manner in which they were to conduct themselves towards God: namely, that they should continually read and ponder on God's Law, and should ever fear and obey God. Moreover, He decided how they should behave towards their subjects: namely, that they should not proudly despise them, or ill-treat them, and that they should not depart from the paths of justice.

Reply to Objection 3: The division of the kingdom, and a number of kings, was rather a punishment inflicted on that people for their many dissensions, specially against the just rule of David, than a benefit conferred on them for their profit. Hence it is written (Osee 13:11): "I will give thee a king in My wrath"; and (Osee 8:4): "They have reigned, but not by Me: they have been princes, and I knew not."

Reply to Objection 4: The priestly office was bequeathed by succession from father to son: and this, in order that it might be held in greater respect, if not any man from the people could become a priest: since honor was given to them out of reverence for the divine worship. Hence it was necessary to put aside certain things for them both as to tithes and as to first-fruits, and, again, as to oblations and sacrifices, that they might be afforded a means of livelihood. On the other hand, the rulers, as stated above, were chosen from the whole people; wherefore they had their own possessions, from which to derive a living: and so much the more, since the Lord forbade even a king to have superabundant wealth to make too much show of magnificence: both because he could scarcely avoid the excesses of pride and tyranny, arising from such things, and because, if the rulers were not very rich, and if their office involved much work and anxiety, it would not tempt the ambition of the common people; and would not become an occasion of sedition.

Reply to Objection 5: That right was not given to the king by Divine institution: rather was it foretold that kings would usurp that right, by framing unjust laws, and by degenerating into tyrants who preyed on their subjects. This is clear from the context that follows: "And you shall be his slaves [Douay: 'servants']": which is significative of tyranny, since a tyrant rules is subjects as though they were his slaves. Hence Samuel spoke these words to deter them from asking for a king; since the narrative continues: "But the people would not hear the voice of Samuel." It may happen, however, that even a good king, without being a tyrant, may take away the sons, and make them tribunes and centurions; and may take many things from his subjects in order to secure the common weal.

Article: 2

Whether the judicial precepts were suitably framed as to the relations of one man with another?

Objection 1: It would seem that the judicial precepts were not suitably framed as regards the relations of one man with another. Because men cannot live together in peace, if one man takes what belongs to another. But this seems to have been approved by the Law: since it is written (Dt. 23:24): "Going into thy neighbor's vineyard, thou mayest eat as many grapes as thou pleasest." Therefore the Old Law did not make suitable provisions for man's peace.

Objection 2: Further, one of the chief causes of the downfall of states has been the holding of property by women, as the Philosopher says (Polit. ii, 6). But this was introduced by the Old Law; for it is written (Num. 27:8): "When a man dieth without a son, his inheritance shall pass to his daughter." Therefore the Law made unsuitable provision for the welfare of the people.

Objection 3: Further, it is most conducive to the preservation of human society that men may provide themselves with necessaries by buying and selling, as stated in Polit. i. But the Old Law took away the force of sales; since it prescribes that in the 50th year of the jubilee all that is sold shall return to the vendor (Lev. 25:28). Therefore in this matter the Law gave the people an unfitting command.

Objection 4: Further, man's needs require that men should be ready to lend: which readiness ceases if the creditors do not return the pledges: hence it is written (Ecclus. 29:10): "Many have refused to lend, not out of wickedness, but they were afraid to be defrauded without cause." And yet this was encouraged by the Law. First, because it prescribed (Dt. 15:2): "He to whom any thing is owing from his friend or neighbor or brother, cannot demand it again, because it is the year of remission of the Lord"; and (Ex. 22:15) it is stated that if a borrowed animal should die while the owner is present, the borrower is not bound to make restitution. Secondly, because the security acquired through the pledge is lost: for it is written (Dt. 24:10): "When thou shalt demand of thy neighbor any thing that he oweth thee, thou shalt not go into his house to take away a pledge"; and again (Dt. 24:12,13): "The pledge shall not lodge with thee that night, but thou shalt restore it to him presently." Therefore the Law made insufficient provision in the matter of loans.

Objection 5: Further, considerable risk attaches to goods deposited with a fraudulent depositary: wherefore great caution should be observed in such matters: hence it is stated in 2 Mach 3:15 that "the priests . . . called upon Him from heaven, Who made the law concerning things given to be kept, that He would preserve them safe, for them that had deposited them." But the precepts of the Old Law observed little caution in regard to deposits: since it is prescribed (Ex. 22:10,11) that when goods deposited are lost, the owner is to stand by the oath of the depositary. Therefore the Law made unsuitable provision in this matter.

Objection 6: Further, just as a workman offers his work for hire, so do men let houses and so forth. But there is no need for the tenant to pay his rent as soon as he takes a house. Therefore it seems an unnecessarily hard prescription (Lev. 19:13) that "the wages of him that hath been hired by thee shall not abide with thee until morning."

Objection 7: Further, since there is often pressing need for a judge, it should be easy to gain access to one. It was therefore unfitting that the Law (Dt. 17:8,9) should command them to go to a fixed place to ask for judgment on doubtful matters.

Objection 8: Further, it is possible that not only two, but three or more, should agree to tell a lie. Therefore it is unreasonably stated (Dt. 19:15) that "in the mouth of two or three witnesses every word shall stand."

Objection 9: Further, punishment should be fixed according to the gravity of the fault: for which reason also it is written (Dt. 25:2): "According to the measure of the sin, shall the measure also of the stripes be." Yet the Law fixed unequal punishments for certain faults: for it is written (Ex. 22:1) that the thief "shall restore five oxen for one ox, and four sheep for one sheep." Moreover, certain slight offenses are severely punished: thus (Num. 15:32, seqq.) a man is stoned for gathering sticks on the sabbath day: and (Dt. 21:18, seqq.) the unruly son is commanded to be stoned on account of certain small transgressions, viz. because "he gave himself to revelling . . . and banquetings." Therefore the Law prescribed punishments in an unreasonable manner.

Objection 1:: Further, as Augustine says (De Civ. Dei xxi, 11), "Tully writes that the laws recognize eight forms of punishment, indemnity, prison, stripes, retaliation, public disgrace, exile, death, slavery." Now some of these were prescribed by the Law. "Indemnity," as when a thief was condemned to make restitution fivefold or fourfold. "Prison," as when (Num. 15:34) a certain man is ordered to be imprisoned. "Stripes"; thus (Dt. 25:2), "if they see that the offender be worthy of stripes; they shall lay him down, and shall cause him to be beaten before them." "Public disgrace" was brought on to him who refused to take to himself the wife of his deceased brother, for she took "off his shoe from his foot, and" did "spit in his face" (Dt. 25:9). It prescribed the "death" penalty, as is clear from (Lev. 20:9): "He that curseth his father, or mother, dying let him die." The Law also recognized the "lex talionis," by prescribing (Ex. 21:24): "Eye for eye, tooth for tooth." Therefore it seems unreasonable that the Law should not have inflicted the two other punishments, viz. "exile" and "slavery."

Objection 1:: Further, no punishment is due except for a fault. But dumb animals cannot commit a fault. Therefore the Law is unreasonable in punishing them (Ex. 21:29): "If the ox . . . shall kill a man or a woman," it "shall be stoned": and (Lev. 20:16): "The woman that shall lie under any beast, shall be killed together with the same." Therefore it seems that matters pertaining to the relations of one man with another were unsuitably regulated by the Law.

Objection 1:: Further, the Lord commanded (Ex. 21:12) a murderer to be punished with death. But the death of a dumb animal is reckoned of much less account than the slaying of a man. Hence murder cannot be sufficiently punished by the slaying of a dumb animal. Therefore it is unfittingly prescribed (Dt. 21:1,4) that "when there shall be found . . . the corpse of a man slain, and it is not known who is guilty of the murder . . . the ancients" of the nearest city "shall take a heifer of the herd, that hath not drawn in the yoke, nor ploughed the ground, and they shall bring her into a rough and stony valley, that never was ploughed, nor sown; and there they shall strike off the head of the heifer."

On the contrary, It is recalled as a special blessing (Ps. 147:20) that "He hath not done in like manner to every nation; and His judgments He hath not made manifest to them."

I answer that, As Augustine says (De Civ. Dei ii, 21), quoting Tully, "a nation is a body of men united together by consent to the law and by community of welfare." Consequently it is of the essence of a nation that the mutual relations of the citizens be ordered by just laws. Now the relations of one man with another are twofold: some are effected under the guidance of those in authority: others are effected by the will of private individuals. And since whatever is subject to the power of an individual can be disposed of according to his will, hence it is that the decision of matters between one man and another, and the punishment of evildoers, depend on the direction of those in authority, to whom men are subject. On the other hand, the power of private persons is exercised over the things they possess: and consequently their dealings with one another, as regards such things, depend on their own will, for instance in buying, selling, giving, and so forth. Now the Law provided sufficiently in respect of each of these relations between one man and another. For it established judges, as is clearly indicated in Dt. 16:18: "Thou shalt appoint judges and magistrates in all its [Vulg.: 'thy'] gates . . . that they may judge the people with just judgment." It is also directed the manner of pronouncing just judgments, according to Dt. 1:16,17: "Judge that which is just, whether he be one of your own country or a stranger: there shall be no difference of persons." It also removed an occasion of pronouncing unjust judgment, by forbidding judges to accept bribes (Ex. 23:8; Dt. 16:19). It prescribed the number of witnesses, viz. two or three: and it appointed certain punishments to certain crimes, as we shall state farther on (ad 10).

But with regard to possessions, it is a very good thing, says the Philosopher (Polit. ii, 2) that the things possessed should be distinct, and the use thereof should be partly common, and partly granted to others by the will of the possessors. These three points were provided for by the Law. Because, in the first place, the possessions themselves were divided among individuals: for it is written (Num. 33:53,54): "I have given you" the land "for a possession: and you shall divide it among you by lot." And since many states have been ruined through want of regulations in the matter of possessions, as the Philosopher observes (Polit. ii, 6); therefore the Law provided a threefold remedy against the regularity of possessions. The first was that they should be divided equally, wherefore it is written (Num. 33:54): "To the more you shall give a larger part, and to the fewer, a lesser." A second remedy was that possessions could not be alienated for ever, but after a certain lapse of time should return to their former owner, so as to avoid confusion of possessions (cf. ad 3). The third remedy aimed at the removal of this confusion, and provided that the dead should be succeeded by their next of kin: in the first place, the son; secondly, the daughter; thirdly, the brother; fourthly, the father's brother; fifthly, any other next of kin.

Furthermore, in order to preserve the distinction of property, the Law enacted that heiresses should marry within their own tribe, as recorded in Num. 36:6.

Secondly, the Law commanded that, in some respects, the use of things should belong to all in common. Firstly, as regards the care of them; for it was prescribed (Dt. 22:1-4): "Thou shalt not pass by, if thou seest thy brother's ox or his sheep go astray; but thou shalt bring them back to thy brother," and in like manner as to other things. Secondly, as regards fruits. For all alike were allowed on entering a friend's vineyard to eat of the fruit, but not to take any away. And, specially, with respect to the poor, it was prescribed that the forgotten sheaves, and the bunches of grapes and fruit, should be left behind for them (Lev. 19:9; Dt. 24:19). Moreover, whatever grew in the seventh year was common property, as stated in Ex. 23:11 and Lev. 25:4.

Thirdly, the law recognized the transference of goods by the owner. There was a purely gratuitous transfer: thus it is written (Dt. 14:28,29): "The third day thou shalt separate another tithe . . . and the Levite . . . and the stranger, and the fatherless, and the widow . . . shall come and shall eat and be filled." And there was a transfer for a consideration, for instance, by selling and buying, by letting out and hiring, by loan and also by deposit, concerning all of which we find that the Law made ample provision. Consequently it is clear that the Old Law provided sufficiently concerning the mutual relations of one man with another.

Reply to Objection 1: As the Apostle says (Rm. 13:8), "he that loveth his neighbor hath fulfilled the Law": because, to wit, all the precepts of the Law, chiefly those concerning our neighbor, seem to aim at the end that men should love one another. Now it is an effect of love that men give their own goods to others: because, as stated in 1 Jn. 3:17: "He that . . . shall see his brother in need, and shall shut up his bowels from him: how doth the charity of God abide in him?" Hence the purpose of the Law was to accustom men to give of their own to others readily: thus the Apostle (1 Tim. 6:18) commands the rich "to give easily and to communicate to others." Now a man does not give easily to others if he will not suffer another man to take some little thing from him without any great injury to him. And so the Law laid down that it should be lawful for a man, on entering his neighbor's vineyard, to eat of the fruit there: but not to carry any away, lest this should lead to the infliction of a grievous harm, and cause a disturbance of the peace: for among well-behaved people, the taking of a little does not disturb the peace; in fact, it rather strengthens friendship and accustoms men to give things to one another.

Reply to Objection 2: The Law did not prescribe that women should succeed to their father's estate except in default of male issue: failing which it was necessary that succession should be granted to the female line in order to comfort the father, who would have been sad to think that his estate would pass to strangers. Nevertheless the Law observed due caution in the matter, by providing that those women who succeeded to their father's estate, should marry within their own tribe, in order to avoid confusion of tribal possessions, as stated in Num. 36:7,8.

Reply to Objection 3: As the Philosopher says (Polit. ii, 4), the regulation of possessions conduces much to the preservation of a state or nation. Consequently, as he himself observes, it was forbidden by the law in some of the heathen states, "that anyone should sell his possessions, except to avoid a manifest loss." For if possessions were to be sold indiscriminately, they might happen to come into the hands of a few: so that it might become necessary for a state or country to become void of inhabitants. Hence the Old Law, in order to remove this danger, ordered things in such a way that while provision was made for men's needs, by allowing the sale of possessions to avail for a certain period, at the same time the said danger was removed, by prescribing the return of those possessions after that period had elapsed. The reason for this law was to prevent confusion of possessions, and to ensure the continuance of a definite distinction among the tribes.

But as the town houses were not allotted to distinct estates, therefore the Law allowed them to be sold in perpetuity, like movable goods. Because the number of houses in a town was not fixed, whereas there was a fixed limit to the amount of estates, which could not be exceeded, while the number of houses in a town could be increased. On the other hand, houses situated not in a town, but "in a village that hath no walls," could not be sold in perpetuity: because such houses are built merely with a view to the cultivation and care of possessions; wherefore the Law rightly made the same prescription in regard to both (Lev. 25).

Reply to Objection 4: As stated above (ad 1), the purpose of the Law was to accustom men to its precepts, so as to be ready to come to one another's assistance: because this is a very great incentive to friendship. The Law granted these facilities for helping others in the matter not only of gratuitous and absolute donations, but also of mutual transfers: because the latter kind of succor is more frequent and benefits the greater number: and it granted facilities for this purpose in many ways. First of all by prescribing that men should be ready to lend, and that they should not be less inclined to do so as the year of remission drew nigh, as stated in Dt. 15:7, seqq. Secondly, by forbidding them to burden a man to whom they might grant a loan, either by exacting usury, or by accepting necessities of life in security; and by prescribing that when this had been done they should be restored at once. For it is written (Dt. 23:19): "Thou shalt not lend to thy brother money to usury": and (Dt. 24:6): "Thou shalt not take the nether nor the upper millstone to pledge; for he hath pledged his life to thee": and (Ex. 22:26): "If thou take of thy neighbor a garment in pledge, thou shalt give it him again before sunset." Thirdly, by forbidding them to be importunate in exacting payment. Hence it is written (Ex. 22:25): "If thou lend money to any of my people that is poor that dwelleth with thee, thou shalt not be hard upon them as an extortioner." For this reason, too, it is enacted (Dt. 24:10,11): "When thou shalt demand of thy neighbor anything that he oweth thee, thou shalt not go into his house to take away a pledge, but thou shalt stand without, and he shall bring out to thee what he hath": both because a man's house is his surest refuge, wherefore it is offensive to a man to be set upon in his own house; and because the Law does not allow the creditor to take away whatever he likes in security, but rather permits the debtor to give what he needs least. Fourthly, the Law prescribed that debts should cease together after the lapse of seven years. For it was probable that those who could conveniently pay their debts, would do so before the seventh year, and would not defraud the lender without cause. But if they were altogether insolvent, there was the same reason for remitting the debt from love for them, as there was for renewing the loan on account of their need.

As regards animals granted in loan, the Law enacted that if, through the neglect of the person to whom they were lent, they perished or deteriorated in his absence, he was bound to make restitution. But if they perished or deteriorated while he was present and taking proper care of them, he was not bound to make restitution, especially if they were hired for a consideration: because they might have died or deteriorated in the same way if they had remained in possession of the lender, so that if the animal had been saved through being lent, the lender would have gained something by the loan which would no longer have been gratuitous. And especially was this to be observed when animals were hired for a consideration: because then the owner received a certain price for the use of the animals; wherefore he had no right to any profit, by receiving indemnity for the animal, unless the person who had charge of it were negligent. In the case, however, of animals not hired for a consideration, equity demanded that he should receive something by way of restitution at least to the value of the hire of the animal that had perished or deteriorated.

Reply to Objection 5: The difference between a loan and a deposit is that a loan is in respect of goods transferred for the use of the person to whom they are transferred, whereas a deposit is for the benefit of the depositor. Hence in certain cases there was a stricter obligation of returning a loan than of restoring goods held in deposit. Because the latter might be lost in two ways. First, unavoidably: i.e. either through a natural cause, for instance if an animal held in deposit were to die or depreciate in value; or through an extrinsic cause, for instance, if it were taken by an enemy, or devoured by a beast (in which case, however, a man was bound to restore to the owner what was left of the animal thus slain): whereas in the other cases mentioned above, he was not bound to make restitution; but only to take an oath in order to clear himself of suspicion. Secondly, the goods deposited might be lost through an avoidable cause, for instance by theft: and then the depositary was bound to restitution on account of his neglect. But, as stated above (ad 4), he who held an animal on loan, was bound to restitution, even if he were absent when it depreciated or died: because he was held responsible for less negligence than a depositary, who was only held responsible in case of theft.

Reply to Objection 6: Workmen who offer their labor for hire, are poor men who toil for their daily bread: and therefore the Law commanded wisely that they should be paid at once, lest they should lack food. But they who offer other commodities for hire, are wont to be rich: nor are they in such need of their price in order to gain a livelihood: and consequently the comparison does not hold.

Reply to Objection 7: The purpose for which judges are appointed among men, is that they may decide doubtful points in matters of justice. Now a matter may be doubtful in two ways. First, among simple-minded people: and in order to remove doubts of this kind, it was prescribed (Dt. 16:18) that "judges and magistrates" should be appointed in each tribe, "to judge the people with just judgment." Secondly, a matter may be doubtful even among experts: and therefore, in order to remove doubts of this kind, the Law prescribed that all should foregather in some chief place chosen by God, where there would be both the high-priest, who would decide doubtful matters relating to the ceremonies of divine worship; and the chief judge of the people, who would decide matters relating to the judgments of men: just as even now cases are taken from a lower to a higher court either by appeal or by consultation. Hence it is written (Dt. 17:8,9): "If thou perceive that there be among you a hard and doubtful matter in judgment . . . and thou see that the words of the judges within thy gates do vary; arise and go up to the place, which the Lord thy God shall choose; and thou shalt come to the priests of the Levitical race, and to the judge that shall be at that time." But such like doubtful matters did not often occur for judgment: wherefore the people were not burdened on this account.

Reply to Objection 8: In the business affairs of men, there is no such thing as demonstrative and infallible proof, and we must be content with a certain conjectural probability, such as that which an orator employs to persuade. Consequently, although it is quite possible for two or three witnesses to agree to a falsehood, yet it is neither easy nor probable that they succeed in so doing: wherefore their testimony is taken as being true, especially if they do not waver in giving it, or are not otherwise suspect. Moreover, in order that witnesses might not easily depart from the truth, the Law commanded that they should be most carefully examined, and that those who were found untruthful should be severely punished, as stated in Dt. 19:16, seqq.

There was, however, a reason for fixing on this particular number, in token of the unerring truth of the Divine Persons, Who are sometimes mentioned as two, because the Holy Ghost is the bond of the other two Persons; and sometimes as three: as Augustine observes on Jn. 8:17: "In your law it is written that the testimony of two men is true."

Reply to Objection 9: A severe punishment is inflicted not only on account of the gravity of a fault, but also for other reasons. First, on account of the greatness of the sin, because a greater sin, other things being equal, deserves a greater punishment. Secondly, on account of a habitual sin, since men are not easily cured of habitual sin except by severe punishments. Thirdly, on account of a great desire for or a great pleasure in the sin: for men are not easily deterred from such sins unless they be severely punished. Fourthly, on account of the facility of committing a sin and of concealing it: for such like sins, when discovered, should be more severely punished in order to deter others from committing them.

Again, with regard to the greatness of a sin, four degrees may be observed, even in respect of one single deed. The first is when a sin is committed unwillingly; because then, if the sin be altogether involuntary, man is altogether excused from punishment; for it is written (Dt. 22:25, seqq.) that a damsel who suffers violence in a field is not guilty of death, because "she cried, and there was no man to help her." But if a man sinned in any way voluntarily, and yet through weakness, as for instance when a man sins from passion, the sin is diminished: and the punishment, according to true judgment, should be diminished also; unless perchance the common weal requires that the sin be severely punished in order to deter others from committing such sins, as stated above. The second degree is when a man sins through ignorance: and then he was held to be guilty to a certain extent, on account of his negligence in acquiring knowledge: yet he was not punished by the judges but expiated his sin by sacrifices. Hence it is written (Lev. 4:2): "The soul that sinneth through ignorance," etc. This is, however, to be taken as applying to ignorance of fact; and not to ignorance of the Divine precept, which all were bound to know. The third degree was when a man sinned from pride, i.e. through deliberate choice or malice: and then he was punished according to the greatness of the sin [*Cf. Dt. 25:2]. The fourth degree was when a man sinned from stubbornness or obstinacy: and then he was to be utterly cut off as a rebel and a destroyer of the commandment of the Law [*Cf. Num. 15:30,31].

Accordingly we must say that, in appointing the punishment for theft, the Law considered what would be likely to happen most frequently (Ex. 22:1-9): wherefore, as regards theft of other things which can easily be safeguarded from a thief, the thief restored only twice their value. But sheep cannot be easily safeguarded from a thief, because they graze in the fields: wherefore it happened more frequently that sheep were stolen in the fields. Consequently the Law inflicted a heavier penalty, by ordering four sheep to be restored for the theft of one. As to cattle, they were yet more difficult to safeguard, because they are kept in the fields, and do not graze in flocks as sheep do; wherefore a yet more heavy penalty was inflicted in their regard, so that five oxen were to be restored for one ox. And this I say, unless perchance the animal itself were discovered in the thief's possession: because in that case he had to restore only twice the number, as in the case of other thefts: for there was reason to presume that he intended to restore the animal, since he kept it alive. Again, we might say, according to a gloss, that "a cow is useful in five ways: it may be used for sacrifice, for ploughing, for food, for milk, and its hide is employed for various purposes": and therefore for one cow five had to be restored. But the sheep was useful in four ways: "for sacrifice, for meat, for milk, and for its wool." The unruly son was slain, not because he ate and drank: but on account of his stubbornness and rebellion, which was always punished by death, as stated above. As to the man who gathered sticks on the sabbath, he was stoned as a breaker of the Law, which commanded the sabbath to be observed, to testify the belief in the newness of the world, as stated above (Question [100], Article [5]): wherefore he was slain as an unbeliever.

Reply to Objection 1:: The Old Law inflicted the death penalty for the more grievous crimes, viz. for those which are committed against God, and for murder, for stealing a man, irreverence towards one's parents, adultery and incest. In the case of thief of other things it inflicted punishment by indemnification: while in the case of blows and mutilation it authorized punishment by retaliation; and likewise for the sin of bearing false witness. In other faults of less degree it prescribed the punishment of stripes or of public disgrace.

The punishment of slavery was prescribed by the Law in two cases. First, in the case of a slave who was unwilling to avail himself of the privilege granted by the Law, whereby he was free to depart in the seventh year of remission: wherefore he was punished by remaining a slave for ever. Secondly, in the case of a thief, who had not wherewith to make restitution, as stated in Ex. 22:3.

The punishment of absolute exile was not prescribed by the Law: because God was worshipped by that people alone, whereas all other nations were given to idolatry: wherefore if any man were exiled from that people absolutely, he would be in danger of falling into idolatry. For this reason it is related (1 Kgs. 26:19) that David said to Saul: "They are cursed in the sight of the Lord, who have case me out this day, that I should not dwell in the inheritance of the Lord, saying: Go, serve strange gods." There was, however, a restricted sort of exile: for it is written in Dt. 19:4 [*Cf. Num. 35:25] that "he that striketh [Vulg.: 'killeth'] his neighbor ignorantly, and is proved to have had no hatred against him, shall flee to one of the cities" of refuge and "abide there until the death of the high-priest." For then it became lawful for him to return home, because when the whole people thus suffered a loss they forgot their private quarrels, so that the next of kin of the slain were not so eager to kill the slayer.

Reply to Objection 1:: Dumb animals were ordered to be slain, not on account of any fault of theirs; but as a punishment to their owners, who had not safeguarded their beasts from these offenses. Hence the owner was more severely punished if his ox had butted anyone "yesterday or the day before" (in which case steps might have been taken to butting suddenly). Or again, the animal was slain in detestation of the sin; and lest men should be horrified at the sight thereof.

Reply to Objection 1:: The literal reason for this commandment, as Rabbi Moses declares (Doct. Perplex. iii), was because the slayer was frequently from the nearest city: wherefore the slaying of the calf was a means of investigating the hidden murder. This was brought about in three ways. In the first place the elders of the city swore that they had taken every measure for safeguarding the roads. Secondly, the owner of the heifer was indemnified for the slaying of his beast, and if the murder was previously discovered, the beast was not slain. Thirdly, the place, where the heifer was slain, remained uncultivated. Wherefore, in order to avoid this twofold loss, the men of the city would readily make known the murderer, if they knew who he was: and it would seldom happen but that some word or sign would escape about the matter. Or again, this was done in order to frighten people, in detestation of murder. Because the slaying of a heifer, which is a useful animal and full of strength, especially before it has been put under the yoke, signified that whoever committed murder, however useful and strong he might be, was to forfeit his life; and that, by a cruel death, which was implied by the striking off of its head; and that the murderer, as vile and abject, was to be cut off from the fellowship of men, which was betokened by the fact that the heifer after being slain was left to rot in a rough and uncultivated place.

Mystically, the heifer taken from the herd signifies the flesh of Christ; which had not drawn a yoke, since it had done no sin; nor did it plough the ground, i.e. it never knew the stain of revolt. The fact of the heifer being killed in an uncultivated valley signified the despised death of Christ, whereby all sins are washed away, and the devil is shown to be the arch-murderer.

Article: 3

Whether the judicial precepts regarding foreigners were framed in a suitable manner?

Objection 1: It would seem that the judicial precepts regarding foreigners were not suitably framed. For Peter said (Acts 10:34,35): "In very deed I perceive that God is not a respecter of persons, but in every nation, he that feareth Him and worketh justice is acceptable to Him." But those who are acceptable to God should not be excluded from the Church of God. Therefore it is unsuitably commanded (Dt. 23:3) that "the Ammonite and the Moabite, even after the tenth generation, shall not enter into the church of the Lord for ever": whereas, on the other hand, it is prescribed (Dt. 23:7) to be observed with regard to certain other nations: "Thou shalt not abhor the Edomite, because he is thy brother; nor the Egyptian because thou wast a stranger in his land."

Objection 2: Further, we do not deserve to be punished for those things which are not in our power. But it is not in man's power to be an eunuch, or born of a prostitute. Therefore it is unsuitably commanded (<u>Dt. 23:1,2</u>) that "an eunuch and one born of a prostitute shalt not enter into the church of the Lord."

Objection 3: Further, the Old Law mercifully forbade strangers to be molested: for it is written (<u>Ex. 22:21</u>): "Thou shalt not molest a stranger, nor afflict him; for yourselves also were strangers in the land of Egypt": and (<u>Ex. 23:9</u>): "Thou shalt not molest a stranger, for you know the hearts of strangers, for you also were strangers in the land of Egypt." But it is an affliction to be burdened with usury. Therefore the Law unsuitably permitted them (<u>Dt. 23:19,20</u>) to lend money to the stranger for usury.

Objection 4: Further, men are much more akin to us than trees. But we should show greater care and love for these things that are nearest to us, according to Ecclus. 13:19: "Every beast loveth its like: so also every man him that is nearest to himself." Therefore the Lord unsuitably commanded (<u>Dt. 20:13-19</u>) that all the inhabitants of a captured hostile city were to be slain, but that the fruit-trees should not be cut down.

Objection 5: Further, every one should prefer the common good of virtue to the good of the individual. But the common good is sought in a war which men fight against their enemies. Therefore it is unsuitably commanded (<u>Dt. 20:5-7</u>) that certain men should be sent home, for instance a man that had built a new house, or who had planted a vineyard, or who had married a wife.

Objection 6: Further, no man should profit by his own fault. But it is a man's fault if he be timid or faint-hearted: since this is contrary to the virtue of fortitude. Therefore the timid and faint-hearted are unfittingly excused from the toil of battle (<u>Dt. 20:8</u>).

On the contrary, Divine Wisdom declares (<u>Prov. 8:8</u>): "All my words are just, there is nothing wicked nor perverse in them."

I answer that, Man's relations with foreigners are twofold: peaceful, and hostile: and in directing both kinds of relation the Law contained suitable precepts. For the Jews were offered three opportunities of peaceful relations with foreigners. First, when foreigners passed through their land as travelers. Secondly, when they came to dwell in their land as newcomers. And in both these respects the Law made kind provision in its precepts: for it is written (<u>Ex. 22:21</u>): "Thou shalt not molest a stranger [advenam]"; and again (<u>Ex. 22:9</u>): "Thou shalt not molest a stranger [peregrino]." Thirdly, when any foreigners wished to be admitted entirely to their fellowship and mode of worship. With regard to these a certain order was observed. For they were not at once admitted to citizenship: just as it was law with some nations that no one was deemed a citizen except after two or three generations, as the Philosopher says (Polit. iii, 1). The reason for this was that if foreigners were allowed to meddle with the affairs of a nation as soon as they settled down in its midst, many dangers might occur, since the foreigners not yet having the common good firmly at heart might attempt something hurtful to the people. Hence it was that the Law prescribed in respect of certain nations that had close relations with the Jews (viz., the Egyptians among whom they were born and educated, and the Idumeans, the children of Esau, Jacob's brother), that they should be admitted to the fellowship of the people after the third generation; whereas others (with whom their relations had been hostile, such as the Ammonites and Moabites) were never to be admitted to citizenship; while the Amalekites, who were yet more hostile to them, and had no fellowship of kindred with them, were to be held as foes in perpetuity: for it is written (Ex. 17:16): "The war of the Lord shall be against Amalec from generation to generation."

In like manner with regard to hostile relations with foreigners, the Law contained suitable precepts. For, in the first place, it commanded that war should be declared for a just cause: thus it is commanded (Dt. 20:10) that when they advanced to besiege a city, they should at first make an offer of peace. Secondly, it enjoined that when once they had entered on a war they should undauntedly persevere in it, putting their trust in God. And in order that they might be the more heedful of this command, it ordered that on the approach of battle the priest should hearten them by promising them God's aid. Thirdly, it prescribed the removal of whatever might prove an obstacle to the fight, and that certain men, who might be in the way, should be sent home. Fourthly, it enjoined that they should use moderation in pursuing the advantage of victory, by sparing women and children, and by not cutting down fruit-trees of that country.

Reply to Objection 1: The Law excluded the men of no nation from the worship of God and from things pertaining to the welfare of the soul: for it is written (Ex. 12:48): "If any stranger be willing to dwell among you, and to keep the Phase of the Lord; all his males shall first be circumcised, and then shall he celebrate it according to the manner, and he shall be as that which is born in the land." But in temporal matters concerning the public life of the people, admission was not granted to everyone at once, for the reason given above: but to some, i.e. the Egyptians and Idumeans, in the third generation; while others were excluded in perpetuity, in detestation of their past offense, i.e. the peoples of Moab, Ammon, and Amalec. For just as one man is punished for a sin committed by him, in order that others seeing this may be deterred and refrain from sinning; so too may one nation or city be punished for a crime, that others may refrain from similar crimes.

Nevertheless it was possible by dispensation for a man to be admitted to citizenship on account of some act of virtue: thus it is related (Judith 14:6) that Achior, the captain of the children of Ammon, "was joined to the people of Israel, with all the succession of his kindred." The same applies to Ruth the Moabite who was "a virtuous woman" (Ruth 3:11): although it may be said that this prohibition regarded men and not women, who are not competent to be citizens absolutely speaking.

Reply to Objection 2: As the Philosopher says (Polit. iii, 3), a man is said to be a citizen in two ways: first, simply; secondly, in a restricted sense. A man is a citizen simply if he has all the rights of citizenship, for instance, the right of debating or voting in the popular assembly. On the other hand, any man may be called citizen, only in a restricted sense, if he dwells within the state, even common people or children or old men, who are not fit to enjoy power in matters pertaining to the common weal. For this reason bastards, by reason of their base origin, were excluded from the "ecclesia," i.e. from the popular assembly, down to the tenth generation. The same applies to eunuchs, who were not competent to receive the honor due to a father, especially among the Jews, where the divine worship was continued through carnal generation: for even among the heathens, those who had many children were marked with special honor, as the Philosopher remarks (Polit. ii, 6). Nevertheless, in matters pertaining to the grace of God, eunuchs were not discriminated from others, as neither were strangers, as already stated: for it is written (Iss 56:3): "Let not the son of the stranger that adhereth to the Lord speak, saying: The Lord will divide and separate me from His people. And let not the eunuch say: Behold I am a dry tree."

Reply to Objection 3: It was not the intention of the Law to sanction the acceptance of usury from strangers, but only to tolerate it on account of the proneness of the Jews to avarice; and in order to promote an amicable feeling towards those out of whom they made a profit.

Reply to Objection 4: A distinction was observed with regard to hostile cities. For some of them were far distant, and were not among those which had been promised to them. When they had taken these cities, they killed all the men who had fought against God's people; whereas the women and children were spared. But in the neighboring cities which had been promised to them, all were ordered to be slain, on account of their former crimes, to punish which God sent the Israelites as executor of Divine justice: for it is written (Dt. 9:5) "because they have done wickedly, they are destroyed at thy coming in." The fruit-trees were commanded to be left untouched, for the use of the people themselves, to whom the city with its territory was destined to be subjected.

Reply to Objection 5: The builder of a new house, the planter of a vineyard, the newly married husband, were excluded from fighting, for two reasons. First, because man is wont to give all his affection to those things which he has lately acquired, or is on the point of having, and consequently he is apt to dread the loss of these above other things. Wherefore it was likely enough that on account of this affection they would fear death all the more, and be so much the less brave in battle. Secondly, because, as the Philosopher says (Phys. ii, 5), "it is a misfortune for a man if he is prevented from obtaining something good when it is within his grasp." And so lest the surviving relations should be the more grieved at the death of these men who had not entered into the possession of the good things prepared for them; and also lest the people should be horror-stricken at the sight of their misfortune: these men were taken away from the danger of death by being removed from the battle.

Reply to Objection 6: The timid were sent back home, not that they might be the gainers thereby; but lest the people might be the losers by their presence, since their timidity and flight might cause others to be afraid and run away.

Article: 4

Whether the Old Law set forth suitable precepts about the members of the household?

Objection 1: It would seem that the Old Law set forth unsuitable precepts about the members of the household. For a slave "is in every respect his master's property," as the Philosopher states (Polit. i, 2). But that which is a man's property should be his always. Therefore it was unfitting for the Law to command (Ex. 21:2) that slaves should "go out free" in the seventh year.

Objection 2: Further, a slave is his master's property, just as an animal, e.g. an ass or an ox. But it is commanded (Dt. 22:1-3) with regard to animals, that they should be brought back to the owner if they be found going astray. Therefore it was unsuitably commanded (Dt. 23:15): "Thou shalt not deliver to his master the servant that is fled to thee."

Objection 3: Further, the Divine Law should encourage mercy more even than the human law. But according to human laws those who ill-treat their servants and maidservants are severely punished: and the worse treatment of all seems to be that which results in death. Therefore it is unfittingly commanded (Ex. 21:20,21) that "he that striketh his bondman or bondwoman with a rod, and they die under his hands . . . if the party remain alive a day . . . he shall not be subject to the punishment, because it is his money."

Objection 4: Further, the dominion of a master over his slave differs from that of the father over his son (Polit. i, 3). But the dominion of master over slave gives the former the right to sell his servant or maidservant. Therefore it was unfitting for the Law to allow a man to sell his daughter to be a servant or handmaid (Ex. 21:7).

Objection 5: Further, a father has power over his son. But he who has power over the sinner has the right to punish him for his offenses. Therefore it is unfittingly commanded (Dt. 21:18, seqq.) that a father should bring his son to the ancients of the city for punishment.

Objection 6: Further, the Lord forbade them (Dt. 7:3, seqq.) to make marriages with strange nations; and commanded the dissolution of such as had been contracted (1 Esdras 10). Therefore it was unfitting to allow them to marry captive women from strange nations (Dt. 21:10, seqq.).

Objection 7: Further, the Lord forbade them to marry within certain degrees of consanguinity and affinity, according to Lev. 18. Therefore it was unsuitably commanded (Dt. 25:5) that if any man died without issue, his brother should marry his wife.

Objection 8: Further, as there is the greatest familiarity between man and wife, so should there be the staunchest fidelity. But this is impossible if the marriage bond can be sundered. Therefore it was unfitting for the Lord to allow (Dt. 24:1-4) a man to put his wife away, by writing a bill of divorce; and besides, that he could not take her again to wife.

Objection 9: Further, just as a wife can be faithless to her husband, so can a slave be to his master, and a son to his father. But the Law did not command any sacrifice to be offered in order to investigate the injury done by a servant to his master, or by a son to his father. Therefore it seems to have been superfluous for the Law to prescribe the "sacrifice of jealousy" in order to investigate a wife's adultery (Num. 5:12, seqq.). Consequently it seems that the Law put forth unsuitable judicial precepts about the members of the household.

On the contrary, It is written (Ps. 18:10): "The judgments of the Lord are true, justified in themselves."

I answer that, The mutual relations of the members of a household regard everyday actions directed to the necessities of life, as the Philosopher states (Polit. i, 1). Now the preservation of man's life may be considered from two points of view. First, from the point of view of the individual, i.e. in so far as man preserves his individuality: and for the purpose of the preservation of life, considered from this standpoint, man has at his service external goods, by means of which he provides himself with food and clothing and other such necessaries of life: in the handling of which he has need of servants. Secondly man's life is preserved from the point of view of the species, by means of generation, for which purpose man needs a wife, that she may bear him children. Accordingly the mutual relations of the members of a household admit of a threefold combination: viz. those of master and servant, those of husband and wife, and those of father and son: and in respect of all these relationships the Old Law contained fitting precepts. Thus, with regard to servants, it commanded them to be treated with moderation---both as to their work, lest, to wit, they should be burdened with excessive labor, wherefore the Lord commanded (Dt. 5:14) that on the Sabbath day "thy manservant and thy maidservant" should "rest even as thyself"---and also as to the infliction of punishment, for it ordered those who maimed their servants, to set them free (Ex. 21:26,27). Similar provision was made in favor of a maidservant when married to anyone (Ex. 21:7, seqq.). Moreover, with regard to those servants in particular who were taken from among the people, the Law prescribed that they should go out free in the seventh year taking whatever they brought with them, even their clothes (Ex. 21:2, seqq.): and furthermore it was commanded (Dt. 15:13) that they should be given provision for the journey.

With regard to wives the Law made certain prescriptions as to those who were to be taken in marriage: for instance, that they should marry a wife from their own tribe (Num. 36:6): and this lest confusion should ensue in the property of various tribes. Also that a man should marry the wife of his deceased brother when the latter died without issue, as prescribed in Dt. 25:5,6: and this in order that he who could not have successors according to carnal origin, might at least have them by a kind of adoption, and that thus the deceased might not be entirely forgotten. It also forbade them to marry certain women; to wit, women of strange nations, through fear of their losing their faith; and those of their near kindred, on account of the natural respect due to them. Furthermore it prescribed in what way wives were to be treated after marriage. To wit, that they should not be slandered without grave reason: wherefore it ordered punishment to be inflicted on the man who falsely accused his wife of a crime (Dt. 22:13, seqq.). Also that a man's hatred of his wife should not be detrimental to his son (Dt. 21:15, seqq.). Again, that a man should not ill-use his wife through hatred of her, but rather that he should write a bill of divorce and send her away (Dt. 24:1). Furthermore, in order to foster conjugal love from the very outset, it was prescribed that no public duties should be laid on a recently married man, so that he might be free to rejoice with his wife.

With regard to children, the Law commanded parents to educate them by instructing them in the faith: hence it is written (Ex. 12:26, seqq.): "When your children shall say to you: What is the meaning of this service? You shall say to them: It is the victim of the passage of the Lord." Moreover, they are commanded to teach them the rules of right conduct: wherefore it is written (Dt. 21:20) that the parents had to say: "He slighteth hearing our admonitions, he giveth himself to revelling and to debauchery."

Reply to Objection 1: As the children of Israel had been delivered by the Lord from slavery, and for this reason were bound to the service of God, He did not wish them to be slaves in perpetuity. Hence it is written (Lev. 25:39, seqq.): "If thy brother, constrained by poverty, sell himself to thee, thou shalt not oppress him with the service of bondservants: but he shall be as a hireling and a sojourner . . . for they are My servants, and I brought them out of the land of Egypt: let them not be sold as bondmen": and consequently, since they were slaves, not absolutely but in a restricted sense, after a lapse of time they were set free.

Reply to Objection 2: This commandment is to be understood as referring to a servant whom his master seeks to kill, or to help him in committing some sin.

Reply to Objection 3: With regard to the ill-treatment of servants, the Law seems to have taken into consideration whether it was certain or not: since if it were certain, the Law fixed a penalty: for maiming, the penalty was forfeiture of the servant, who was ordered to be given his liberty: while for slaying, the punishment was that of a murderer, when the slave died under the blow of his master. If, however, the hurt was not certain, but only probable, the Law did not impose any penalty as regards a man's own servant: for instance if the servant did not die at once after being struck, but after some days: for it would be uncertain whether he died as a result of the blows he received. For when a man struck a free man, yet so that he did not die at once, but "walked abroad again upon his staff," he that struck him was quit of murder, even though afterwards he died. Nevertheless he was bound to pay the doctor's fees incurred by the victim of his assault. But this was not the case if a man killed his own servant: because whatever the servant had, even his very person, was the property of his master. Hence the reason for his not being subject to a pecuniary penalty is set down as being "because it is his money."

Reply to Objection 4: As stated above (ad 1), no Jew could own a Jew as a slave absolutely: but only in a restricted sense, as a hireling for a fixed time. And in this way the Law permitted that through stress of poverty a man might sell his son or daughter. This is shown by the very words of the Law, where we read: "If any man sell his daughter to be a servant, she shall not go out as bondwomen are wont to go out." Moreover, in this way a man might sell not only his son, but even himself, rather as a hireling than as a slave, according to Lev. 25:39,40: "If thy brother, constrained by poverty, sell himself to thee, thou shalt not oppress him with the service of bondservants: but he shall be as a hireling and a sojourner."

Reply to Objection 5: As the Philosopher says (Ethic. x, 9), the paternal authority has the power only of admonition; but not that of coercion, whereby rebellious and headstrong persons can be compelled. Hence in this case the Lord commanded the stubborn son to be punished by the rulers of the city.

Reply to Objection 6: The Lord forbade them to marry strange women on account of the danger of seduction, lest they should be led astray into idolatry. And specially did this prohibition apply with respect to those nations who dwelt near them, because it was more probable that they would adopt their religious practices. When, however, the woman was willing to renounce idolatry, and become an adherent of the Law, it was lawful to take her in marriage: as was the case with Ruth whom Booz married. Wherefore she said to her mother-in-law (Ruth 1:16): "Thy people shall be my people, and thy God my God." Accordingly it was not permitted to marry a captive woman unless she first shaved her hair, and pared her nails, and put off the raiment wherein she was taken, and mourned for her father and mother, in token that she renounced idolatry for ever.

Reply to Objection 7: As Chrysostom says (Hom. xlviii super Matth.), "because death was an unmitigated evil for the Jews, who did everything with a view to the present life, it was ordained that children should be born to the dead man through his brother: thus affording a certain mitigation to his death. It was not, however, ordained that any other than his brother or one next of kin should marry the wife of the deceased, because" the offspring of this union "would not be looked upon as that of the deceased: and moreover, a stranger would not be under the obligation to support the household of the deceased, as his brother would be bound to do from motives of justice on account of his relationship." Hence it is evident that in marrying the wife of his dead brother, he took his dead brother's place.

Reply to Objection 8: The Law permitted a wife to be divorced, not as though it were just absolutely speaking, but on account of the Jews' hardness of heart, as Our Lord declared (Mt. 19:8). Of this, however, we must speak more fully in the treatise on Matrimony (SP, Question [67]).

Reply to Objection 9: Wives break their conjugal faith by adultery, both easily, for motives of pleasure, and hiddenly, since "the eye of the adulterer observeth darkness" (Job 24:15). But this does not apply to a son in respect of his father, or to a servant in respect of his master: because the latter infidelity is not the result of the lust of pleasure, but rather of malice: nor can it remain hidden like the infidelity of an adulterous woman.

OF THE LAW OF THE GOSPEL, CALLED THE NEW LAW, CONSIDERED IN ITSELF (FOUR ARTICLES)

In proper sequence we have to consider now the Law of the Gospel which is called the New Law: and in the first place we must consider it in itself; secondly, in comparison with the Old Law; thirdly, we shall treat of those things that are contained in the New Law. Under the first head there are four points of inquiry:

(1) What kind of law is it? i.e. Is it a written law or is it instilled in the heart?
(2) Of its efficacy, i.e. does it justify?
(3) Of its beginning: should it have been given at the beginning of the world?
(4) Of its end: i.e. whether it will last until the end, or will another law take its place?

Question 106 Article: 1

Whether the New Law is a written law?

Objection 1: It would seem that the New Law is a written law. For the New Law is just the same as the Gospel. But the Gospel is set forth in writing, according to Jn. 20:31: "But these are written that you may believe." Therefore the New Law is a written law.

Objection 2: Further, the law that is instilled in the heart is the natural law, according to Rm. 2:14,15: "(The Gentiles) do by nature those things that are of the law . . . who have [Vulg.: 'show'] the work of the law written in their hearts." If therefore the law of the Gospel were instilled in our hearts, it would not be distinct from the law of nature.

Objection 3: Further, the law of the Gospel is proper to those who are in the state of the New Testament. But the law that is instilled in the heart is common to those who are in the New Testament and to those who are in the Old Testament: for it is written (Wis. 7:27) that Divine Wisdom "through nations conveyeth herself into holy souls, she maketh the friends of God and prophets." Therefore the New Law is not instilled in our hearts.

On the contrary, The New Law is the law of the New Testament. But the law of the New Testament is instilled in our hearts. For the Apostle, quoting the authority of Jeremias 31:31,33: "Behold the days shall come, saith the Lord; and I will perfect unto the house of Israel, and unto the house of Judah, a new testament," says, explaining what this statement is (Heb. 8:8,10): "For this is the testament which I will make to the house of Israel . . . by giving [Vulg.: 'I will give'] My laws into their mind, and in their heart will I write them." Therefore the New Law is instilled in our hearts.

To be greater in number or importance

I answer that, "Each thing appears to be that which preponderates in it," as the Philosopher states (Ethic. ix, 8). Now that which is preponderant in the law of the New Testament, and whereon all its efficacy is based, is the grace of the Holy Ghost, which is given through faith in Christ. Consequently the New Law is chiefly the grace itself of the Holy Ghost, which is given to those who believe in Christ. This is manifestly stated by the Apostle who says (Rm. 3:27): "Where is . . . thy boasting? It is excluded. By what law? Of works? No, but by the law of faith": for he calls the grace itself of faith "a law." And still more clearly it is written (Rm. 8:2): "The law of the spirit of life, in Christ Jesus, hath delivered me from the law of sin and of death." Hence Augustine says (De Spir. et Lit. xxiv) that "as the law of deeds was written on tables of stone, so is the law of faith inscribed on the hearts of the faithful": and elsewhere, in the same book (xxi): "What else are the Divine laws written by God Himself on our hearts, but the very presence of His Holy Spirit?"

Nevertheless the New Law contains certain things that dispose us to receive the grace of the Holy Ghost, and pertaining to the use of that grace: such things are of secondary importance, so to speak, in the New Law; and the faithful need to be instructed concerning them, both by word and writing, both as to what they should believe and as to what they should do. Consequently we must say that the New Law is in the first place a law that is inscribed on our hearts, but that secondarily it is a written law.

Reply to Objection 1: The Gospel writings contain only such things as pertain to the grace of the Holy Ghost, either by disposing us thereto, or by directing us to the use thereof. Thus with regard to the intellect, the Gospel contains certain matters pertaining to the manifestation of Christ's Godhead or humanity, which dispose us by means of faith through which we receive the grace of the Holy Ghost: and with regard to the affections, it contains matters touching the contempt of the world, whereby man is rendered fit to receive the grace of the Holy Ghost: for "the world," i.e. worldly men, "cannot receive" the Holy Ghost (Jn. 14:17). As to the use of spiritual grace, this consists in works of virtue to which the writings of the New Testament exhort men in divers ways.

Reply to Objection 2: There are two ways in which a thing may be instilled into man. First, through being part of his nature, and thus the natural law is instilled into man. Secondly, a thing is instilled into man by being, as it were, added on to his nature by a gift of grace. In this way the New Law is instilled into man, not only by indicating to him what he should do, but also by helping him to accomplish it.

Reply to Objection 3: No man ever had the grace of the Holy Ghost except through faith in Christ either explicit or implicit: and by faith in Christ man belongs to the New Testament. Consequently whoever had the law of grace instilled into them belonged to the New Testament.

Article: 2

Whether the New Law justifies?

Objection 1: It would seem that the New Law does not justify. For no man is justified unless he obeys God's law, according to Heb. 5:9: "He," i.e. Christ, "became to all that obey Him the cause of eternal salvation." But the Gospel does not always cause men to believe in it: for it is written (Rm. 10:16): "All do not obey the Gospel." Therefore the New Law does not justify.

Objection 2: Further, the Apostle proves in his epistle to the Romans that the Old Law did not justify, because transgression increased at its advent: for it is stated (Rm. 4:15): "The Law worketh wrath: for where there is no law, neither is there transgression." But much more did the New Law increase transgression: since he who sins after the giving of the New Law deserves greater punishment, according to Heb. 10:28,29: "A man making void the Law of Moses dieth without any mercy under two or three witnesses. How much more, do you think, he deserveth worse punishments, who hath trodden underfoot the Son of God," etc.? Therefore the New Law, like the Old Law, does not justify.

Objection 3: Further, justification is an effect proper to God, according to Rm. 8:33: "God that justifieth." But the Old Law was from God just as the New Law. Therefore the New Law does not justify any more than the Old Law.

On the contrary, The Apostle says (Rm. 1:16): "I am not ashamed of the Gospel: for it is in the power of God unto salvation to everyone that believeth." But there is no salvation but to those who are justified. Therefore the Law of the Gospel justifies.

I answer that, As stated above (Article [1]), there is a twofold element in the Law of the Gospel. There is the chief element, viz. the grace of the Holy Ghost bestowed inwardly. And as to this, the New Law justifies. Hence Augustine says (De Spir. et Lit. xvii): "There," i.e. in the Old Testament, "the Law was set forth in an outward fashion, that the ungodly might be afraid"; "here," i.e. in the New Testament, "it is given in an inward manner, that they may be justified." The other element of the Evangelical Law is secondary: namely, the teachings of faith, and those commandments which direct human affections and human actions. And as to this, the New Law does not justify. Hence the Apostle says (2 Cor. 3:6) "The letter killeth, but the spirit quickeneth": and Augustine explains this (De Spir. et Lit. xiv, xvii) by saying that the letter denotes any writing external to man, even that of the moral precepts such as are contained in the Gospel. Wherefore the letter, even of the Gospel would kill, unless there were the inward presence of the healing grace of faith.

Reply to Objection 1: This argument holds true of the New Law, not as to its principal, but as to its secondary element: i.e. as to the dogmas and precepts outwardly put before man either in words or in writing.

Reply to Objection 2: Although the grace of the New Testament helps man to avoid sin, yet it does not so confirm man in good that he cannot sin: for this belongs to the state of glory. Hence if a man sin after receiving the grace of the New Testament, he deserves greater punishment, as being ungrateful for greater benefits, and as not using the help given to him. And this is why the New Law is not said to "work wrath": because as far as it is concerned it gives man sufficient help to avoid sin.

Reply to Objection 3: The same God gave both the New and the Old Law, but in different ways. For He gave the Old Law written on tables of stone: whereas He gave the New Law written "in the fleshly tables of the heart," as the Apostle expresses it (2 Cor. 3:3). Wherefore, as Augustine says (De Spir. et Lit. xviii), "the Apostle calls this letter which is written outside man, a ministration of death and a ministration of condemnation: whereas he calls the other letter, i.e. the Law of the New Testament, the ministration of the spirit and the ministration of justice: because through the gift of the Spirit we work justice, and are delivered from the condemnation due to transgression."

Article: 3

Whether the New Law should have been given from the beginning of the world?

Objection 1: It would seem that the New Law should have been given from the beginning of the world. "For there is no respect of persons with God" (Rm. 2:11). But "all" men "have sinned and do need the glory of God" (Rm. 3:23). Therefore the Law of the Gospel should have been given from the beginning of the world, in order that it might bring succor to all.

Objection 2: Further, as men dwell in various places, so do they live in various times. But God, "Who will have all men to be saved" (1 Tim. 2:4), commanded the Gospel to be preached in all places, as may be seen in the last chapters of Matthew and Mark. Therefore the Law of the Gospel should have been at hand for all times, so as to be given from the beginning of the world.

Objection 3: Further, man needs to save his soul, which is for all eternity, more than to save his body, which is a temporal matter. But God provided man from the beginning of the world with things that are necessary for the health of his body, by subjecting to his power whatever was created for the sake of man (Gn. 1:26-29). Therefore the New Law also, which is very necessary for the health of the soul, should have been given to man from the beginning of the world.

On the contrary, The Apostle says (1 Cor. 15:46): "That was not first which is spiritual, but that which is natural." But the New Law is highly spiritual. Therefore it was not fitting for it to be given from the beginning of the world.

I answer that, Three reasons may be assigned why it was not fitting for the New Law to be given from the beginning of the world. The first is because the New Law, as stated above (Article [1]), consists chiefly in the grace of the Holy Ghost: which it behoved not to be given abundantly until sin, which is an obstacle to grace, had been cast out of man through the accomplishment of his redemption by Christ: wherefore it is written (Jn. 7:39): "As yet the Spirit was not given, because Jesus was not yet glorified." This reason the Apostle states clearly (Rm. 8:2, seqq.) where, after speaking of "the Law of the Spirit of life," he adds: "God sending His own Son, in the likeness of sinful flesh, of sin* hath condemned sin in the flesh, that the justification of the Law might be fulfilled in us." [*St. Thomas, quoting perhaps from memory, omits the "et" (and), after "sinful flesh." The text quoted should read thus: "in the likeness of sinful flesh, and a sin offering ({peri hamartias}), hath," etc.]

A second reason may be taken from the perfection of the New Law. Because a thing is not brought to perfection at once from the outset, but through an orderly succession of time; thus one is at first a boy, and then a man. And this reason is stated by the Apostle (Gal. 3:24,25): "The Law was our pedagogue in Christ that we might be justified by faith. But after the faith is come, we are no longer under a pedagogue."

The third reason is found in the fact that the New Law is the law of grace: wherefore it behoved man first of all to be left to himself under the state of the Old Law, so that through falling into sin, he might realize his weakness, and acknowledge his need of grace. This reason is set down by the Apostle (Rm. 5:20): "The Law entered in, that sin might abound: and when sin abounded grace did more abound."

Reply to Objection 1: Mankind on account of the sin of our first parents deserved to be deprived of the aid of grace: and so "from whom it is withheld it is justly withheld, and to whom it is given, it is mercifully given," as Augustine states (De Perfect. Justit. iv) [*Cf. Ep. ccvii; De Pecc. Mer. et Rem. ii, 19]. Consequently it does not follow that there is respect of persons with God, from the fact that He did not offer the Law of grace to all from the beginning of the world, which Law was to be published in due course of time, as stated above.

Reply to Objection 2: The state of mankind does not vary according to diversity of place, but according to succession of time. Hence the New Law avails for all places, but not for all times: although at all times there have been some persons belonging to the New Testament, as stated above (Article [1], ad 3).

Reply to Objection 3: Things pertaining to the health of the body are of service to man as regards his nature, which sin does not destroy: whereas things pertaining to the health of the soul are ordained to grace, which is forfeit through sin. Consequently the comparison will not hold.

Article: 4

Whether the New Law will last till the end of the world?

Objection 1: It would seem that the New Law will not last until the end of the world. Because, as the Apostle says (1 Cor. 13:10), "when that which is perfect is come, that which is in part shall be done away." But the New Law is "in part," since the Apostle says (1 Cor. 13:9): "We know in part and we prophesy in part." Therefore the New Law is to be done away, and will be succeeded by a more perfect state.

Objection 2: Further, Our Lord (Jn. 16:13) promised His disciples the knowledge of all truth when the Holy Ghost, the Comforter, should come. But the Church knows not yet all truth in the state of the New Testament. Therefore we must look forward to another state, wherein all truth will be revealed by the Holy Ghost.

Objection 3: Further, just as the Father is distinct from the Son and the Son from the Father, so is the Holy Ghost distinct from the Father and the Son. But there was a state corresponding with the Person of the Father, viz. the state of the Old Law, wherein men were intent on begetting children: and likewise there is a state corresponding to the Person of the Son: viz. the state of the New Law, wherein the clergy who are intent on wisdom (which is appropriated to the Son) hold a prominent place. Therefore there will be a third state corresponding to the Holy Ghost, wherein spiritual men will hold the first place.

Objection 4: Further, Our Lord said (Mt. 24:14): "This Gospel of the kingdom shall be preached in the whole world . . . and then shall the consummation come." But the Gospel of Christ is already preached throughout the whole world: and yet the consummation has not yet come. Therefore the Gospel of Christ is not the Gospel of the kingdom, but another Gospel, that of the Holy Ghost, is to come yet, like unto another Law.

On the contrary, Our Lord said (Mt. 24:34): "I say to you that this generation shall not pass till all (these) things be done": which passage Chrysostom (Hom.

lxxvii) explains as referring to "the generation of those that believe in Christ." Therefore the state of those who believe in Christ will last until the consummation of the world.

I answer that, The state of the world may change in two ways. In one way, according to a change of law: and thus no other state will succeed this state of the New Law. Because the state of the New Law succeeded the state of the Old Law, as a more perfect law a less perfect one. Now no state of the present life can be more perfect that the state of the New Law: since nothing can approach nearer to the last end than that which is the immediate cause of our being brought to the last end. But the New Law does this: wherefore the Apostle says (Heb. 10:19-22): "Having therefore, brethren, a confidence in the entering into the Holies by the blood of Christ, a new . . . way which He hath dedicated for us . . . let us draw near." Therefore no state of the present life can be more perfect than that of the New Law, since the nearer a thing is to the last end the more perfect it is.

In another way the state of mankind may change according as man stands in relation to one and the same law more or less perfectly. And thus the state of the Old Law underwent frequent changes, since at times the laws were very well kept, and at other times were altogether unheeded. Thus, too, the state of the New Law is subject to change with regard to various places, times, and persons, according as the grace of the Holy Ghost dwells in man more or less perfectly. Nevertheless we are not to look forward to a state wherein man is to possess the grace of the Holy Ghost more perfectly than he has possessed it hitherto, especially the apostles who "received the firstfruits of the Spirit, i.e. sooner and more abundantly than others," as a gloss expounds on Rm. 8:23.

Reply to Objection 1: As Dionysius says (Eccl. Hier. v), there is a threefold state of mankind; the first was under the Old Law; the second is that of the New Law; the third will take place not in this life, but in heaven. But as the first state is figurative and imperfect in comparison with the state of the Gospel; so is the present state figurative and imperfect in comparison with the heavenly state, with the advent of which the present state will be done away as expressed in that very passage (1 Cor. 13:12): "We see now through a glass in a dark manner; but then face to face."

Reply to Objection 2: As Augustine says (Contra Faust. xix, 31), Montanus and Priscilla pretended that Our Lord's promise to give the Holy Ghost was fulfilled, not in the apostles, but in themselves. In like manner the Manicheans maintained that it was fulfilled in Manes whom they held to be the Paraclete. Hence none of the above received the Acts of the Apostles, where it is clearly shown that the aforesaid promise was fulfilled in the apostles: just as Our Lord promised them a second time (Acts 1:5): "You shall be baptized with the Holy Ghost, not many days hence": which we read as having been fulfilled in Acts 2. However, these foolish notions are refuted by the statement (Jn. 7:39) that "as yet the Spirit was not given, because Jesus was not yet glorified"; from which we gather that the

Holy Ghost was given as soon as Christ was glorified in His Resurrection and Ascension. Moreover, this puts out of court the senseless idea that the Holy Ghost is to be expected to come at some other time.

Now the Holy Ghost taught the apostles all truth in respect of matters necessary for salvation; those things, to wit, that we are bound to believe and to do. But He did not teach them about all future events: for this did not regard them according to Acts 1:7: "It is not for you to know the times or moments which the Father hath put in His own power."

Reply to Objection 3: The Old Law corresponded not only to the Father, but also to the Son: because Christ was foreshadowed in the Old Law. Hence Our Lord said (Jn. 5:46): "If you did believe Moses, you would perhaps believe me also; for he wrote of Me." In like manner the New Law corresponds not only to Christ, but also to the Holy Ghost; according to Rm. 8:2: "The Law of the Spirit of life in Christ Jesus," etc. Hence we are not to look forward to another law corresponding to the Holy Ghost.

Reply to Objection 4: Since Christ said at the very outset of the preaching of the Gospel: "The kingdom of heaven is at hand" (Mt. 4:17), it is most absurd to say that the Gospel of Christ is not the Gospel of the kingdom. But the preaching of the Gospel of Christ may be understood in two ways. First, as denoting the spreading abroad of the knowledge of Christ: and thus the Gospel was preached throughout the world even at the time of the apostles, as Chrysostom states (Hom. lxxv in Matth.). And in this sense the words that follow---"and then shall the consummation come," refer to the destruction of Jerusalem, of which He was speaking literally. Secondly, the preaching of the Gospel may be understood as extending throughout the world and producing its full effect, so that, to wit, the Church would be founded in every nation. And in these sense, as Augustine writes to Hesychius (Epist. cxcix), the Gospel is not preached to the whole world yet, but, when it is, the consummation of the world will come.

OF THE NEW LAW AS COMPARED WITH THE OLD (FOUR ARTICLES)

We must now consider the New Law as compared with the Old: under which head there are four points of inquiry:

(1) Whether the New Law is distinct from the Old Law?
(2) Whether the New Law fulfils the Old?
(3) Whether the New Law is contained in the Old?
(4) Which is the more burdensome, the New or the Old Law?

Question 107 Article: 1

Whether the New Law is distinct from the Old Law?

Objection 1: It would seem that the New Law is not distinct from the Old. Because both these laws were given to those who believe in God: since "without faith it is impossible to please God," according to Heb. 11:6. But the faith of olden times and of nowadays is the same, as the gloss says on Mt. 21:9. Therefore the law is the same also.

Objection 2: Further, Augustine says (Contra Adamant. Manich. discip. xvii) that "there is little difference between the Law and Gospel" [*The 'little difference' refers to the Latin words 'timor' and 'amor']---"fear and love." But the New and Old Laws cannot be differentiated in respect of these two things: since even the Old Law comprised precepts of charity: "Thou shalt love thy neighbor" (Lev. 19:18), and: "Thou shalt love the Lord thy God" (Dt. 6:5). In like manner neither can they differ according to the other difference which Augustine assigns (Contra Faust. iv, 2), viz. that "the Old Testament contained temporal promises, whereas the New Testament contains spiritual and eternal promises": since even the New Testament contains temporal promises, according to Mk. 10:30: He shall receive "a hundred times as much . . . in this time, houses and brethren," etc.: while in the Old Testament they hoped in promises spiritual and eternal, according to Heb. 11:16: "But now they desire a better, that is to say, a heavenly country," which is said of the patriarchs. Therefore it seems that the New Law is not distinct from the Old.

Objection 3: Further, the Apostle seems to distinguish both laws by calling the Old Law "a law of works," and the New Law "a law of faith" (Rm. 3:27). But the Old Law was also a law of faith, according to Heb. 11:39: "All were [Vulg.: 'All these being'] approved by the testimony of faith," which he says of the fathers of the Old Testament. In like manner the New Law is a law of works: since it is written (Mt. 5:44): "Do good to them that hate you"; and (Lk. 22:19): "Do this for a commemoration of Me." Therefore the New Law is not distinct from the Old.

On the contrary, the Apostle says (Heb. 7:12): "The priesthood being translated it is necessary that a translation also be made of the Law." But the priesthood of the New Testament is distinct from that of the Old, as the Apostle shows in the same place. Therefore the Law is also distinct.

I answer that, As stated above (Question [90], Article [2]; Question [91], Article [4]), every law ordains human conduct to some end. Now things ordained to an end may be divided in two ways, considered from the point of view of the end. First, through being ordained to different ends: and this difference will be specific, especially if such ends are proximate. Secondly, by reason of being closely or remotely connected with the end. Thus it is clear that movements differ in species through being directed to different terms: while according as one part of a movement is nearer to the term than another part, the difference of perfect and imperfect movement is assessed.

Accordingly then two laws may be distinguished from one another in two ways. First, through being altogether diverse, from the fact that they are ordained to diverse ends; thus a state-law ordained to democratic government, would differ specifically from a law ordained to government by the aristocracy. Secondly, two laws may be distinguished from one another, through one of them being more closely connected with the end, and the other more remotely; thus in one and the same state there is one law enjoined on men of mature age, who can forthwith accomplish that which pertains to the common good; and another law regulating the education of children who need to be taught how they are to achieve manly deeds later on.

We must therefore say that, according to the first way, the New Law is not distinct from the Old Law: because they both have the same end, namely, man's subjection to God; and there is but one God of the New and of the Old Testament, according to Rm. 3:30: "It is one God that justifieth circumcision by faith, and uncircumcision through faith." According to the second way, the New Law is distinct from the Old Law: because the Old Law is like a pedagogue of children, as the Apostle says (Gal. 3:24), whereas the New Law is the law of perfection, since it is the law of charity, of which the Apostle says (Col. 3:14) that it is "the bond of perfection."

Reply to Objection 1: The unity of faith under both Testaments witnesses to the unity of end: for it has been stated above (Question [62], Article [2]) that the object of the theological virtues, among which is faith, is the last end. Yet faith had a different state in the Old and in the New Law: since what they believed as future, we believe as fact.

Reply to Objection 2: All the differences assigned between the Old and New Laws are gathered from their relative perfection and imperfection. For the precepts of every law prescribe acts of virtue. Now the imperfect, who as yet are not possessed of a virtuous habit, are directed in one way to perform virtuous acts, while those who are perfected by the possession of virtuous habits are directed in another way. For those who as yet are not endowed with virtuous habits, are directed to the performance of virtuous acts by reason of some outward cause: for instance, by the threat of punishment, or the promise of some extrinsic rewards, such as honor, riches, or the like. Hence the Old Law, which was given to men who were imperfect, that is, who had not yet received spiritual grace, was called the "law of fear," inasmuch as it induced men to observe its commandments by threatening them with penalties; and is spoken of as containing temporal promises. On the other hand, those who are possessed of virtue, are inclined to do virtuous deeds through love of virtue, not on account of some extrinsic punishment or reward. Hence the New Law which derives its pre-eminence from the spiritual grace instilled into our hearts, is called the "Law of love": and it is described as containing spiritual and eternal promises, which are objects of the virtues, chiefly of charity. Accordingly such persons are inclined of themselves to those objects, not as to something foreign but as to something of their own. For this reason, too, the Old Law is described as "restraining the hand, not the will" [*Peter Lombard, Sent. iii, D, 40]; since when a man refrains from some sins through fear of being punished, his will does not shrink simply from sin, as does the will of a man who refrains from sin through love of righteousness: and hence the New Law, which is the Law of love, is said to restrain the will.

Nevertheless there were some in the state of the Old Testament who, having charity and the grace of the Holy Ghost, looked chiefly to spiritual and eternal promises: and in this respect they belonged to the New Law. In like manner in the New Testament there are some carnal men who have not yet attained to the perfection of the New Law; and these it was necessary, even under the New Testament, to lead to virtuous action by the fear of punishment and by temporal promises.

But although the Old Law contained precepts of charity, nevertheless it did not confer the Holy Ghost by Whom "charity . . . is spread abroad in our hearts" (Rm. 5:5).

Reply to Objection 3: As stated above (Question [106], Articles [1],2), the New Law is called the law of faith, in so far as its pre-eminence is derived from that very grace which is given inwardly to believers, and for this reason is called the grace of faith. Nevertheless it consists secondarily in certain deeds, moral and sacramental: but the New Law does not consist chiefly in these latter things, as did the Old Law. As to those under the Old Testament who through faith were acceptable to God, in this respect they belonged to the New Testament: for they were not justified except through faith in Christ, Who is the Author of the New Testament. Hence of Moses the Apostle says (Heb. 11:26) that he esteemed "the reproach of Christ greater riches than the treasure of the Egyptians."

Article: 2 Whether the New Law fulfils the Old?

Objection 1: It would seem that the New Law does not fulfil the Old. Because to fulfil and to void are contrary. But the New Law voids or excludes the observances of the Old Law: for the Apostle says (Gal. 5:2): "If you be circumcised, Christ shall profit you nothing." Therefore the New Law is not a fulfilment of the Old.

Objection 2: Further, one contrary is not the fulfilment of another. But Our Lord propounded in the New Law precepts that were contrary to precepts of the Old Law. For we read (Mt. 5:27-32): You have heard that it was said to them of old: . . . "Whosoever shall put away his wife, let him give her a bill of divorce. But I say to you that whosoever shall put away his wife . . . maketh her to commit adultery." Furthermore, the same evidently applies to the prohibition against swearing, against retaliation, and against hating one's enemies. In like manner Our Lord seems to have done away with the precepts of the Old Law relating to the different kinds of foods (Mt. 15:11): "Not that which goeth into the mouth defileth the man: but what cometh out of the mouth, this defileth a man." Therefore the New Law is not a fulfilment of the Old.

Objection 3: Further, whoever acts against a law does not fulfil the law. But Christ in certain cases acted against the Law. For He touched the leper (Mt. 8:3), which was contrary to the Law. Likewise He seems to have frequently broken the sabbath; since the Jews used to say of Him (Jn. 9:16): "This man is not of God, who keepeth not the sabbath." Therefore Christ did not fulfil the Law: and so the New Law given by Christ is not a fulfilment of the Old.

Objection 4: Further, the Old Law contained precepts, moral, ceremonial, and judicial, as stated above (Question [99], Article [4]). But Our Lord (Mt. 5) fulfilled the Law in some respects, but without mentioning the judicial and ceremonial precepts. Therefore it seems that the New Law is not a complete fulfilment of the Old.

On the contrary, Our Lord said (Mt. 5:17): "I am not come to destroy, but to fulfil": and went on to say (Mt. 5:18): "One jot or one tittle shall not pass of the Law till all be fulfilled."

I answer that, As stated above (Article [1]), the New Law is compared to the Old as the perfect to the imperfect. Now everything perfect fulfils that which is lacking in the imperfect. And accordingly the New Law fulfils the Old by supplying that which was lacking in the Old Law.

Now two things of every law is to make men righteous and virtuous as was stated above (Question [92], Article [1]): and consequently the end of the Old Law was the justification of men. The Law, however, could not accomplish this:

273

but foreshadowed it by certain ceremonial actions, and promised it in words. And in this respect, the New Law fulfils the Old by justifying men through the power of Christ's Passion. This is what the Apostle says (Rm. 8:3,4): "What the Law could not do . . . God sending His own Son in the likeness of sinful flesh . . . hath condemned sin in the flesh, that the justification of the Law might be fulfilled in us." And in this respect, the New Law gives what the Old Law promised, according to 2 Cor. 1:20: "Whatever are the promises of God, in Him," i.e. in Christ, "they are 'Yea'." [*The Douay version reads thus: "All the promises of God are in Him, 'It is'."] Again, in this respect, it also fulfils what the Old Law foreshadowed. Hence it is written (Col. 2:17) concerning the ceremonial precepts that they were "a shadow of things to come, but the body is of Christ"; in other words, the reality is found in Christ. Wherefore the New Law is called the law of reality; whereas the Old Law is called the law of shadow or of figure.

Now Christ fulfilled the precepts of the Old Law both in His works and in His doctrine. In His works, because He was willing to be circumcised and to fulfil the other legal observances, which were binding for the time being; according to Gal. 4:4: "Made under the Law." In His doctrine He fulfilled the precepts of the Law in three ways. First, by explaining the true sense of the Law. This is clear in the case of murder and adultery, the prohibition of which the Scribes and Pharisees thought to refer only to the exterior act: wherefore Our Lord fulfilled the Law by showing that the prohibition extended also to the interior acts of sins. Secondly, Our Lord fulfilled the precepts of the Law by prescribing the safest way of complying with the statutes of the Old Law. Thus the Old Law forbade perjury: and this is more safely avoided, by abstaining altogether from swearing, save in cases of urgency. Thirdly, Our Lord fulfilled the precepts of the Law, by adding some counsels of perfection; this is clearly seen in Mt. 19:21, where Our Lord said to the man who affirmed that he had kept all the precepts of the Old Law: "One thing is wanting to thee: If thou wilt be perfect, go, sell whatsoever thou hast," etc. [*St. Thomas combines Mt. 19:21 with Mk. 10:21].

Reply to Objection 1: The New Law does not void observance of the Old Law except in the point of ceremonial precepts, as stated above (Question [103], Articles [3],4). Now the latter were figurative of something to come. Wherefore from the very fact that the ceremonial precepts were fulfilled when those things were accomplished which they foreshadowed, it follows that they are no longer to be observed: for if they were to be observed, this would mean that something is still to be accomplished and is not yet fulfilled. Thus the promise of a future gift holds no longer when it has been fulfilled by the presentation of the gift. In this way the legal ceremonies are abolished by being fulfilled.

Reply to Objection 2: As Augustine says (Contra Faust. xix, 26), those precepts of Our Lord are not contrary to the precepts of the Old Law. For what Our Lord commanded about a man not putting away his wife, is not contrary to what the Law prescribed. "For the Law did not say: 'Let him that wills, put his wife away':

the contrary of which would be not to put her away. On the contrary, the Law was unwilling that a man should put away his wife, since it prescribed a delay, so that excessive eagerness for divorce might cease through being weakened during the writing of the bill. Hence Our Lord, in order to impress the fact that a wife ought not easily to be put away, allowed no exception save in the case of fornication." The same applies to the prohibition about swearing, as stated above. The same is also clear with respect to the prohibition of retaliation. For the Law fixed a limit to revenge, by forbidding men to seek vengeance unreasonably: whereas Our Lord deprived them of vengeance more completely by commanding them to abstain from it altogether. With regard to the hatred of one's enemies, He dispelled the false interpretation of the Pharisees, by admonishing us to hate, not the person, but his sin. As to discriminating between various foods, which was a ceremonial matter, Our Lord did not forbid this to be observed: but He showed that no foods are naturally unclean, but only in token of something else, as stated above (Question [102], Article [6], ad 1).

Reply to Objection 3: It was forbidden by the Law to touch a leper; because by doing so, man incurred a certain uncleanness of irregularity, as also by touching the dead, as stated above (Question [102], Article [5], ad 4). But Our Lord, Who healed the leper, could not contract an uncleanness. By those things which He did on the sabbath, He did not break the sabbath in reality, as the Master Himself shows in the Gospel: both because He worked miracles by His Divine power, which is ever active among things; and because He worked miracles by His Divine power, which is ever active among things; and because His works were concerned with the salvation of man, while the Pharisees were concerned for the well-being of animals even on the sabbath; and again because on account of urgency He excused His disciples for gathering the ears of corn on the sabbath. But He did seem to break the sabbath according to the superstitious interpretation of the Pharisees, who thought that man ought to abstain from doing even works of kindness on the sabbath; which was contrary to the intention of the Law.

Reply to Objection 4: The reason why the ceremonial precepts of the Law are not mentioned in Mt. 5 is because, as stated above (ad 1), their observance was abolished by their fulfilment. But of the judicial precepts He mentioned that of retaliation: so that what He said about it should refer to all the others. With regard to this precept, He taught that the intention of the Law was that retaliation should be sought out of love of justice, and not as a punishment out of revengeful spite, which He forbade, admonishing man to be ready to suffer yet greater insults; and this remains still in the New Law.

Article: 3 Whether the New Law is contained in the Old?

Objection 1: It would seem that the New Law is not contained in the Old. Because the New Law consists chiefly in faith: wherefore it is called the "law of faith" (Rm. 3:27). But many points of faith are set forth in the New Law, which are not contained in the Old. Therefore the New Law is not contained in the Old.

Objection 2: Further, a gloss says on Mt. 5:19, "He that shall break one of these least commandments," that the lesser commandments are those of the Law, and the greater commandments, those contained in the Gospel. Now the greater cannot be contained in the lesser. Therefore the New Law is not contained in the Old.

Objection 3: Further, who holds the container holds the contents. If, therefore, the New Law is contained in the Old, it follows that whoever had the Old Law had the New: so that it was superfluous to give men a New Law when once they had the Old. Therefore the New Law is not contained in the Old.

On the contrary, As expressed in Ezech. 1:16, there was "a wheel in the midst of a wheel," i.e. "the New Testament within the Old," according to Gregory's exposition.

I answer that, One thing may be contained in another in two ways. First, actually; as a located thing is in a place. Secondly, virtually; as an effect in its cause, or as the complement in that which is incomplete; thus a genus contains its species, and a seed contains the whole tree virtually. It is in this way that the New Law is contained in the Old: for it has been stated (Article [1]) that the New Law is compared to the Old as perfect to imperfect. Hence Chrysostom, expounding Mk. 4:28, "The earth of itself bringeth forth fruit, first the blade, then the ear, afterwards the full corn in the ear," expresses himself as follows: "He brought forth first the blade, i.e. the Law of Nature; then the ear, i.e. the Law of Moses; lastly, the full corn, i.e. the Law of the Gospel." Hence then the New Law is in the Old as the corn in the ear.

Reply to Objection 1: Whatsoever is set down in the New Testament explicitly and openly as a point of faith, is contained in the Old Testament as a matter of belief, but implicitly, under a figure. And accordingly, even as to those things which we are bound to believe, the New Law is contained in the Old.

Reply to Objection 2: The precepts of the New Law are said to be greater than those of the Old Law, in the point of their being set forth explicitly. But as to the substance itself of the precepts of the New Testament, they are all contained in the Old. Hence Augustine says (Contra Faust. xix, 23,28) that "nearly all Our Lord's admonitions or precepts, where He expressed Himself by saying: 'But I say unto you,' are to be found also in those ancient books. Yet, since they thought that murder was only the slaying of the human body, Our Lord declared to them that every wicked impulse to hurt our brother is to be looked on as a kind of murder." And it is in the point of declarations of this kind that the precepts of the New Law are said to be greater than those of the Old. Nothing, however, prevents the greater from being contained in the lesser virtually; just as a tree is contained in the seed.

Reply to Objection 3: What is set forth implicitly needs to be declared explicitly. Hence after the publishing of the Old Law, a New Law also had to be given.

Article: 4

Whether the New Law is more burdensome than the Old?

Objection 1: It would seem that the New Law is more burdensome than the Old. For Chrysostom (Opus Imp. in Matth., Hom. x [*The work of an unknown author]) say: "The commandments given to Moses are easy to obey: Thou shalt not kill; Thou shalt not commit adultery: but the commandments of Christ are difficult to accomplish, for instance: Thou shalt not give way to anger, or to lust." Therefore the New Law is more burdensome than the Old.

Objection 2: Further, it is easier to make use of earthly prosperity than to suffer tribulations. But in the Old Testament observance of the Law was followed by temporal prosperity, as may be gathered from Dt. 28:1-14; whereas many kinds of trouble ensue to those who observe the New Law, as stated in 2 Cor. 6:4-10: "Let us exhibit ourselves as the ministers of God, in much patience, in tribulation, in necessities, in distresses," etc. Therefore the New Law is more burdensome than the Old.

Objection 3: The more one has to do, the more difficult it is. But the New Law is something added to the Old. For the Old Law forbade perjury, while the New Law proscribed even swearing: the Old Law forbade a man to cast off his wife without a bill of divorce, while the New Law forbade divorce altogether; as is clearly stated in Mt. 5:31, seqq., according to Augustine's expounding. Therefore the New Law is more burdensome than the Old.

On the contrary, It is written (Mt. 11:28): "Come to Me, all you that labor and are burdened": which words are expounded by Hilary thus: "He calls to Himself all those that labor under the difficulty of observing the Law, and are burdened with the sins of this world." And further on He says of the yoke of the Gospel: "For My yoke is sweet and My burden light." Therefore the New Law is a lighter burden than the Old.

I answer that, A twofold difficult may attach to works of virtue with which the precepts of the Law are concerned. One is on the part of the outward works which of themselves are, in a way, difficult and burdensome. And in this respect the Old Law is a much heavier burden than the New: since the Old Law by its numerous ceremonies prescribed many more outward acts than the New Law, which, in the teaching of Christ and the apostles, added very few precepts to those of the natural law; although afterwards some were added, through being instituted by the holy Fathers. Even in these Augustine says that moderation should be observed, lest good conduct should become a burden to the faithful. For he says in reply to the queries of Januarius (Ep. lv) that, "whereas God in His mercy wished religion to be a free service rendered by the public solemnization of a small number of most manifest sacraments, certain persons make it a slave's burden; so much so that the state of the Jews who were subject to the sacraments of the Law, and not to the presumptuous devices of man, was more tolerable."

The other difficulty attaches to works of virtue as to interior acts; for instance, that a virtuous deed be done with promptitude and pleasure. It is this difficulty that virtue solves: because to act thus is difficult for a man without virtue: but through virtue it becomes easy for him. In this respect the precepts of the New Law are more burdensome than those of the Old; because the New Law prohibits certain interior movements of the soul, which were not expressly forbidden in the Old Law in all cases, although they were forbidden in some, without, however, any punishment being attached to the prohibition. Now this is very difficult to a man without virtue: thus even the Philosopher states (Ethic. v, 9) that it is easy to do what a righteous man does; but that to do it in the same way, viz. with pleasure and promptitude, is difficult to a man who is not righteous. Accordingly we read also (1 Jn. 5:3) that "His commandments are not heavy": which words Augustine expounds by saying that "they are not heavy to the man that loveth; whereas they are a burden to him that loveth not."

Reply to Objection 1: The passage quoted speaks expressly of the difficulty of the New Law as to the deliberate curbing of interior movements.

Reply to Objection 2: The tribulations suffered by those who observe the New Law are not imposed by the Law itself. Moreover they are easily borne, on account of the love in which the same Law consists: since, as Augustine says (De Verb. Dom., Serm. lxx), "love makes light and nothing of things that seem arduous and beyond our power."

Reply to Objection 3: The object of these additions to the precepts of the Old Law was to render it easier to do what it prescribed, as Augustine states [*De Serm. Dom. in Monte i, 17,21; xix, 23,26]. Accordingly this does not prove that the New Law is more burdensome, but rather that it is a lighter burden.

THINGS THAT ARE CONTAINED IN THE NEW LAW (4 ARTICLES)

We must now consider those things that are contained in the New Law: under which head there are four points of inquiry:

(1) Whether the New Law ought to prescribe or to forbid any outward works?
(2) Whether the New Law makes sufficient provision in prescribing and forbidding external acts?
(3) Whether in the matter of internal acts it directs man sufficiently?
(4) Whether it fittingly adds counsels to precepts?

Question 108 Article: 1

Whether the New Law ought to prescribe or prohibit any external acts?

Objection 1: It would seem that the New Law should not prescribe or prohibit any external acts. For the New Law is the Gospel of the kingdom, according to Mt. 24:14: "This Gospel of the kingdom shall be preached in the whole world." But the kingdom of God consists not in exterior, but only in interior acts, according to Lk. 17:21: "The kingdom of God is within you"; and Rm. 14:17: "The kingdom of God is not meat and drink; but justice and peace and joy in the Holy Ghost." Therefore the New Law should not prescribe or forbid any external acts.

Objection 2: Further, the New Law is "the law of the Spirit" (Rm. 8:2). But "where the Spirit of the Lord is, there is liberty" (2 Cor. 3:17). Now there is no liberty when man is bound to do or avoid certain external acts. Therefore the New Law does not prescribe or forbid any external acts.

Objection 3: Further, all external acts are understood as referable to the hand, just as interior acts belong to the mind. But this is assigned as the difference between the New and Old Laws that the "Old Law restrains the hand, whereas the New Law curbs the will" [*Peter Lombard, Sent. iii, D, 40]. Therefore the New Law should not contain prohibitions and commands about exterior deeds, but only about interior acts.

On the contrary, Through the New Law, men are made "children of light": wherefore it is written (Jn. 12:36): "Believe in the light that you may be the children of light." Now it is becoming that children of the light should do deeds of light and cast aside deeds of darkness, according to Eph. 5:8: "You were heretofore darkness, but now light in the Lord. Walk . . . as children of the light." Therefore the New Law had to forbid certain external acts and prescribe others.

I answer that, As stated above (Question [106], Articles [1],2), the New Law consists chiefly in the grace of the Holy Ghost, which is shown forth by faith that worketh through love. Now men become receivers of this grace through God's Son made man, Whose humanity grace filled first, and thence flowed forth to us. Hence it is written (Jn. 1:14): "The Word was made flesh," and afterwards: "full of grace and truth"; and further on: "Of His fulness we all have received, and grace for grace." Hence it is added that "grace and truth came by Jesus Christ." Consequently it was becoming that the grace flows from the incarnate Word should be given to us by means of certain external sensible objects; and that from this inward grace, whereby the flesh is subjected to the Spirit, certain external works should ensue.

Accordingly external acts may have a twofold connection with grace. In the first place, as leading in some way to grace. Such are the sacramental acts which are instituted in the New Law, e.g. Baptism, the Eucharist, and the like.

In the second place there are those external acts which ensue from the promptings of grace: and herein we must observe a difference. For there are some which are necessarily in keeping with, or in opposition to inward grace consisting in faith that worketh through love. Such external works are prescribed or forbidden in the New Law; thus confession of faith is prescribed, and denial of faith is forbidden; for it is written (Mt. 10:32,33) "(Every one) that shall confess Me before men, I will also confess him before My Father . . . But he that shall deny Me before men, I will also deny him before My Father." On the other hand, there are works which are not necessarily opposed to, or in keeping with faith that worketh through love. Such works are not prescribed or forbidden in the New Law, by virtue of its primitive institution; but have been left by the Lawgiver, i.e. Christ, to the discretion of each individual. And so to each one it is free to decide what he should do or avoid; and to each superior, to direct his subjects in such matters as regards what they must do or avoid. Wherefore also in this respect the Gospel is called the "law of liberty" [*Cf. Reply Objection [2]]: since the Old Law decided many points and left few to man to decide as he chose.

Reply to Objection 1: The kingdom of God consists chiefly in internal acts: but as a consequence all things that are essential to internal acts belong also to the kingdom of God. Thus if the kingdom of God is internal righteousness, peace, and spiritual joy, all external acts that are incompatible with righteousness, peace, and spiritual joy, are in opposition to the kingdom of God; and consequently should be forbidden in the Gospel of the kingdom. On the other hand, those things that are indifferent as regards the aforesaid, for instance, to eat of this or that food, are not part of the kingdom of God; wherefore the Apostle says before the words quoted: "The kingdom of God is not meat and drink."

Reply to Objection 2: According to the Philosopher (Metaph. i, 2), what is "free is cause of itself." Therefore he acts freely, who acts of his own accord. Now man does of his own accord that which he does from a habit that is suitable to his nature: since a habit inclines one as a second nature. If, however, a habit be in opposition to nature, man would not act according to his nature, but according to some corruption affecting that nature. Since then the grace of the Holy Ghost is like an interior habit bestowed on us and inclining us to act aright, it makes us do freely those things that are becoming to grace, and shun what is opposed to it.

Accordingly the New Law is called the law of liberty in two respects. First, because it does not bind us to do or avoid certain things, except such as are of themselves necessary or opposed to salvation, and come under the prescription or prohibition of the law. Secondly, because it also makes us comply freely with these precepts and prohibitions, inasmuch as we do so through the promptings of grace. It is for these two reasons that the New Law is called "the law of perfect liberty" (James 1:25).

Reply to Objection 3: The New Law, by restraining the mind from inordinate movements, must needs also restrain the hand from inordinate acts, which ensue from inward movements.

Article: 2

Whether the New Law made sufficient ordinations about external acts?

Objection 1: It would seem that the New Law made insufficient ordinations about external acts. Because faith that worketh through charity seems chiefly to belong to the New Law, according to Gal. 5:6: "In Christ Jesus neither circumcision availeth anything, nor uncircumcision: but faith that worketh through charity." But the New Law declared explicitly certain points of faith which were not set forth explicitly in the Old Law; for instance, belief in the Trinity. Therefore it should also have added certain outward moral deeds, which were not fixed in the Old Law.

Objection 2: Further, in the Old Law not only were sacraments instituted, but also certain sacred things, as stated above (Question [101], Article [4]; Question [102], Article [4]). But in the New Law, although certain sacraments are instituted by Our Lord; for instance, pertaining either to the sanctification of a temple or of the vessels, or to the celebration of some particular feast. Therefore the New Law made insufficient ordinations about external matters.

Objection 3: Further, in the Old Law, just as there were certain observances pertaining to God's ministers, so also were there certain observances pertaining to the people: as was stated above when we were treating of the ceremonial of the Old Law (Question [101], Article [4]; Question [102], Article [6]). Now in the

New Law certain observances seem to have been prescribed to the ministers of God; as may be gathered from Mt. 10:9: "Do not possess gold, nor silver, nor money in your purses," nor other things which are mentioned here and Lk. 9,10. Therefore certain observances pertaining to the faithful should also have been instituted in the New Law.

Objection 4: Further, in the Old Law, besides moral and ceremonial precepts, there were certain judicial precepts. But in the New Law there are no judicial precepts. Therefore the New Law made insufficient ordinations about external works.

On the contrary, Our Lord said (Mt. 7:24): "Every one . . . that heareth these My words, and doth them, shall be likened to a wise man that built his house upon a rock." But a wise builder leaves out nothing that is necessary to the building. Therefore Christ's words contain all things necessary for man's salvation.

I answer that, as stated above (Article [1]), the New Law had to make such prescriptions or prohibitions alone as are essential for the reception or right use of grace. And since we cannot of ourselves obtain grace, but through Christ alone, hence Christ of Himself instituted the sacraments whereby we obtain grace: viz. Baptism, Eucharist, Orders of the ministers of the New Law, by the institution of the apostles and seventy-two disciples, Penance, and indissoluble Matrimony. He promised Confirmation through the sending of the Holy Ghost: and we read that by His institution the apostles healed the sick by anointing them with oil (Mk. 6:13). These are the sacraments of the New Law.

The right use of grace is by means of works of charity. These, in so far as they are essential to virtue, pertain to the moral precepts, which also formed part of the Old Law. Hence, in this respect, the New Law had nothing to add as regards external action. The determination of these works in their relation to the divine worship, belongs to the ceremonial precepts of the Law; and, in relation to our neighbor, to the judicial precepts, as stated above (Question [99], Article [4]). And therefore, since these determinations are not in themselves necessarily connected with inward grace wherein the Law consists, they do not come under a precept of the New Law, but are left to the decision of man; some relating to inferiors---as when a precept is given to an individual; others, relating to superiors, temporal or spiritual, referring, namely, to the common good.

Accordingly the New Law had no other external works to determine, by prescribing or forbidding, except the sacraments, and those moral precepts which have a necessary connection with virtue, for instance, that one must not kill, or steal, and so forth.

Reply to Objection 1: Matters of faith are above human reason, and so we cannot attain to them except through grace. Consequently, when grace came to be bestowed more abundantly, the result was an increase in the number of explicit points of faith. On the other hand, it is through human reason that we are directed to works of virtue, for it is the rule of human action, as stated above (Question [19], Article [3]; Question [63], Article [2]). Wherefore in such matters as these there was no need for any precepts to be given besides the moral precepts of the Law, which proceed from the dictate of reason.

Reply to Objection 2: In the sacraments of the New Law grace is bestowed, which cannot be received except through Christ: consequently they had to be instituted by Him. But in the sacred things no grace is given: for instance, in the consecration of a temple, an altar or the like, or, again, in the celebration of feasts. Wherefore Our Lord left the institution of such things to the discretion of the faithful, since they have not of themselves any necessary connection with inward grace.

Reply to Objection 3: Our Lord gave the apostles those precepts not as ceremonial observances, but as moral statutes: and they can be understood in two ways. First, following Augustine (De Consensu Evang. 30), as being not commands but permissions. For He permitted them to set forth to preach without scrip or stick, and so on, since they were empowered to accept their livelihood from those to whom they preached: wherefore He goes on to say: "For the laborer is worthy of his hire." Nor is it a sin, but a work of supererogation for a preacher to take means of livelihood with him, without accepting supplies from those to whom he preaches; as Paul did (1 Cor. 9:4, seqq.).

Secondly, according to the explanation of other holy men, they may be considered as temporal commands laid upon the apostles for the time during which they were sent to preach in Judea before Christ's Passion. For the disciples, being yet as little children under Christ's care, needed to receive some special commands from Christ, such as all subjects receive from their superiors: and especially so, since they were to be accustomed little by little to renounce the care of temporalities, so as to become fitted for the preaching of the Gospel throughout the whole world. Nor must we wonder if He established certain fixed modes of life, as long as the state of the Old Law endured and the people had not as yet achieved the perfect liberty of the Spirit. These statutes He abolished shortly before His Passion, as though the disciples had by their means become sufficiently practiced. Hence He said (Lk. 22:35,36) "When I sent you without purse and scrip and shoes, did you want anything? But they said: Nothing. Then said He unto them: But now, he that hath a purse, let him take it, and likewise a scrip." Because the time of perfect liberty was already at hand, when they would be left entirely to their own judgment in matters not necessarily connected with virtue.

Reply to Objection 4: Judicial precepts also, are not essential to virtue in respect of any particular determination, but only in regard to the common notion of justice. Consequently Our Lord left the judicial precepts to the discretion of those

283

who were to have spiritual or temporal charge of others. But as regards the judicial precepts of the Old Law, some of them He explained, because they were misunderstood by the Pharisees, as we shall state later on (Article [3], ad 2).

Article: 3

Whether the New Law directed man sufficiently as regards interior actions?

Objection 1: It would seem that the New Law directed man insufficiently as regards interior actions. For there are ten commandments of the decalogue directing man to God and his neighbor. But Our Lord partly fulfilled only three of them: as regards, namely, the prohibition of murder, of adultery, and of perjury. Therefore it seems that, by omitting to fulfil the other precepts, He directed man insufficiently.

Objection 2: Further, as regards the judicial precepts, Our Lord ordained nothing in the Gospel, except in the matter of divorcing of wife, of punishment by retaliation, and of persecuting one's enemies. But there are many other judicial precepts of the Old Law, as stated above (Question [104], Article [4]; Question [105]). Therefore, in this respect, He directed human life insufficiently.

Objection 3: Further, in the Old Law, besides moral and judicial, there were ceremonial precepts about which Our Lord made no ordination. Therefore it seems that He ordained insufficiently.

Objection 4: Further, in order that the mind be inwardly well disposed, man should do no good deed for any temporal whatever. But there are many other temporal goods besides the favor of man: and there are many other good works besides fasting, alms-deeds, and prayer. Therefore Our Lord unbecomingly taught that only in respect of these three works, and of no other earthly goods ought we to shun the glory of human favor.

Objection 5: Further, solicitude for the necessary means of livelihood is by nature instilled into man, and this solicitude even other animals share with man: wherefore it is written (Prov. 6:6,8): "Go to the ant, O sluggard, and consider her ways . . . she provideth her meat for herself in the summer, and gathereth her food in the harvest." But every command issued against the inclination of nature is an unjust command, forasmuch as it is contrary to the law of nature. Therefore it seems that Our Lord unbecomingly forbade solicitude about food and raiment.

Objection 6: Further, no act of virtue should be the subject of a prohibition. Now judgment is an act of justice, according to Ps. 18:15: "Until justice be turned into judgment." Therefore it seems that Our Lord unbecomingly forbade judgment:

and consequently that the New Law directed man insufficiently in the matter of interior acts.

On the contrary, Augustine says (De Serm. Dom. in Monte i, 1): We should take note that, when He said: "'He that heareth these My words,' He indicates clearly that this sermon of the Lord is replete with all the precepts whereby a Christian's life is formed."

I answer that, As is evident from Augustine's words just quoted, the sermon, contains the whole process of forming the life of a Christian. Therein man's interior movements are ordered. Because after declaring that his end is Beatitude and after commending the authority of the apostles, through whom the teaching of the Gospel was to be promulgated, He orders man's interior movements, first in regard to man himself, secondly in regard to his neighbor.

This he does in regard to man himself, in two ways, corresponding to man's two interior movements in respect of any prospective action, viz. volition of what has to be done, and intention of the end. Wherefore, in the first place, He directs man's will in respect of the various precepts of the Law: by prescribing that man should refrain not merely from those external works that are evil in themselves, but also from internal acts, and from the occasions of evil deeds. In the second place He directs man's intention, by teaching that in our good works, we should seek neither human praise, nor worldly riches, which is to lay up treasures on earth.

Afterwards He directs man's interior movement in respect of his neighbor, by forbidding us, on the one hand, to judge him rashly, unjustly, or presumptuously; and, on the other, to entrust him too readily with sacred things if he be unworthy.

Lastly, He teaches us how to fulfil the teaching of the Gospel; viz. by imploring the help of God; by striving to enter by the narrow door of perfect virtue; and by being wary lest we be led astray by evil influences. Moreover, He declares that we must observe His commandments, and that it is not enough to make profession of faith, or to work miracles, or merely to hear His words.

Reply to Objection 1: Our Lord explained the manner of fulfilling those precepts which the Scribes and Pharisees did not rightly understand: and this affected chiefly those precepts of the decalogue. For they thought that the prohibition of adultery and murder covered the external act only, and not the internal desire. And they held this opinion about murder and adultery rather than about theft and false witness, because the movement of anger tending to murder, and the movement of desire tending to adultery, seem to be in us from nature somewhat, but not the desire of stealing or bearing false witness. They held a false opinion about perjury, for they thought that perjury indeed was a sin; but that oaths were of themselves to be desired and to be taken frequently, since they seem to proceed from reverence to God. Hence Our Lord shows that an oath is not desirable as a good thing; and that it is better to speak without oaths, unless necessity forces us to have recourse to them.

Reply to Objection 2: The Scribes and Pharisees erred about the judicial precepts in two ways. First, because they considered certain matters contained in the Law of Moses by way of permission, to be right in themselves: namely, divorce of a wife, and the taking of usury from strangers. Wherefore Our Lord forbade a man to divorce his wife (Mt. 5:32); and to receive usury (Lk. 6:35), when He said: "Lend, hoping for nothing thereby."

In another way they erred by thinking that certain things which the Old Law commanded to be done for justice's sake, should be done out of desire for revenge, or out of lust for temporal goods, or out of hatred of one's enemies; and this in respect of three precepts. For they thought that desire for revenge was lawful, on account of the precept concerning punishment by retaliation: whereas this precept was given that justice might be safeguarded, not that man might seek revenge. Wherefore, in order to do away with this, Our Lord teaches that man should be prepared in his mind to suffer yet more if necessary. They thought that movements of covetousness were lawful on account of those judicial precepts which prescribed restitution of what had been purloined, together with something added thereto, as stated above (Question [105], Article [2], ad 9); whereas the Law commanded this to be done in order to safeguard justice, not to encourage covetousness. Wherefore Our Lord teaches that we should not demand our goods from motives of cupidity, and that we should be ready to give yet more if necessary. They thought that the movement of hatred was lawful, on account of the commandments of the Law about the slaying of one's enemies: whereas the Law ordered this for the fulfilment of justice, as stated above (Question [105], Article [3], ad 4), not to satisfy hatred. Wherefore Our Lord teaches us that we ought to love our enemies, and to be ready to do good to them if necessary. For these precepts are to be taken as binding "the mind to be prepared to fulfil them," as Augustine says (De Serm. Dom. in Monte i, 19).

Reply to Objection 3: The moral precepts necessarily retained their force under the New Law, because they are of themselves essential to virtue: whereas the judicial precepts did not necessarily continue to bind in exactly the same way as had been fixed by the Law: this was left to man to decide in one way or another. Hence Our Lord directed us becomingly with regard to these two kinds of precepts. On the other hand, the observance of the ceremonial precepts was totally abolished by the advent of the reality; wherefore in regard to these precepts He commanded nothing on this occasion when He was giving the general points of His doctrine. Elsewhere, however, He makes it clear that the entire bodily worship which was fixed by the Law, was to be changed into spiritual worship: as is evident from Jn. 4:21,23, where He says: "The hour cometh when you shall neither on this mountain, nor in Jerusalem adore the Father . . . but . . . the true adorers shall adore the Father in spirit and in truth."

Reply to Objection 4: All worldly goods may be reduced to three---honors, riches, and pleasures; according to 1 Jn. 2:16: "All that is in the world is the concupiscence of the flesh," which refers to pleasures of the flesh, "and the concupiscence of the eyes," which refers to riches, "and the pride of life," which refers to ambition for renown and honor. Now the Law did not promise an abundance of carnal pleasures; on the contrary, it forbade them. But it did promise exalted honors and abundant riches; for it is written in reference to the former (Dt. 28:1): "If thou wilt hear the voice of the Lord thy God . . . He will make thee higher than all the nations"; and in reference to the latter, we read a little further on (Dt. 28:11): "He will make thee abound with all goods." But the Jews so distorted the true meaning of these promises, as to think that we ought to serve God, with these things as the end in view. Wherefore Our Lord set this aside by teaching, first of all, that works of virtue should not be done for human glory. And He mentions three works, to which all others may be reduced: since whatever a man does in order to curb his desires, comes under the head of fasting; and whatever a man does for the love of his neighbor, comes under the head of alms-deeds; and whatever a man does for the worship of God, comes under the head of prayer. And He mentions these three specifically, as they hold the principal place, and are most often used by men in order to gain glory. In the second place He taught us that we must not place our end in riches, when He said: "Lay not up to yourselves treasures on earth" (Mt. 6:19).

Reply to Objection 5: Our Lord forbade, not necessary, but inordinate solicitude. Now there is a fourfold solicitude to be avoided in temporal matters. First, we must not place our end in them, nor serve God for the sake of the necessities of food and raiment. Wherefore He says: "Lay not up for yourselves," etc. Secondly, we must not be so anxious about temporal things, as to despair of God's help: wherefore Our Lord says (Mt. 6:32): "Your Father knoweth that you have need of all these things." Thirdly, we must not add presumption to our solicitude; in other words, we must not be confident of getting the necessaries of life by our own efforts without God's help: such solicitude Our Lord sets aside by saying that a man cannot add anything to his stature (Mt. 6:27). We must not anticipate the time for anxiety; namely, by being solicitous now, for the needs, not of the present, but of a future time: wherefore He says (Mt. 6:34): "Be not . . . solicitous for tomorrow."

Reply to Objection 6: Our Lord did not forbid the judgment of justice, without which holy things could not be withdrawn from the unworthy. But he forbade inordinate judgment, as stated above.

Counsel - instruction
Counsel - advice
↳ Poverty, Chastity, Obedience → advice to live our forth & shortly

Article: 4 Whether certain counsels are fittingly proposed in the New Law?

Objection 1: It would seem that certain definite counsels are not fittingly proposed in the New Law. For counsels are given about that which is expedient for an end, as we stated above, when treating of counsel (Question [14], Article [2]). But the same things are not expedient for all. Therefore certain definite counsels should not be proposed to all.

Objection 2: Further, counsels regard a greater good. But there are no definite degrees to the greater good. Therefore definite counsels should not be given.

Objection 3: Further, counsels pertain to the life of perfection. But obedience pertains to the life of perfection. Therefore it was unfitting that no counsel of obedience should be contained in the Gospel.

Objection 4: Further, many matters pertaining to the life of perfection are found among the commandments, as, for instance, "Love your enemies" (Mt. 5:44), and those precepts which Our Lord gave His apostles (Mt. 10). Therefore the counsels are unfittingly given in the New Law: both because they are not all mentioned; and because they are not distinguished from the commandments.

On the contrary, The counsels of a wise friend are of great use, according to Prov. (27:9): "Ointment and perfumes rejoice the heart: and the good counsels of a friend rejoice the soul." But Christ is our wisest and greatest friend. Therefore His counsels are supremely useful and becoming.

I answer that, The difference between a counsel and a commandment is that a commandment implies obligation, whereas a counsel is left to the option of the one to whom it is given. Consequently in the New Law, which is the law of liberty, counsels are added to the commandments, and not in the Old Law, which is the law of bondage. We must therefore understand the commandments of the New Law to have been given about matters that are necessary to gain the end of eternal bliss, to which end the New Law brings us forthwith: but that the counsels are about matters that render the gaining of this end more assured and expeditious.

Now man is placed between the things of this world, and spiritual goods wherein eternal happiness consists: so that the more he cleaves to the one, the more he withdraws from the other, and conversely. Wherefore he that cleaves wholly to the things of this world, so as to make them his end, and to look upon them as the reason and rule of all he does, falls away altogether from spiritual goods. Hence this disorder is removed by the commandments. Nevertheless, for man to gain the end aforesaid, he does not need to renounce the things of the world altogether: since he can, while using the things of this world, attain to eternal happiness, provided he does not place his end in them: but he will attain

288

more speedily thereto by giving up the goods of this world entirely: wherefore the evangelical counsels are given for this purpose.

Now the goods of this world which come into use in human life, consist in three things: viz. in external wealth pertaining to the "concupiscence of the eyes"; carnal pleasures pertaining to the "concupiscence of the flesh"; and honors, which pertain to the "pride of life," according to 1 Jn. 2:16: and it is in renouncing these altogether, as far as possible, that the evangelical counsels consist. Moreover, every form of the religious life that professes the state of perfection is based on these three: since riches are renounced by poverty; carnal pleasures by perpetual chastity; and the pride of life by the bondage of obedience.

Now if a man observe these absolutely, this is in accordance with the counsels as they stand. But if a man observe any one of them in a particular case, this is taking that counsel in a restricted sense, namely, as applying to that particular case. For instance, when anyone gives an alms to a poor man, not being bound so to do, he follows the counsels in that particular case. In like manner, when a man for some fixed time refrains from carnal pleasures that he may give himself to prayer, he follows the counsel for that particular time. And again, when a man follows not his will as to some deed which he might do lawfully, he follows the counsel in that particular case: for instance, if he do good to his enemies when he is not bound to, or if he forgive an injury of which he might justly seek to be avenged. In this way, too, all particular counsels may be reduced to these three general and perfect counsels.

Reply to Objection 1: The aforesaid counsels, considered in themselves, are expedient to all; but owing to some people being ill-disposed, it happens that some of them are inexpedient, because their disposition is not inclined to such things. Hence Our Lord, in proposing the evangelical counsels, always makes mention of man's fitness for observing the counsels. For in giving the counsel of perpetual poverty (Mt. 19:21), He begins with the words: "If thou wilt be perfect," and then He adds: "Go, sell all [Vulg.: 'what'] thou hast." In like manner when He gave the counsel of perpetual chastity, saying (Mt. 19:12): "There are eunuchs who have made themselves eunuchs for the kingdom of heaven," He adds straightway: "He that can take, let him take it." And again, the Apostle (1 Cor. 7:35), after giving the counsel of virginity, says: "And this I speak for your profit; not to cast a snare upon you."

Reply to Objection 2: The greater goods are not definitely fixed in the individual; but those which are simply and absolutely the greater good in general are fixed: and to these all the above particular goods may be reduced, as stated above.

Reply to Objection 3: Even the counsel of obedience is understood to have been given by Our Lord in the words: "And [let him] follow Me." For we follow Him not only by imitating His works, but also by obeying His commandments, according to Jn. 10:27: "My sheep hear My voice . . . and they follow Me."

Reply to Objection 4: Those things which Our Lord prescribed about the true love of our enemies, and other similar sayings (<u>Mt. 5; Lk. 6</u>), may be referred to the preparation of the mind, and then they are necessary for salvation; for instance, that man be prepared to do good to his enemies, and other similar actions, when there is need. Hence these things are placed among the precepts. But that anyone should actually and promptly behave thus towards an enemy when there is no special need, is to be referred to the particular counsels, as stated above. As to those matters which are set down in Mt. 10 and Lk. 9 and 10, they were either disciplinary commands for that particular time, or concessions, as stated above (<u>Article [2]</u>, ad 3). Hence they are not set down among the counsels.

------------------ END OF TREATISE ON LAW ------------------

TREATISE ON GRACE (Questions 109-114)
OF THE NECESSITY OF GRACE (TEN ARTICLES)

We must now consider the exterior principle of human acts, i.e. God, in so far as, through grace, we are helped by Him to do right: and, first, we must consider the grace of God; secondly, its cause; thirdly, its effects.

The first point of consideration will be threefold: for we shall consider (1) The necessity of grace; (2) grace itself, as to its essence; (3) its division.

Under the first head there are ten points of inquiry:

(1) Whether without grace man can know anything?
(2) Whether without God's grace man can do or wish any good?
(3) Whether without grace man can love God above all things?
(4) Whether without grace man can keep the commandments of the Law?
(5) Whether without grace he can merit eternal life?
(6) Whether without grace man can prepare himself for grace?
(7) Whether without grace he can rise from sin?
(8) Whether without grace man can avoid sin?
(9) Whether man having received grace can do good and avoid sin without any further Divine help?
(10) Whether he can of himself persevere in good?

Question 109 Article: 1

Whether without grace man can know any truth?

Objection 1: It would seem that without grace man can know no truth. For, on 1 Cor. 12:3: "No man can say, the Lord Jesus, but by the Holy Ghost," a gloss says: "Every truth, by whomsoever spoken is from the Holy Ghost." Now the Holy Ghost dwells in us by grace. Therefore we cannot know truth without grace.

Objection 2: Further, Augustine says (Solil. i, 6) that "the most certain sciences are like things lit up by the sun so as to be seen. Now God Himself is He Whom sheds the light. And reason is in the mind as sight is in the eye. And the eyes of the mind are the senses of the soul." Now the bodily senses, however pure, cannot see any visible object, without the sun's light. Therefore the human mind, however perfect, cannot, by reasoning, know any truth without Divine light: and this pertains to the aid of grace.

Objection 3: Further, the human mind can only understand truth by thinking, as is clear from Augustine (De Trin. xiv, 7). But the Apostle says (2 Cor. 3:5): "Not that we are sufficient to think anything of ourselves, as of ourselves; but our sufficiency is from God." Therefore man cannot, of himself, know truth without the help of grace.

On the contrary, Augustine says (Retract. i, 4): "I do not approve having said in the prayer, O God, Who dost wish the sinless alone to know the truth; for it may be answered that many who are not sinless know many truths." Now man is cleansed from sin by grace, according to Ps. 50:12: "Create a clean heart in me, O God, and renew a right spirit within my bowels." Therefore without grace man of himself can know truth.

I answer that, To know truth is a use or act of intellectual light, since, according to the Apostle (Eph. 5:13): "All that is made manifest is light." Now every use implies movement, taking movement broadly, so as to call thinking and willing movements, as is clear from the Philosopher (De Anima iii, 4). Now in corporeal things we see that for movement there is required not merely the form which is the principle of the movement or action, but there is also required the motion of the first mover. Now the first mover in the order of corporeal things is the heavenly body. Hence no matter how perfectly fire has heat, it would not bring about alteration, except by the motion of the heavenly body. But it is clear that as all corporeal movements are reduced to the motion of the heavenly body as to the first corporeal mover, so all movements, both corporeal and spiritual, are reduced to the simple First Mover, Who is God. And hence no matter how perfect a corporeal or spiritual nature is supposed to be, it cannot proceed to its act unless it be moved by God; but this motion is according to the plan of His providence, and not by necessity of nature as the motion of the heavenly body. Now not only is every motion from God as from the First Mover, but all formal perfection is from Him as from the First Act. And thus the act of the intellect or of any created being whatsoever depends upon God in two ways: first, inasmuch as it is from Him that it has the form whereby it acts; secondly, inasmuch as it is moved by Him to act.

Now every form bestowed on created things by God has power for a determined act, which it can bring about in proportion to its own proper endowment; and beyond which it is powerless, except by a superadded form, as water can only heat when heated by the fire. And thus the human understanding has a form, viz. intelligible light, which of itself is sufficient for knowing certain intelligible things, viz. those we can come to know through the senses. Higher intelligible things of the human intellect cannot know, unless it be perfected by a stronger light, viz. the light of faith or prophecy which is called the "light of grace," inasmuch as it is added to nature.

Hence we must say that for the knowledge of any truth whatsoever man needs Divine help, that the intellect may be moved by God to its act. But he does not need a new light added to his natural light, in order to know the truth in all things, but only in some that surpass his natural knowledge. And yet at times God miraculously instructs some by His grace in things that can be known by

292

natural reason, even as He sometimes brings about miraculously what nature can do.

Reply to Objection 1: Every truth by whomsoever spoken is from the Holy Ghost as bestowing the natural light, and moving us to understand and speak the truth, but not as dwelling in us by sanctifying grace, or as bestowing any habitual gift superadded to nature. For this only takes place with regard to certain truths that are known and spoken, and especially in regard to such as pertain to faith, of which the Apostle speaks.

Reply to Objection 2: The material sun sheds its light outside us; but the intelligible Sun, Who is God, shines within us. Hence the natural light bestowed upon the soul is God's enlightenment, whereby we are enlightened to see what pertains to natural knowledge; and for this there is required no further knowledge, but only for such things as surpass natural knowledge.

Reply to Objection 3: We always need God's help for every thought, inasmuch as He moves the understanding to act; for actually to understand anything is to think, as is clear from Augustine (De Trin. xiv, 7).

Article: 2

Whether man can wish or do any good without grace?

Objection 1: It would seem that man can wish and do good without grace. For that is in man's power, whereof he is master. Now man is master of his acts, and especially of his willing, as stated above (Question [1], Article [1]; Question [13], Article [6]). Hence man, of himself, can wish and do good without the help of grace.

Objection 2: Further, man has more power over what is according to his nature than over what is beyond his nature. Now sin is against his nature, as Damascene says (De Fide Orth. ii, 30); whereas deeds of virtue are according to his nature, as stated above (Question [71], Article [1]). Therefore since man can sin of himself he can wish and do good.

Objection 3: Further, the understanding's good is truth, as the Philosopher says (Ethic. vi, 2). Now the intellect can of itself know truth, even as every other thing can work its own operation of itself. Therefore, much more can man, of himself, do and wish good.

On the contrary, The Apostle says (Rm. 9:16): "It is not of him that willeth," namely, to will, "nor of him that runneth," namely to run, "but of God that showeth mercy." And Augustine says (De Corrept. et Gratia ii) that "without grace men do nothing good when they either think or wish or love or act."

293

I answer that, Man's nature may be looked at in two ways: first, in its integrity, as it was in our first parent before sin; secondly, as it is corrupted in us after the sin of our first parent. Now in both states human nature needs the help of God as First Mover, to do or wish any good whatsoever, as stated above (Article [1]). But in the state of integrity, as regards the sufficiency of the operative power, man by his natural endowments could wish and do the good proportionate to his nature, such as the good of acquired virtue; but not surpassing good, as the good of infused virtue. But in the state of corrupt nature, man falls short of what he could do by his nature, so that he is unable to fulfil it by his own natural powers. Yet because human nature is not altogether corrupted by sin, so as to be shorn of every natural good, even in the state of corrupted nature it can, by virtue of its natural endowments, work some particular good, as to build dwellings, plant vineyards, and the like; yet it cannot do all the good natural to it, so as to fall short in nothing; just as a sick man can of himself make some movements, yet he cannot be perfectly moved with the movements of one in health, unless by the help of medicine he be cured.

And thus in the state of perfect nature man needs a gratuitous strength superadded to natural strength for one reason, viz. in order to do and wish supernatural good; but for two reasons, in the state of corrupt nature, viz. in order to be healed, and furthermore in order to carry out works of supernatural virtue, which are meritorious. Beyond this, in both states man needs the Divine help, that he may be moved to act well.

Reply to Objection 1: Man is master of his acts and of his willing or not willing, because of his deliberate reason, which can be bent to one side or another. And although he is master of his deliberating or not deliberating, yet this can only be by a previous deliberation; and since it cannot go on to infinity, we must come at length to this, that man's free-will is moved by an extrinsic principle, which is above the human mind, to wit by God, as the Philosopher proves in the chapter "On Good Fortune" (Ethic. Eudem. vii). Hence the mind of man still unweakened is not so much master of its act that it does not need to be moved by God; and much more the free-will of man weakened by sin, whereby it is hindered from good by the corruption of the nature.

Reply to Objection 2: To sin is nothing else than to fail in the good which belongs to any being according to its nature. Now as every created thing has its being from another, and, considered in itself, is nothing, so does it need to be preserved by another in the good which pertains to its nature. For it can of itself fail in good, even as of itself it can fall into non-existence, unless it is upheld by God.

Reply to Objection 3: Man cannot even know truth without Divine help, as stated above (Article [1]). And yet human nature is more corrupt by sin in regard to the desire for good, than in regard to the knowledge of truth.

Article: 3 Whether by his own natural powers and without grace man can love God above all things?

Objection 1: It would seem that without grace man cannot love God above all things by his own natural powers. For to love God above all things is the proper and principal act of charity. Now man cannot of himself possess charity, since the "charity of God is poured forth in our hearts by the Holy Ghost Who is given to us," as is said Rm. 5:5. Therefore man by his natural powers alone cannot love God above all things.

Objection 2: Further, no nature can rise above itself. But to love God above all things is to tend above oneself. Therefore without the help of grace no created nature can love God above itself.

Objection 3: Further, to God, Who is the Highest Good, is due the best love, which is that He be loved above all things. Now without grace man is not capable of giving God the best love, which is His due; otherwise it would be useless to add grace. Hence man, without grace and with his natural powers alone, cannot love God above all things.

On the contrary, As some maintain, man was first made with only natural endowments; and in this state it is manifest that he loved God to some extent. But he did not love God equally with himself, or less than himself, otherwise he would have sinned. Therefore he loved God above himself. Therefore man, by his natural powers alone, can love God more than himself and above all things.

I answer that, As was said above (FP, Question [60], Article [5]), where the various opinions concerning the natural love of the angels were set forth, man in a state of perfect nature, could by his natural power, do the good natural to him without the addition of any gratuitous gift, though not without the help of God moving him. Now to love God above all things is natural to man and to every nature, not only rational but irrational, and even to inanimate nature according to the manner of love which can belong to each creature. And the reason of this is that it is natural to all to seek and love things according as they are naturally fit (to be sought and loved) since "all things act according as they are naturally fit" as stated in Phys. ii, 8. Now it is manifest that the good of the part is for the good of the whole; hence everything, by its natural appetite and love, loves its own proper good on account of the common good of the whole universe, which is God. Hence Dionysius says (Div. Nom. iv) that "God leads everything to love of Himself." Hence in the state of perfect nature man referred the love of himself and of all other things to the love of God as to its end; and thus he loved God more than himself and above all things. But in the state of corrupt nature man falls short of this in the appetite of his rational will, which, unless it is cured by God's grace, follows its private good, on account of the corruption of nature. And hence we must say that in the state of perfect nature man did not need the gift of grace added to his natural endowments, in order to love God above all things naturally, although he needed God's help to move him to it; but in the state of corrupt nature man needs, even for this, the help of grace to heal his nature.

Reply to Objection 1: Charity loves God above all things in a higher way than nature does. For nature loves God above all things inasmuch as He is the beginning and the end of natural good; whereas charity loves Him, as He is the object of beatitude, and inasmuch as man has a spiritual fellowship with God. Moreover charity adds to natural love of God a certain quickness and joy, in the same way that every habit of virtue adds to the good act which is done merely by the natural reason of a man who has not the habit of virtue.

Reply to Objection 2: When it is said that nature cannot rise above itself, we must not understand this as if it could not be drawn to any object above itself, for it is clear that our intellect by its natural knowledge can know things above itself, as is shown in our natural knowledge of God. But we are to understand that nature cannot rise to an act exceeding the proportion of its strength. Now to love God above all things is not such an act; for it is natural to every creature, as was said above.

Reply to Objection 3: Love is said to be best, both with respect to degree of love, and with regard to the motive of loving, and the mode of love. And thus the highest degree of love is that whereby charity loves God as the giver of beatitude, as was said above.

Article: 4

Whether man without grace and by his own natural powers can fulfil the commandments of the Law?

Objection 1: It would seem that man without grace, and by his own natural powers, can fulfil the commandments of the Law. For the Apostle says (Rm. 2:14) that "the Gentiles who have not the law, do by nature those things that are of the Law." Now what a man does naturally he can do of himself without grace. Hence a man can fulfil the commandments of the Law without grace.

Objection 2: Further, Jerome says (Expos. Cathol. Fide [*Symboli Explanatio ad Damasum, among the supposititious works of St. Jerome: now ascribed to Pelagius]) that "they are anathema who say God has laid impossibilities upon man." Now what a man cannot fulfil by himself is impossible to him. Therefore a man can fulfil all the commandments of himself.

Objection 3: Further, of all the commandments of the Law, the greatest is this, "Thou shalt love the Lord thy God with thy whole heart" (Mt. 27:37). Now man with his natural endowments can fulfil this command by loving God above all things, as stated above (Article [3]). Therefore man can fulfil all the commandments of the Law without grace.

On the contrary, Augustine says (De Haeres. lxxxviii) that it is part of the Pelagian heresy that "they believe that without grace man can fulfil all the Divine commandments."

I answer that, There are two ways of fulfilling the commandments of the Law. The first regards the substance of the works, as when a man does works of justice, fortitude, and of other virtues. And in this way man in the state of perfect nature could fulfil all the commandments of the Law; otherwise he would have been unable to sin in that state, since to sin is nothing else than to transgress the Divine commandments. But in the state of corrupted nature man cannot fulfil all the Divine commandments without healing grace. Secondly, the commandments of the law can be fulfilled, not merely as regards the substance of the act, but also as regards the mode of acting, i.e. their being done out of charity. And in this way, neither in the state of perfect nature, nor in the state of corrupt nature can man fulfil the commandments of the law without grace. Hence, Augustine (De Corrupt. et Grat. ii) having stated that "without grace men can do no good whatever," adds: "Not only do they know by its light what to do, but by its help they do lovingly what they know." Beyond this, in both states they need the help of God's motion in order to fulfil the commandments, as stated above (Articles [2],3).

Reply to Objection 1: As Augustine says (De Spir. et Lit. xxvii), "do not be disturbed at his saying that they do by nature those things that are of the Law; for the Spirit of grace works this, in order to restore in us the image of God, after which we were naturally made."

Reply to Objection 2: What we can do with the Divine assistance is not altogether impossible to us; according to the Philosopher (Ethic. iii, 3): "What we can do through our friends, we can do, in some sense, by ourselves." Hence Jerome [*Symboli Explanatio ad Damasum, among the supposititious works of St. Jerome: now ascribed to Pelagius] concedes that "our will is in such a way free that we must confess we still require God's help."

Reply to Objection 3: Man cannot, with his purely natural endowments, fulfil the precept of the love of God, as stated above (Article [3]).

Article: 5

Whether man can merit everlasting life without grace?

Objection 1: It would seem that man can merit everlasting life without grace. For Our Lord says (Mt. 19:17): "If thou wilt enter into life, keep the commandments"; from which it would seem that to enter into everlasting life rests with man's will. But what rests with our will, we can do of ourselves. Hence it seems that man can merit everlasting life of himself.

Objection 2: Further, eternal life is the wage of reward bestowed by God on men, according to Mt. 5:12: "Your reward is very great in heaven." But wage or reward is meted by God to everyone according to his works, according to Ps. 61:12: "Thou wilt render to every man according to his works." Hence, since man is master of his works, it seems that it is within his power to reach everlasting life.

Objection 3: Further, everlasting life is the last end of human life. Now every natural thing by its natural endowments can attain its end. Much more, therefore, may man attain to life everlasting by his natural endowments, without grace.

On the contrary, The Apostle says (Rm. 6:23): "The grace of God is life everlasting." And as a gloss says, this is said "that we may understand that God, of His own mercy, leads us to everlasting life."

I answer that, Acts conducing to an end must be proportioned to the end. But no act exceeds the proportion of its active principle; and hence we see in natural things, that nothing can by its operation bring about an effect which exceeds its active force, but only such as is proportionate to its power. Now everlasting life is an end exceeding the proportion of human nature, as is clear from what we have said above (Question [5], Article [5]). Hence man, by his natural endowments, cannot produce meritorious works proportionate to everlasting life; and for this a higher force is needed, viz. the force of grace. And thus without grace man cannot merit everlasting life; yet he can perform works conducing to a good which is natural to man, as "to toil in the fields, to drink, to eat, or to have friends," and the like, as Augustine says in his third Reply to the Pelagians [*Hypognosticon iii, among the spurious works of St. Augustine].

Reply to Objection 1: Man, by his will, does works meritorious of everlasting life; but as Augustine says, in the same book, for this it is necessary that the will of man should be prepared with grace by God.

Reply to Objection 2: As the gloss upon Rm. 6:23, "The grace of God is life everlasting," says, "It is certain that everlasting life is meter to good works; but the works to which it is meted, belong to God's grace." And it has been said (Article [4]), that to fulfil the commandments of the Law, in their due way, whereby their fulfilment may be meritorious, requires grace.

Reply to Objection 3: This objection has to do with the natural end of man. Now human nature, since it is nobler, can be raised by the help of grace to a higher end, which lower natures can nowise reach; even as a man who can recover his health by the help of medicines is better disposed to health than one who can nowise recover it, as the Philosopher observes (De Coelo ii, 12).

Article: 6

Whether a man, by himself and without the external aid of grace, can prepare himself for grace?

Objection 1: It would seem that man, by himself and without the external help of grace, can prepare himself for grace. For nothing impossible is laid upon man, as stated above (Article [4], ad 1). But it is written (Zach. 1:3): "Turn ye to Me . . . and I will turn to you." Now to prepare for grace is nothing more than to turn to God. Therefore it seems that man of himself, and without the external help of grace, can prepare himself for grace.

Objection 2: Further, man prepares himself for grace by doing what is in him to do, since if man does what is in him to do, God will not deny him grace, for it is written (Mt. 7:11) that God gives His good Spirit "to them that ask Him." But what is in our power is in us to do. Therefore it seems to be in our power to prepare ourselves for grace.

Objection 3: Further, if a man needs grace in order to prepare for grace, with equal reason will he need grace to prepare himself for the first grace; and thus to infinity, which is impossible. Hence it seems that we must not go beyond what was said first, viz. that man, of himself and without grace, can prepare himself for grace.

Objection 4: Further, it is written (Prov. 16:1) that "it is the part of man to prepare the soul." Now an action is said to be part of a man, when he can do it by himself. Hence it seems that man by himself can prepare himself for grace.

On the contrary, It is written (Jn. 6:44): "No man can come to Me except the Father, Who hath sent Me, draw him." But if man could prepare himself, he would not need to be drawn by another. Hence man cannot prepare himself without the help of grace.

I answer that, The preparation of the human will for good is twofold: the first, whereby it is prepared to operate rightly and to enjoy God; and this preparation of the will cannot take place without the habitual gift of grace, which is the principle of meritorious works, as stated above (Article [5]). There is a second way in which the human will may be taken to be prepared for the gift of habitual grace itself. Now in order that man prepare himself to receive this gift, it is not necessary to presuppose any further habitual gift in the soul, otherwise we should go on to infinity. But we must presuppose a gratuitous gift of God, Who moves the soul inwardly or inspires the good wish. For in these two ways do we need the Divine assistance, as stated above (Articles [2],3). Now that we need the help of God to move us, is manifest. For since every agent acts for an end, every cause must direct is effect to its end, and hence since the order of ends is according to the order of agents or movers, man must be directed to the last end by the motion of the first mover, and to the proximate end by the motion of any of the subordinate movers; as the spirit of the soldier is bent towards seeking the victory by the motion of the leader of the army---and towards following the standard of a regiment by the motion of the standard-bearer. And thus since God is the First Mover, simply, it is by His motion that everything seeks to be likened to God in its own way. Hence Dionysius says (Div. Nom. iv) that "God turns all to Himself." But He directs righteous men to Himself as to a special end, which they seek, and to which they wish to cling, according to Ps. 72:28, "it is good for Me to adhere to my God." And that they are "turned" to God can only spring from God's having "turned" them. Now to prepare oneself for grace is, as it were, to be turned to God; just as, whoever has his eyes turned away from the light of the sun, prepares himself to receive the sun's light, by turning his eyes towards the sun. Hence it is clear that man cannot prepare himself to receive the light of grace except by the gratuitous help of God moving him inwardly.

Reply to Objection 1: Man's turning to God is by free-will; and thus man is bidden to turn himself to God. But free-will can only be turned to God, when God turns it, according to Jer. 31:18: "Convert me and I shall be converted, for Thou art the Lord, my God"; and Lam. 5:21: "Convert us, O Lord, to Thee, and we shall be converted."

Reply to Objection 2: Man can do nothing unless moved by God, according to Jn. 15:5: "Without Me, you can do nothing." Hence when a man is said to do what is in him to do, this is said to be in his power according as he is moved by God.

Reply to Objection 3: This objection regards habitual grace, for which some preparation is required, since every form requires a disposition in that which is to be its subject. But in order that man should be moved by God, no further motion is presupposed since God is the First Mover. Hence we need not go to infinity.

Reply to Objection 4: It is the part of man to prepare his soul, since he does this by his free-will. And yet he does not do this without the help of God moving him, and drawing him to Himself, as was said above.

Article: 7 Whether man can rise from sin without the help of grace?

Objection 1: It would seem that man can rise from sin without the help of grace. For what is presupposed to grace, takes place without grace. But to rise to sin is presupposed to the enlightenment of grace; since it is written (Eph. 5:14): "Arise from the dead and Christ shall enlighten thee." Therefore man can rise from sin without grace.

Objection 2: Further, sin is opposed to virtue as illness to health, as stated above (Question [71], Article [1], ad 3). Now, man, by force of his nature, can rise from illness to health, without the external help of medicine, since there still remains in him the principle of life, from which the natural operation proceeds. Hence it seems that, with equal reason, man may be restored by himself, and return from the state of sin to the state of justice without the help of external grace.

Objection 3: Further, every natural thing can return by itself to the act befitting its nature, as hot water returns by itself to its natural coldness, and a stone cast upwards returns by itself to its natural movement. Now a sin is an act against nature, as is clear from Damascene (De Fide Orth. ii, 30). Hence it seems that man by himself can return from sin to the state of justice.

On the contrary, The Apostle says (Gal. 2:21; Cf. Gal. 3:21): "For if there had been a law given which could give life---then Christ died in vain," i.e. to no purpose. Hence with equal reason, if man has a nature, whereby he can he justified, "Christ died in vain," i.e. to no purpose. But this cannot fittingly be said. Therefore by himself he cannot be justified, i.e. he cannot return from a state of sin to a state of justice.

I answer that, Man by himself can no wise rise from sin without the help of grace. For since sin is transient as to the act and abiding in its guilt, as stated above (Question [87], Article [6]), to rise from sin is not the same as to cease the act of sin; but to rise from sin means that man has restored to him what he lost by sinning. Now man incurs a triple loss by sinning, as was clearly shown above (Question [85], Article [1]; Question [86], Article [1]; Question [87], Article [1]), viz. stain, corruption of natural good, and debt of punishment. He incurs a stain, inasmuch as he forfeits the lustre of grace through the deformity of sin. Natural good is corrupted, inasmuch as man's nature is disordered by man's will not being subject to God's; and this order being overthrown, the consequence is that the whole nature of sinful man remains disordered. Lastly, there is the debt of punishment, inasmuch as by sinning man deserves everlasting damnation.

Now it is manifest that none of these three can be restored except by God. For since the lustre of grace springs from the shedding of Divine light, this lustre cannot be brought back, except God sheds His light anew: hence a habitual gift is necessary, and this is the light of grace. Likewise, the order of nature can only be restored, i.e. man's will can only be subject to God when God draws man's will to Himself, as stated above (Article [6]). So, too, the guilt of eternal punishment can be remitted by God alone, against Whom the offense was committed and Who is man's Judge. And thus in order that man rise from sin there is required the help of grace, both as regards a habitual gift, and as regards the internal motion of God.

Reply to Objection 1: To man is bidden that which pertains to the act of free-will, as this act is required in order that man should rise from sin. Hence when it is said, "Arise, and Christ shall enlighten thee," we are not to think that the complete rising from sin precedes the enlightenment of grace; but that when man by his free-will, moved by God, strives to rise from sin, he receives the light of justifying grace.

Reply to Objection 2: The natural reason is not the sufficient principle of the health that is in man by justifying grace. This principle is grace which is taken away by sin. Hence man cannot be restored by himself; but he requires the light of grace to be poured upon him anew, as if the soul were infused into a dead body for its resurrection.

Reply to Objection 3: When nature is perfect, it can be restored by itself to its befitting and proportionate condition; but without exterior help it cannot be restored to what surpasses its measure. And thus human nature undone by reason of the act of sin, remains no longer perfect, but corrupted, as stated above (Question [85]); nor can it be restored, by itself, to its connatural good, much less to the supernatural good of justice.

Article: 8

Whether man without grace can avoid sin?

Objection 1: It would seem that without grace man can avoid sin. Because "no one sins in what he cannot avoid," as Augustine says (De Duab. Anim. x, xi; De Libero Arbit. iii, 18). Hence if a man in mortal sin cannot avoid sin, it would seem that in sinning he does not sin, which is impossible.

Objection 2: Further, men are corrected that they may not sin. If therefore a man in mortal sin cannot avoid sin, correction would seem to be given to no purpose; which is absurd.

Objection 3: Further, it is written (Ecclus. 15:18): "Before man is life and death, good and evil; that which he shall choose shall be given him." But by sinning no one ceases to be a man. Hence it is still in his power to choose good or evil; and thus man can avoid sin without grace.

On the contrary, Augustine says (De Perfect Just. xxi): "Whoever denies that we ought to say the prayer 'Lead us not into temptation' (and they deny it who maintain that the help of God's grace is not necessary to man for salvation, but that the gift of the law is enough for the human will) ought without doubt to be removed beyond all hearing, and to be anathematized by the tongues of all."

I answer that, We may speak of man in two ways: first, in the state of perfect nature; secondly, in the state of corrupted nature. Now in the state of perfect nature, man, without habitual grace, could avoid sinning either mortally or venially; since to sin is nothing else than to stray from what is according to our nature---and in the state of perfect nature man could avoid this. Nevertheless he could not have done it without God's help to uphold him in good, since if this had been withdrawn, even his nature would have fallen back into nothingness.

But in the state of corrupt nature man needs grace to heal his nature in order that he may entirely abstain from sin. And in the present life this healing is wrought in the mind---the carnal appetite being not yet restored. Hence the Apostle (Rm. 7:25) says in the person of one who is restored: "I myself, with the mind, serve the law of God, but with the flesh, the law of sin." And in this state man can abstain from all mortal sin, which takes its stand in his reason, as stated above (Question [74], Article [5]); but man cannot abstain from all venial sin on account of the corruption of his lower appetite of sensuality. For man can, indeed, repress each of its movements (and hence they are sinful and voluntary), but not all, because whilst he is resisting one, another may arise, and also because the reason is always alert to avoid these movements, as was said above (Question [74], Article [3], ad 2).

So, too, before man's reason, wherein is mortal sin, is restored by justifying grace, he can avoid each mortal sin, and for a time, since it is not necessary that he should be always actually sinning. But it cannot be that he remains for a long time without mortal sin. Hence Gregory says (Super Ezech. Hom. xi) that " a sin not at once taken away by repentance, by its weight drags us down to other sins": and this because, as the lower appetite ought to be subject to the reason, so should the reason be subject to God, and should place in Him the end of its will. Now it is by the end that all human acts ought to be regulated, even as it is by the judgment of the reason that the movements of the lower appetite should be regulated. And thus, even as inordinate movements of the sensitive appetite cannot help occurring since the lower appetite is not subject to reason, so likewise, since man's reason is not entirely subject to God, the consequence is that many disorders occur in the reason. For when man's heart is not so fixed on God as to be unwilling to be parted from Him for the sake of finding any good or avoiding any evil, many things happen for the achieving or avoiding of which a man strays from God and breaks His commandments, and thus sins mortally: especially since, when surprised, a man acts according to his preconceived end and his pre-existing habits, as the Philosopher says (Ethic. iii); although with premeditation of his reason a man may do something outside the order of his preconceived end and the inclination of his habit. But because a man cannot always have this premeditation, it cannot help occurring that he acts in accordance with his will turned aside from God, unless, by grace, he is quickly brought back to the due order.

Reply to Objection 1: Man can avoid each but every act of sin, except by grace, as stated above. Nevertheless, since it is by his own shortcoming that he does not prepare himself to have grace, the fact that he cannot avoid sin without grace does not excuse him from sin.

Reply to Objection 2: Correction is useful "in order that out of the sorrow of correction may spring the wish to be regenerate; if indeed he who is corrected is a son of promise, in such sort that whilst the noise of correction is outwardly resounding and punishing, God by hidden inspirations is inwardly causing to will," as Augustine says (De Corr. et Gratia vi). Correction is therefore necessary, from the fact that man's will is required in order to abstain from sin; yet it is not sufficient without God's help. Hence it is written (Eccles. 7:14): "Consider the works of God that no man can correct whom He hath despised."

Reply to Objection 3: As Augustine says (Hypognosticon iii [*Among the spurious works of St. Augustine]), this saying is to be understood of man in the state of perfect nature, when as yet he was not a slave of sin. Hence he was able to sin and not to sin. Now, too, whatever a man wills, is given to him; but his willing good, he has by God's assistance.

Article: 9

Whether one who has already obtained grace, can, of himself and without further help of grace, do good and avoid sin?

Objection 1: It would seem that whoever has already obtained grace, can by himself and without further help of grace, do good and avoid sin. For a thing is useless or imperfect, if it does not fulfil what it was given for. Now grace is given to us that we may do good and keep from sin. Hence if with grace man cannot do this, it seems that grace is either useless or imperfect.

Objection 2: Further, by grace the Holy Spirit dwells in us, according to 1 Cor. 3:16: "Know you not that you are the temple of God, and that the Spirit of God dwelleth in you?" Now since the Spirit of God is omnipotent, He is sufficient to ensure our doing good and to keep us from sin. Hence a man who has obtained grace can do the above two things without any further assistance of grace.

Objection 3: Further, if a man who has obtained grace needs further aid of grace in order to live righteously and to keep free from sin, with equal reason, will he need yet another grace, even though he has obtained this first help of grace.

Therefore we must go on to infinity; which is impossible. Hence whoever is in grace needs no further help of grace in order to do righteously and to keep free from sin.

On the contrary, Augustine says (De Natura et Gratia xxvi) that "as the eye of the body though most healthy cannot see unless it is helped by the brightness of light, so, neither can a man, even if he is most righteous, live righteously unless he be helped by the eternal light of justice." But justification is by grace, according to Rm. 3:24: "Being justified freely by His grace." Hence even a man who already possesses grace needs a further assistance of grace in order to live righteously.

I answer that, As stated above (Article [5]), in order to live righteously a man needs a twofold help of God---first, a habitual gift whereby corrupted human nature is healed, and after being healed is lifted up so as to work deeds meritoriously of everlasting life, which exceed the capability of nature. Secondly, man needs the help of grace in order to be moved by God to act.

Now with regard to the first kind of help, man does not need a further help of grace, e.g. a further infused habit. Yet he needs the help of grace in another way, i.e. in order to be moved by God to act righteously, and this for two reasons: first, for the general reason that no created thing can put forth any act, unless by virtue of the Divine motion. Secondly, for this special reason---the condition of the state of human nature. For although healed by grace as to the mind, yet it remains corrupted and poisoned in the flesh, whereby it serves "the law of sin," Rm. 7:25. In the intellect, too, there seems the darkness of ignorance, whereby, as is written (Rm. 8:26): "We know not what we should pray for as we ought"; since on account of the various turns of circumstances, and because we do not know ourselves perfectly, we cannot fully know what is for our good, according to Wis. 9:14: "For the thoughts of mortal men are fearful and our counsels uncertain." Hence we must be guided and guarded by God, Who knows and can do all things. For which reason also it is becoming in those who have been born again as sons of God, to say: "Lead us not into temptation," and "Thy Will be done on earth as it is in heaven," and whatever else is contained in the Lord's Prayer pertaining to this.

Reply to Objection 1: The gift of habitual grace is not therefore given to us that we may no longer need the Divine help; for every creature needs to be preserved in the good received from Him. Hence if after having received grace man still needs the Divine help, it cannot be concluded that grace is given to no purpose, or that it is imperfect, since man will need the Divine help even in the state of glory, when grace shall be fully perfected. But here grace is to some extent imperfect, inasmuch as it does not completely heal man, as stated above.

Reply to Objection 2: The operation of the Holy Ghost, which moves and protects, is not circumscribed by the effect of habitual grace which it causes in us; but beyond this effect He, together with the Father and the Son, moves and protects us.

Reply to Objection 3: This argument merely proves that man needs no further habitual grace.

Article: 10

Whether man possessed of grace needs the help of grace in order to persevere?

Objection 1: It would seem that man possessed of grace needs no help to persevere. For perseverance is something less than virtue, even as continence is, as is clear from the Philosopher (Ethic. vii, 7,9). Now since man is justified by grace, he needs no further help of grace in order to have the virtues. Much less, therefore, does he need the help of grace to have perseverance.

Objection 2: Further, all the virtues are infused at once. But perseverance is put down as a virtue. Hence it seems that, together with grace, perseverance is given to the other infused virtues.

Objection 3: Further, as the Apostle says (Rm. 5:20) more was restored to man by Christ's gift, than he had lost by Adam's sin. But Adam received what enabled him to persevere; and thus man does not need grace in order to persevere.

On the contrary, Augustine says (De Persev. ii): "Why is perseverance besought of God, if it is not bestowed by God? For is it not a mocking request to seek what we know He does not give, and what is in our power without His giving it?" Now perseverance is besought by even those who are hallowed by grace; and this is seen, when we say "Hallowed be Thy name," which Augustine confirms by the words of Cyprian (De Correp. et Grat. xii). Hence man, even when possessed of grace, needs perseverance to be given to him by God.

I answer that, Perseverance is taken in three ways. First, to signify a habit of the mind whereby a man stands steadfastly, lest he be moved by the assault of sadness from what is virtuous. And thus perseverance is to sadness as continence is to concupiscence and pleasure, as the Philosopher says (Ethic. vii, 7). Secondly, perseverance may be called a habit, whereby a man has the purpose of persevering in good unto the end. And in both these ways perseverance is infused together with grace, even as continence and the other virtues are. Thirdly, perseverance is called the abiding in good to the end of life. And in order to have this perseverance man does not, indeed, need another habitual grace, but he needs the Divine assistance guiding and guarding him against the attacks of the passions, as appears from the preceding article. And hence after anyone has been justified by grace, he still needs to beseech God for the aforesaid gift of perseverance, that he may be kept from evil till the end of his life. For to many grace is given to whom perseverance in grace is not given.

Reply to Objection 1: This objection regards the first mode of perseverance, as the second objection regards the second.

Hence the solution of the second objection is clear.

Reply to Objection 3: As Augustine says (De Natura et Gratia xliii) [*Cf. De Correp. et Grat. xii]: "in the original state man received a gift whereby he could persevere, but to persevere was not given him. But now, by the grace of Christ, many receive both the gift of grace whereby they may persevere, and the further gift of persevering," and thus Christ's gift is greater than Adam's fault. Nevertheless it was easier for man to persevere, with the gift of grace in the state of innocence in which the flesh was not rebellious against the spirit, than it is now. For the restoration by Christ's grace, although it is already begun in the mind, is not yet completed in the flesh, as it will be in heaven, where man will not merely be able to persevere but will be unable to sin.

OF THE GRACE OF GOD AS REGARDS ITS ESSENCE (FOUR ARTICLES)

We must now consider the grace of God as regards its essence; and under this head there are four points of inquiry:

(1) Whether grace implies something in the soul?
(2) Whether grace is a quality?
(3) Whether grace differs from infused virtue?
(4) Of the subject of grace.

Question 110 Article: 1

Whether grace implies anything in the soul?

Objection 1: It would seem that grace does not imply anything in the soul. For man is said to have the grace of God even as the grace of man. Hence it is written (Gn. 39:21) that the Lord gave to Joseph "grace [Douay: 'favor'] in the sight of the chief keeper of the prison." Now when we say that a man has the favor of another, nothing is implied in him who has the favor of the other, but an acceptance is implied in him whose favor he has. Hence when we say that a man has the grace of God, nothing is implied in his soul; but we merely signify the Divine acceptance.

Objection 2: Further, as the soul quickens the body so does God quicken the soul; hence it is written (Dt. 30:20): "He is thy life." Now the soul quickens the body immediately. Therefore nothing can come as a medium between God and the soul. Hence grace implies nothing created in the soul.

Objection 3: Further, on Rm. 1:7, "Grace to you and peace," the gloss says: "Grace, i.e. the remission of sins." Now the remission of sin implies nothing in the soul, but only in God, Who does not impute the sin, according to Ps. 31:2: "Blessed is the man to whom the Lord hath not imputed sin." Hence neither does grace imply anything in the soul.

On the contrary, Light implies something in what is enlightened. But grace is a light of the soul; hence Augustine says (De Natura et Gratia xxii): "The light of truth rightly deserts the prevaricator of the law, and those who have been thus deserted become blind." Therefore grace implies something in the soul.

I answer that, According to the common manner of speech, grace is usually taken in three ways. First, for anyone's love, as we are accustomed to say that the soldier is in the good graces of the king, i.e. the king looks on him with favor. Secondly, it is taken for any gift freely bestowed, as we are accustomed to say: I do you this act of grace. Thirdly, it is taken for the recompense of a gift given "gratis," inasmuch as we are said to be "grateful" for benefits. Of these three the second depends on the first, since one bestows something on another "gratis" from the love wherewith he receives him into his good "graces." And from the second proceeds the third, since from benefits bestowed "gratis" arises "gratitude."

Now as regards the last two, it is clear that grace implies something in him who receives grace: first, the gift given gratis; secondly, the acknowledgment of the gift. But as regards the first, a difference must be noted between the grace of God and the grace of man; for since the creature's good springs from the Divine will, some good in the creature flows from God's love, whereby He wishes the good of the creature. On the other hand, the will of man is moved by the good pre-existing in things; and hence man's love does not wholly cause the good of the thing, but pre-supposes it either in part or wholly. Therefore it is clear that every love of God is followed at some time by a good caused in the creature, but not co-eternal with the eternal love. And according to this difference of good the love of God to the creature is looked at differently. For one is common, whereby He loves "all things that are" (Wis. 11:25), and thereby gives things their natural being. But the second is a special love, whereby He draws the rational creature above the condition of its nature to a participation of the Divine good; and according to this love He is said to love anyone simply, since it is by this love that God simply wishes the eternal good, which is Himself, for the creature.

Accordingly when a man is said to have the grace of God, there is signified something bestowed on man by God. Nevertheless the grace of God sometimes signifies God's eternal love, as we say the grace of predestination, inasmuch as God gratuitously and not from merits predestines or elects some; for it is written (Eph. 1:5): "He hath predestinated us into the adoption of children . . . unto the praise of the glory of His grace."

Reply to Objection 1: Even when a man is said to be in another's good graces, it is understood that there is something in him pleasing to the other; even as anyone is said to have God's grace---with this difference, that what is pleasing to a man in another is presupposed to his love, but whatever is pleasing to God in a man is caused by the Divine love, as was said above.

Reply to Objection 2: God is the life of the soul after the manner of an efficient cause; but the soul is the life of the body after the manner of a formal cause. Now there is no medium between form and matter, since the form, of itself, "informs" the matter or subject; whereas the agent "informs" the subject, not by its substance, but by the form, which it causes in the matter.

Reply to Objection 3: Augustine says (Retract. i, 25): "When I said that grace was for the remission of sins, and peace for our reconciliation with God, you must not take it to mean that peace and reconciliation do not pertain to general peace, but that the special name of grace signifies the remission of sins." Not only grace, therefore, but many other of God's gifts pertain to grace. And hence the remission of sins does not take place without some effect divinely caused in us, as will appear later (Question [113], Article [2]).

Article: 2

Whether grace is a quality of the soul?

Objection 1: It would seem that grace is not a quality of the soul. For no quality acts on its subject, since the action of a quality is not without the action of its subject, and thus the subject would necessarily act upon itself. But grace acts upon the soul, by justifying it. Therefore grace is not a quality.

Objection 2: Furthermore, substance is nobler than quality. But grace is nobler than the nature of the soul, since we can do many things by grace, to which nature is not equal, as stated above (Question [109], Articles [1],2,3). Therefore grace is not a quality.

Objection 3: Furthermore, no quality remains after it has ceased to be in its subject. But grace remains; since it is not corrupted, for thus it would be reduced to nothing, since it was created from nothing; hence it is called a "new creature"(Gal. 6:15).

On the contrary, on Ps. 103:15: "That he may make the face cheerful with oil"; the gloss says: "Grace is a certain beauty of soul, which wins the Divine love." But beauty of soul is a quality, even as beauty of body. Therefore grace is a quality.

I answer that, As stated above (Article [1]), there is understood to be an effect of God's gratuitous will in whoever is said to have God's grace. Now it was stated (Question [109], Article [1]) that man is aided by God's gratuitous will in two ways: first, inasmuch as man's soul is moved by God to know or will or do something, and in this way the gratuitous effect in man is not a quality, but a movement of the soul; for "motion is the act of the mover in the moved." Secondly, man is helped by God's gratuitous will, inasmuch as a habitual gift is infused by God into the soul; and for this reason, that it is not fitting that God should provide less for those He loves, that they may acquire supernatural good, than for creatures, whom He loves that they may acquire natural good. Now He so provides for natural creatures, that not merely does He move them to their natural acts, but He bestows upon them certain forms and powers, which are the principles of acts, in order that they may of themselves be inclined to these movements, and thus the movements whereby they are moved by God become natural and easy to creatures, according to Wis. 8:1: "she . . . ordereth all things sweetly." Much more therefore does He infuse into such as He moves towards the acquisition of supernatural good, certain forms or supernatural qualities, whereby they may be moved by Him sweetly and promptly to acquire eternal good; and thus the gift of grace is a quality.

Reply to Objection 1: Grace, as a quality, is said to act upon the soul, not after the manner of an efficient cause, but after the manner of a formal cause, as whiteness makes a thing white, and justice, just.

Reply to Objection 2: Every substance is either the nature of the thing whereof it is the substance or is a part of the nature, even as matter and form are called substance. And because grace is above human nature, it cannot be a substance or a substantial form, but is an accidental form of the soul. Now what is substantially in God, becomes accidental in the soul participating the Divine goodness, as is clear in the case of knowledge. And thus because the soul participates in the Divine goodness imperfectly, the participation of the Divine goodness, which is grace, has its being in the soul in a less perfect way than the soul subsists in itself. Nevertheless, inasmuch as it is the expression or participation of the Divine goodness, it is nobler than the nature of the soul, though not in its mode of being.

Reply to Objection 3: As Boethius [*Pseudo-Bede, Sent. Phil. ex Artist] says, the "being of an accident is to inhere." Hence no accident is called being as if it had being, but because by it something is; hence it is said to belong to a being rather to be a being (Metaph. vii, text. 2). And because to become and to be corrupted belong to what is, properly speaking, no accident comes into being or is corrupted, but is said to come into being and to be corrupted inasmuch as its subject begins or ceases to be in act with this accident. And thus grace is said to be created inasmuch as men are created with reference to it, i.e. are given a new being out of nothing, i.e. not from merits, according to Eph. 2:10, "created in Jesus Christ in good works."

Article: 3

Whether grace is the same as virtue?

Objection 1: It would seem that grace is the same as virtue. For Augustine says (De Spir. et Lit. xiv) that "operating grace is faith that worketh by charity." But faith that worketh by charity is a virtue. Therefore grace is a virtue.

Objection 2: Further, what fits the definition, fits the defined. But the definitions of virtue given by saints and philosophers fit grace, since "it makes its subject good, and his work good," and "it is a good quality of the mind, whereby we live righteously," etc. Therefore grace is virtue.

Objection 3: Further, grace is a quality. Now it is clearly not in the "fourth" species of quality; viz. "form" which is the "abiding figure of things," since it does not belong to bodies. Nor is it in the "third," since it is not a "passion nor a passion-like quality," which is in the sensitive part of the soul, as is proved in Physic. viii; and grace is principally in the mind. Nor is it in the "second" species, which is "natural power" or "impotence"; since grace is above nature and does not regard good and evil, as does natural power. Therefore it must be in the "first" species which is "habit" or "disposition." Now habits of the mind are virtues; since even knowledge itself is a virtue after a manner, as stated above (Question [57], Articles [1],2). Therefore grace is the same as virtue.

On the contrary, If grace is a virtue, it would seem before all to be one of the three theological virtues. But grace is neither faith nor hope, for these can be without sanctifying grace. Nor is it charity, since "grace foreruns charity," as Augustine says in his book on the Predestination of the Saints (De Dono Persev. xvi). Therefore grace is not virtue.

I answer that, Some held that grace and virtue were identical in essence, and differed only logically---in the sense that we speak of grace inasmuch as it makes man pleasing to God, or is given gratuitously---and of virtue inasmuch as it empowers us to act rightly. And the Master seems to have thought this (Sent. ii, D 27).

But if anyone rightly considers the nature of virtue, this cannot hold, since, as the Philosopher says (Physic. vii, text. 17), "virtue is disposition of what is perfect--- and I call perfect what is disposed according to its nature." Now from this it is clear that the virtue of a thing has reference to some pre-existing nature, from the fact that everything is disposed with reference to what befits its nature. But it is manifest that the virtues acquired by human acts of which we spoke above (Question [55], seqq.) are dispositions, whereby a man is fittingly disposed with reference to the nature whereby he is a man; whereas infused virtues dispose man in a higher manner and towards a higher end, and consequently in relation to some higher nature, i.e. in relation to a participation of the Divine Nature, according to 2 Pt. 1:4: "He hath given us most great and most precious promises; that by these you may be made partakers of the Divine Nature." And it is in respect of receiving this nature that we are said to be born again sons of God.

And thus, even as the natural light of reason is something besides the acquired virtues, which are ordained to this natural light, so also the light of grace which is a participation of the Divine Nature is something besides the infused virtues which are derived from and are ordained to this light, hence the Apostle says (Eph. 5:8): "For you were heretofore darkness, but now light in the Lord. Walk then as children of the light." For as the acquired virtues enable a man to walk, in accordance with the natural light of reason, so do the infused virtues enable a man to walk as befits the light of grace.

Reply to Objection 1: Augustine calls "faith that worketh by charity" grace, since the act of faith of him that worketh by charity is the first act by which sanctifying grace is manifested.

Reply to Objection 2: Good is placed in the definition of virtue with reference to its fitness with some pre-existing nature essential or participated. Now good is not attributed to grace in this manner, but as to the root of goodness in man, as stated above.

Reply to Objection 3: Grace is reduced to the first species of quality; and yet it is not the same as virtue, but is a certain disposition which is presupposed to the infused virtues, as their principle and root.

Article: 4

Whether grace is in the essence of the soul as in a subject, or in one of the powers?

Objection 1: It would seem that grace is not in the essence of the soul, as in a subject, but in one of the powers. For Augustine says (Hypognosticon iii [*Among the spurious works of St. Augustine]) that grace is related to the will or to the free will "as a rider to his horse." Now the will or the free will is a power, as stated above (FP, Question [83], Article [2]). Hence grace is in a power of the soul, as in a subject.

Objection 2: Further, "Man's merit springs from grace" as Augustine says (De Gratia et Lib. Arbit. vi). Now merit consists in acts, which proceed from a power. Hence it seems that grace is a perfection of a power of the soul.

Objection 3: Further, if the essence of the soul is the proper subject of grace, the soul, inasmuch as it has an essence, must be capable of grace. But this is false; since it would follow that every soul would be capable of grace. Therefore the essence of the soul is not the proper subject of grace.

Objection 4: Further, the essence of the soul is prior to its powers. Now what is prior may be understood without what is posterior. Hence it follows that grace may be taken to be in the soul, although we suppose no part or power of the soul---viz. neither the will, nor the intellect, nor anything else; which is impossible.

On the contrary, By grace we are born again sons of God. But generation terminates at the essence prior to the powers. Therefore grace is in the soul's essence prior to being in the powers.

I answer that, This question depends on the preceding. For if grace is the same as virtue, it must necessarily be in the powers of the soul as in a subject; since the soul's powers are the proper subject of virtue, as stated above (Question [56], Article [1]). But if grace differs from virtue, it cannot be said that a power of the soul is the subject of grace, since every perfection of the soul's powers has the nature of virtue, as stated above (Question [55], Article [1]; Question [56], Article [1]). Hence it remains that grace, as it is prior to virtue, has a subject prior to the powers of the soul, so that it is in the essence of the soul. For as man in his intellective powers participates in the Divine knowledge through the virtue of faith, and in his power of will participates in the Divine love through the virtue of charity, so also in the nature of the soul does he participate in the Divine Nature, after the manner of a likeness, through a certain regeneration or re-creation.

Reply to Objection 1: As from the essence of the soul flows its powers, which are the principles of deeds, so likewise the virtues, whereby the powers are moved to act, flow into the powers of the soul from grace. And thus grace is compared to the will as the mover to the moved, which is the same comparison as that of a horseman to the horse—but not as an accident to a subject.

And thereby is made clear the Reply to the Second Objection. For grace is the principle of meritorious works through the medium of virtues, as the essence of the soul is the principal of vital deeds through the medium of the powers.

Reply to Objection 3: The soul is the subject of grace, as being in the species of intellectual or rational nature. But the soul is not classed in a species by any of its powers, since the powers are natural properties of the soul following upon the species. Hence the soul differs specifically in its essence from other souls, viz. of dumb animals, and of plants. Consequently it does not follow that, if the essence of the human soul is the subject of grace, every soul may be the subject of grace; since it belongs to the essence of the soul, inasmuch as it is of such a species.

Reply to Objection 4: Since the powers of the soul are natural properties following upon the species, the soul cannot be without them. Yet, granted that it was without them, the soul would still be called intellectual or rational in its species, not that it would actually have these powers, but on account of the essence of such a species, from which these powers naturally flow.

OF THE DIVISION OF GRACE (FIVE ARTICLES)

We must now consider the division of grace; under which head there are five points of inquiry:

(1) Whether grace is fittingly divided into gratuitous grace and sanctifying grace?

(2) Of the division into operating and cooperating grace;

(3) Of the division of it into prevenient and subsequent grace;

(4) Of the division of gratuitous grace;

(5) Of the comparison between sanctifying and gratuitous grace.

Question 111 Article: 1

Whether grace is fittingly divided into sanctifying grace and gratuitous grace?

Objection 1: It would seem that grace is not fittingly divided into sanctifying grace and gratuitous grace. For grace is a gift of God, as is clear from what has been already stated (Question [110], Article [1]). But man is not therefore pleasing to God because something is given him by God, but rather on the contrary; since something is freely given by God, because man is pleasing to Him. Hence there is no sanctifying grace.

Objection 2: Further, whatever is not given on account of preceding merits is given gratis. Now even natural good is given to man without preceding merit, since nature is presupposed to merit. Therefore nature itself is given gratuitously by God. But nature is condivided with grace. Therefore to be gratuitously given is not fittingly set down as a difference of grace, since it is found outside the genus of grace.

Objection 3: Further, members of a division are mutually opposed. But even sanctifying grace, whereby we are justified, is given to us gratuitously, according to Rm. 3:24: "Being justified freely [gratis] by His grace." Hence sanctifying grace ought not to be divided against gratuitous grace.

On the contrary, The Apostle attributes both to grace, viz. to sanctify and to be gratuitously given. For with regard to the first he says (Eph. 1:6): "He hath graced us in His beloved son." And with regard to the second (Rm. 2:6): "And if by grace, it is not now by works, otherwise grace is no more grace." Therefore grace can be distinguished by its having one only or both.

I answer that, As the Apostle says (Rm. 13:1), "those things that are of God are well ordered [Vulg.: 'those that are, are ordained by God]." Now the order of things consists in this, that things are led to God by other things, as Dionysius says (Coel. Hier. iv). And hence since grace is ordained to lead men to God, this takes place in a certain order, so that some are led to God by others.

And thus there is a twofold grace: one whereby man himself is united to God, and this is called "sanctifying grace"; the other is that whereby one man cooperates with another in leading him to God, and this gift is called "gratuitous grace," since it is bestowed on a man beyond the capability of nature, and beyond the merit of the person. But whereas it is bestowed on a man, not to justify him, but rather that he may cooperate in the justification of another, it is not called sanctifying grace. And it is of this that the Apostle says (1 Cor. 12:7): "And the manifestation of the Spirit is given to every man unto utility," i.e. of others.

Reply to Objection 1: Grace is said to make pleasing, not efficiently but formally, i.e. because thereby a man is justified, and is made worthy to be called pleasing to God, according to Col. 1:21: "He hath made us worthy to be made partakers of the lot of the saints in light."

Reply to Objection 2: Grace, inasmuch as it is gratuitously given, excludes the notion of debt. Now debt may be taken in two ways: first, as arising from merit; and this regards the person whose it is to do meritorious works, according to Rm. 4:4: "Now to him that worketh, the reward is not reckoned according to grace, but according to debt." The second debt regards the condition of nature. Thus we say it is due to a man to have reason, and whatever else belongs to human nature. Yet in neither way is debt taken to mean that God is under an obligation to His creature, but rather that the creature ought to be subject to God, that the Divine ordination may be fulfilled in it, which is that a certain nature should have certain conditions or properties, and that by doing certain works it should attain to something further. And hence natural endowments are not a debt in the first sense but in the second. Hence they especially merit the name of grace.

Reply to Objection 3: Sanctifying grace adds to the notion of gratuitous grace something pertaining to the nature of grace, since it makes man pleasing to God. And hence gratuitous grace which does not do this keeps the common name, as happens in many other cases; and thus the two parts of the division are opposed as sanctifying and non-sanctifying grace.

Article: 2

Whether grace is fittingly divided into operating and cooperating grace?

Objection 1: It would seem that grace is not fittingly divided into operating and cooperating grace. For grace is an accident, as stated above (Question

[110], Article [2]). Now no accident can act upon its subject. Therefore no grace can be called operating.

Objection 2: Further, if grace operates anything in us it assuredly brings about justification. But not only grace works this. For Augustine says, on Jn. 14:12, "the works that I do he also shall do," says (Serm. clxix): "He Who created thee without thyself, will not justify thee without thyself." Therefore no grace ought to be called simply operating.

Objection 3: Further, to cooperate seems to pertain to the inferior agent, and not to the principal agent. But grace works in us more than free-will, according to Rm. 9:16: "It is not of him that willeth, nor of him that runneth, but of God that sheweth mercy." Therefore no grace ought to be called cooperating.

Objection 4: Further, division ought to rest on opposition. But to operate and to cooperate are not opposed; for one and the same thing can both operate and cooperate. Therefore grace is not fittingly divided into operating and cooperating.

On the contrary, Augustine says (De Gratia et Lib. Arbit. xvii): "God by cooperating with us, perfects what He began by operating in us, since He who perfects by cooperation with such as are willing, beings by operating that they may will." But the operations of God whereby He moves us to good pertain to grace. Therefore grace is fittingly divided into operating and cooperating.

I answer that, As stated above (Question [110], Article [2]) grace may be taken in two ways; first, as a Divine help, whereby God moves us to will and to act; secondly, as a habitual gift divinely bestowed on us.

Now in both these ways grace is fittingly divided into operating and cooperating. For the operation of an effect is not attributed to the thing moved but to the mover. Hence in that effect in which our mind is moved and does not move, but in which God is the sole mover, the operation is attributed to God, and it is with reference to this that we speak of "operating grace." But in that effect in which our mind both moves and is moved, the operation is not only attributed to God, but also to the soul; and it is with reference to this that we speak of "cooperating grace." Now there is a double act in us. First, there is the interior act of the will, and with regard to this act the will is a thing moved, and God is the mover; and especially when the will, which hitherto willed evil, begins to will good. And hence, inasmuch as God moves the human mind to this act, we speak of operating grace. But there is another, exterior act; and since it is commanded by the will, as was shown above (Question [17], Article [9]) the operation of this act is attributed to the will. And because God assists us in this act, both by strengthening our will interiorly so as to attain to the act, and by granting outwardly the capability of operating, it is with respect to this that we speak of cooperating grace. Hence after the aforesaid words Augustine subjoins: "He operates that we may will; and when we will, He cooperates that we may perfect." And thus if grace is taken for God's gratuitous motion whereby He moves us to meritorious good, it is fittingly divided into operating and cooperating grace.

But if grace is taken for the habitual gift, then again there is a double effect of grace, even as of every other form; the first of which is "being," and the second, "operation"; thus the work of heat is to make its subject hot, and to give heat outwardly. And thus habitual grace, inasmuch as it heals and justifies the soul, or makes it pleasing to God, is called operating grace; but inasmuch as it is the principle of meritorious works, which spring from the free-will, it is called cooperating grace.

Reply to Objection 1: Inasmuch as grace is a certain accidental quality, it does not act upon the soul efficiently, but formally, as whiteness makes a surface white.

Reply to Objection 2: God does not justify us without ourselves, because whilst we are being justified we consent to God's justification [justitiae] by a movement of our free-will. Nevertheless this movement is not the cause of grace, but the effect; hence the whole operation pertains to grace.

Reply to Objection 3: One thing is said to cooperate with another not merely when it is a secondary agent under a principal agent, but when it helps to the end intended. Now man is helped by God to will the good, through the means of operating grace. And hence, the end being already intended, grace cooperates with us.

Reply to Objection 4: Operating and cooperating grace are the same grace; but are distinguished by their different effects, as is plain from what has been said.

Article: 3

Whether grace is fittingly divided into prevenient and subsequent grace?

Objection 1: It would seem that grace is not fittingly divided into prevenient and subsequent. For grace is an effect of the Divine love. But God's love is never subsequent, but always prevenient, according to 1 Jn. 4:10: "Not as though we had loved God, but because He hath first loved us." Therefore grace ought not to be divided into prevenient and subsequent.

Objection 2: Further, there is but one sanctifying grace in man, since it is sufficient, according to 2 Cor. 12:9: "My grace is sufficient for thee." But the same thing cannot be before and after. Therefore grace is not fittingly divided into prevenient and subsequent.

Objection 3: Further, grace is known by its effects. Now there are an infinite number of effects---one preceding another. Hence it with regard to these, grace must be divided into prevenient and subsequent, it would seem that there are infinite species of grace. Now no art takes note of the infinite in number. Hence grace is not fittingly divided into prevenient and subsequent.

On the contrary, God's grace is the outcome of His mercy. Now both are said in Ps. 58:11: "His mercy shall prevent me," and again, Ps. 22:6: "Thy mercy will follow me." Therefore grace is fittingly divided into prevenient and subsequent.

I answer that, As grace is divided into operating and cooperating, with regard to its diverse effects, so also is it divided into prevenient and subsequent, howsoever we consider grace. Now there are five effects of grace in us: of these, the first is, to heal the soul; the second, to desire good; the third, to carry into effect the good proposed; the fourth, to persevere in good; the fifth, to reach glory. And hence grace, inasmuch as it causes the first effect in us, is called prevenient with respect to the second, and inasmuch as it causes the second, it is called subsequent with respect to the first effect. And as one effect is posterior to this effect, and prior to that, so may grace be called prevenient and subsequent on account of the same effect viewed relatively to divers others. And this is what Augustine says (De Natura et Gratia xxxi): "It is prevenient, inasmuch as it heals, and subsequent, inasmuch as, being healed, we are strengthened; it is prevenient, inasmuch as we are called, and subsequent, inasmuch as we are glorified."

Reply to Objection 1: God's love signifies something eternal; and hence can never be called anything but prevenient. But grace signifies a temporal effect, which can precede and follow another; and thus grace may be both prevenient and subsequent.

Reply to Objection 2: The division into prevenient and subsequent grace does not divide grace in its essence, but only in its effects, as was already said of operating and cooperating grace. For subsequent grace, inasmuch as it pertains to glory, is not numerically distinct from prevenient grace whereby we are at present justified. For even as the charity of the earth is not voided in heaven, so must the same be said of the light of grace, since the notion of neither implies imperfection.

Reply to Objection 3: Although the effects of grace may be infinite in number, even as human acts are infinite, nevertheless all reduced to some of a determinate species, and moreover all coincide in this---that one precedes another.

Article: 4 Whether gratuitous grace is rightly divided by the Apostle?

Objection 1: It would seem that gratuitous grace is not rightly divided by the Apostle. For every gift vouchsafed to us by God, may be called a gratuitous grace. Now there are an infinite number of gifts freely bestowed on us by God as regards both the good of the soul and the good of the body---and yet they do not make us pleasing to God. Hence gratuitous graces cannot be contained under any certain division.

Objection 2: Further, gratuitous grace is distinguished from sanctifying grace. But faith pertains to sanctifying grace, since we are justified by it, according to Rm. 5:1: "Being justified therefore by faith." Hence it is not right to place faith amongst the gratuitous graces, especially since the other virtues are not so placed, as hope and charity.

Objection 3: Further, the operation of healing, and speaking divers tongues are miracles. Again, the interpretation of speeches pertains either to wisdom or to knowledge, according to Dan. 1:17: "And to these children God gave knowledge and understanding in every book and wisdom." Hence it is not correct to divide the grace of healing and kinds of tongues against the working of miracles; and the interpretation of speeches against the word of wisdom and knowledge.

Objection 4: Further, as wisdom and knowledge are gifts of the Holy Ghost, so also are understanding, counsel, piety, fortitude, and fear, as stated above (Question [68], Article [4]). Therefore these also ought to be placed amongst the gratuitous gifts.

On the contrary, The Apostle says (1 Cor. 12:8,9,10): "To one indeed by the Spirit is given the word of wisdom; and to another the word of knowledge, according to the same Spirit; to another, the working of miracles; to another, prophecy; to another, the discerning of spirits; to another divers kinds of tongues; to another interpretation of speeches."

I answer that, As was said above (Article [1]), gratuitous grace is ordained to this, viz. that a man may help another to be led to God. Now no man can help in this by moving interiorly (for this belongs to God alone), but only exteriorly by teaching or persuading. Hence gratuitous grace embraces whatever a man needs in order to instruct another in Divine things which are above reason. Now for this three things are required: first, a man must possess the fullness of knowledge of Divine things, so as to be capable of teaching others. Secondly, he must be able to confirm or prove what he says, otherwise his words would have no weight. Thirdly, he must be capable of fittingly presenting to his hearers what he knows.

Now as regards the first, three things are necessary, as may be seen in human teaching. For whoever would teach another in any science must first be certain of the principles of the science, and with regard to this there is "faith," which is certitude of invisible things, the principles of Catholic doctrine. Secondly, it behooves the teacher to know the principal conclusions of the science, and hence we have the word of "wisdom," which is the knowledge of Divine things. Thirdly, he ought to abound with examples and a knowledge of effects, whereby at times he needs to manifest causes; and thus we have the word of "knowledge," which is the knowledge of human things, since "the invisible things of Him . . . are clearly seen, being understood by the things that are made" (Rm. 1:20).

Now the confirmation of such things as are within reason rests upon arguments; but the confirmation of what is above reason rests on what is proper to the Divine power, and this in two ways: first, when the teacher of sacred doctrine does what God alone can do, in miraculous deeds, whether with respect to bodily health---and thus there is the "grace of healing," or merely for the purpose of manifesting the Divine power; for instance, that the sun should stand still or darken, or that the sea should be divided---and thus there is the "working of miracles." Secondly, when he can manifest what God alone can know, and these are either future contingents---and thus there is "prophecy," or also the secrets of hearts---and thus there is the "discerning of spirits."

But the capability of speaking can regard either the idiom in which a person can be understood, and thus there is "kinds of tongues"; or it can regard the sense of what is said, and thus there is the "interpretation of speeches."

Reply to Objection 1: As stated above (Article [1]), not all the benefits divinely conferred upon us are called gratuitous graces, but only those that surpass the power of nature---e.g. that a fisherman should be replete with the word of wisdom and of knowledge and the like; and such as these are here set down as gratuitous graces.

Reply to Objection 2: Faith is enumerated here under the gratuitous graces, not as a virtue justifying man in himself, but as implying a super-eminent certitude of faith, whereby a man is fitted for instructing others concerning such things as belong to the faith. With regard to hope and charity, they belong to the appetitive power, according as man is ordained thereby to God.

Reply to Objection 3: The grace of healing is distinguished from the general working of miracles because it has a special reason for inducing one to the faith, since a man is all the more ready to believe when he has received the gift of bodily health through the virtue of faith. So, too, to speak with divers tongues and to interpret speeches have special efficacy in bestowing faith. Hence they are set down as special gratuitous graces.

Reply to Objection 4: Wisdom and knowledge are not numbered among the gratuitous graces in the same way as they are reckoned among the gifts of the Holy Ghost, i.e. inasmuch as man's mind is rendered easily movable by the Holy Ghost to the things of wisdom and knowledge; for thus they are gifts of the Holy Ghost, as stated above (Question [68], Articles [1],4). But they are numbered amongst the gratuitous graces, inasmuch as they imply such a fullness of knowledge and wisdom that a man may not merely think aright of Divine things, but may instruct others and overpower adversaries. Hence it is significant that it is the "word" of wisdom and the "word" of knowledge that are placed in the gratuitous graces, since, as Augustine says (De Trin. xiv, 1), "It is one thing merely to know what a man must believe in order to reach everlasting life, and another thing to know how this may benefit the godly and may be defended against the ungodly."

Article: 5

Whether gratuitous grace is nobler than sanctifying grace?

Objection 1: It would seem that gratuitous grace is nobler than sanctifying grace. For "the people's good is better than the individual good," as the Philosopher says (Ethic. i, 2). Now sanctifying grace is ordained to the good of one man alone, whereas gratuitous grace is ordained to the common good of the whole Church, as stated above (Articles [1],4). Hence gratuitous grace is nobler than sanctifying grace.

Objection 2: Further, it is a greater power that is able to act upon another, than that which is confined to itself, even as greater is the brightness of the body that can illuminate other bodies, than of that which can only shine but cannot illuminate; and hence the Philosopher says (Ethic. v, 1) "that justice is the most excellent of the virtues," since by it a man bears himself rightly towards others. But by sanctifying grace a man is perfected only in himself; whereas by gratuitous grace a man works for the perfection of others. Hence gratuitous grace is nobler than sanctifying grace.

Objection 3: Further, what is proper to the best is nobler than what is common to all; thus to reason, which is proper to man is nobler than to feel, which is common to all animals. Now sanctifying grace is common to all members of the Church, but gratuitous grace is the proper gift of the more exalted members of the Church. Hence gratuitous grace is nobler than sanctifying grace.

On the contrary, The Apostle (1 Cor. 12:31), having enumerated the gratuitous graces adds: "And I shew unto you yet a more excellent way"; and as the sequel proves he is speaking of charity, which pertains to sanctifying grace. Hence sanctifying grace is more noble than gratuitous grace.

I answer that, The higher the good to which a virtue is ordained, the more excellent is the virtue. Now the end is always greater than the means. But sanctifying grace ordains a man immediately to a union with his last end, whereas gratuitous grace ordains a man to what is preparatory to the end; i.e. by prophecy and miracles and so forth, men are induced to unite themselves to their last end. And hence sanctifying grace is nobler than gratuitous grace.

Reply to Objection 1: As the Philosopher says (Metaph. xii, text. 52), a multitude, as an army, has a double good; the first is in the multitude itself, viz. the order of the army; the second is separate from the multitude, viz. the good of the leader---and this is better good, since the other is ordained to it. Now gratuitous grace is ordained to the common good of the Church, which is ecclesiastical order, whereas sanctifying grace is ordained to the separate common good, which is God. Hence sanctifying grace is the nobler.

Reply to Objection 2: If gratuitous grace could cause a man to have sanctifying grace, it would follow that the gratuitous grace was the nobler; even as the brightness of the sun that enlightens is more excellent than that of an object that is lit up. But by gratuitous grace a man cannot cause another to have union with God, which he himself has by sanctifying grace; but he causes certain dispositions towards it. Hence gratuitous grace needs not to be the more excellent, even as in fire, the heat, which manifests its species whereby it produces heat in other things, is not more noble than its substantial form.

Reply to Objection 3: Feeling is ordained to reason, as to an end; and thus, to reason is nobler. But here it is the contrary; for what is proper is ordained to what is common as to an end. Hence there is no comparison.

OF THE CAUSE OF GRACE (FIVE ARTICLES)

We must now consider the cause of grace; and under this head there are five points of inquiry:

(1) Whether God alone is the efficient cause of grace?
(2) Whether any disposition towards grace is needed on the part of the recipient, by an act of free-will?
(3) Whether such a disposition can make grace follow of necessity?
(4) Whether grace is equal in all?
(5) Whether anyone may know that he has grace?

Question 112 Article: 1

Whether God alone is the cause of grace?

Objection 1: It would seem that God alone is not the cause of grace. For it is written (Jn. 1:17): "Grace and truth came by Jesus Christ." Now, by the name of Jesus Christ is understood not merely the Divine Nature assuming, but the created nature assumed. Therefore a creature may be the cause of grace.

Objection 2: Further, there is this difference between the sacraments of the New Law and those of the Old, that the sacraments of the New Law cause grace, whereas the sacraments of the Old Law merely signify it. Now the sacraments of the New Law are certain visible elements. Therefore God is not the only cause of grace.

Objection 3: Further, according to Dionysius (Coel. Hier. iii, iv, vii, viii), "Angels cleanse, enlighten, and perfect both lesser angels and men." Now the rational creature is cleansed, enlightened, and perfected by grace. Therefore God is not the only cause of grace.

On the contrary, It is written (Ps. 83:12): "The Lord will give grace and glory."

I answer that, Nothing can act beyond its species, since the cause must always be more powerful than its effect. Now the gift of grace surpasses every capability of created nature, since it is nothing short of a partaking of the Divine Nature, which exceeds every other nature. And thus it is impossible that any creature should cause grace. For it is as necessary that God alone should deify, bestowing a partaking of the Divine Nature by a participated likeness, as it is impossible that anything save fire should enkindle.

Reply to Objection 1: Christ's humanity is an "organ of His Godhead," as Damascene says (De Fide Orth. iii, 19). Now an instrument does not bring forth the action of the principal agent by its own power, but in virtue of the principal agent. Hence Christ's humanity does not cause grace by its own power, but by virtue of the Divine Nature joined to it, whereby the actions of Christ's humanity are saving actions.

Reply to Objection 2: As in the person of Christ the humanity causes our salvation by grace, the Divine power being the principal agent, so likewise in the sacraments of the New Law, which are derived from Christ, grace is instrumentally caused by the sacraments, and principally by the power of the Holy Ghost working in the sacraments, according to Jn. 3:5: "Unless a man be born again of water and the Holy Ghost he cannot enter into the kingdom of God."

Reply to Objection 3: Angels cleanse, enlighten, and perfect angels or men, by instruction, and not by justifying them through grace. Hence Dionysius says (Coel. Hier. vii) that "this cleansing and enlightenment and perfecting is nothing else than the assumption of Divine knowledge."

Article: 2

Whether any preparation and disposition for grace is required on man's part?

Objection 1: It would seem that no preparation or disposition for grace is required on man's part, since, as the Apostle says (Rm. 4:4), "To him that worketh, the reward is not reckoned according to grace, but according to debt." Now a man's preparation by free-will can only be through some operation. Hence it would do away with the notion of grace.

Objection 2: Further, whoever is going on sinning, is not preparing himself to have grace. But to some who are going on sinning grace is given, as is clear in the case of Paul, who received grace whilst he was "breathing our threatenings and slaughter against the disciples of the Lord" (Act 9:1). Hence no preparation for grace is required on man's part.

Objection 3: Further, an agent of infinite power needs no disposition in matter, since it does not even require matter, as appears in creation, to which grace is compared, which is called "a new creature" (Gal. 6:15). But only God, Who has infinite power, causes grace, as stated above (Article [1]). Hence no preparation is required on man's part to obtain grace.

On the contrary, It is written (Amos 4:12): "Be prepared to meet thy God, O Israel," and (1 Kgs. 7:3): "Prepare your hearts unto the Lord."

 I answer that, As stated above (Question [111], Article [2]), grace is taken in two ways: first, as a habitual gift of God. Secondly, as a help from God, Who moves the soul to good. Now taking grace in the first sense, a certain preparation of grace is required for it, since a form can only be in disposed matter. But if we speak of grace as it signifies a help from God to move us to good, no preparation is required on man's part, that, as it were, anticipates the Divine help, but rather, every preparation in man must be by the help of God moving the soul to good. And thus even the good movement of the free-will, whereby anyone is prepared for receiving the gift of grace is an act of the free-will moved by God. And thus man is said to prepare himself, according to Prov. 16:1: "It is the part of man to prepare the soul"; yet it is principally from God, Who moves the free-will. Hence it is said that man's will is prepared by God, and that man's steps are guided by God.

Reply to Objection 1: A certain preparation of man for grace is simultaneous with the infusion of grace; and this operation is meritorious, not indeed of grace, which is already possessed---but of glory which is not yet possessed. But there is another imperfect preparation, which sometimes precedes the gift of sanctifying grace, and yet it is from God's motion. But it does not suffice for merit, since man is not yet justified by grace, and merit can only arise from grace, as will be seen further on (Question [114], Article [2]).

Reply to Objection 2: Since a man cannot prepare himself for grace unless God prevent and move him to good, it is of no account whether anyone arrive at perfect preparation instantaneously, or step by step. For it is written (Ecclus. 11:23): "It is easy in the eyes of God on a sudden to make the poor man rich." Now it sometimes happens that God moves a man to good, but not perfect good, and this preparation precedes grace. But He sometimes moves him suddenly and perfectly to good, and man receives grace suddenly, according to Jn. 6:45: "Every one that hath heard of the Father, and hath learned, cometh to Me." And thus it happened to Paul, since, suddenly when he was in the midst of sin, his heart was perfectly moved by God to hear, to learn, to come; and hence he received grace suddenly.

Reply to Objection 3: An agent of infinite power needs no matter or disposition of matter, brought about by the action of something else; and yet, looking to the condition of the thing caused, it must cause, in the thing caused, both the matter and the due disposition for the form. So likewise, when God infuses grace into a soul, no preparation is required which He Himself does not bring about.

Article: 3

Whether grace is necessarily given to whoever prepares himself for it, or to whoever does what he can?

Objection 1: It would seem that grace is necessarily given to whoever prepares himself for grace, or to whoever does what he can, because, on Rm. 5:1, "Being justified . . . by faith, let us have peace," etc. the gloss says: "God welcomes whoever flies to Him, otherwise there would be injustice with Him." But it is impossible for injustice to be with God. Therefore it is impossible for God not to welcome whoever flies to Him. Hence he receives grace of necessity.

Objection 2: Further, Anselm says (De Casu Diaboli. iii) that the reason why God does not bestow grace on the devil, is that he did not wish, nor was he prepared, to receive it. But if the cause be removed, the effect must needs be removed also. Therefore, if anyone is willing to receive grace it is bestowed on them of necessity.

Objection 3: Further, good is diffusive of itself, as appears from Dionysius (Div. Nom. iv). Now the good of grace is better than the good of nature. Hence, since natural forms necessarily come to disposed matter, much more does it seem that grace is necessarily bestowed on whoever prepares himself for grace.

On the contrary, Man is compared to God as clay to the potter, according to Jer. 18:6: "As clay is in the hand of the potter, so are you in My hand." But however much the clay is prepared, it does not necessarily receive its shape from the potter. Hence, however much a man prepares himself, he does not necessarily receive grace from God.

I answer that, As stated above (Article [2]), man's preparation for grace is from God, as Mover, and from the free-will, as moved. Hence the preparation may be looked at in two ways: first, as it is from free-will, and thus there is no necessity that it should obtain grace, since the gift of grace exceeds every preparation of human power. But it may be considered, secondly, as it is from God the Mover, and thus it has a necessity---not indeed of coercion, but of infallibility---as regards what it is ordained to by God, since God's intention cannot fail, according to the saying of Augustine in his book on the Predestination of the Saints (De Dono Persev. xiv) that "by God's good gifts whoever is liberated, is most certainly liberated." Hence if God intends, while moving, that the one whose heart He moves should attain to grace, he will infallibly attain to it, according to Jn. 6:45: "Every one that hath heard of the Father, and hath learned, cometh to Me."

Reply to Objection 1: This gloss is speaking of such as fly to God by a meritorious act of their free-will, already "informed" with grace; for if they did not receive grace, it would be against the justice which He Himself established. Or if it refers to the movement of free-will before grace, it is speaking in the sense that man's flight to God is by a Divine motion, which ought not, in justice, to fail.

Reply to Objection 2: The first cause of the defect of grace is on our part; but the first cause of the bestowal of grace is on God's according to Osee 13:9: "Destruction is thy own, O Israel; thy help is only in Me."

Reply to Objection 3: Even in natural things, the form does not necessarily ensue the disposition of the matter, except by the power of the agent that causes the disposition.

Article: 4

Whether grace is greater in one than in another?

Objection 1: It would seem that grace is not greater in one than in another. For grace is caused in us by the Divine love, as stated above (Question [110], Article [1]). Now it is written (Wis. 6:8): "He made the little and the great and He hath equally care of all." Therefore all obtain grace from Him equally.

Objection 2: Further, whatever is the greatest possible, cannot be more or less. But grace is the greatest possible, since it joins us with our last end. Therefore there is no greater or less in it. Hence it is not greater in one than in another.

Objection 3: Further, grace is the soul's life, as stated above (Question [110], Article [1], ad 2). But there is no greater or less in life. Hence, neither is there in grace.

On the contrary, It is written (Eph. 4:7): "But to every one of us is given grace according to the measure of the giving of Christ." Now what is given in measure, is not given to all equally. Hence all have not an equal grace.

I answer that, As stated above (Question [52], Articles [1],2; Question [56], Articles [1],2), habits can have a double magnitude: one, as regards the end or object, as when a virtue is said to be more noble through being ordained to a greater good; the other on the part of the subject, which more or less participates in the habit inhering to it.

Now as regards the first magnitude, sanctifying grace cannot be greater or less, since, of its nature, grace joins man to the Highest Good, which is God. But as regards the subject, grace can receive more or less, inasmuch as one may be more perfectly enlightened by grace than another. And a certain reason for this is on the part of him who prepares himself for grace; since he who is better prepared for grace, receives more grace. Yet it is not here that we must seek the first cause of this diversity, since man prepares himself, only inasmuch as his free-will is prepared by God. Hence the first cause of this diversity is to be sought on the part of the God, Who dispenses His gifts of grace variously, in order that the beauty and perfection of the Church may result from these various degree; even as He instituted the various conditions of things, that the universe might be perfect. Hence after the Apostle had said (Eph. 4:7): "To every one of us is given grace according to the measure of the giving of Christ," having enumerated the various graces, he adds (Eph. 4:12): "For the perfecting of the saints . . . for the edifying of the body of Christ."

Reply to Objection 1: The Divine care may be looked at in two ways: first, as regards the Divine act, which is simple and uniform; and thus His care looks equally to all, since by one simple act He administers great things and little. But, "secondly," it may be considered in those things which come to be considered by the Divine care; and thus, inequality is found, inasmuch as God by His care provides greater gifts to some, and lesser gifts for others.

Reply to Objection 2: This objection is based on the first kind of magnitude of grace; since grace cannot be greater by ordaining to a greater good, but inasmuch as it more or less ordains to a greater or less participation of the same good. For there may be diversity of intensity and remissness, both in grace and in final glory as regards the subjects' participation.

Reply to Objection 3: Natural life pertains to man's substance, and hence cannot be more or less; but man partakes of the life of grace accidentally, and hence man may possess it more or less.

Article: 5

Whether man can know that he has grace?

Objection 1: It would seem that man can know that he has grace. For grace by its physical reality is in the soul. Now the soul has most certain knowledge of those things that are in it by their physical reality, as appears from Augustine (Gen. ad lit. xii, 31). Hence grace may be known most certainly by one who has grace.

Objection 2: Further, as knowledge is a gift of God, so is grace. But whoever receives knowledge from God, knows that he has knowledge, according to Wis. 7:17: The Lord "hath given me the true knowledge of the things that are." Hence, with equal reason, whoever receives grace from God, knows that he has grace.

Objection 3: Further, light is more knowable than darkness, since, according to the Apostle (Eph. 5:13), "all that is made manifest is light," Now sin, which is spiritual darkness, may be known with certainty by one that is in sin. Much more, therefore, may grace, which is spiritual light, be known.

Objection 4: Further, the Apostle says (1 Cor. 2:12): "Now we have received not the Spirit of this world, but the Spirit that is of God; that we may know the things that are given us from God." Now grace is God's first gift. Hence, the man who receives grace by the Holy Spirit, by the same Holy Spirit knows the grace given to him.

Objection 5: Further, it was said by the Lord to Abraham (Gn. 22:12): "Now I know that thou fearest God," i.e. "I have made thee know." Now He is speaking there of chaste fear, which is not apart from grace. Hence a man may know that he has grace.

On the contrary, It is written (Eccles. 9:1): "Man knoweth not whether he be worthy of love or hatred." Now sanctifying grace maketh a man worthy of God's love. Therefore no one can know whether he has sanctifying grace.

I answer that, There are three ways of knowing a thing: first, by revelation, and thus anyone may know that he has grace, for God by a special privilege reveals this at times to some, in order that the joy of safety may begin in them even in this life, and that they may carry on toilsome works with greater trust and greater energy, and may bear the evils of this present life, as when it was said to Paul (2 Cor. 12:9): "My grace is sufficient for thee."

Secondly, a man may, of himself, know something, and with certainty; and in this way no one can know that he has grace. For certitude about a thing can only be had when we may judge of it by its proper principle. Thus it is by undemonstrable universal principles that certitude is obtained concerning demonstrative conclusions. Now no one can know he has the knowledge of a conclusion if he does not know its principle. But the principle of grace and its object is God, Who by reason of His very excellence is unknown to us, according to Job 36:26: "Behold God is great, exceeding our knowledge." And hence His presence in us and His absence cannot be known with certainty, according to Job 9:11: "If He come to me, I shall not see Him; if He depart I shall not understand." And hence man cannot judge with certainty that he has grace, according to 1 Cor. 4:3,4: "But neither do I judge my own self . . . but He that judgeth me is the Lord."

Thirdly, things are known conjecturally by signs; and thus anyone may know he has grace, when he is conscious of delighting in God, and of despising worldly things and inasmuch as a man is not conscious of any mortal sin. And thus it is written (Apoc. 2:17): "To him that overcometh I will give the hidden manna . . . which no man knoweth, but he that receiveth it," because whoever receives it knows, by experiencing a certain sweetness, which he who does not receive it, does not experience. Yet this knowledge is imperfect; hence the Apostle says (1 Cor. 4:4): "I am not conscious to myself of anything, yet am I not hereby justified," since, according to Ps. 18:13: "Who can understand sins? From my secret ones cleanse me, O Lord, and from those of others spare Thy servant."

Reply to Objection 1: Those things which are in the soul by their physical reality, are known through experimental knowledge; in so far as through acts man has experience of their inward principles: thus when we wish, we perceive that we have a will; and when we exercise the functions of life, we observe that there is life in us.

Reply to Objection 2: It is an essential condition of knowledge that a man should have certitude of the objects of knowledge; and again, it is an essential condition of faith that a man should be certain of the things of faith, and this, because certitude belongs to the perfection of the intellect, wherein these gifts exist. Hence, whoever has knowledge or faith is certain that he has them. But it is otherwise with grace and charity and such like, which perfect the appetitive faculty.

Reply to Objection 3: Sin has for its principal object commutable good, which is known to us. But the object or end of grace is unknown to us on account of the greatness of its light, according to 1 Tim. 6:16: "Who . . . inhabiteth light inaccessible."

Reply to Objection 4: The Apostle is here speaking of the gifts of glory, which have been given to us in hope, and these we know most certainly by faith, although we do not know for certain that we have grace to enable us to merit them. Or it may be said that he is speaking of the privileged knowledge, which comes of revelation. Hence he adds (1 Cor. 2:10): "But to us God hath revealed them by His Spirit."

Reply to Objection 5: What was said to Abraham may refer to experimental knowledge which springs from deeds of which we are cognizant. For in the deed that Abraham had just wrought, he could know experimentally that he had the fear of God. Or it may refer to a revelation.

OF THE EFFECTS OF GRACE (TEN ARTICLES)

We have now to consider the effect of grace; (1) the justification of the ungodly, which is the effect of operating grace; and (2) merit, which is the effect of cooperating grace. Under the first head there are ten points of inquiry:

(1) What is the justification of the ungodly?
(2) Whether grace is required for it?
(3) Whether any movement of the free-will is required?
(4) Whether a movement of faith is required?
(5) Whether a movement of the free-will against sin is required?
(6) Whether the remission of sins is to be reckoned with the foregoing?
(7) Whether the justification of the ungodly is a work of time or is sudden?
(8) Of the natural order of the things concurring to justification;
(9) Whether the justification of the ungodly is God's greatest work?
(10) Whether the justification of the ungodly is miraculous?

Question 113 Article: 1

Whether the justification of the ungodly is the remission of sins?

Objection 1: It would seem that the justification of the ungodly is not the remission of sins. For sin is opposed not only to justice, but to all the other virtues, as stated above (Question [71], Article [1]). Now justification signifies a certain movement towards justice. Therefore not even remission of sin is justification, since movement is from one contrary to the other.

Objection 2: Further, everything ought to be named from what is predominant in it, according to De Anima ii, text. 49. Now the remission of sins is brought about chiefly by faith, according to Acts 15:9: "Purifying their hearts by faith"; and by charity, according to Prov. 10:12: "Charity covereth all sins." Therefore the remission of sins ought to be named after faith or charity rather than justice.

Objection 3: Further, the remission of sins seems to be the same as being called, for whoever is called is afar off, and we are afar off from God by sin. But one is called before being justified according to Rm. 8:30: "And whom He called, them He also justified." Therefore justification is not the remission of sins.

On the contrary, On Rm. 8:30, "Whom He called, them He also justified," the gloss says i.e. "by the remission of sins." Therefore the remission of sins is justification.

I answer that, Justification taken passively implies a movement towards heat. But since justice, by its nature, implies a certain rectitude of order, it may be taken in two ways: first, inasmuch as it implies a right order in man's act, and thus justice is placed amongst the virtues---either as particular justice, which directs a man's acts by regulating them in relation to his fellowman---or as legal justice, which directs a man's acts by regulating them in their relation to the common good of society, as appears from Ethic. v, 1.

Secondly, justice is so-called inasmuch as it implies a certain rectitude of order in the interior disposition of a man, in so far as what is highest in man is subject to God, and the inferior powers of the soul are subject to the superior, i.e. to the reason; and this disposition the Philosopher calls "justice metaphorically speaking" (Ethic. v, 11). Now this justice may be in man in two ways: first, by simple generation, which is from privation to form; and thus justification may belong even to such as are not in sin, when they receive this justice from God, as Adam is said to have received original justice. Secondly, this justice may be brought about in man by a movement from one contrary to the other, and thus justification implies a transmutation from the state of injustice to the aforesaid state of justice. And it is thus we are now speaking of the justification of the ungodly, according to the Apostle (Rm. 4:5): "But to him that worketh not, yet believeth in Him that justifieth the ungodly," etc. And because movement is named after its term "whereto" rather than from its term "whence," the transmutation whereby anyone is changed by the remission of sins from the state of ungodliness to the state of justice, borrows its name from its term "whereto," and is called "justification of the ungodly."

Reply to Objection 1: Every sin, inasmuch as it implies the disorder of a mind not subject to God, may be called injustice, as being contrary to the aforesaid justice, according to 1 Jn. 3:4: "Whosoever committeth sin, committeth also iniquity; and sin is iniquity." And thus the removal of any sin is called the justification of the ungodly.

Reply to Objection 2: Faith and charity imply a special directing of the human mind to God by the intellect and will; whereas justice implies a general rectitude of order. Hence this transmutation is named after justice rather than after charity or faith.

Reply to Objection 3: Being called refers to God's help moving and exciting our mind to give up sin, and this motion of God is not the remission of sins, but its cause.

Article: 2

Whether the infusion of grace is required for the remission of guilt, i.e. for the justification of the ungodly?

Objection 1: It would seem that for the remission of guilt, which is the justification of the ungodly, no infusion of grace is required. For anyone may be moved from one contrary without being led to the other, if the contraries are not immediate. Now the state of guilt and the state of grace are not immediate contraries; for there is the middle state of innocence wherein a man has neither grace nor guilt. Hence a man may be pardoned his guilt without his being brought to a state of grace.

Objection 2: Further, the remission of guilt consists in the Divine imputation, according to Ps. 31:2: "Blessed is the man to whom the Lord hath not imputed sin." Now the infusion of grace puts something into our soul, as stated above (Question [110], Article [1]). Hence the infusion of grace is not required for the remission of guilt.

Objection 3: Further, no one can be subject to two contraries at once. Now some sins are contraries, as wastefulness and miserliness. Hence whoever is subject to the sin of wastefulness is not simultaneously subject to the sin of miserliness, yet it may happen that he has been subject to it hitherto. Hence by sinning with the vice of wastefulness he is freed from the sin of miserliness. And thus a sin is remitted without grace.

On the contrary, It is written (Rm. 3:24): "Justified freely by His grace."

I answer that, by sinning a man offends God as stated above (Question [71], Article [5]). Now an offense is remitted to anyone, only when the soul of the offender is at peace with the offended. Hence sin is remitted to us, when God is at peace with us, and this peace consists in the love whereby God loves us. Now God's love, considered on the part of the Divine act, is eternal and unchangeable; whereas, as regards the effect it imprints on us, it is sometimes interrupted, inasmuch as we sometimes fall short of it and once more require it. Now the effect of the Divine love in us, which is taken away by sin, is grace, whereby a man is made worthy of eternal life, from which sin shuts him out. Hence we could not conceive the remission of guilt, without the infusion of grace.

Reply to Objection 1: More is required for an offender to pardon an offense, than for one who has committed no offense, not to be hated. For it may happen amongst men that one man neither hates nor loves another. But if the other offends him, then the forgiveness of the offense can only spring from a special goodwill. Now God's goodwill is said to be restored to man by the gift of grace; and hence although a man before sinning may be without grace and without guilt, yet that he is without guilt after sinning can only be because he has grace.

Reply to Objection 2: As God's love consists not merely in the act of the Divine will but also implies a certain effect of grace, as stated above (Question [110], Article [1]), so likewise, when God does not impute sin to a man, there is implied a certain effect in him to whom the sin is not imputed; for it proceeds from the Divine love, that sin is not imputed to a man by God.

Reply to Objection 3: As Augustine says (De Nup. et Concup. i, 26), if to leave off sinning was the same as to have no sin, it would be enough if Scripture warned us thus: "'My son, hast thou sinned? do so no more?' Now this is not enough, but it is added: 'But for thy former sins also pray that they may be forgiven thee.'" For the act of sin passes, but the guilt remains, as stated above (Question [87], Article [6]). Hence when anyone passes from the sin of one vice to the sin of a contrary vice, he ceases to have the act of the former sin, but he does not cease to have the guilt, hence he may have the guilt of both sins at once. For sins are not contrary to each other on the part of their turning from God, wherein sin has its guilt.

Article: 3

Whether for the justification of the ungodly is required a movement of the free-will?

Objection 1: It would seem that no movement of the free-will is required for the justification of the ungodly. For we see that by the sacrament of Baptism, infants and sometimes adults are justified without a movement of their free-will: hence Augustine says (Confess. iv) that when one of his friends was taken with a fever, "he lay for a long time senseless and in a deadly sweat, and when he was despaired of, he was baptized without his knowing, and was regenerated"; which is effected by sanctifying grace. Now God does not confine His power to the sacraments. Hence He can justify a man without the sacraments, and without any movement of the free-will.

Objection 2: Further, a man has not the use of reason when asleep, and without it there can be no movement of the free-will. But Solomon received from God the gift of wisdom when asleep, as related in 3 Kgs. 3 and 2 Paral 1. Hence with equal reason the gift of sanctifying grace is sometimes bestowed by God on man without the movement of his free-will.

Objection 3: Further, grace is preserved by the same cause as brings it into being, for Augustine says (Gen. ad lit. viii, 12) that "so ought man to turn to God as he is ever made just by Him." Now grace is preserved in man without a movement of his free-will. Hence it can be infused in the beginning without a movement of the free-will.

On the contrary, It is written (Jn. 6:45): "Every one that hath heard of the Father, and hath learned, cometh to Me." Now to learn cannot be without a movement of the free-will, since the learner assents to the teacher. Hence, no one comes to the Father by justifying grace without a movement of the free-will.

I answer that, The justification of the ungodly is brought about by God moving man to justice. For He it is "that justifieth the ungodly" according to Rm. 4:5.

Now God moves everything in its own manner, just as we see that in natural things, what is heavy and what is light are moved differently, on account of their diverse natures. Hence He moves man to justice according to the condition of his human nature. But it is man's proper nature to have free-will. Hence in him who has the use of reason, God's motion to justice does not take place without a movement of the free-will; but He so infuses the gift of justifying grace that at the same time He moves the free-will to accept the gift of grace, in such as are capable of being moved thus.

Reply to Objection 1: Infants are not capable of the movement of their free-will; hence it is by the mere infusion of their souls that God moves them to justice. Now this cannot be brought about without a sacrament; because as original sin, from which they are justified, does not come to them from their own will, but by carnal generation, so also is grace given them by Christ through spiritual regeneration. And the same reason holds good with madmen and idiots that have never had the use of their free-will. But in the case of one who has had the use of his free-will and afterwards has lost it either through sickness or sleep, he does not obtain justifying grace by the exterior rite of Baptism, or of any other sacrament, unless he intended to make use of this sacrament, and this can only be by the use of his free-will. And it was in this way that he of whom Augustine speaks was regenerated, because both previously and afterwards he assented to the Baptism.

Reply to Objection 2: Solomon neither merited nor received wisdom whilst asleep; but it was declared to him in his sleep that on account of his previous desire wisdom would be infused into him by God. Hence it is said in his person (Wis. 7:7): "I wished, and understanding was given unto me."

Or it may be said that his sleep was not natural, but was the sleep of prophecy, according to Num. 12:6: "If there be among you a prophet of the Lord, I will appear to him in a vision, or I will speak to him in a dream." In such cases the use of free-will remains.

And yet it must be observed that the comparison between the gift of wisdom and the gift of justifying grace does not hold. For the gift of justifying grace especially ordains a man to good, which is the object of the will; and hence a man is moved to it by a movement of the will which is a movement of free-will. But wisdom perfects the intellect which precedes the will; hence without any complete movement of the free-will, the intellect can be enlightened with the gift of wisdom, even as we see that things are revealed to men in sleep, according to Job 33:15,16: "When deep sleep falleth upon men and they are sleeping in their beds, then He openeth the ears of men, and teaching, instructeth them in what they are to learn."

Reply to Objection 3: In the infusion of justifying grace there is a certain transmutation of the human soul, and hence a proper movement of the human soul is required in order that the soul may be moved in its own manner. But the conservation of grace is without transmutation: no movement on the part of the soul is required but only a continuation of the Divine influx.

Article: 4

Whether a movement of faith is required for the justification of the ungodly?

Objection 1: It would seem that no movement of faith is required for the justification of the ungodly. For as a man is justified by faith, so also by other things, viz. by fear, of which it is written (Ecclus. 1:27): "The fear of the Lord driveth out sin, for he that is without fear cannot be justified"; and again by charity, according to Lk. 7:47: "Many sins are forgiven her because she hath loved much"; and again by humility, according to James 4:6: "God resisteth the proud and giveth grace to the humble"; and again by mercy, according to Prov. 15:27: "By mercy and faith sins are purged away." Hence the movement of faith is no more required for the justification of the ungodly, than the movements of the aforesaid virtues.

Objection 2: Further, the act of faith is required for justification only inasmuch as a man knows God by faith. But a man may know God in other ways, viz. by natural knowledge, and by the gift of wisdom. Hence no act of faith is required for the justification of the ungodly.

Objection 3: Further, there are several articles of faith. Therefore if the act of faith is required for the justification of the ungodly, it would seem that a man ought to think on every article of faith when he is first justified. But this seems inconvenient, since such thought would require a long delay of time. Hence it seems that an act of faith is not required for the justification of the ungodly.

On the contrary, It is written (Rm. 5:1): "Being justified therefore by faith, let us have peace with God."

I answer that, As stated above (Article [3]) a movement of free-will is required for the justification of the ungodly, inasmuch as man's mind is moved by God. Now God moves man's soul by turning it to Himself according to Ps. 84:7 (Septuagint): "Thou wilt turn us, O God, and bring us to life." Hence for the justification of the ungodly a movement of the mind is required, by which it is turned to God. Now the first turning to God is by faith, according to Heb. 11:6: "He that cometh to God must believe that He is." Hence a movement of faith is required for the justification of the ungodly.

Reply to Objection 1: The movement of faith is not perfect unless it is quickened by charity; hence in the justification of the ungodly, a movement of charity is infused together with the movement of faith. Now free-will is moved to God by being subject to Him; hence an act of filial fear and an act of humility also concur. For it may happen that one and the same act of free-will springs from different virtues, when one commands and another is commanded, inasmuch as the act may be ordained to various ends. But the act of mercy counteracts sin either by way of satisfying for it, and thus it follows justification; or by way of preparation, inasmuch as the merciful obtain mercy; and thus it can either precede justification, or concur with the other virtues towards justification, inasmuch as mercy is included in the love of our neighbor.

Reply to Objection 2: By natural knowledge a man is not turned to God, according as He is the object of beatitude and the cause of justification. Hence such knowledge does not suffice for justification. But the gift of wisdom presupposes the knowledge of faith, as stated above (Question [68], Article [4], ad 3).

Reply to Objection 3: As the Apostle says (Rm. 4:5), "to him that . . . believeth in Him that justifieth the ungodly his faith is reputed to justice, according to the purpose of the grace of God." Hence it is clear that in the justification of the ungodly an act of faith is required in order that a man may believe that God justifies man through the mystery of Christ.

Article: 5

Whether for the justification of the ungodly there is required a movement of the free-will towards sin?

Objection 1: It would seem that no movement of the free-will towards sin is required for the justification of the ungodly. For charity alone suffices to take away sin, according to Prov. 10:12: "Charity covereth all sins." Now the object of charity is not sin. Therefore for this justification of the ungodly no movement of the free-will towards sin is required.

Objection 2: Further, whoever is tending onward, ought not to look back, according to Phil. 3:13,14: "Forgetting the things that are behind, and stretching forth myself to those that are before, I press towards the mark, to the prize of the supernal vocation." But whoever is stretching forth to righteousness has his sins behind him. Hence he ought to forget them, and not stretch forth to them by a movement of his free-will.

Objection 3: Further, in the justification of the ungodly one sin is not remitted without another, for "it is irreverent to expect half a pardon from God" [*Cap., Sunt. plures: Dist. iii, De Poenit.]. Hence, in the justification of the ungodly, if man's free-will must move against sin, he ought to think of all his sins. But this is unseemly, both because a great space of time would be required for such thought, and because a man could not obtain the forgiveness of such sins as he had forgotten. Hence for the justification of the ungodly no movement of the free-will is required.

On the contrary, It is written (Ps. 31:5): "I will confess against myself my injustice to the Lord; and Thou hast forgiven the wickedness of my sin."

I answer that, As stated above (Article [1]), the justification of the ungodly is a certain movement whereby the human mind is moved by God from the state of sin to the state of justice. Hence it is necessary for the human mind to regard both extremes by an act of free-will, as a body in local movement is related to both terms of the movement. Now it is clear that in local movement the moving body leaves the term "whence" and nears the term "whereto." Hence the human mind whilst it is being justified, must, by a movement of its free-will withdraw from sin and draw near to justice.

Now to withdraw from sin and to draw near to justice, in an act of free-will, means detestation and desire. For Augustine says on the words "the hireling fleeth," etc. (Jn. 10:12): "Our emotions are the movements of our soul; joy is the soul's outpouring; fear is the soul's flight; your soul goes forward when you seek; your soul flees, when you are afraid." Hence in the justification of the ungodly there must be two acts of the free-will---one, whereby it tends to God's justice; the other whereby it hates sin.

Reply to Objection 1: It belongs to the same virtue to seek one contrary and to avoid the other; and hence, as it belongs to charity to love God, so likewise, to detest sin whereby the soul is separated from God.

Reply to Objection 2: A man ought not to return to those things that are behind, by loving them; but, for that matter, he ought to forget them, lest he be drawn to them. Yet he ought to recall them to mind, in order to detest them; for this is to fly from them.

Reply to Objection 3: Previous to justification a man must detest each sin he remembers to have committed, and from this remembrance the soul goes on to have a general movement of detestation with regard to all sins committed, in which are included such sins as have been forgotten. For a man is then in such a frame of mind that he would be sorry even for those he does not remember, if they were present to his memory; and this movement cooperates in his justification.

Article: 6 Whether the remission of sins ought to be reckoned amongst the things required for justification?

Objection 1: It would seem that the remission of sins ought not to be reckoned amongst the things required for justification. For the substance of a thing is not reckoned together with those that are required for a thing; thus a man is not reckoned together with his body and soul. But the justification of the ungodly is itself the remission of sins, as stated above (Article [1]). Therefore the remission of sins ought not to be reckoned among the things required for the justification of the ungodly.

Objection 2: Further, infusion of grace and remission of sins are the same; as illumination and expulsion of darkness are the same. But a thing ought not to be reckoned together with itself; for unity is opposed to multitude. Therefore the remission of sins ought not to be reckoned with the infusion of grace.

Objection 3: Further, the remission of sin follows as effect from cause, from the free-will's movement towards God and sin; since it is by faith and contrition that sin is forgiven. But an effect ought not to be reckoned with its cause; since things thus enumerated together, and, as it were, condivided, are by nature simultaneous. Hence the remission of sins ought not to be reckoned with the things required for the justification of the ungodly.

On the contrary, In reckoning what is required for a thing we ought not to pass over the end, which is the chief part of everything. Now the remission of sins is the end of the justification of the ungodly; for it is written (Is. 27:9): "This is all the fruit, that the sin thereof should be taken away." Hence the remission of sins ought to be reckoned amongst the things required for justification.

I answer that, There are four things which are accounted to be necessary for the justification of the ungodly, viz. the infusion of grace, the movement of the free-will towards God by faith, the movement of the free-will towards sin, and the remission of sins. The reason for this is that, as stated above (Article [1]), the justification of the ungodly is a movement whereby the soul is moved by God from a state of sin to a state of justice. Now in the movement whereby one thing is moved by another, three things are required: first, the motion of the mover; secondly, the movement of the moved; thirdly, the consummation of the movement, or the attainment of the end. On the part of the Divine motion, there is the infusion of grace; on the part of the free-will which is moved, there are two movements---of departure from the term "whence," and of approach to the term "whereto"; but the consummation of the movement or the attainment of the end of the movement is implied in the remission of sins; for in this is the justification of the ungodly completed.

Reply to Objection 1: The justification of the ungodly is called the remission of sins, even as every movement has its species from its term. Nevertheless, many other things are required in order to reach the term, as stated above (Article [5]).

Reply to Objection 2: The infusion of grace and the remission of sin may be considered in two ways: first, with respect to the substance of the act, and thus they are the same; for by the same act God bestows grace and remits sin. Secondly, they may be considered on the part of the objects; and thus they differ by the difference between guilt, which is taken away, and grace, which is infused; just as in natural things generation and corruption differ, although the generation of one thing is the corruption of another.

Reply to Objection 3: This enumeration is not the division of a genus into its species, in which the things enumerated must be simultaneous; but it is division of the things required for the completion of anything; and in this enumeration we may have what precedes and what follows, since some of the principles and parts of a composite thing may precede and some follow.

Article: 7

Whether the justification of the ungodly takes place in an instant or successively?

Objection 1: It would seem that the justification of the ungodly does not take place in an instant, but successively, since, as already stated (Article [3]), for the justification of the ungodly, there is required a movement of free-will. Now the act of the free-will is choice, which requires the deliberation of counsel, as stated above (Question [13], Article [1]). Hence, since deliberation implies a certain reasoning process, and this implies succession, the justification of the ungodly would seem to be successive.

Objection 2: Further, the free-will's movement is not without actual consideration. But it is impossible to understand many things actually and at once, as stated above (FP, Question [85], Article [4]). Hence, since for the justification of the ungodly there is required a movement of the free-will towards several things, viz. towards God and towards sin, it would seem impossible for the justification of the ungodly to be in an instant.

Objection 3: Further, a form that may be greater or less, e.g. blackness or whiteness, is received successively by its subject. Now grace may be greater or less, as stated above (Question [112], Article [4]). Hence it is not received suddenly by its subject. Therefore, seeing that the infusion of grace is required for the justification of the ungodly, it would seem that the justification of the ungodly cannot be in an instant.

Objection 4: Further, the free-will's movement, which cooperates in justification, is meritorious; and hence it must proceed from grace, without which there is no merit, as we shall state further on (Question [114], Article [2]). Now a thing receives its form before operating by this form. Hence grace is first infused, and then the free-will is moved towards God and to detest sin. Hence justification is not all at once.

Objection 5: Further, if grace is infused into the soul, there must be an instant when it first dwells in the soul; so, too, if sin is forgiven there must be a last instant that man is in sin. But it cannot be the same instant, otherwise opposites would be in the same simultaneously. Hence they must be two successive instants; between which there must be time, as the Philosopher says (Phys. vi, 1). Therefore the justification of the ungodly takes place not all at once, but successively.

On the contrary, The justification of the ungodly is caused by the justifying grace of the Holy Spirit. Now the Holy Spirit comes to men's minds suddenly, according to Acts 2:2: "And suddenly there came a sound from heaven as of a mighty wind coming," upon which the gloss says that "the grace of the Holy Ghost knows no tardy efforts." Hence the justification of the ungodly is not successive, but instantaneous.

I answer that, The entire justification of the ungodly consists as to its origin in the infusion of grace. For it is by grace that free-will is moved and sin is remitted. Now the infusion of grace takes place in an instant and without succession. And the reason of this is that if a form be not suddenly impressed upon its subject, it is either because that subject is not disposed, or because the agent needs time to dispose the subject. Hence we see that immediately the matter is disposed by a preceding alteration, the substantial form accrues to the matter; thus because the atmosphere of itself is disposed to receive light, it is suddenly illuminated by a body actually luminous. Now it was stated (Question [112], Article [2]) that God, in order to infuse grace into the soul, needs no disposition, save what He Himself has made. And sometimes this sufficient disposition for the reception of grace He makes suddenly, sometimes gradually and successively, as stated above (Question [112], Article [2], ad 2). For the reason why a natural agent cannot suddenly dispose matter is that in the matter there is a resistant which has some disproportion with the power of the agent; and hence we see that the stronger the agent, the more speedily is the matter disposed. Therefore, since the Divine power is infinite, it can suddenly dispose any matter whatsoever to its form; and much more man's free-will, whose movement is by nature instantaneous. Therefore the justification of the ungodly by God takes place in an instant.

Reply to Objection 1: The movement of the free-will, which concurs in the justification of the ungodly, is a consent to detest sin, and to draw near to God; and this consent takes place suddenly. Sometimes, indeed, it happens that deliberation precedes, yet this is not of the substance of justification, but a way of justification; as local movement is a way of illumination, and alteration to generation.

Reply to Objection 2: As stated above (FP, Question [85], Article [5]), there is nothing to prevent two things being understood at once, in so far as they are somehow one; thus we understand the subject and predicate together, inasmuch as they are united in the order of one affirmation. And in the same manner can the free-will be moved to two things at once in so far as one is ordained to the other. Now the free-will's movement towards sin is ordained to the free-will's movement towards God, since a man detests sin, as contrary to God, to Whom he wishes to cling. Hence in the justification of the ungodly the free-will simultaneously detests sin and turns to God, even as a body approaches one point and withdraws from another simultaneously.

Reply to Objection 3: The reason why a form is not received instantaneously in the matter is not the fact that it can inhere more or less; for thus the light would not be suddenly received in the air, which can be illumined more or less. But the reason is to be sought on the part of the disposition of the matter or subject, as stated above.

Reply to Objection 4: The same instant the form is acquired, the thing begins to operate with the form; as fire, the instant it is generated moves upwards, and if its movement was instantaneous, it would be terminated in the same instant. Now to will and not to will---the movements of the free-will---are not successive, but instantaneous. Hence the justification of the ungodly must not be successive.

Reply to Objection 5: The succession of opposites in the same subject must be looked at differently in the things that are subject to time and in those that are above time. For in those that are in time, there is no last instant in which the previous form inheres in the subject; but there is the last time, and the first instant that the subsequent form inheres in the matter or subject; and this for the reason, that in time we are not to consider one instant, since neither do instants succeed each other immediately in time, nor points in a line, as is proved in Physic. vi, 1. But time is terminated by an instant. Hence in the whole of the previous time wherein anything is moving towards its form, it is under the opposite form; but in the last instant of this time, which is the first instant of the subsequent time, it has the form which is the term of the movement.

But in those that are above time, it is otherwise. For if there be any succession of affections or intellectual conceptions in them (as in the angels), such succession is not measured by continuous time, but by discrete time, even as the things measured are not continuous, as stated above (FP, Question [53], Articles [2],3). In these, therefore, there is a last instant in which the preceding is, and a first instant in which the subsequent is. Nor must there be time in between, since there is no continuity of time, which this would necessitate.

Now the human mind, which is justified, is, in itself, above time, but is subject to time accidentally, inasmuch as it understands with continuity and time, with respect to the phantasms in which it considers the intelligible species, as stated above (FP, Question [85], Articles [1],2). We must, therefore, decide from this about its change as regards the condition of temporal movements, i.e. we must say that there is no last instant that sin inheres, but a last time; whereas there is a first instant that grace inheres; and in all the time previous sin inhered.

Article: 8

Whether the infusion of grace is naturally the first of the things required for the justification of the ungodly?

Objection 1: It would seem that the infusion of grace is not what is naturally required first for the justification of the ungodly. For we withdraw from evil before drawing near to good, according to Ps. 33:15: "Turn away from evil, and do good." Now the remission of sins regards the turning away from evil, and the infusion of grace regards the turning to good. Hence the remission of sin is naturally before the infusion of grace.

Objection 2: Further, the disposition naturally precedes the form to which it disposes. Now the free-will's movement is a disposition for the reception of grace. Therefore it naturally precedes the infusion of grace.

Objection 3: Further, sin hinders the soul from tending freely to God. Now a hindrance to movement must be removed before the movement takes place. Hence the remission of sin and the free-will's movement towards sin are naturally before the infusion of grace.

On the contrary, The cause is naturally prior to its effect. Now the infusion of grace is the cause of whatever is required for the justification of the ungodly, as stated above (Article [7]). Therefore it is naturally prior to it.

I answer that, The aforesaid four things required for the justification of the ungodly are simultaneous in time, since the justification of the ungodly is not successive, as stated above (Article [7]); but in the order of nature, one is prior to another; and in their natural order the first is the infusion of grace; the second, the free-will's movement towards God; the third, the free-will's movement towards sin; the fourth, the remission of sin.

The reason for this is that in every movement the motion of the mover is naturally first; the disposition of the matter, or the movement of the moved, is second; the end or term of the movement in which the motion of the mover rests, is last. Now the motion of God the Mover is the infusion of grace, as stated above (Article [6]); the movement or disposition of the moved is the free-will's double movement; and the term or end of the movement is the remission of sin, as stated above (Article [6]). Hence in their natural order the first in the justification of the ungodly is the infusion of grace; the second is the free-will's movement towards God; the third is the free-will's movement towards sin, for he who is being justified detests sin because it is against God, and thus the free-will's movement towards God naturally precedes the free-will's movement towards sin, since it is its cause and reason; the fourth and last is the remission of sin, to which this transmutation is ordained as to an end, as stated above (Articles [1],6).

Reply to Objection 1: The withdrawal from one term and approach to another may be looked at in two ways: first, on the part of the thing moved, and thus the withdrawal from a term naturally precedes the approach to a term, since in the subject of movement the opposite which is put away is prior to the opposite which the subject moved attains to by its movement. But on the part of the agent it is the other way about, since the agent, by the form pre-existing in it, acts for the removal of the opposite form; as the sun by its light acts for the removal of darkness, and hence on the part of the sun, illumination is prior to the removal of darkness; but on the part of the atmosphere to be illuminated, to be freed from darkness is, in the order of nature, prior to being illuminated, although both are simultaneous in time. And since the infusion of grace and the remission of sin regard God Who justifies, hence in the order of nature the infusion of grace is prior to the freeing from sin. But if we look at what is on the part of the man justified, it is the other way about, since in the order of nature the being freed from sin is prior to the obtaining of justifying grace. Or it may be said that the term "whence" of justification is sin; and the term "whereto" is justice; and that grace is the cause of the forgiveness of sin and of obtaining of justice.

Reply to Objection 2: The disposition of the subject precedes the reception of the form, in the order of nature; yet it follows the action of the agent, whereby the subject is disposed. And hence the free-will's movement precedes the reception of grace in the order of nature, and follows the infusion of grace.

Reply to Objection 3: As the Philosopher says (Phys. ii, 9), in movements of the soul the movement toward the speculative principle or the practical end is the very first, but in exterior movements the removal of the impediment precedes the attainment of the end. And as the free-will's movement is a movement of the soul, in the order of nature it moves towards God as to its end, before removing the impediment of sin.

Article: 9

Whether the justification of the ungodly is God's greatest work?

Objection 1: It would seem that the justification of the ungodly is not God's greatest work. For it is by the justification of the ungodly that we attain the grace of a wayfarer. Now by glorification we receive heavenly grace, which is greater. Hence the glorification of angels and men is a greater work than the justification of the ungodly.

Objection 2: Further, the justification of the ungodly is ordained to the particular good of one man. But the good of the universe is greater than the good of one man, as is plain from Ethic. i, 2. Hence the creation of heaven and earth is a greater work than the justification of the ungodly.

Objection 3: Further, to make something from nothing, where there is nought to cooperate with the agent, is greater than to make something with the cooperation of the recipient. Now in the work of creation something is made from nothing, and hence nothing can cooperate with the agent; but in the justification of the ungodly God makes something from something, i.e. a just man from a sinner, and there is a cooperation on man's part, since there is a movement of the free-will, as stated above (Article [3]). Hence the justification of the ungodly is not God's greatest work.

On the contrary, It is written (Ps. 144:9): "His tender mercies are over all His works," and in a collect [*Tenth Sunday after Pentecost] we say: "O God, Who dost show forth Thine all-mightiness most by pardoning and having mercy," and Augustine, expounding the words, "greater than these shall he do" (Jn. 14:12) says that "for a just man to be made from a sinner, is greater than to create heaven and earth."

I answer that, A work may be called great in two ways: first, on the part of the mode of action, and thus the work of creation is the greatest work, wherein something is made from nothing; secondly, a work may be called great on account of what is made, and thus the justification of the ungodly, which terminates at the eternal good of a share in the Godhead, is greater than the creation of heaven and earth, which terminates at the good of mutable nature. Hence, Augustine, after saying that "for a just man to be made from a sinner is greater than to create heaven and earth," adds, "for heaven and earth shall pass away, but the justification of the ungodly shall endure."

Again, we must bear in mind that a thing is called great in two ways: first, in an absolute quantity, and thus the gift of glory is greater than the gift of grace that sanctifies the ungodly; and in this respect the glorification of the just is greater than the justification of the ungodly. Secondly, a thing may be said to be great in proportionate quantity, and thus the gift of grace that justifies the ungodly is greater than the gift of glory that beatifies the just, for the gift of grace exceeds the worthiness of the ungodly, who are worthy of punishment, more than the gift of glory exceeds the worthiness of the just, who by the fact of their justification are worthy of glory. Hence Augustine says: "Let him that can, judge whether it is greater to create the angels just, than to justify the ungodly. Certainly, if they both betoken equal power, one betokens greater mercy."

And thus the reply to the first is clear.

Reply to Objection 2: The good of the universe is greater than the particular good of one, if we consider both in the same genus. But the good of grace in one is greater than the good of nature in the whole universe.

Reply to Objection 3: This objection rests on the manner of acting, in which way creation is God's greatest work.

Article: 10

Whether the justification of the ungodly is a miraculous work?

Objection 1: It would seem that the justification of the ungodly is a miraculous work. For miraculous works are greater than non-miraculous. Now the justification of the ungodly is greater than the other miraculous works, as is clear from the quotation from Augustine (Article [9]). Hence the justification of the ungodly is a miraculous work.

Objection 2: Further, the movement of the will in the soul is like the natural inclination in natural things. But when God works in natural things against their inclination of their nature, it is a miraculous work, as when He gave sight to the blind or raised the dead. Now the will of the ungodly is bent on evil. Hence, since God in justifying a man moves him to good, it would seem that the justification of the ungodly is miraculous.

Objection 3: Further, as wisdom is a gift of God, so also is justice. Now it is miraculous that anyone should suddenly obtain wisdom from God without study. Therefore it is miraculous that the ungodly should be justified by God.

On the contrary, Miraculous works are beyond natural power. Now the justification of the ungodly is not beyond natural power; for Augustine says (De Praed. Sanct. v) that "to be capable of having faith and to be capable of having charity belongs to man's nature; but to have faith and charity belongs to the grace of the faithful." Therefore the justification of the ungodly is not miraculous.

I answer that, In miraculous works it is usual to find three things: the first is on the part of the active power, because they can only be performed by Divine power; and they are simply wondrous, since their cause is hidden, as stated above (FP, Question [105], Article [7]). And thus both the justification of the ungodly and the creation of the world, and, generally speaking, every work that can be done by God alone, is miraculous.

Secondly, in certain miraculous works it is found that the form introduced is beyond the natural power of such matter, as in the resurrection of the dead, life is above the natural power of such a body. And thus the justification of the ungodly is not miraculous, because the soul is naturally capable of grace; since from its having been made to the likeness of God, it is fit to receive God by grace, as Augustine says, in the above quotation.

Thirdly, in miraculous works something is found besides the usual and customary order of causing an effect, as when a sick man suddenly and beyond the wonted course of healing by nature or art, receives perfect health; and thus the justification of the ungodly is sometimes miraculous and sometimes not. For the common and wonted course of justification is that God moves the soul interiorly and that man is converted to God, first by an imperfect conversion, that it may afterwards become perfect; because "charity begun merits increase, and when increased merits perfection," as Augustine says (In Epist. Joan. Tract. v). Yet God sometimes moves the soul so vehemently that it reaches the perfection of justice at once, as took place in the conversion of Paul, which was accompanied at the same time by a miraculous external prostration. Hence the conversion of Paul is commemorated in the Church as miraculous.

Reply to Objection 1: Certain miraculous works, although they are less than the justification of the ungodly, as regards the good caused, are beyond the wonted order of such effects, and thus have more of the nature of a miracle.

Reply to Objection 2: It is not a miraculous work, whenever a natural thing is moved contrary to its inclination, otherwise it would be miraculous for water to be heated, or for a stone to be thrown upwards; but only whenever this takes place beyond the order of the proper cause, which naturally does this. Now no other cause save God can justify the ungodly, even as nothing save fire can heat water. Hence the justification of the ungodly by God is not miraculous in this respect.

Reply to Objection 3: A man naturally acquires wisdom and knowledge from God by his own talent and study. Hence it is miraculous when a man is made wise or learned outside this order. But a man does not naturally acquire justifying grace by his own action, but by God's. Hence there is no parity.

OF MERIT (TEN ARTICLES)

We must now consider merit, which is the effect of cooperating grace; and under this head there are ten points of inquiry:

(1) Whether a man can merit anything from God?
(2) Whether without grace anyone can merit eternal life?
(3) Whether anyone with grace may merit eternal life condignly?
(4) Whether it is chiefly through the instrumentality of charity that grace is the principle of merit?
(5) Whether a man may merit the first grace for himself?
(6) Whether he may merit it for someone else?
(7) Whether anyone can merit restoration after sin?
(8) Whether he can merit for himself an increase of grace or charity?
(9) Whether he can merit final perseverance?
(10) Whether temporal goods fall under merit?

Question 114 Article: 1

Whether a man may merit anything from God?

Objection 1: It would seem that a man can merit nothing from God. For no one, it would seem, merits by giving another his due. But by all the good we do, we cannot make sufficient return to God, since yet more is His due, as also the Philosopher says (Ethic. viii, 14). Hence it is written (Lk. 17:10): "When you have done all these things that are commanded you, say: We are unprofitable servants; we have done that which we ought to do." Therefore a man can merit nothing from God.

Objection 2: Further, it would seem that a man merits nothing from God, by what profits himself only, and profits God nothing. Now by acting well, a man profits himself or another man, but not God, for it is written (Job 35:7): "If thou do justly, what shalt thou give Him, or what shall He receive of thy hand." Hence a man can merit nothing from God.

Objection 3: Further, whoever merits anything from another makes him his debtor; for a man's wage is a debt due to him. Now God is no one's debtor; hence it is written (Rm. 11:35): "Who hath first given to Him, and recompense shall be made to him?" Hence no one can merit anything from God.

On the contrary, It is written (Jer. 31:16): "There is a reward for thy work." Now a reward means something bestowed by reason of merit. Hence it would seem that a man may merit from God.

[Handwritten annotations in bottom margin: "MErit // grace", "Favor that is owed", "favor given freely", "condign // congruous", "appropriate or deserving", "in line / fits with", "impetration - beseech or beg"]

I answer that, Merit and reward refer to the same, for a reward means something given anyone in return for work or toil, as a price for it. Hence, as it is an act of justice to give a just price for anything received from another, so also is it an act of justice to make a return for work or toil. Now justice is a kind of equality, as is clear from the Philosopher (Ethic. v, 3), and hence justice is simply between those that are simply equal; but where there is no absolute equality between them, neither is there abso

lute justice, but there may be a certain manner of justice, as when we speak of a father's or a master's right (Ethic. v, 6), as the Philosopher says. And hence where there is justice simply, there is the character of merit and reward simply. But where there is no simple right, but only relative, there is no character of merit simply, but only relatively, in so far as the character of justice is found there, since the child merits something from his father and the slave from his lord.

Now it is clear that between God and man there is the greatest inequality: for they are infinitely apart, and all man's good is from God. Hence there can be no justice of absolute equality between man and God, but only of a certain proportion, inasmuch as both operate after their own manner. Now the manner and measure of human virtue is in man from God. Hence man's merit with God only exists on the presupposition of the Divine ordination, so that man obtains from God, as a reward of his operation, what God gave him the power of operation for, even as natural things by their proper movements and operations obtain that to which they were ordained by God; differently, indeed, since the rational creature moves itself to act by its free-will, hence its action has the character of merit, which is not so in other creatures.

Reply to Objection 1: Man merits, inasmuch as he does what he ought, by his free-will; otherwise the act of justice whereby anyone discharges a debt would not be meritorious.

Reply to Objection 2: God seeks from our goods not profit, but glory, i.e. the manifestation of His goodness; even as He seeks it also in His own works. Now nothing accrues to Him, but only to ourselves, by our worship of Him. Hence we merit from God, not that by our works anything accrues to Him, but inasmuch as we work for His glory.

Reply to Objection 3: Since our action has the character of merit, only on the presupposition of the Divine ordination, it does not follow that God is made our debtor simply, but His own, inasmuch as it is right that His will should be carried out.

Article: 2 Whether anyone without grace can merit eternal life?

Objection 1: It would seem that without grace anyone can merit eternal life. For man merits from God what he is divinely ordained to, as stated above (Article [1]). Now man by his nature is ordained to beatitude as his end; hence, too, he naturally wishes to be blessed. Hence man by his natural endowments and without grace can merit beatitude which is eternal life.

Objection 2: Further, the less a work is due, the more meritorious it is. Now, less due is that work which is done by one who has received fewer benefits. Hence, since he who has only natural endowments has received fewer gifts from God, than he who has gratuitous gifts as well as nature, it would seem that his works are more meritorious with God. And thus if he who has grace can merit eternal life to some extent, much more may he who has no grace.

Objection 3: Further, God's mercy and liberality infinitely surpass human mercy and liberality. Now a man may merit from another, even though he has not hitherto had his grace. Much more, therefore, would it seem that a man without grace may merit eternal life.

On the contrary, The Apostle says (Rm. 6:23): "The grace of God, life everlasting."

I answer that, Man without grace may be looked at in two states, as was said above (Question [109], Article [2]): the first, a state of perfect nature, in which Adam was before his sin; the second, a state of corrupt nature, in which we are before being restored by grace. Therefore, if we speak of man in the first state, there is only one reason why man cannot merit eternal life without grace, by his purely natural endowments, viz. because man's merit depends on the Divine pre-ordination. Now no act of anything whatsoever is divinely ordained to anything exceeding the proportion of the powers which are the principles of its act; for it is a law of Divine providence that nothing shall act beyond its powers. Now everlasting life is a good exceeding the proportion of created nature; since it exceeds its knowledge and desire, according to 1 Cor. 2:9: "Eye hath not seen, nor ear heard, neither hath it entered into the heart of man." And hence it is that no created nature is a sufficient principle of an act meritorious of eternal life, unless there is added a supernatural gift, which we call grace. But if we speak of man as existing in sin, a second reason is added to this, viz. the impediment of sin. For since sin is an offense against God, excluding us from eternal life, as is clear from what has been said above (Question [71], Article [6]; Question [113], Article [2]), no one existing in a state of mortal sin can merit eternal life unless first he be reconciled to God, through his sin being forgiven, which is brought about by grace. For the sinner deserves not life, but death, according to Rm. 6:23: "The wages of sin is death."

Reply to Objection 1: God ordained human nature to attain the end of eternal life, not by its own strength, but by the help of grace; and in this way its act can be meritorious of eternal life.

Reply to Objection 2: Without grace a man cannot have a work equal to a work proceeding from grace, since the more perfect the principle, the more perfect the action. But the objection would hold good, if we supposed the operations equal in both cases.

Reply to Objection 3: With regard to the first reason adduced, the case is different in God and in man. For a man receives all his power of well-doing from God, and not from man. Hence a man can merit nothing from God except by His gift, which the Apostle expresses aptly saying (Rm. 11:35): "Who hath first given to Him, and recompense shall be made to him?" But man may merit from man, before he has received anything from him, by what he has received from God.

But as regards the second proof taken from the impediment of sin, the case is similar with man and God, since one man cannot merit from another whom he has offended, unless he makes satisfaction to him and is reconciled.

Article: 3

Whether a man in grace can merit eternal life condignly?

Objection 1: It would seem that a man in grace cannot merit eternal life condignly, for the Apostle says (Rm. 8:18): "The sufferings of this time are not worthy [condignae] to be compared with the glory to come, that shall be revealed in us." But of all meritorious works, the sufferings of the saints would seem the most meritorious. Therefore no works of men are meritorious of eternal life condignly.

Objection 2: Further, on Rm. 6:23, "The grace of God, life everlasting," a gloss says: "He might have truly said: 'The wages of justice, life everlasting'; but He preferred to say 'The grace of God, life everlasting,' that we may know that God leads us to life everlasting of His own mercy and not by our merits." Now when anyone merits something condignly he receives it not from mercy, but from merit. Hence it would seem that a man with grace cannot merit life everlasting condignly.

Objection 3: Further, merit that equals the reward, would seem to be condign. Now no act of the present life can equal everlasting life, which surpasses our knowledge and our desire, and moreover, surpasses the charity or love of the wayfarer, even as it exceeds nature. Therefore with grace a man cannot merit eternal life condignly.

On the contrary, What is granted in accordance with a fair judgment, would seem a condign reward. But life everlasting is granted by God, in accordance with the judgment of justice, according to 2 Tim. 4:8: "As to the rest, there is laid up for me a crown of justice, which the Lord, the just judge, will render to me in that day." Therefore man merits everlasting life condignly.

I answer that, Man's meritorious work may be considered in two ways: first, as it proceeds from free-will; secondly, as it proceeds from the grace of the Holy Ghost. If it is considered as regards the substance of the work, and inasmuch as it springs from the free-will, there can be no condignity because of the very great inequality. But there is congruity, on account of an equality of proportion: for it would seem congruous that, if a man does what he can, God should reward him according to the excellence of his power.

If, however, we speak of a meritorious work, inasmuch as it proceeds from the grace of the Holy Ghost moving us to life everlasting, it is meritorious of life everlasting condignly. For thus the value of its merit depends upon the power of the Holy Ghost moving us to life everlasting according to Jn. 4:14: "Shall become in him a fount of water springing up into life everlasting." And the worth of the work depends on the dignity of grace, whereby a man, being made a partaker of the Divine Nature, is adopted as a son of God, to whom the inheritance is due by right of adoption, according to Rm. 8:17: "If sons, heirs also."

Reply to Objection 1: The Apostle is speaking of the substance of these sufferings.

Reply to Objection 2: This saying is to be understood of the first cause of our reaching everlasting life, viz. God's mercy. But our merit is a subsequent cause.

Reply to Objection 3: The grace of the Holy Ghost which we have at present, although unequal to glory in act, is equal to it virtually as the seed of a tree, wherein the whole tree is virtually. So likewise by grace of the Holy Ghost dwells in man; and He is a sufficient cause of life everlasting; hence, 2 Cor. 1:22, He is called the "pledge" of our inheritance.

Article: 4

Whether grace is the principle of merit through charity rather than the other virtues?

Objection 1: It would seem that grace is not the principle of merit through charity rather than the other virtues. For wages are due to work, according to Mt. 20:8: "Call the laborers and pay them their hire." Now every virtue is a principle of some operation, since virtue is an operative habit, as stated above (Question [55], Article [2]). Hence every virtue is equally a principle of merit.

Objection 2: Further, the Apostle says (1 Cor. 3:8): "Every man shall receive his own reward according to his labor." Now charity lessens rather than increases the labor, because as Augustine says (De Verbis Dom., Serm. lxx), "love makes all hard and repulsive tasks easy and next to nothing." Hence charity is no greater principle of merit than any other virtue.

Objection 3: Further, the greatest principle of merit would seem to be the one whose acts are most meritorious. But the acts of faith and patience or fortitude would seem to be the most meritorious, as appears in the martyrs, who strove for the faith patiently and bravely even till death. Hence other virtues are a greater principle of merit than charity.

On the contrary, Our Lord said (Jn. 14:21): "He that loveth Me, shall be loved of My Father; and I will love him and will manifest Myself to him." Now everlasting life consists in the manifest knowledge of God, according to Jn. 17:3: "This is eternal life: that they may know Thee, the only true" and living "God." Hence the merit of eternal life rests chiefly with charity.

I answer that, As we may gather from what has been stated above (Article [1]), human acts have the nature of merit from two causes: first and chiefly from the Divine ordination, inasmuch as acts are said to merit that good to which man is divinely ordained. Secondly, on the part of free-will, inasmuch as man, more than other creatures, has the power of voluntary acts by acting by himself. And in both these ways does merit chiefly rest with charity. For we must bear in mind that everlasting life consists in the enjoyment of God. Now the human mind's movement to the fruition of the Divine good is the proper act of charity, whereby all the acts of the other virtues are ordained to this end, since all the other virtues are commanded by charity. Hence the merit of life everlasting pertains first to charity, and secondly, to the other virtues, inasmuch as their acts are commanded by charity. So, likewise, is it manifest that what we do out of love we do most willingly. Hence, even inasmuch as merit depends on voluntariness, merit is chiefly attributed to charity.

Reply to Objection 1: Charity, inasmuch as it has the last end for object, moves the other virtues to act. For the habit to which the end pertains always commands the habits to which the means pertain, as was said above (Question [9], Article [1]).

Reply to Objection 2: A work can be toilsome and difficult in two ways: first, from the greatness of the work, and thus the greatness of the work pertains to the increase of merit; and thus charity does not lessen the toil---rather, it makes us undertake the greatest toils, "for it does great things, if it exists," as Gregory says (Hom. in Evang. xxx). Secondly, from the defect of the operator; for what is not done with a ready will is hard and difficult to all of us, and this toil lessens merit and is removed by charity.

Reply to Objection 3: The act of faith is not meritorious unless "faith . . . worketh by charity" (Gal. 5:6). So, too, the acts of patience and fortitude are not meritorious unless a man does them out of charity, according to 1 Cor. 13:3: "If I should deliver my body to be burned, and have not charity, it profiteth me nothing."

Article: 5

Whether a man may merit for himself the first grace?

Objection 1: It would seem that a man may merit for himself the first grace, because, as Augustine says (Ep. clxxxvi), "faith merits justification." Now a man is justified by the first grace. Therefore a man may merit the first grace.

Objection 2: Further, God gives grace only to the worthy. Now, no one is said to be worthy of some good, unless he has merited it condignly. Therefore we may merit the first grace condignly.

Objection 3: Further, with men we may merit a gift already received. Thus if a man receives a horse from his master, he merits it by a good use of it in his master's service. Now God is much more bountiful than man. Much more, therefore, may a man, by subsequent works, merit the first grace already received from God.

On the contrary, The nature of grace is repugnant to reward of works, according to Rm. 4:4: "Now to him that worketh, the reward is not reckoned according to grace but according to debt." Now a man merits what is reckoned to him according to debt, as the reward of his works. Hence a man may not merit the first grace.

I answer that, The gift of grace may be considered in two ways: first in the nature of a gratuitous gift, and thus it is manifest that all merit is repugnant to grace, since as the Apostle says (Rm. 11:6), "if by grace, it is not now by works." Secondly, it may be considered as regards the nature of the thing given, and thus, also, it cannot come under the merit of him who has not grace, both because it exceeds the proportion of nature, and because previous to grace a man in the state of sin has an obstacle to his meriting grace, viz. sin. But when anyone has grace, the grace already possessed cannot come under merit, since reward is the term of the work, but grace is the principle of all our good works, as stated above (Question [109]). But of anyone merits a further gratuitous gift by virtue of the preceding grace, it would not be the first grace. Hence it is manifest that no one can merit for himself the first grace.

Reply to Objection 1: As Augustine says (Retract. i, 23), he was deceived on this point for a time, believing the beginning of faith to be from us, and its consummation to be granted us by God; and this he here retracts. And seemingly it is in this sense that he speaks of faith as meriting justification. But if we suppose, as indeed it is a truth of faith, that the beginning of faith is in us from God, the first act must flow from grace; and thus it cannot be meritorious of the first grace. Therefore man is justified by faith, not as though man, by believing, were to merit justification, but that, he believes, whilst he is being justified; inasmuch as a movement of faith is required for the justification of the ungodly, as stated above (Question [113], Article [4]).

Reply to Objection 2: God gives grace to none but to the worthy, not that they were previously worthy, but that by His grace He makes them worthy, Who alone "can make him clean that is conceived of unclean seed" (Job 14:4).

Reply to Objection 3: Man's every good work proceeds from the first grace as from its principle; but not from any gift of man. Consequently, there is no comparison between gifts of grace and gifts of men.

Article: 6

Whether a man can merit the first grace for another?

Objection 1: It would seem that a man can merit the first grace for another. Because on Mt. 9:2: "Jesus seeing their faith," etc. a gloss says: "How much is our personal faith worth with God, Who set such a price on another's faith, as to heal the man both inwardly and outwardly!" Now inward healing is brought about by grace. Hence a man can merit the first grace for another.

Objection 2: Further, the prayers of the just are not void, but efficacious, according to James 5:16: "The continued prayer of a just man availeth much." Now he had previously said: "Pray one for another, that you may be saved." Hence, since man's salvation can only be brought about by grace, it seems that one man may merit for another his first grace.

Objection 3: Further, it is written (Lk. 16:9): "Make unto you friends of the mammon of iniquity, that when you shall fail they may receive you into everlasting dwellings." Now it is through grace alone that anyone is received into everlasting dwellings, for by it alone does anyone merit everlasting life as stated above (Article [2]; Question [109], Article [5]). Hence one man may by merit obtain for another his first grace.

On the contrary, It is written (Jer. 15:1): "If Moses and Samuel shall stand before Me, My soul is not towards this people" ---yet they had great merit with God. Hence it seems that no one can merit the first grace for another.

I answer that, As shown above (Articles [1],3,4), our works are meritorious from two causes: first, by virtue of the Divine motion; and thus we merit condignly; secondly, according as they proceed from free-will in so far as we do them willingly, and thus they have congruous merit, since it is congruous that when a man makes good use of his power God should by His super-excellent power work still higher things. And therefore it is clear that no one can merit condignly for another his first grace, save Christ alone; since each one of us is moved by God to reach life everlasting through the gift of grace; hence condign merit does not reach beyond this motion. But Christ's soul is moved by God through grace, not only so as to reach the glory of life everlasting, but so as to lead others to it, inasmuch as He is the Head of the Church, and the Author of human salvation, according to Heb. 2:10: "Who hath brought many children into glory [to perfect] the Author of their salvation."

But one may merit the first grace for another congruously; because a man in grace fulfils God's will, and it is congruous and in harmony with friendship that God should fulfil man's desire for the salvation of another, although sometimes there may be an impediment on the part of him whose salvation the just man desires. And it is in this sense that the passage from Jeremias speaks.

Reply to Objection 1: A man's faith avails for another's salvation by congruous and not by condign merit.

Reply to Objection 2: The impetration of prayer rests on mercy, whereas condign merit rests on justice; hence a man may impetrate many things from the Divine mercy in prayer, which he does not merit in justice, according to Dan. 9:18: "For it is not for our justifications that we present our prayers before Thy face, but for the multitude of Thy tender mercies."

Reply to Objection 3: The poor who receive alms are said to receive others into everlasting dwellings, either by impetrating their forgiveness in prayer, or by meriting congruously by other good works, or materially speaking, inasmuch as by these good works of mercy, exercised towards the poor, we merit to be received into everlasting dwellings.

Article: 7

Whether a man may merit restoration after a fall?

Objection 1: It would seem that anyone may merit for himself restoration after a fall. For what a man may justly ask of God, he may justly merit. Now nothing may more justly be besought of God than to be restored after a fall, as Augustine says [*Cf. Ennar. i super Ps. lxx.], according to Ps. 70:9: "When my strength shall fail, do not Thou forsake me." Hence a man may merit to be restored after a fall.

Objection 2: Further, a man's works benefit himself more than another. Now a man may, to some extent, merit for another his restoration after a fall, even as his first grace. Much more, therefore, may he merit for himself restoration after a fall.

Objection 3: Further, when a man is once in grace he merits life everlasting by the good works he does, as was shown above (Article [2]; Question [109], Article [5]). Now no one can attain life everlasting unless he is restored by grace. Hence it would seem that he merits for himself restoration.

On the contrary, It is written (Ezech. 18:24): "If the just man turn himself away from his justice and do iniquity . . . all his justices which he hath done shall not be remembered." Therefore his previous merits will nowise help him to rise again. Hence no one can merit for himself restoration after a fall.

I answer that, No one can merit for himself restoration after a future fall, either condignly or congruously. He cannot merit for himself condignly, since the reason of this merit depends on the motion of Divine grace, and this motion is interrupted by the subsequent sin; hence all benefits which he afterwards obtains from God, whereby he is restored, do not fall under merit---the motion of the preceding grace not extending to them. Again, congruous merit, whereby one merits the first grace for another, is prevented from having its effect on account of the impediment of sin in the one for whom it is merited. Much more, therefore, is the efficacy of such merit impeded by the obstacle which is in him who merits, and in him for whom it is merited; for both these are in the same person. And therefore a man can nowise merit for himself restoration after a fall.

Reply to Objection 1: The desire whereby we seek for restoration after a fall is called just, and likewise the prayer whereby this restoration is besought is called just, because it tends to justice; and not that it depends on justice by way of merit, but only on mercy.

Reply to Objection 2: Anyone may congruously merit for another his first grace, because there is no impediment (at least, on the part of him who merits), such as is found when anyone recedes from justice after the merit of grace.

Reply to Objection 3: Some have said that no one "absolutely" merits life everlasting except by the act of final grace, but only "conditionally," i.e. if he perseveres. But it is unreasonable to say this, for sometimes the act of the last grace is not more, but less meritorious than preceding acts, on account of the prostration of illness. Hence it must be said that every act of charity merits eternal life absolutely; but by subsequent sin, there arises an impediment to the preceding merit, so that it does not obtain its effect; just as natural causes fail of their effects on account of a supervening impediment.

Article: 8

Whether a man may merit the increase of grace or charity?

Objection 1: It would seem that a man cannot merit an increase of grace or charity. For when anyone receives the reward he merited no other reward is due to him; thus it was said of some (Mt. 6:2): "They have received their reward." Hence, if anyone were to merit the increase of charity or grace, it would follow that, when his grace has been increased, he could not expect any further reward, which is unfitting.

Objection 2: Further, nothing acts beyond its species. But the principle of merit is grace or charity, as was shown above (Articles [2], 4). Therefore no one can merit greater grace or charity than he has.

Objection 3: Further, what falls under merit a man merits by every act flowing from grace or charity, as by every such act a man merits life everlasting. If, therefore, the increase of grace or charity falls under merit, it would seem that by every act quickened by charity a man would merit an increase of charity. But what a man merits, he infallibly receives from God, unless hindered by subsequent sin; for it is written (2 Tim. 1:12): "I know Whom I have believed, and I am certain that He is able to keep that which I have committed unto Him." Hence it would follow that grace or charity is increased by every meritorious act; and this would seem impossible since at times meritorious acts are not very fervent, and would not suffice for the increase of charity. Therefore the increase of charity does not come under merit.

On the contrary, Augustine says (super Ep. Joan.; cf. Ep. clxxxvi) that "charity merits increase, and being increased merits to be perfected." Hence the increase of grace or charity falls under merit.

I answer that, As stated above (Articles [6],7), whatever the motion of grace reaches to, falls under condign merit. Now the motion of a mover extends not merely to the last term of the movement, but to the whole progress of the movement. But the term of the movement of grace is eternal life; and progress in this movement is by the increase of charity or grace according to Prov. 4:18: "But the path of the just as a shining light, goeth forward and increaseth even to perfect day," which is the day of glory. And thus the increase of grace falls under condign merit.

Reply to Objection 1: Reward is the term of merit. But there is a double term of movement, viz. the last, and the intermediate, which is both beginning and term; and this term is the reward of increase. Now the reward of human favor is as the last end to those who place their end in it; hence such as these receive no other reward.

Reply to Objection 2: The increase of grace is not above the virtuality of the pre-existing grace, although it is above its quantity, even as a tree is not above the virtuality of the seed, although above its quantity.

Reply to Objection 3: By every meritorious act a man merits the increase of grace, equally with the consummation of grace which is eternal life. But just as eternal life is not given at once, but in its own time, so neither is grace increased at once, but in its own time, viz. when a man is sufficiently disposed for the increase of grace.

Article: 9

Whether a man may merit perseverance?

Objection 1: It would seem that anyone may merit perseverance. For what a man obtains by asking, can come under the merit of anyone that is in grace. Now men obtain perseverance by asking it of God; otherwise it would be useless to ask it of God in the petitions of the Lord's Prayer, as Augustine says (De Dono Persev. ii). Therefore perseverance may come under the merit of whoever has grace.

Objection 2: Further, it is more not to be able to sin than not to sin. But not to be able to sin comes under merit, for we merit eternal life, of which impeccability is an essential part. Much more, therefore, may we merit not to sin, i.e. to persevere.

Objection 3: Further, increase of grace is greater than perseverance in the grace we already possess. But a man may merit an increase of grace, as was stated above (Article [8]). Much more, therefore, may he merit perseverance in the grace he has already.

On the contrary, What we merit, we obtain from God, unless it is hindered by sin. Now many have meritorious works, who do not obtain perseverance; nor can it be urged that this takes place because of the impediment of sin, since sin itself is opposed to perseverance; and thus if anyone were to merit perseverance, God would not permit him to fall into sin. Hence perseverance does not come under merit.

I answer that, Since man's free-will is naturally flexible towards good and evil, there are two ways of obtaining from God perseverance in good: first, inasmuch as free-will is determined to good by consummate grace, which will be in glory; secondly, on the part of the Divine motion, which inclines man to good unto the end. Now as explained above (Articles [6],7,8), that which is related as a term to the free-will's movement directed to God the mover, falls under human merit; and not what is related to the aforesaid movement as principle. Hence it is clear that the perseverance of glory which is the term of the aforesaid movement falls under merit; but perseverance of the wayfarer does not fall under merit, since it depends solely on the Divine motion, which is the principle of all merit. Now God freely bestows the good of perseverance, on whomsoever He bestows it.

Reply to Objection 1: We impetrate in prayer things that we do not merit, since God hears sinners who beseech the pardon of their sins, which they do not merit, as appears from Augustine [*Tract. xliv in Joan.] on Jn. 11:31, "Now we know that God doth not hear sinners," otherwise it would have been useless for the publican to say: "O God, be merciful to me a sinner," Lk. 18:13. So too may we impetrate of God in prayer the grace of perseverance either for ourselves or for others, although it does not fall under merit.

Reply to Objection 2: The perseverance which is in heaven is compared as term to the free-will's movement; not so, the perseverance of the wayfarer, for the reason given in the body of the article.

In the same way may we answer the third objection which concerns the increase of grace, as was explained above.

Article: 10

Whether temporal goods fall under merit?

Objection 1: It would seem that temporal goods fall under merit. For what is promised to some as a reward of justice, falls under merit. Now, temporal goods were promised in the Old Law as the reward of justice, as appears from Dt. 28. Hence it seems that temporal goods fall under merit.

Objection 2: Further, that would seem to fall under merit, which God bestows on anyone for a service done. But God sometimes bestows temporal goods on men for services done for Him. For it is written (Ex. 1:21): "And because the midwives feared God, He built them houses"; on which a gloss of Gregory (Moral. xviii, 4) says that "life everlasting might have been awarded them as the fruit of their goodwill, but on account of their sin of falsehood they received an earthly reward." And it is written (Ezech. 29:18): "The King of Babylon hath made his army to undergo hard service against Tyre . . . and there hath been no reward given him," and further on: "And it shall be wages for his army . . . I have given him the land of Egypt because he hath labored for me." Therefore temporal goods fall under merit.

Objection 3: Further, as good is to merit so is evil to demerit. But on account of the demerit of sin some are punished by God with temporal punishments, as appears from the Sodomites, Gn. 19. Hence temporal goods fall under merit.

Objection 4: On the contrary, What falls under merit does not come upon all alike. But temporal goods regard the good and the wicked alike; according to Eccles. 9:2: "All things equally happen to the just and the wicked, to the good and to the evil, to the clean and to the unclean, to him that offereth victims and to him that despiseth sacrifices." Therefore temporal goods do not fall under merit.

I answer that, What falls under merit is the reward or wage, which is a kind of good. Now man's good is twofold: the first, simply; the second, relatively. Now man's good simply is his last end (according to Ps. 72:27: "But it is good for men to adhere to my God") and consequently what is ordained and leads to this end; and these fall simply under merit. But the relative, not the simple, good of man is what is good to him now, or what is a good to him relatively; and this does not fall under merit simply, but relatively.

Hence we must say that if temporal goods are considered as they are useful for virtuous works, whereby we are led to heaven, they fall directly and simply under merit, even as increase of grace, and everything whereby a man is helped to attain beatitude after the first grace. For God gives men, both just and wicked, enough temporal goods to enable them to attain to everlasting life; and thus these temporal goods are simply good. Hence it is written (Ps. 33:10): "For there is no want to them that fear Him," and again, Ps. 36:25: "I have not seen the just forsaken," etc.

But if these temporal goods are considered in themselves, they are not man's good simply, but relatively, and thus they do not fall under merit simply, but relatively, inasmuch as men are moved by God to do temporal works, in which with God's help they reach their purpose. And thus as life everlasting is simply the reward of the works of justice in relation to the Divine motion, as stated above (Articles [3],6), so have temporal goods, considered in themselves, the nature of reward, with respect to the Divine motion, whereby men's wills are moved to undertake these works, even though, sometimes, men have not a right intention in them.

Reply to Objection 1: As Augustine says (Contra Faust. iv, 2), "in these temporal promises were figures of spiritual things to come. For the carnal people were adhering to the promises of the present life; and not merely their speech but even their life was prophetic."

Reply to Objection 2: These rewards are said to have been divinely brought about in relation to the Divine motion, and not in relation to the malice of their wills, especially as regards the King of Babylon, since he did not besiege Tyre as if wishing to serve God, but rather in order to usurp dominion. So, too, although the midwives had a good will with regard to saving the children, yet their will was not right, inasmuch as they framed falsehoods.

Reply to Objection 3: Temporal evils are imposed as a punishment on the wicked, inasmuch as they are not thereby helped to reach life everlasting. But to the just who are aided by these evils they are not punishments but medicines as stated above (Question [87], Article [8]).

Reply to Objection 4: All things happen equally to the good and the wicked, as regards the substance of temporal good or evil; but not as regards the end, since the good and not the wicked are led to beatitude by them.

And now enough has been said regarding morals in general.

------------------ END OF TREATISE ON GRACE ------------------

KOLBE'S GREATEST BOOKS
OF CHRISTIAN CIVILIZATION

52 Saint Joan of Arc

53 Sir Thomas Malory

54 The Golden Legend

55 Nicholas Copernicus

56 St. Thomas More

57 St. Ignatius of Loyola

58 St. Teresa of Avila

59 St. John of the Cross

60 St. Robert Bellarmine

61 William Shakespeare

62 St Francis de sales

63 Venerable Mary
   of Agreda

64 Blaise Pascal

65 Huygens-Boyle

66 Sir Isaac Newton

67 St. Jean Baptist
   de la Salle

68 St. Louis de Montfort

69 St. Alphonsus Ligouri

70 Anton Lavoisier

71 Johan Wolfgang
   von Goethe

72 Jane Austen

73 Federalist Papers

74 Adam Mickiewicz

75 Saint John Newman

Politics – Philosophy – Science – Theology
Education - Literature – Math – History

KOLBE'S GREATEST BOOKS
OF CHRISTIAN CIVILIZATION

76 Pope Leo XIII

77 Charles Dickens

78 St. John Bosco

79 Herman Melville

80 Fydor Dostoevsky

81 Gregor Mendel

82 Louis Pasteur

83 William Prescott

84 Lew Wallace

85 Orestes Brownson

86 Henryk Sienkiewicz

87 Vladimir Soloviev

88 Hilaire Belloc

89 Maria Montessori

90 St .Terese of Lisieux

91 G. K. Chesterton

92 Albert Einstein

93 Abbe Georges Lemaitre

94 Jacques Maritain

95 Christopher Dawson

96 T. S. Eliot

97 St. Edith Stein

98 C. S. Lewis

99 John Haffert

100 Msgr. Philip Hughes

101 Pope John Paul II

Politics – Philosophy – Science – Theology
Education - Literature – Math – History